Blood on the Tracks

volume 12

Shuzo Oshimi

CHAPTER 99 Visitation 003

CHAPTER 100 Mommy 029

CHAPTER 101 Imagination 053

CHAPTER 102 Good News 077

CHAPTER 103 Waiting in Vain 101

CHAPTER 104 Judgment 125

CHAPTER 105 Pointless 149

CHAPTER 106 Announcement 173

CHAPTER 107 Rancor 197

CHAPTER 108 Disposition 221

WAKE UP!

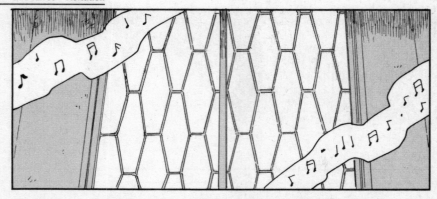

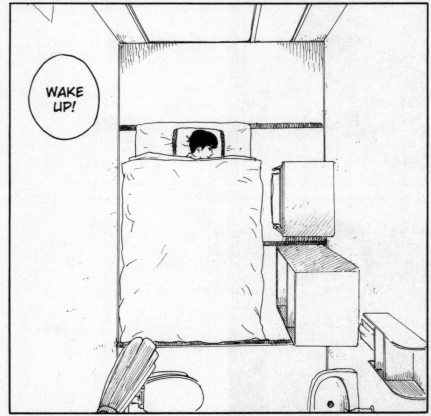

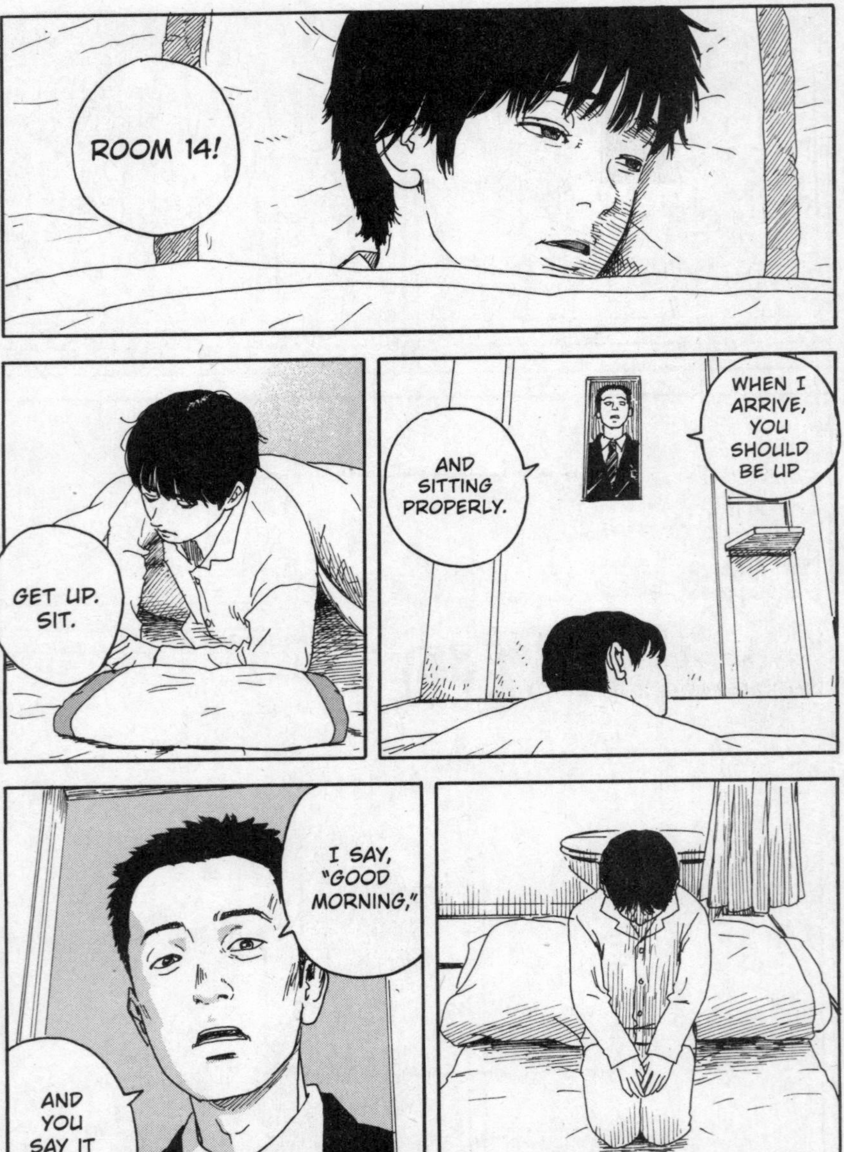
ROOM 14!
WHEN I ARRIVE, YOU SHOULD BE UP
AND SITTING PROPERLY.
GET UP. SIT.
I SAY, "GOOD MORNING,"
AND YOU SAY IT BACK.

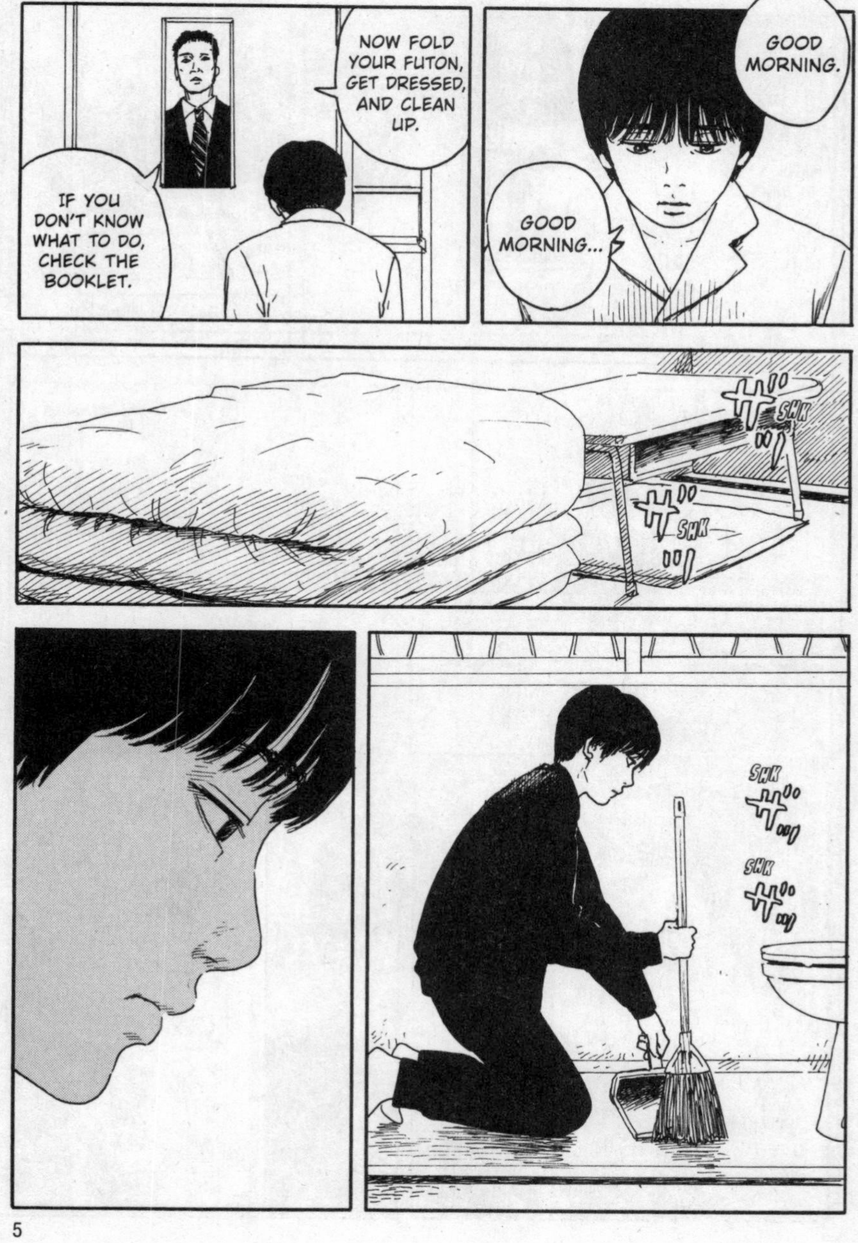
GOOD MORNING.
GOOD MORNING...
NOW FOLD YOUR FUTON, GET DRESSED, AND CLEAN UP.
IF YOU DON'T KNOW WHAT TO DO, CHECK THE BOOKLET.
SHK
SHK
SHK
SHK

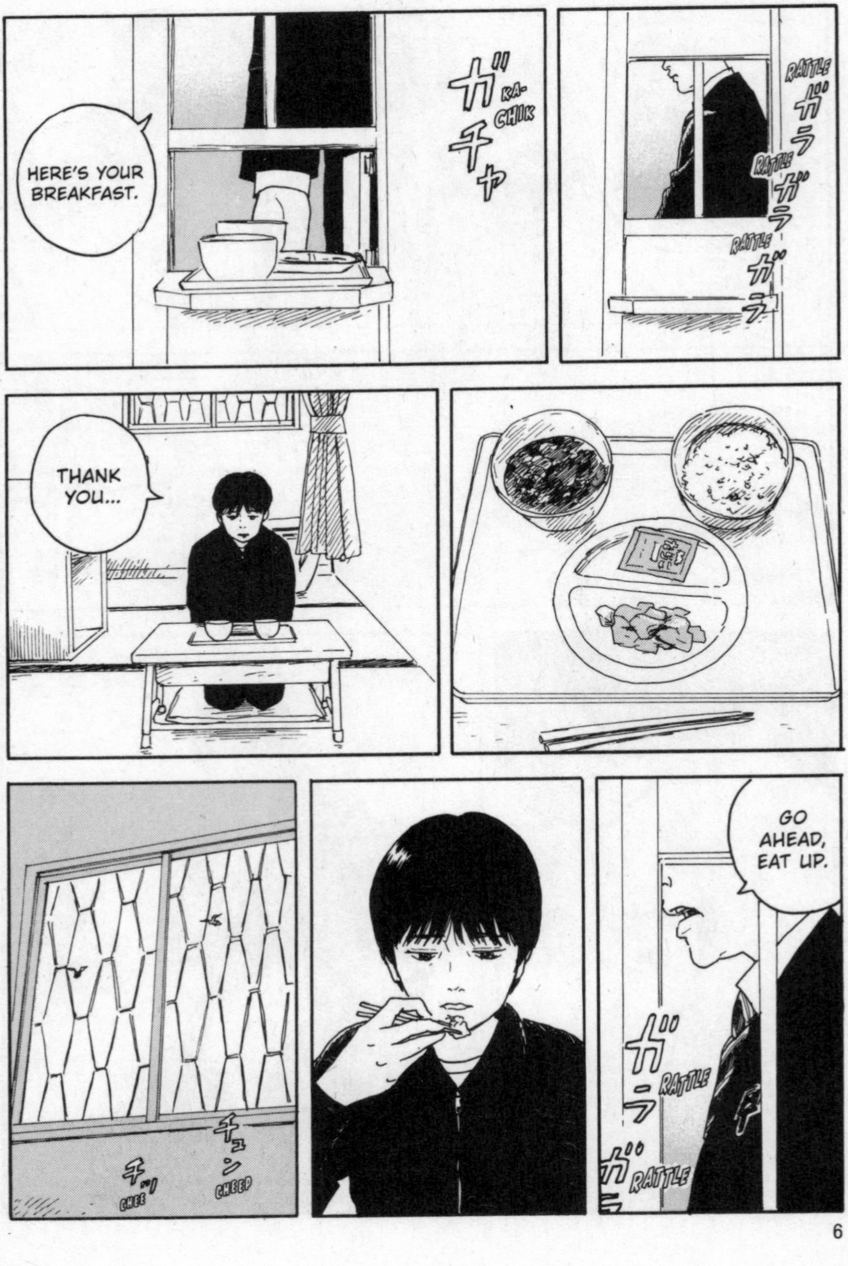

RATTLE
ガラ
RATTLE
ガラ
RATTLE
ガラ
ガチャ
KA-CHIK
HERE'S YOUR BREAKFAST.
THANK YOU...
GO AHEAD, EAT UP.
ガラ
RATTLE
ガラ
RATTLE
チュン
CHEEP
チッ
CHEE

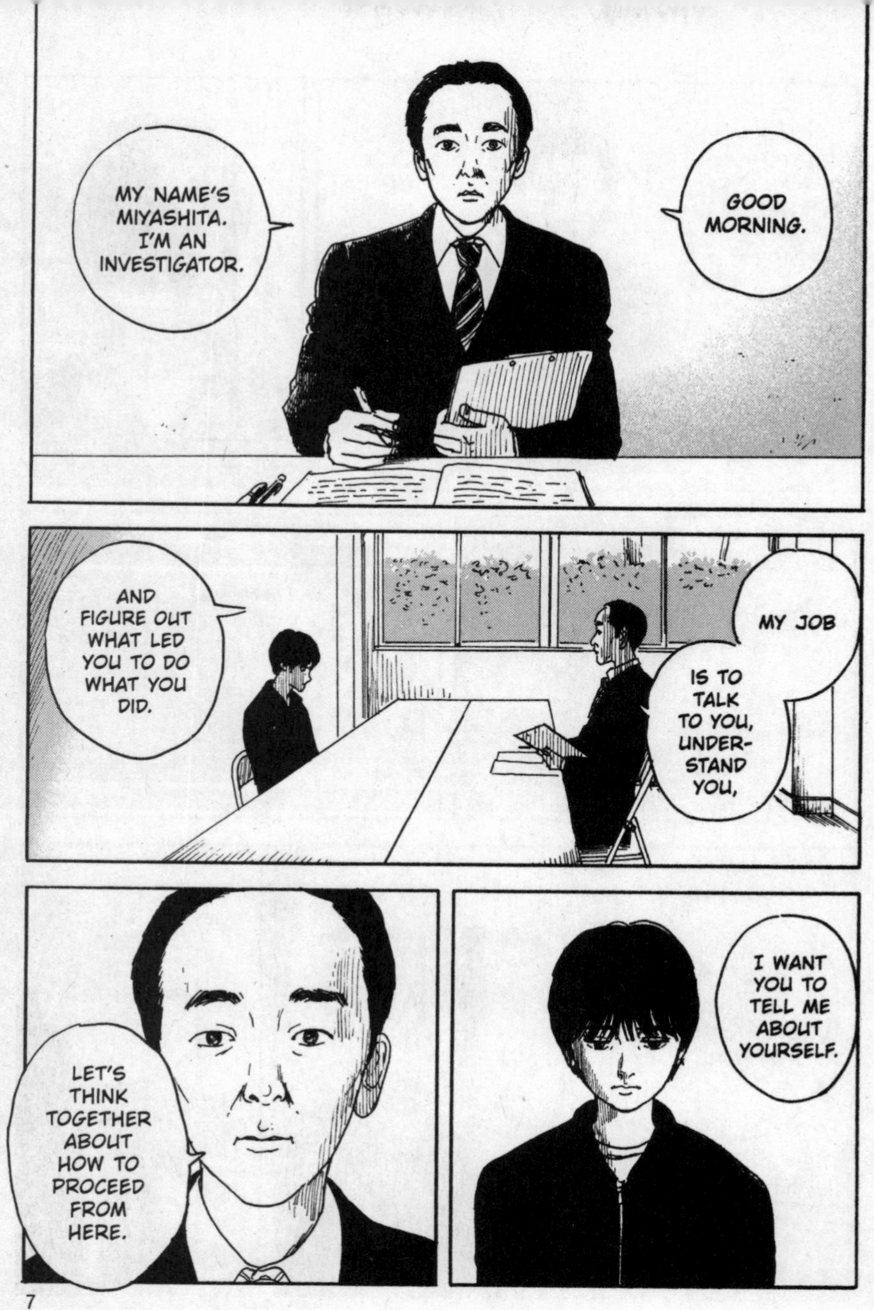
GOOD MORNING.
MY NAME'S MIYASHITA. I'M AN INVESTIGATOR.
MY JOB
IS TO TALK TO YOU, UNDERSTAND YOU,
AND FIGURE OUT WHAT LED YOU TO DO WHAT YOU DID.
I WANT YOU TO TELL ME ABOUT YOURSELF.
LET'S THINK TOGETHER ABOUT HOW TO PROCEED FROM HERE.

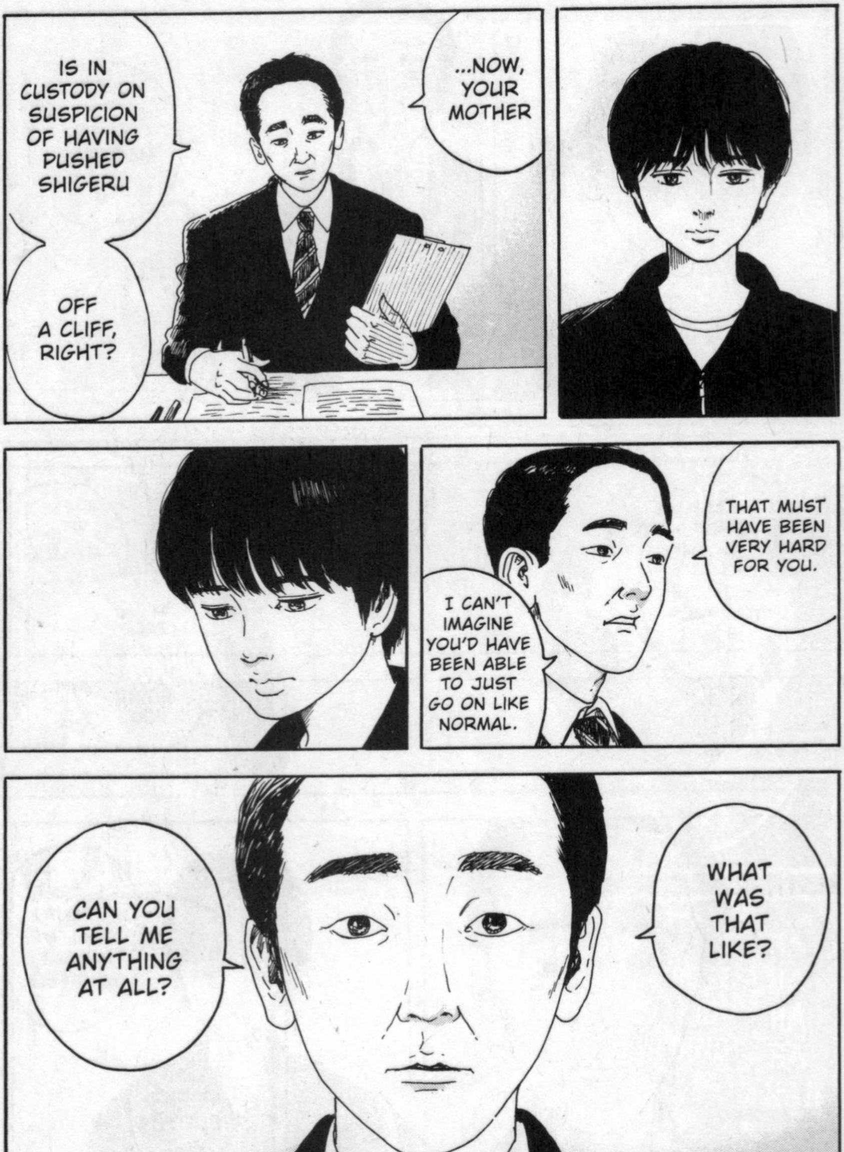
...NOW, YOUR MOTHER
IS IN CUSTODY ON SUSPICION OF HAVING PUSHED SHIGERU
OFF A CLIFF, RIGHT?
THAT MUST HAVE BEEN VERY HARD FOR YOU.
I CAN'T IMAGINE YOU'D HAVE BEEN ABLE TO JUST GO ON LIKE NORMAL.
WHAT WAS THAT LIKE?
CAN YOU TELL ME ANYTHING AT ALL?

...
MAYBE THAT WAS TOO SUDDEN.
ALL RIGHT...
TELL ME ABOUT YOUR MOTHER.
WHAT'S SHE LIKE,
FROM YOUR PER-SPECTIVE?
DO YOU LOVE YOUR MOTHER?

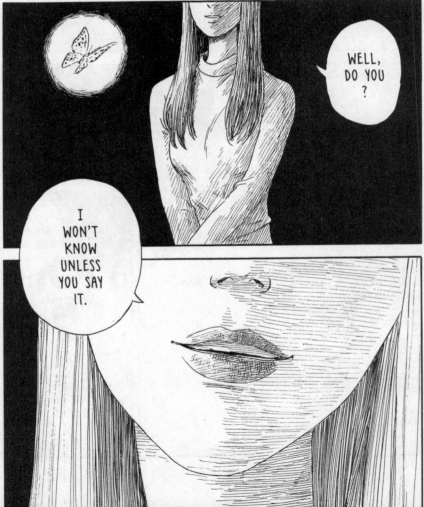

WELL,
DO YOU
?

I
WON'T
KNOW
UNLESS
YOU SAY
IT.

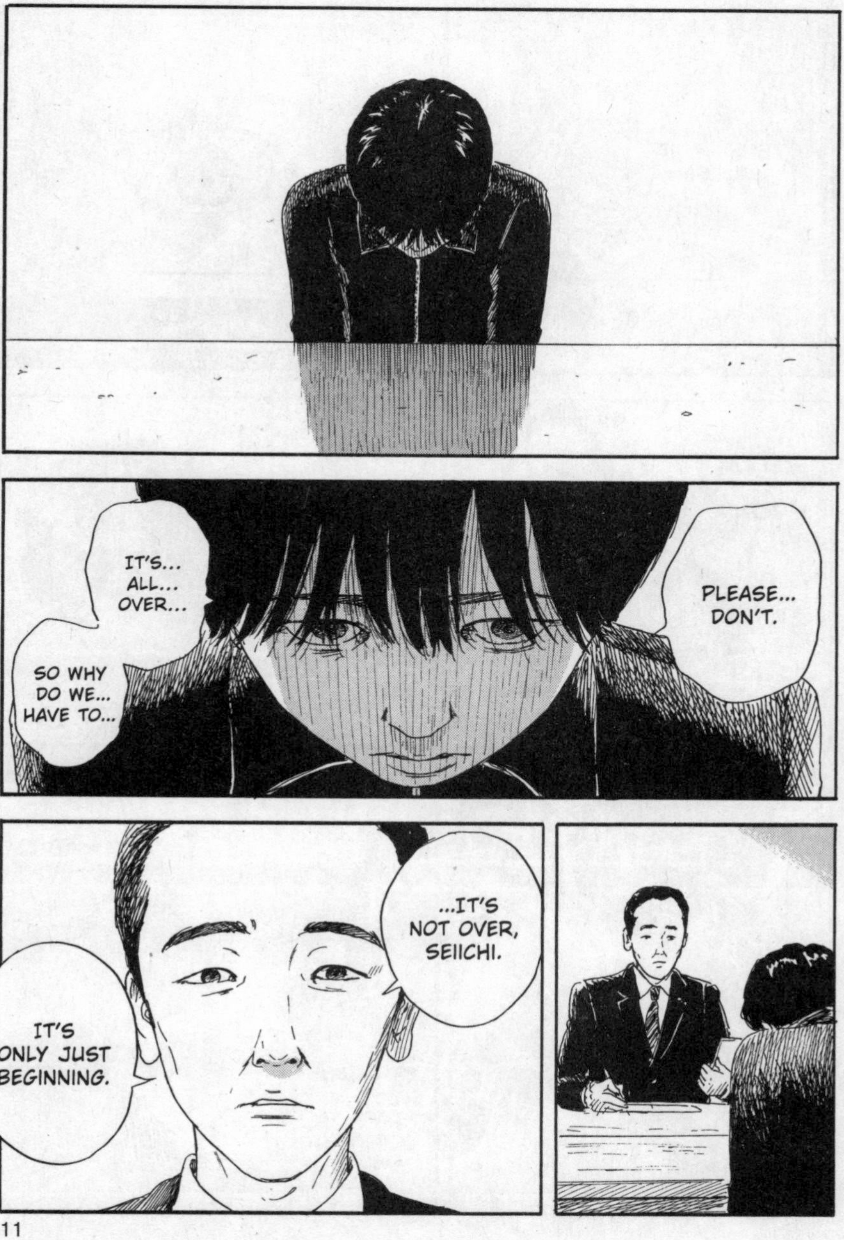
PLEASE... DON'T.
IT'S... ALL... OVER...
SO WHY DO WE... HAVE TO...
...IT'S NOT OVER, SEIICHI.
IT'S ONLY JUST BEGINNING.

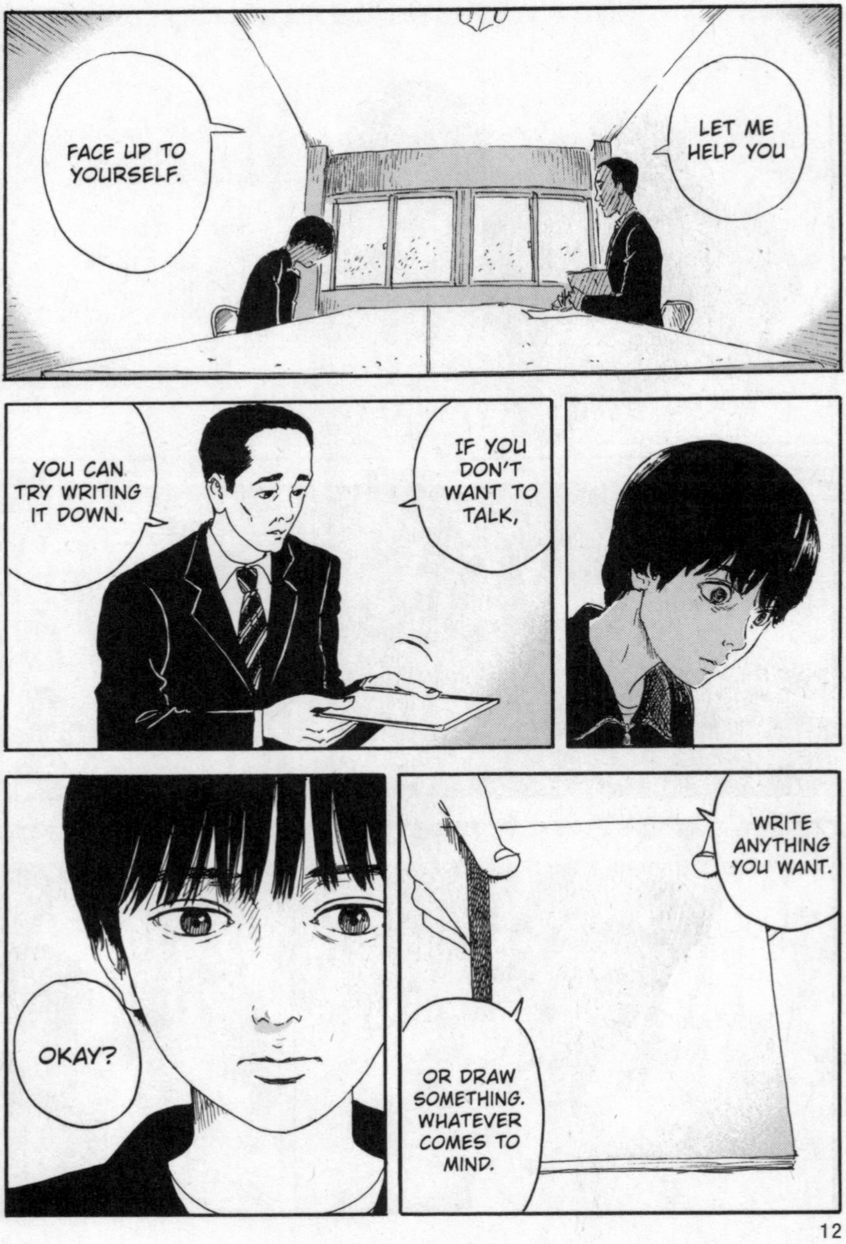
LET ME HELP YOU
FACE UP TO YOURSELF.
IF YOU DON'T WANT TO TALK,
YOU CAN TRY WRITING IT DOWN.
WRITE ANYTHING YOU WANT.
OR DRAW SOMETHING. WHATEVER COMES TO MIND.
OKAY?

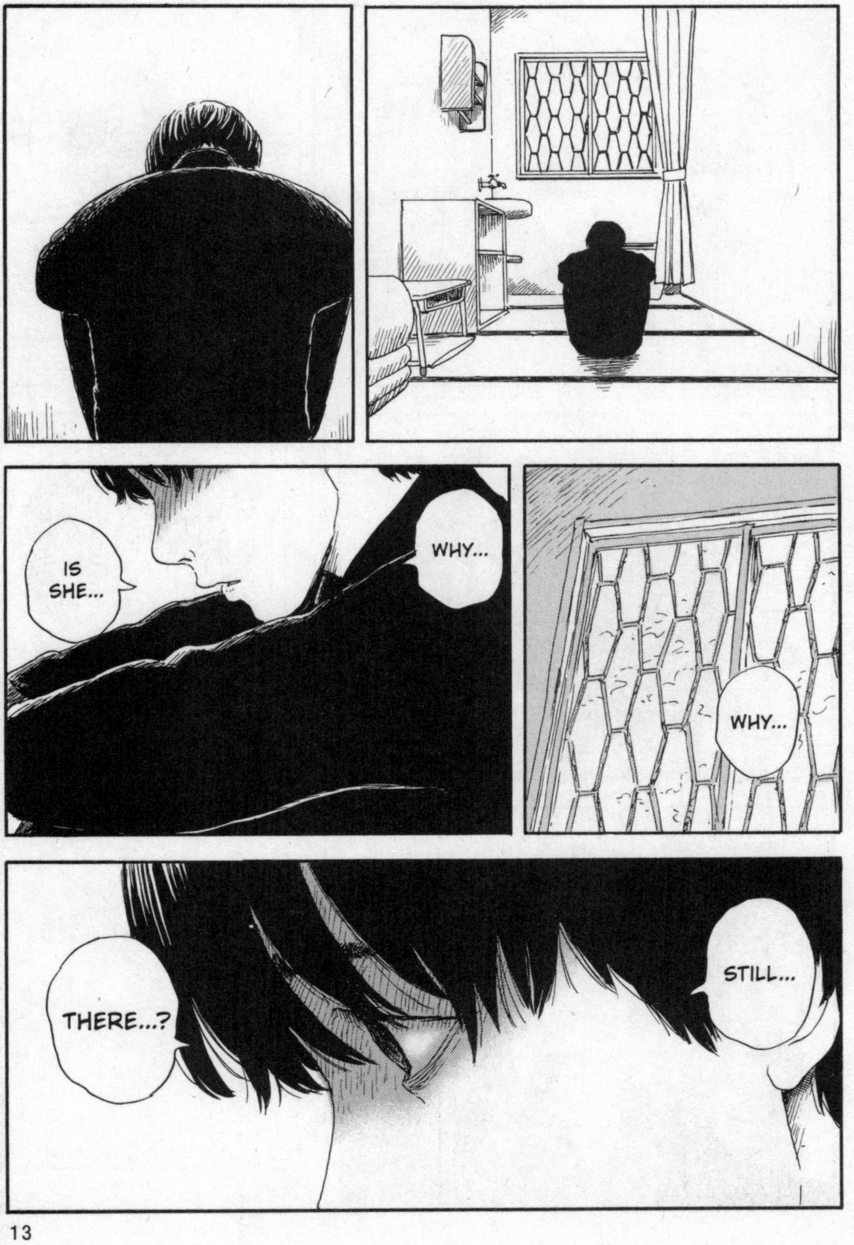
WHY...
WHY...
IS SHE...
STILL...
THERE...?

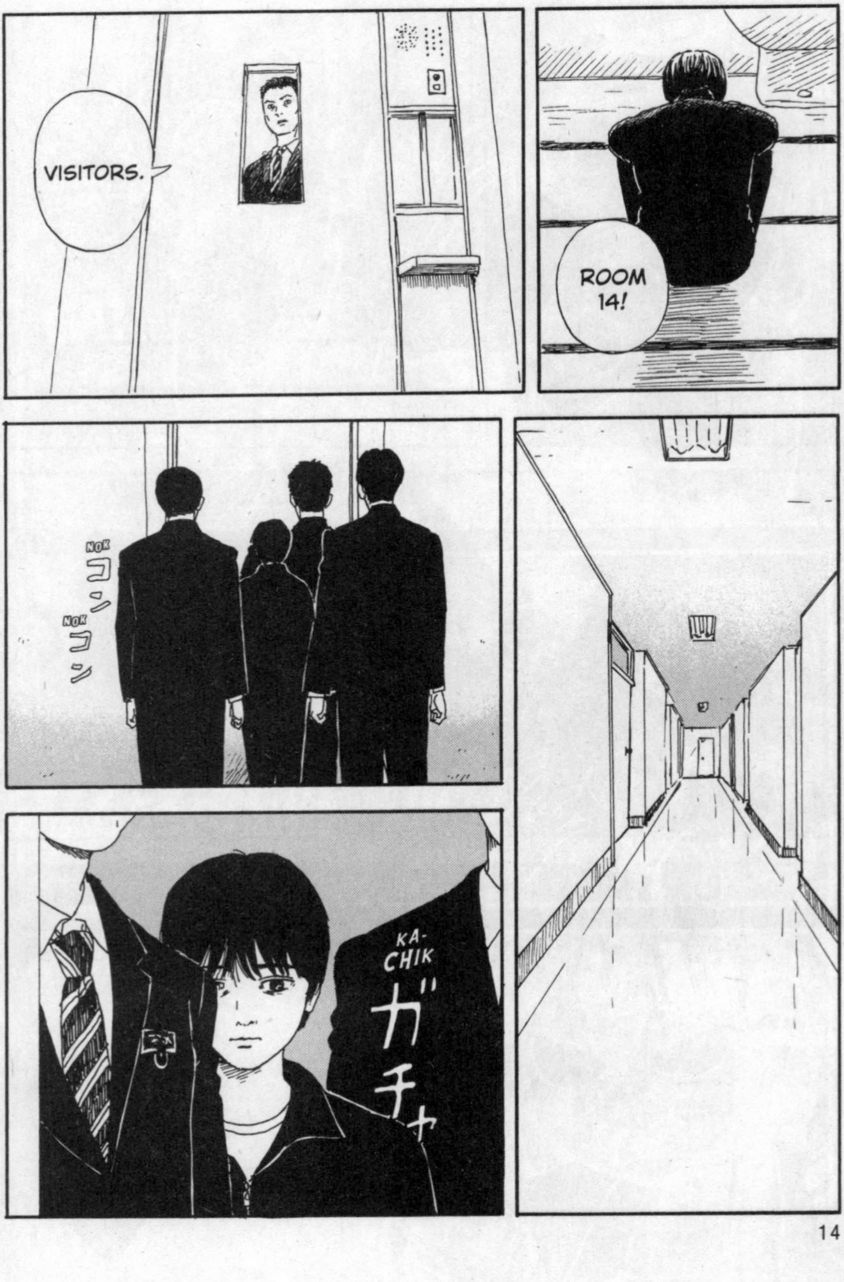
ROOM 14!
VISITORS.
NOK コン
NOK コン
KA-CHIK ガチャ

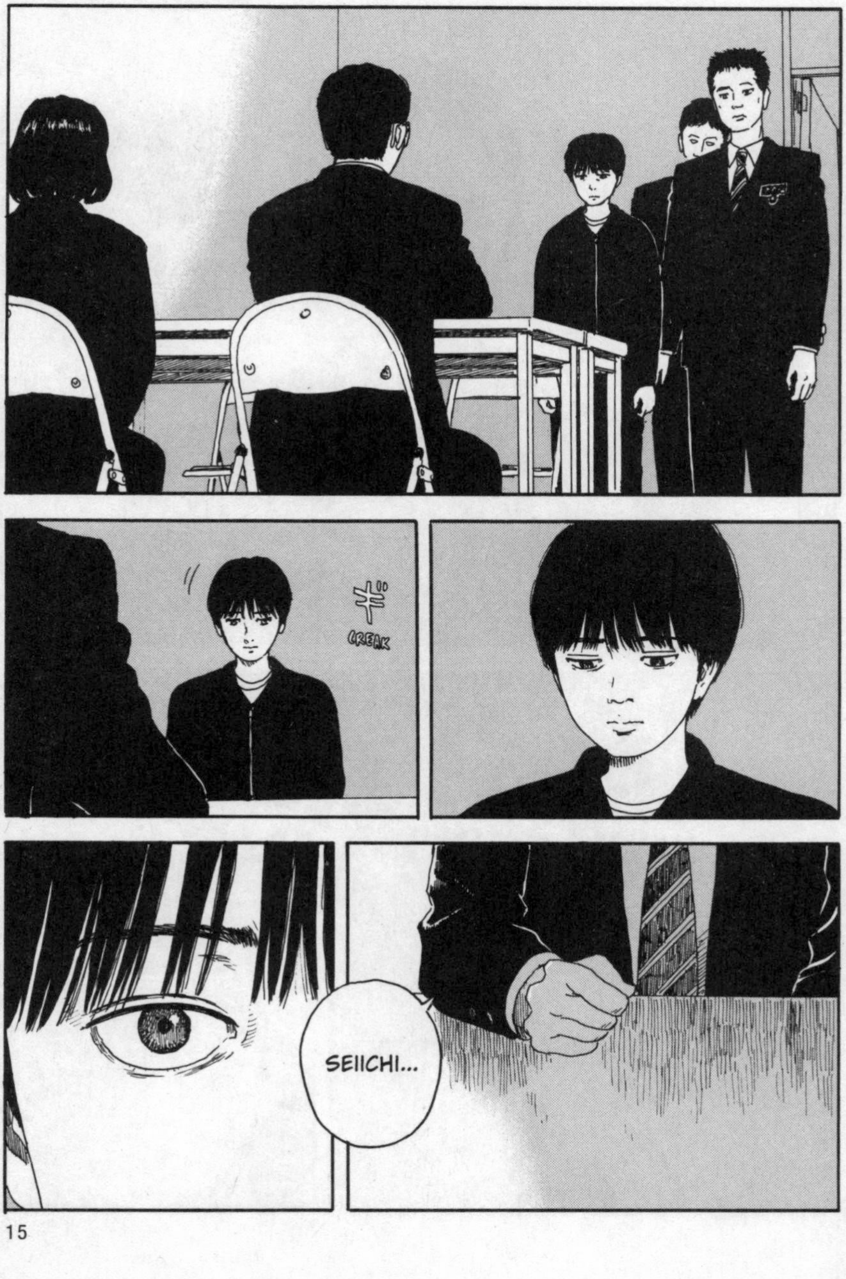
ギ
CREAK
SEIICHI...

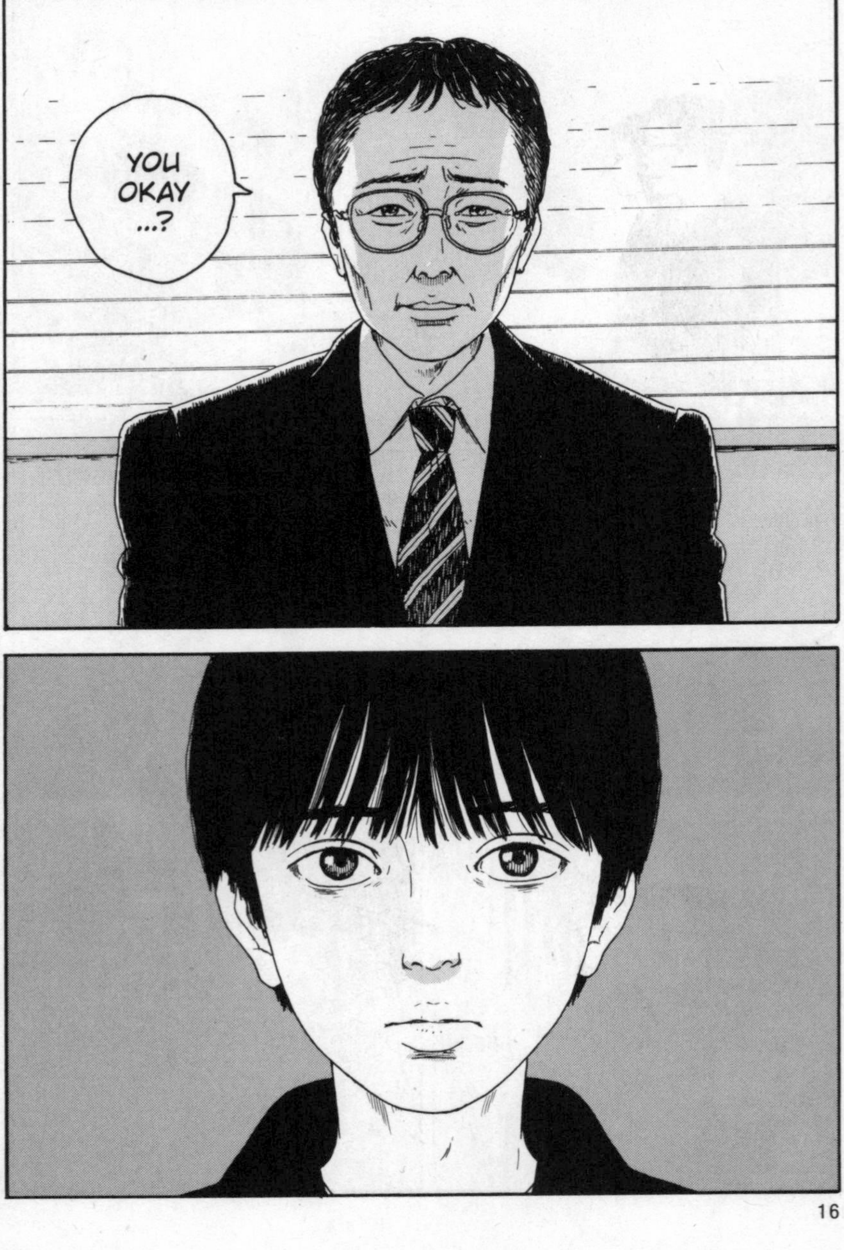
YOU OKAY ...?

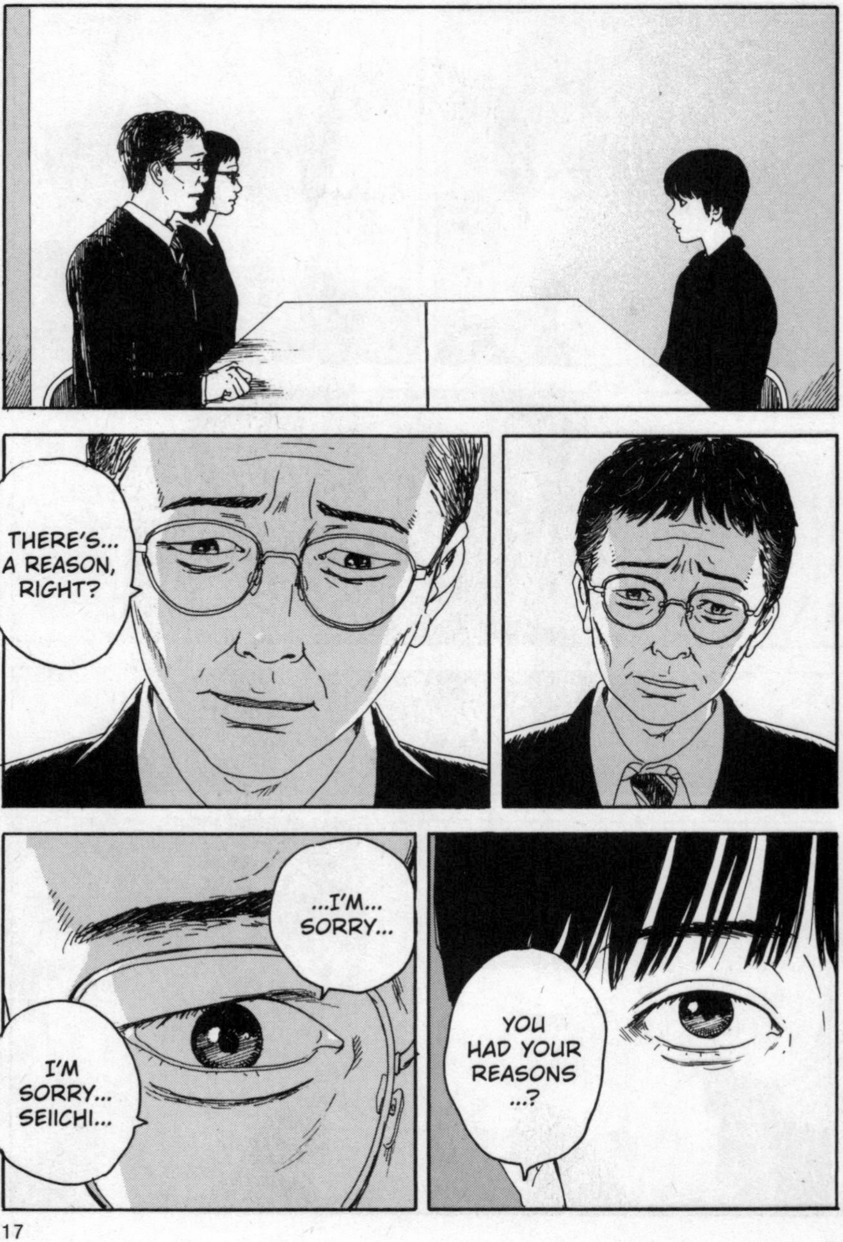
THERE'S... A REASON, RIGHT?
YOU HAD YOUR REASONS ...?
...I'M... SORRY...
I'M SORRY... SEIICHI...

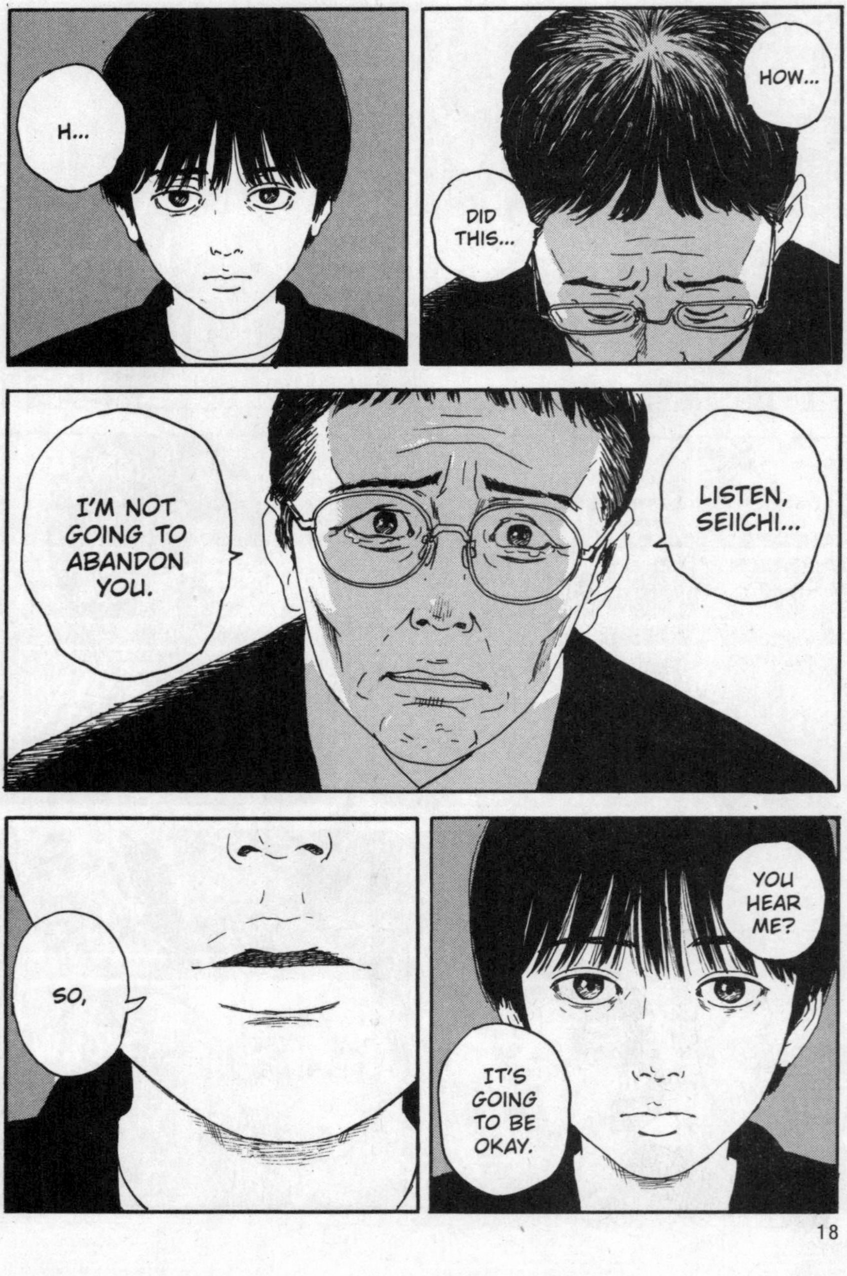
HOW...
DID THIS...
H...
LISTEN, SEIICHI...
I'M NOT GOING TO ABANDON YOU.
YOU HEAR ME?
IT'S GOING TO BE OKAY.
SO,

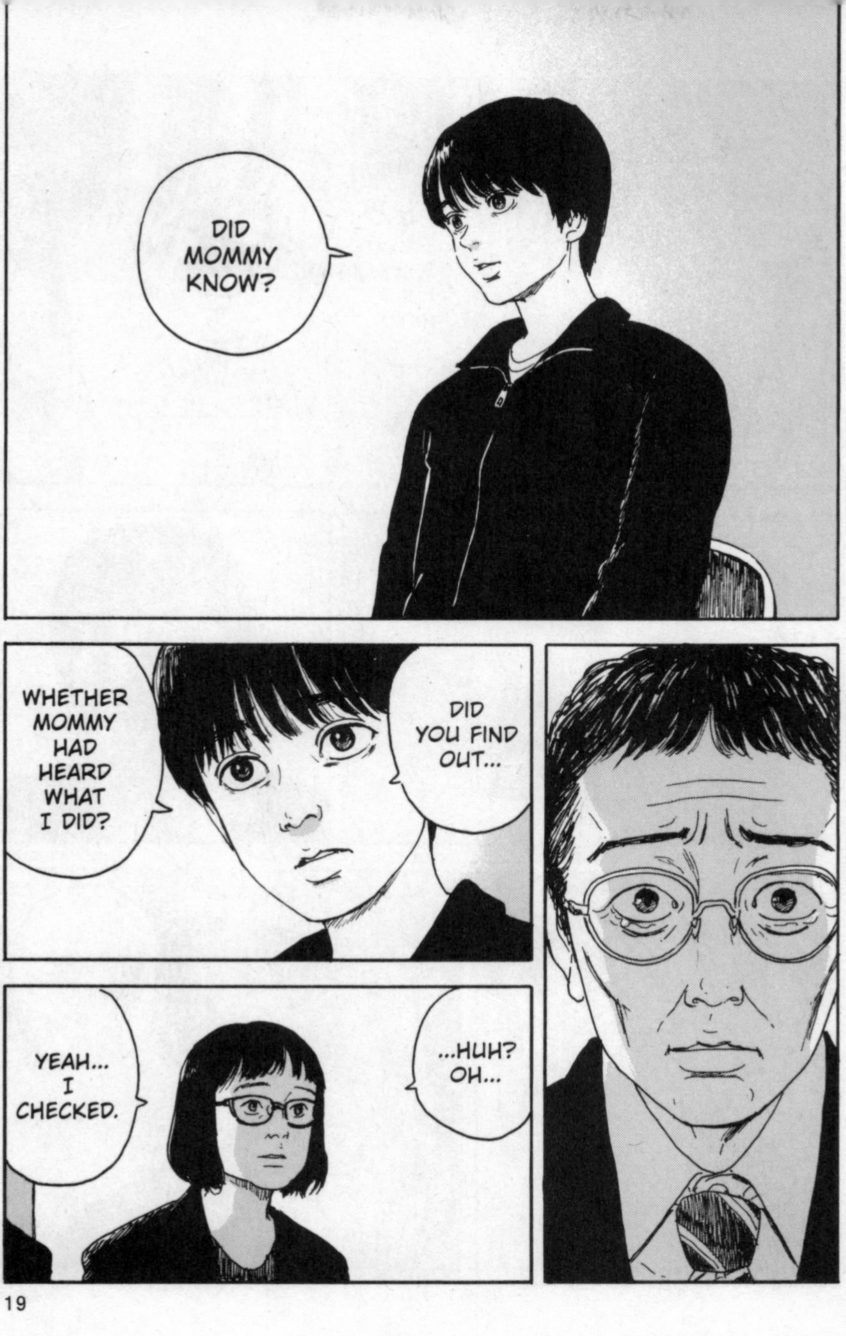
DID MOMMY KNOW?
DID YOU FIND OUT...
WHETHER MOMMY HAD HEARD WHAT I DID?
...HUH? OH...
YEAH... I CHECKED.

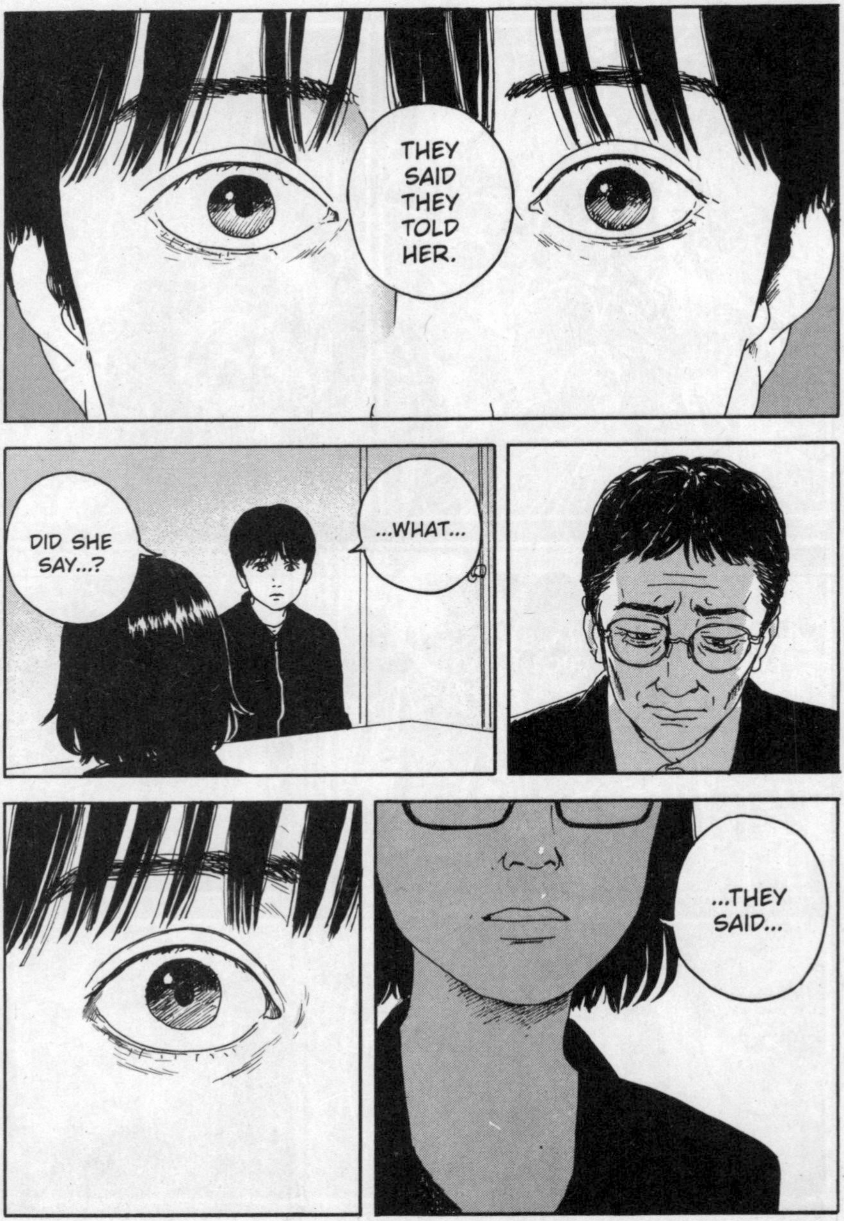
THEY SAID THEY TOLD HER.
...WHAT...
DID SHE SAY...?
...THEY SAID...

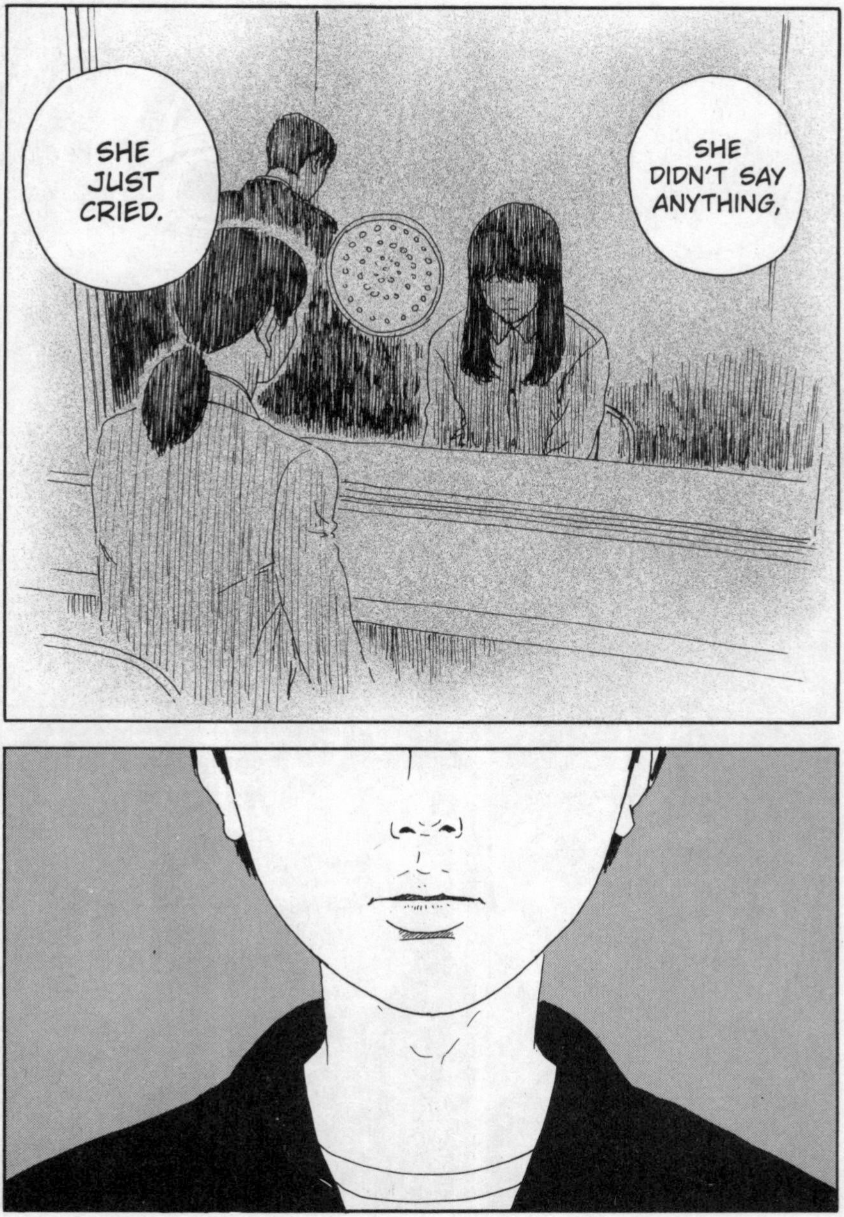
SHE DIDN'T SAY ANYTHING,
SHE JUST CRIED.

THAT'S IT...?

SHE JUST CRIED...

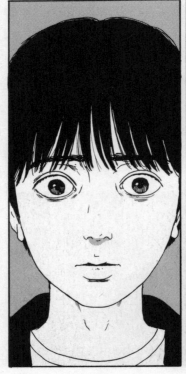

MM-HMM.

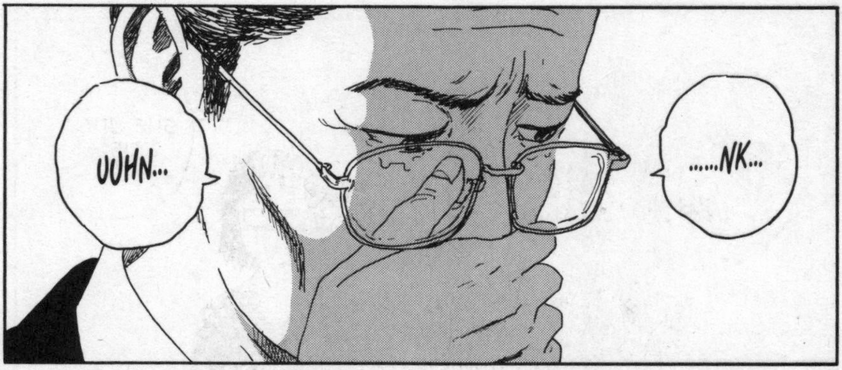
......NK...
UUHN...

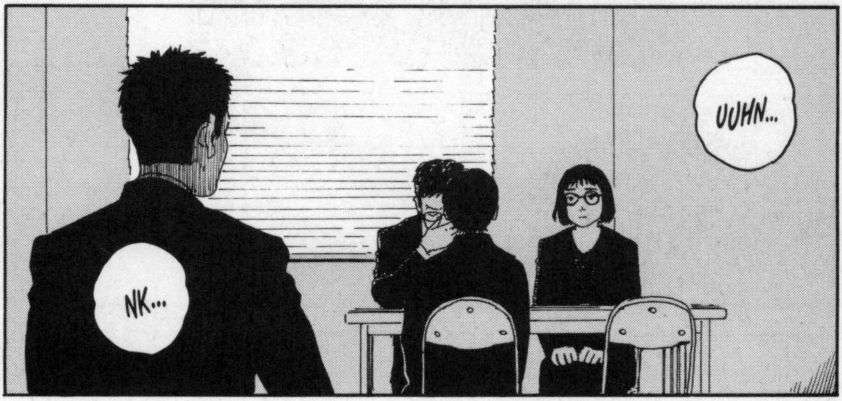
UUHN...
NK...

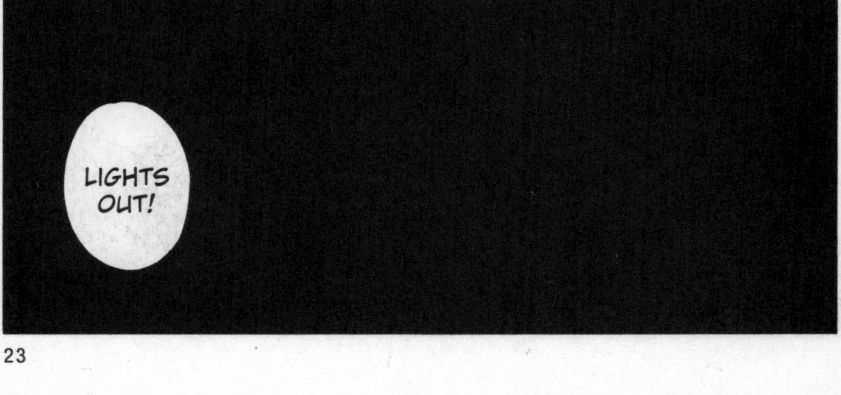
LIGHTS OUT!

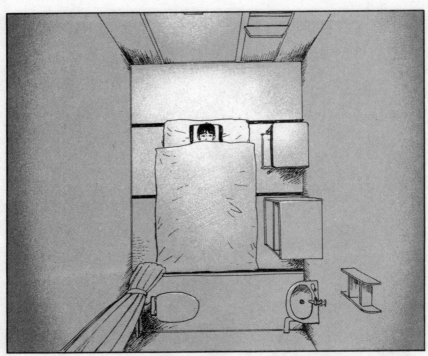

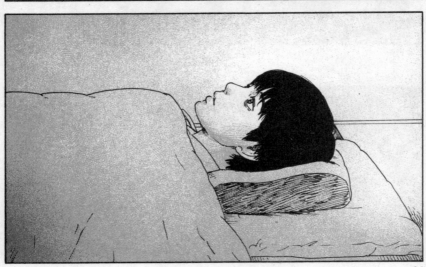

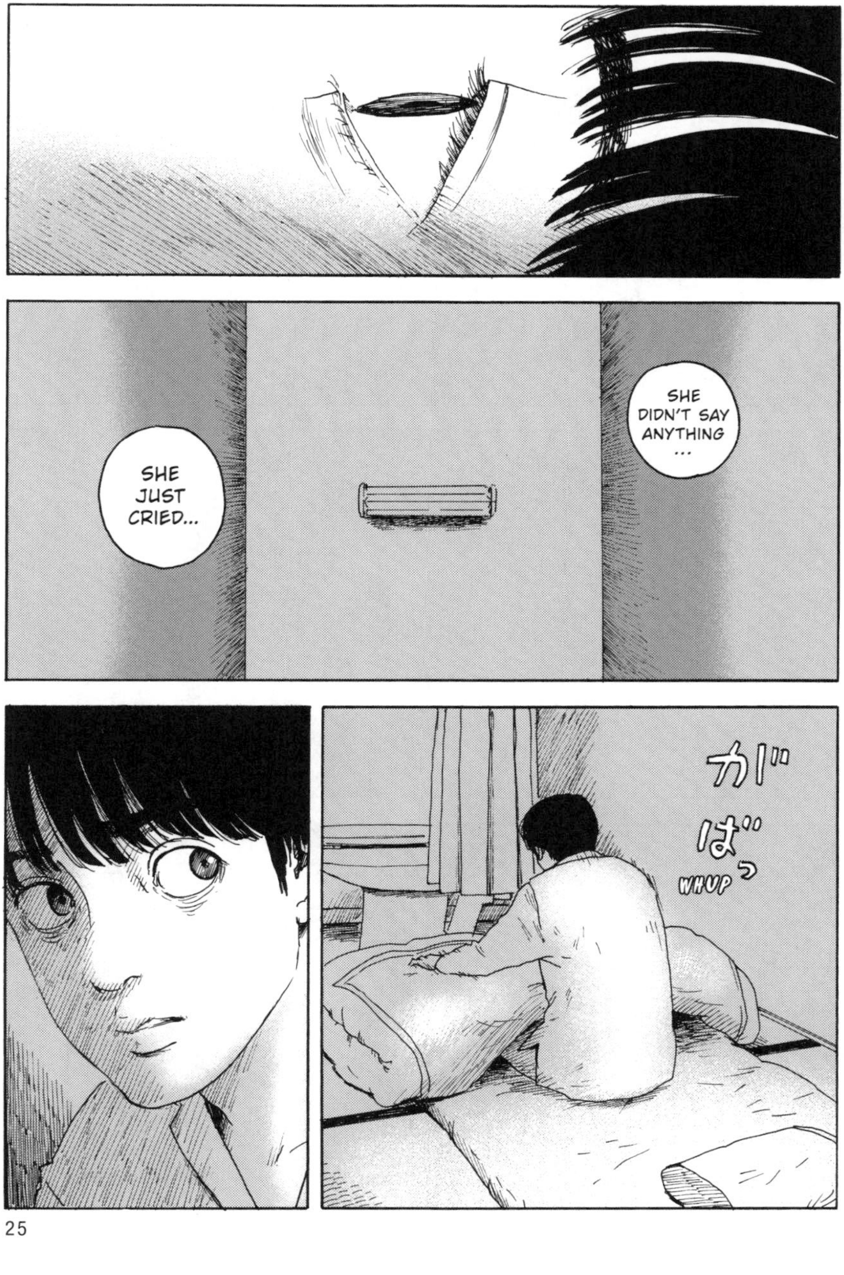
SHE DIDN'T SAY ANYTHING ...
SHE JUST CRIED...
ガばっ
WHUP

FWAP
バサッ

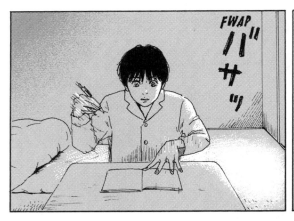

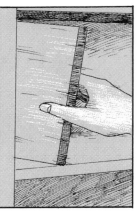

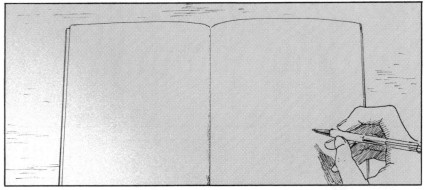

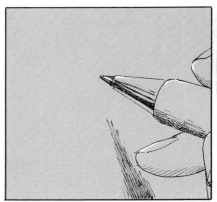

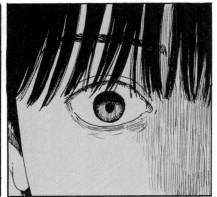

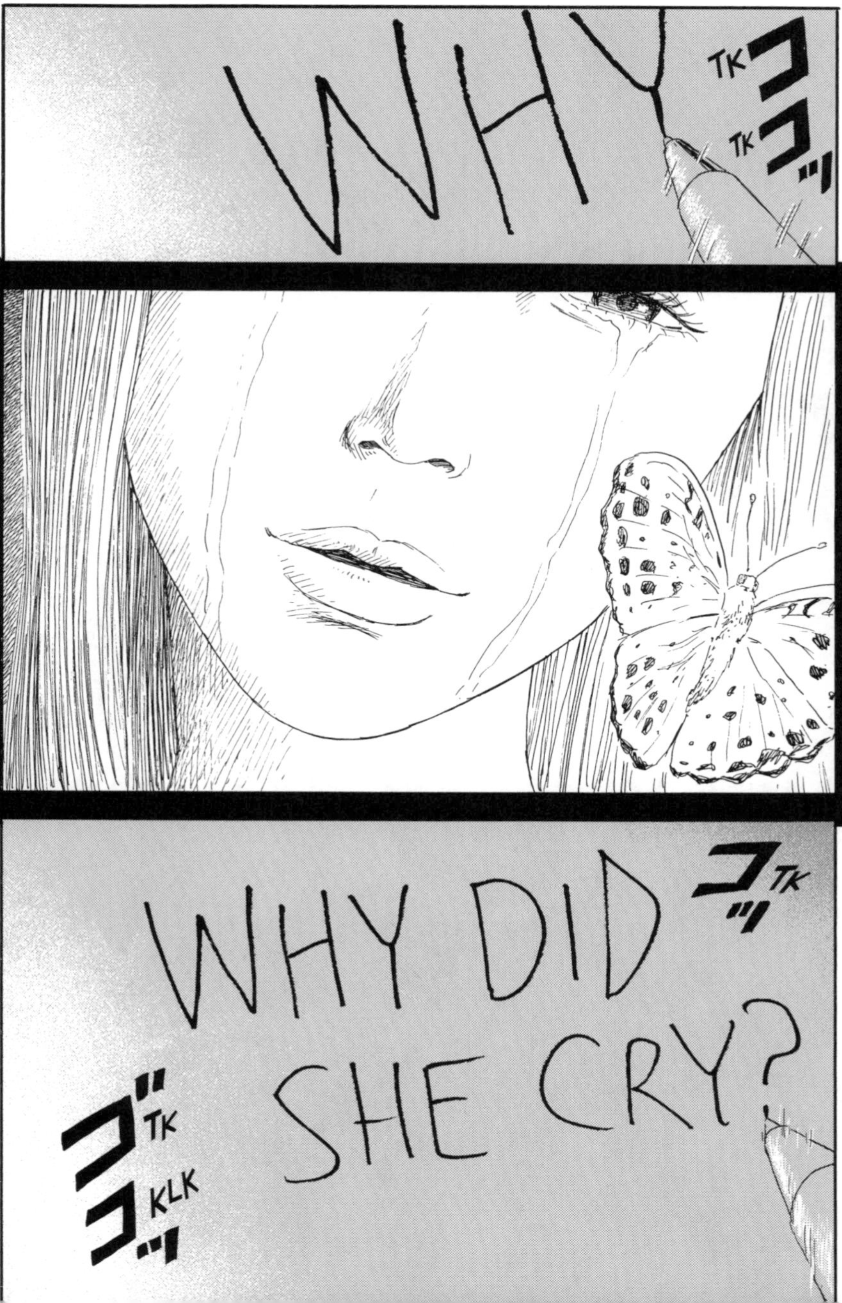
TK
TK
WHY
コッ TK
WHY DID SHE CRY?
ゴ TK
コッ KLK

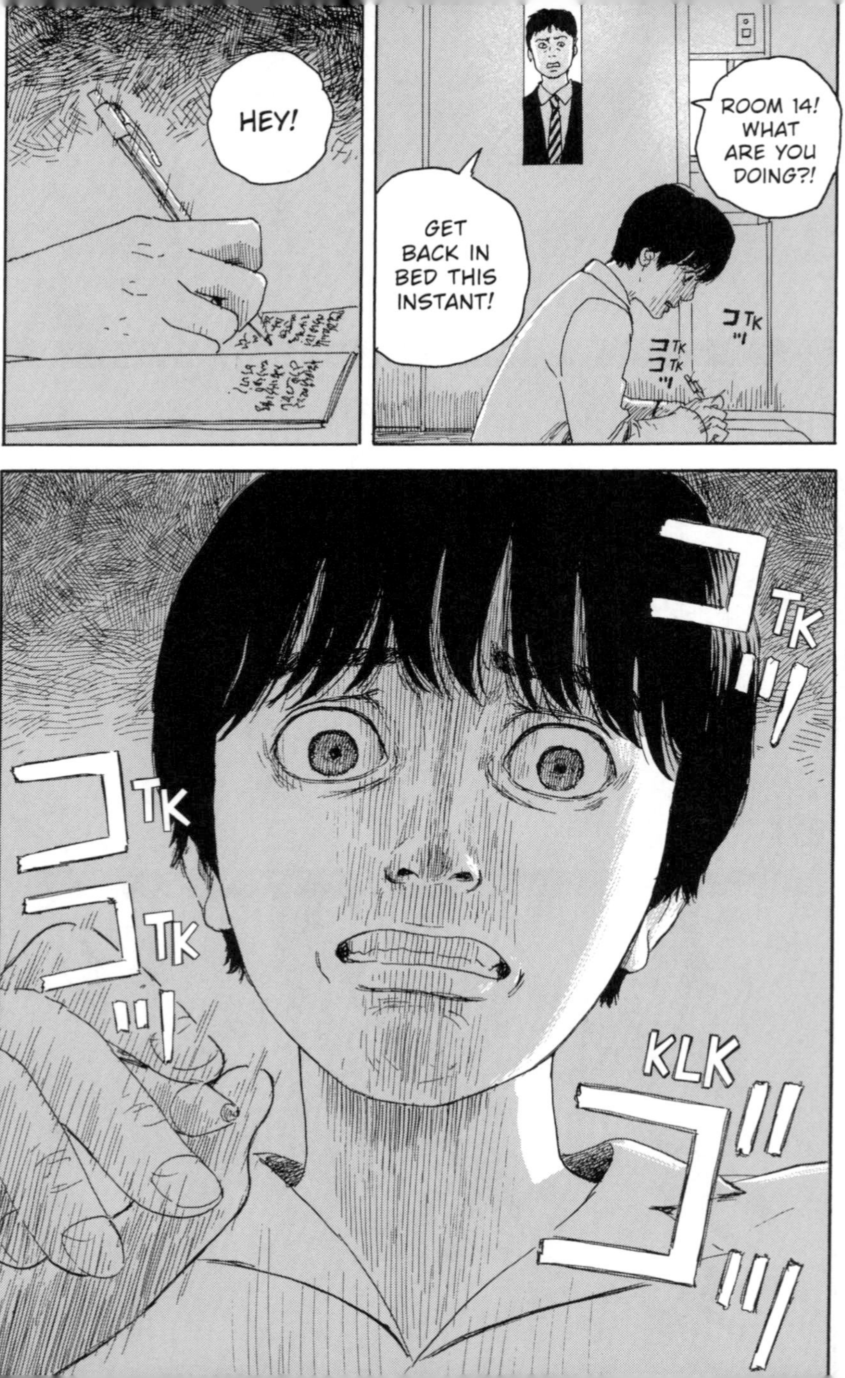
ROOM 14! WHAT ARE YOU DOING?!
GET BACK IN BED THIS INSTANT!
コッ TK
コ TK コッ TK
HEY!
コッ TK
コ TK コッ TK
KLK ゴッゴッ

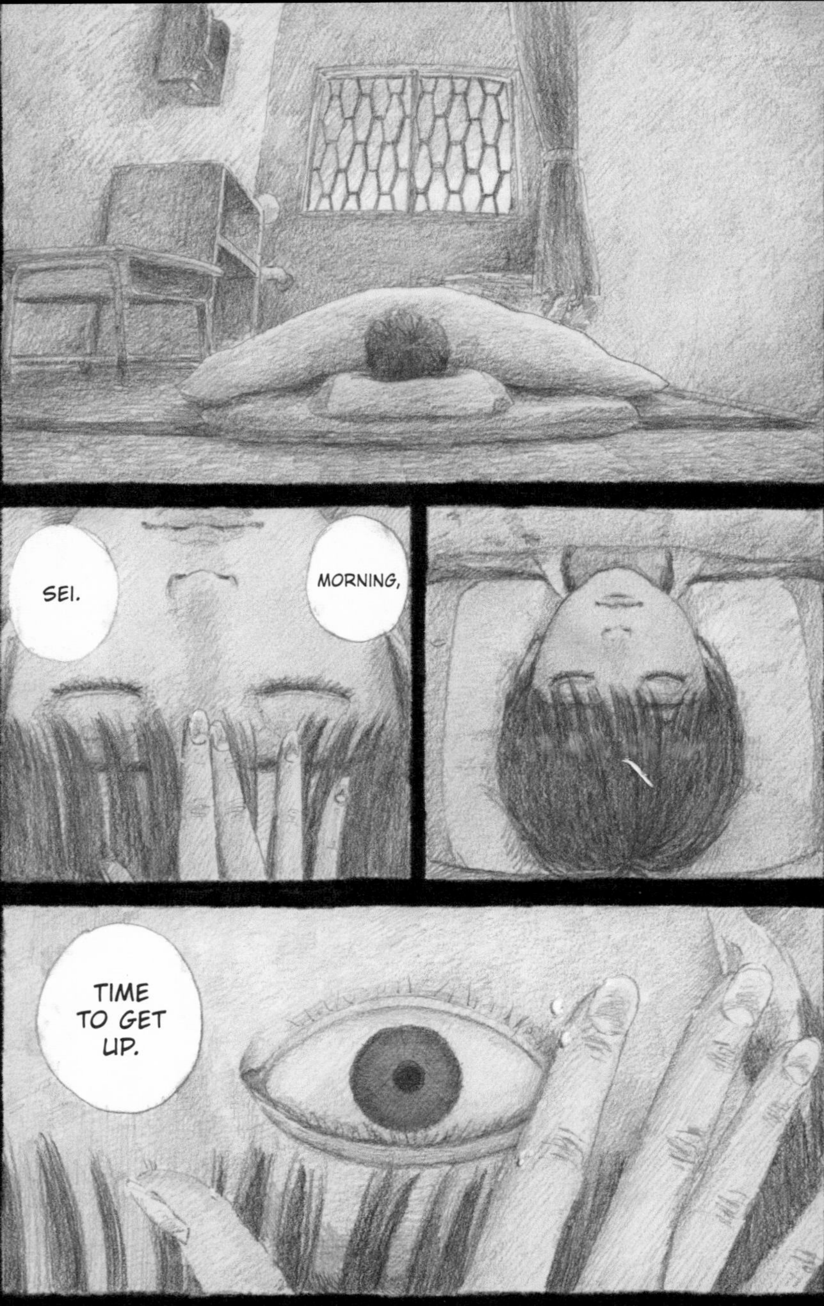
MORNING,
SEI.
TIME TO GET UP.

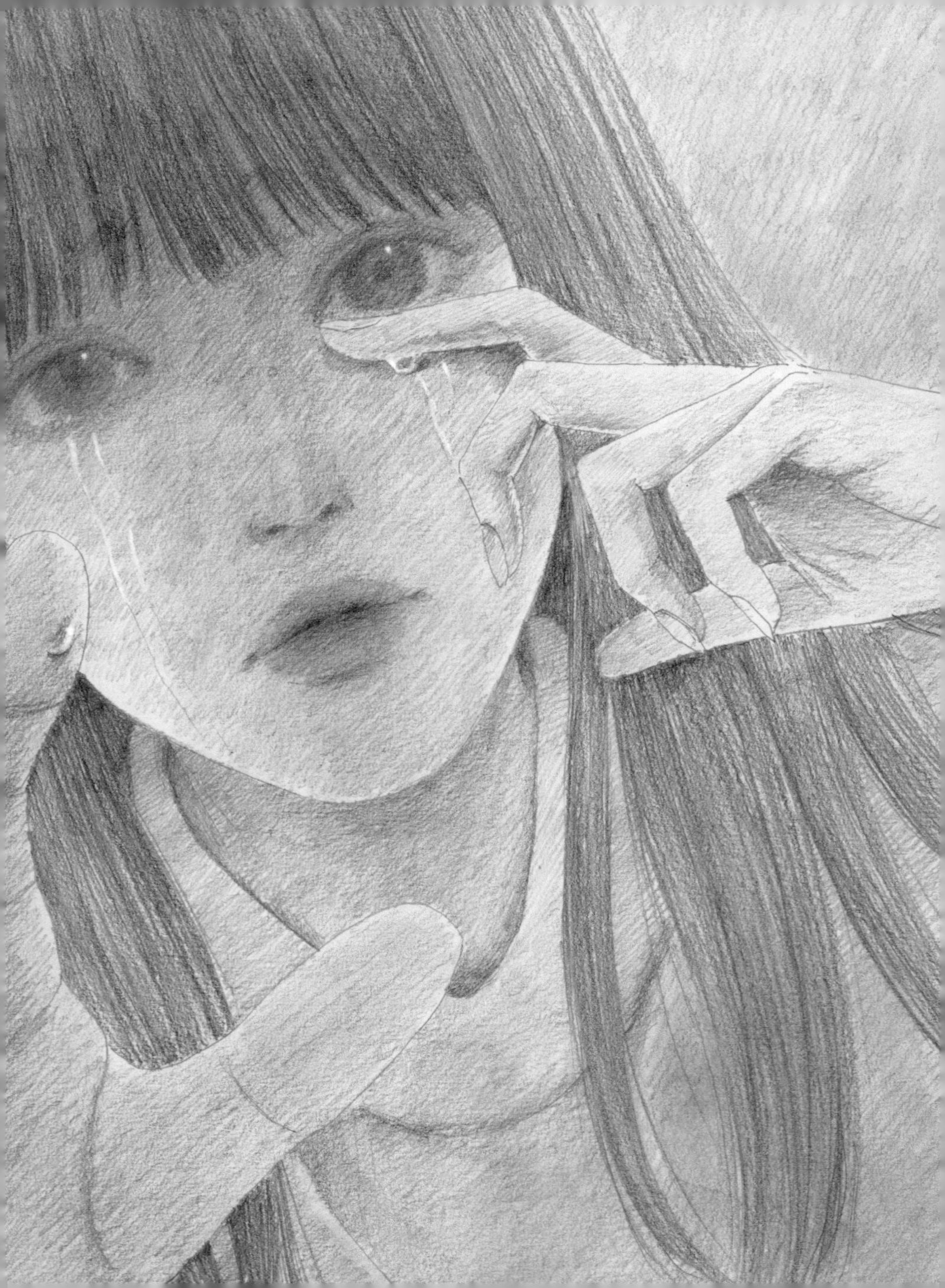

CHAPTER 100 Mommy

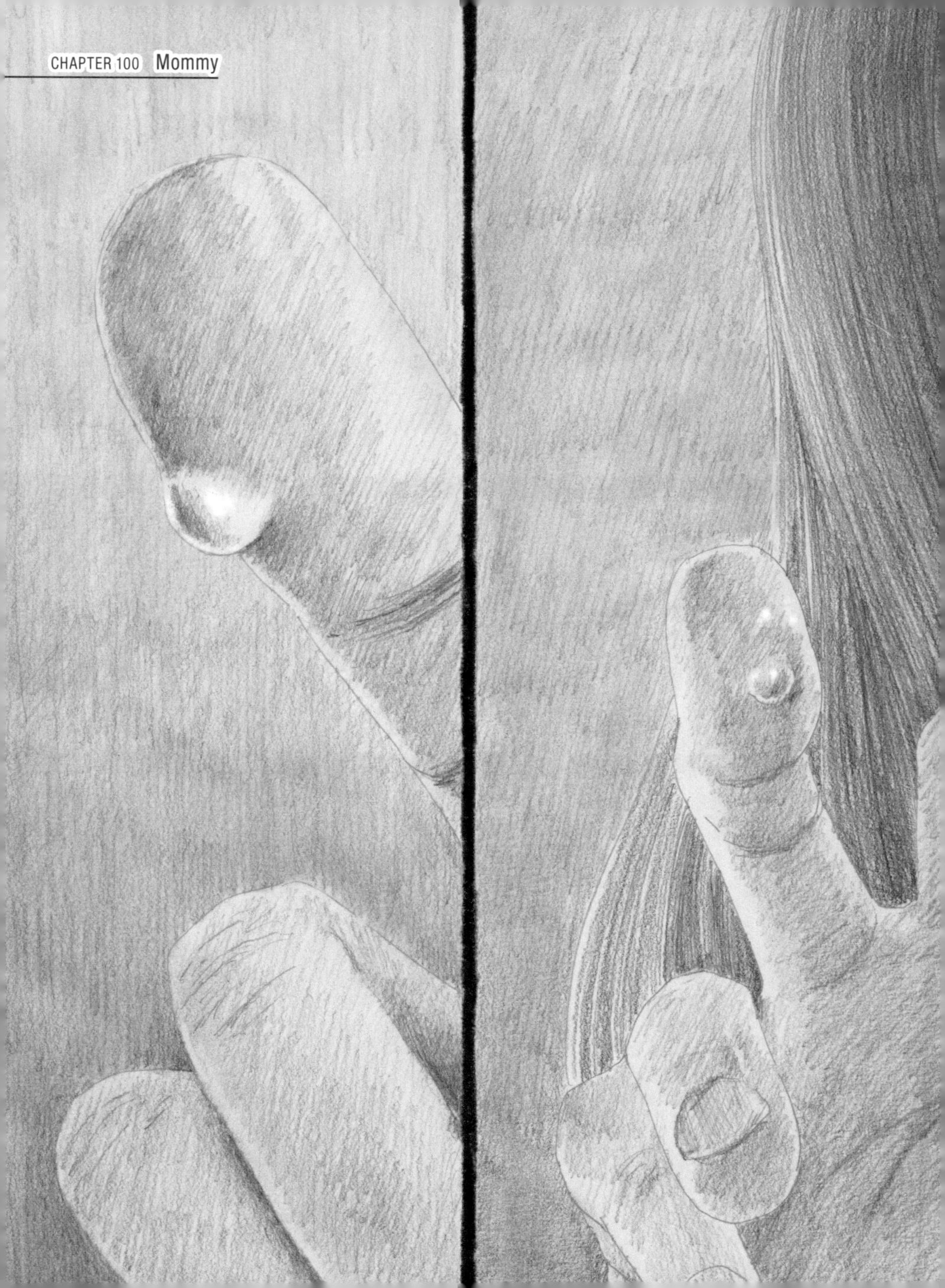

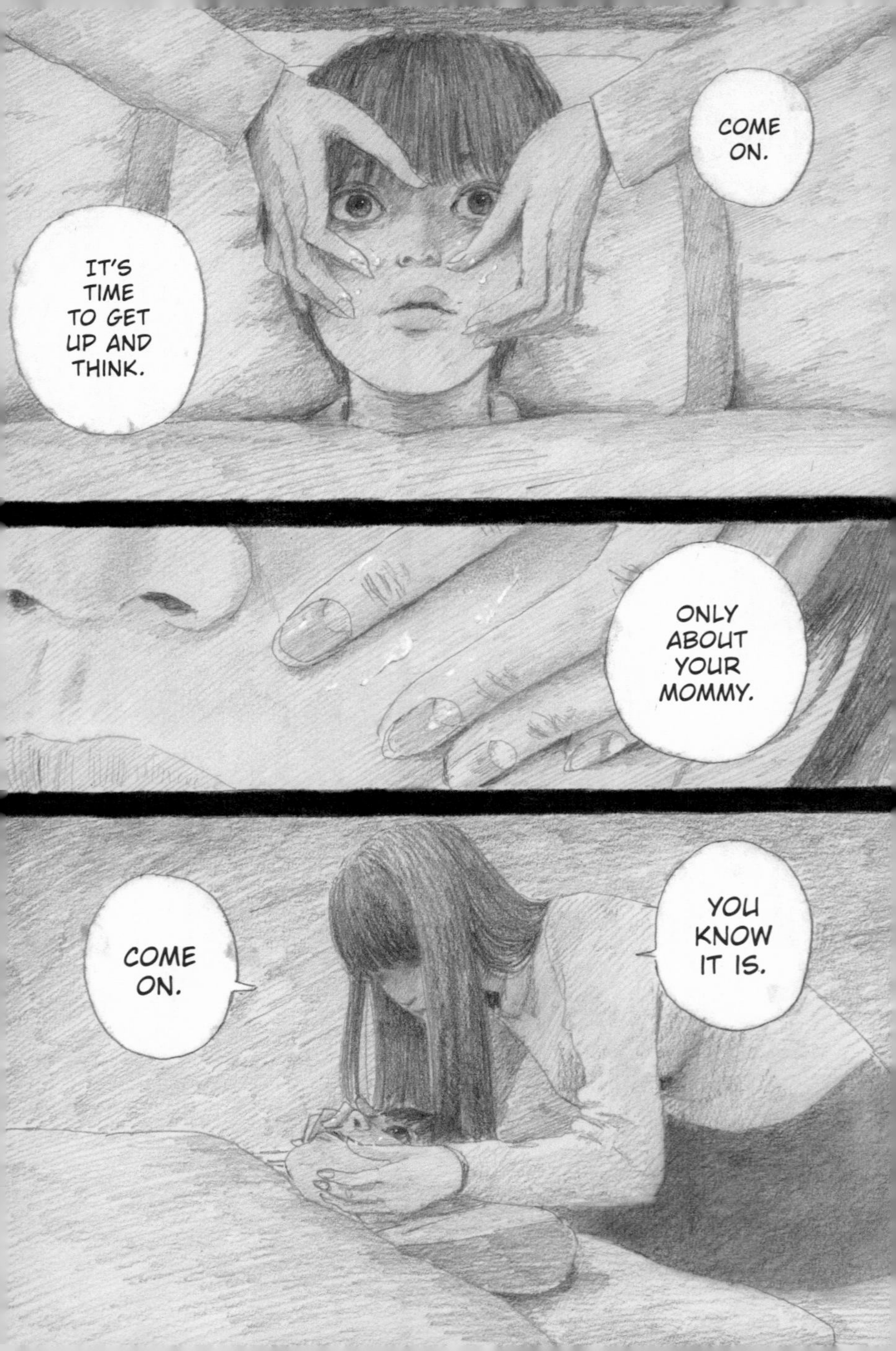
COME ON.
IT'S TIME TO GET UP AND THINK.
ONLY ABOUT YOUR MOMMY.
YOU KNOW IT IS.
COME ON.

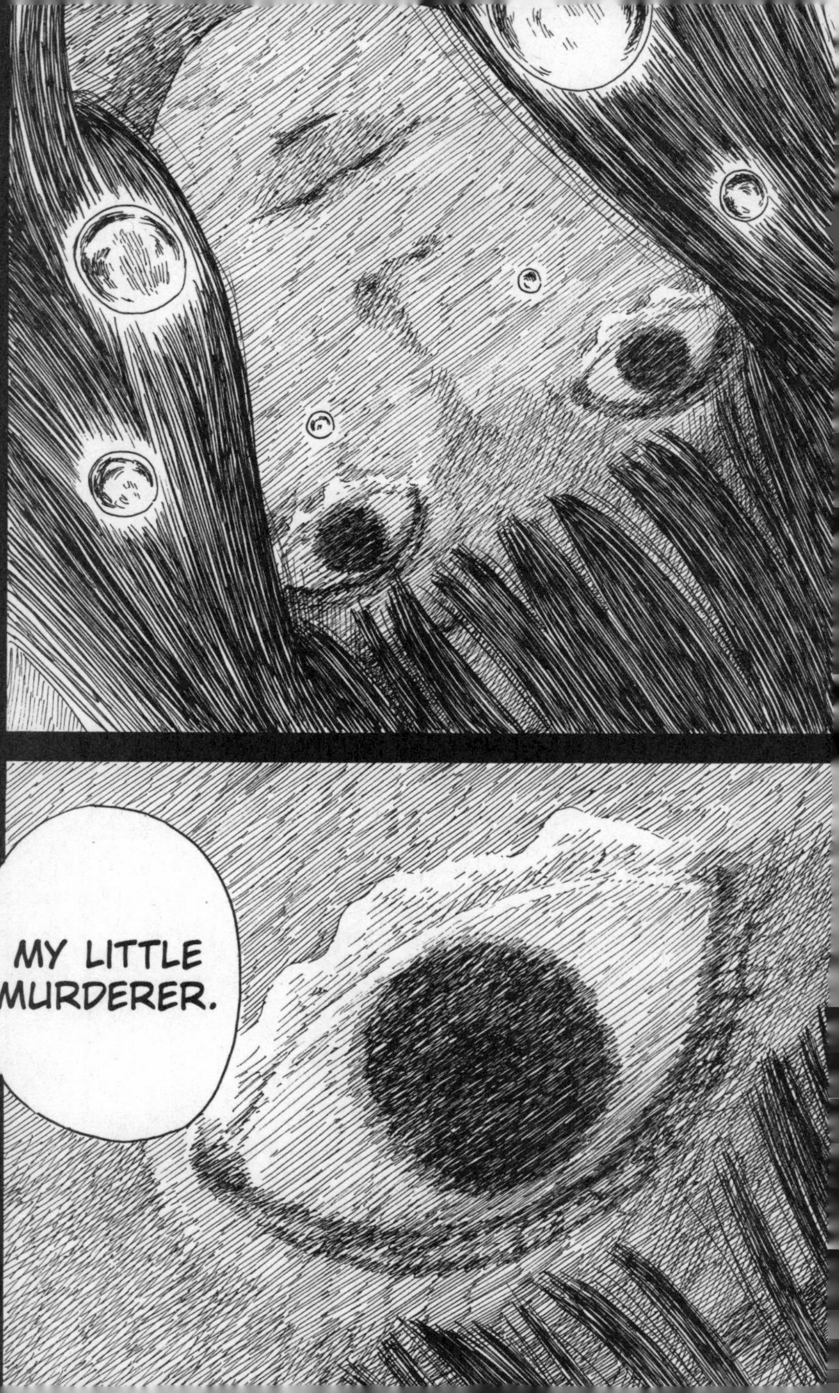
MY LITTLE MURDERER.

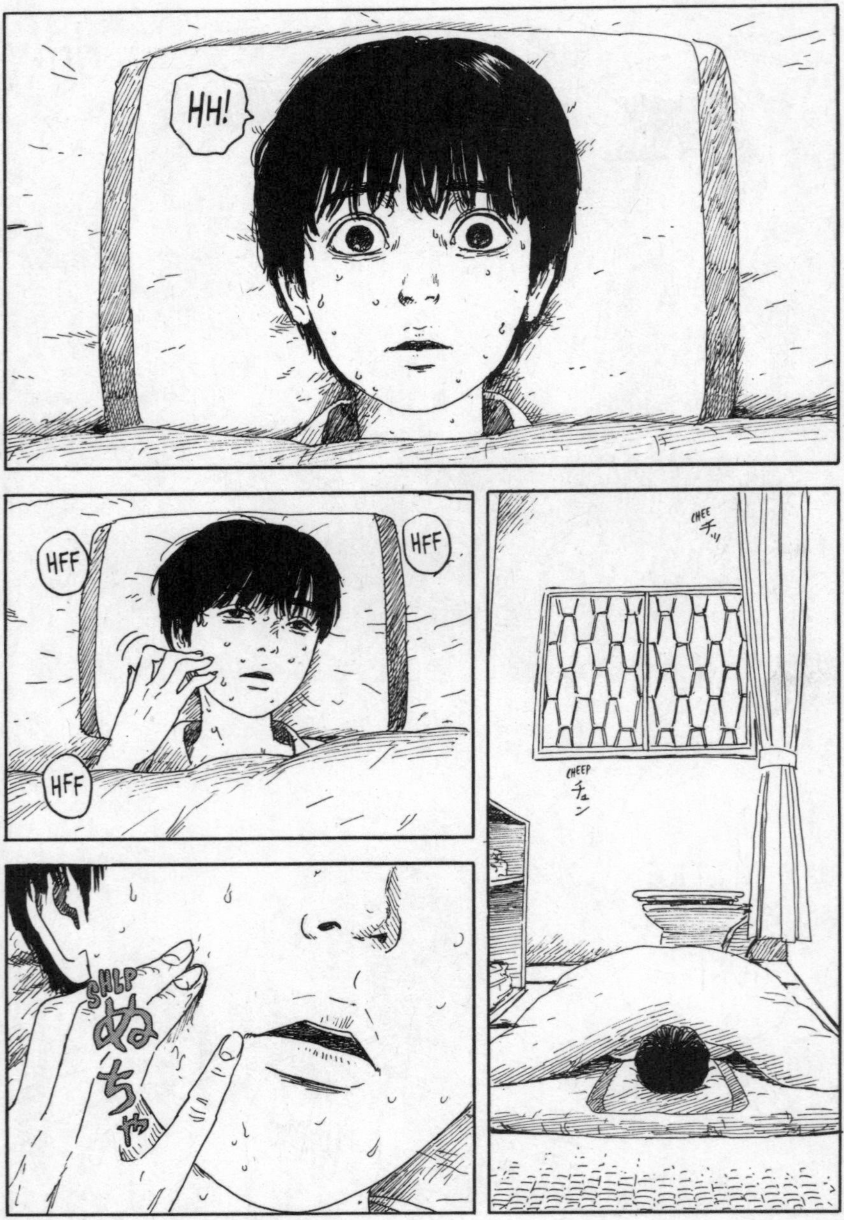
HH!
CHEE
チッ
CHEEP
チュン
HFF
HFF
HFF
SHLP
ぬちゃ

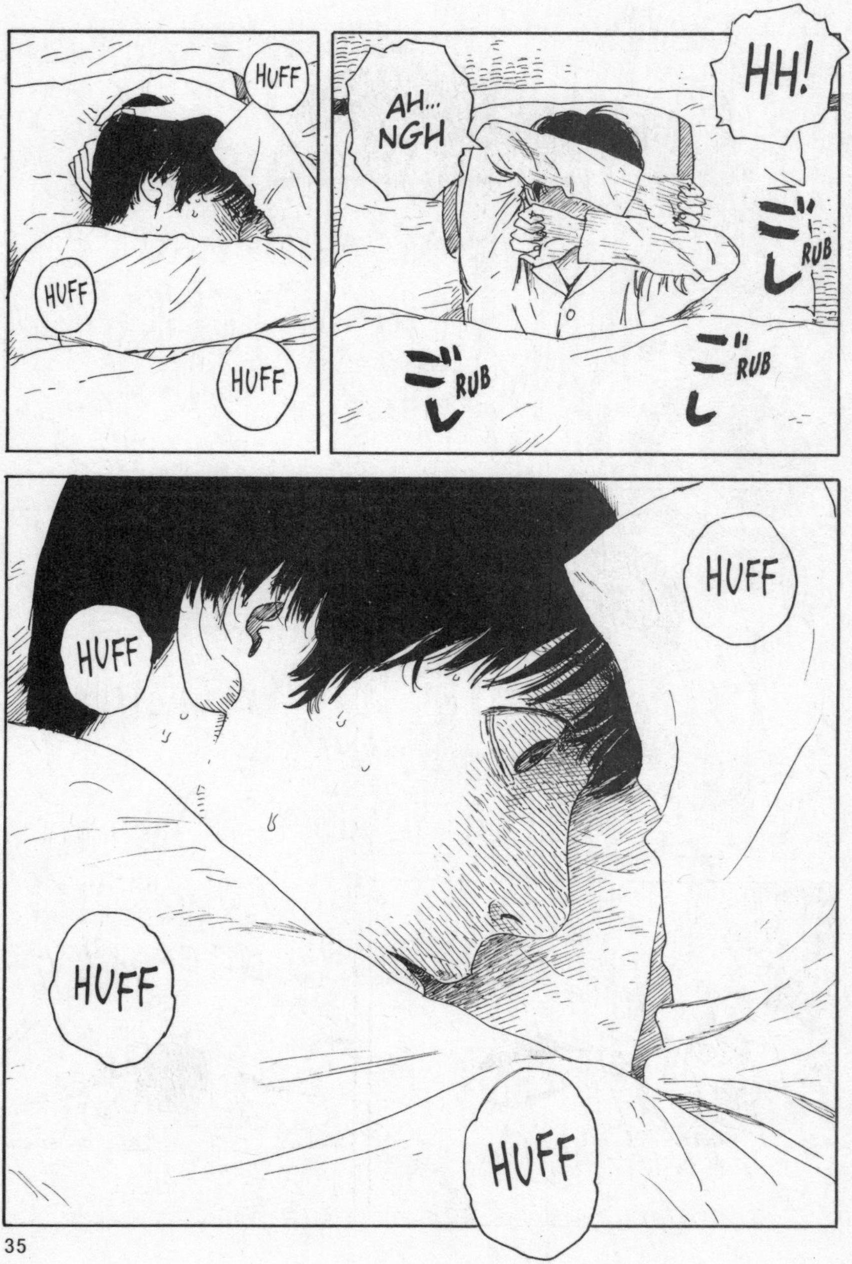
HH!
AH... NGH
ごし RUB
ごし RUB
ごし RUB
HUFF
HUFF
HUFF
HUFF
HUFF
HUFF
HUFF

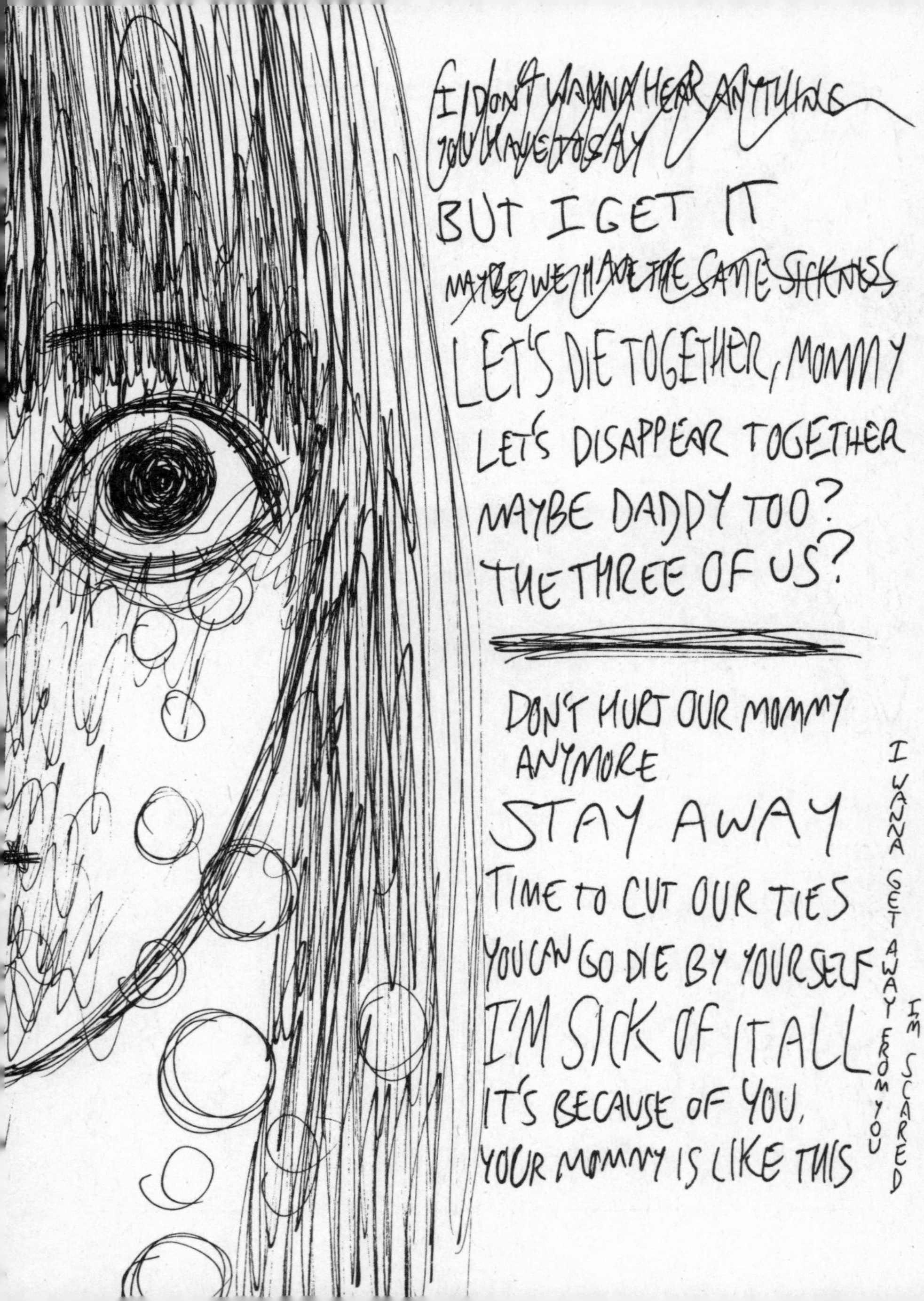

I DON'T WANNA HEAR ANYTHING
YOU HAVE TO SAY

BUT I GET IT

MAYBE WE HAVE THE SAME SICKNESS

LET'S DIE TOGETHER, MOMMY

LET'S DISAPPEAR TOGETHER

MAYBE DADDY TOO?

THE THREE OF US?

DON'T HURT OUR MOMMY
ANYMORE

STAY AWAY

TIME TO CUT OUR TIES

YOU CAN GO DIE BY YOURSELF

I'M SICK OF IT ALL

IT'S BECAUSE OF YOU,
YOUR MOMMY IS LIKE THIS

I WANNA GET AWAY FROM YOU

I'M SCARED

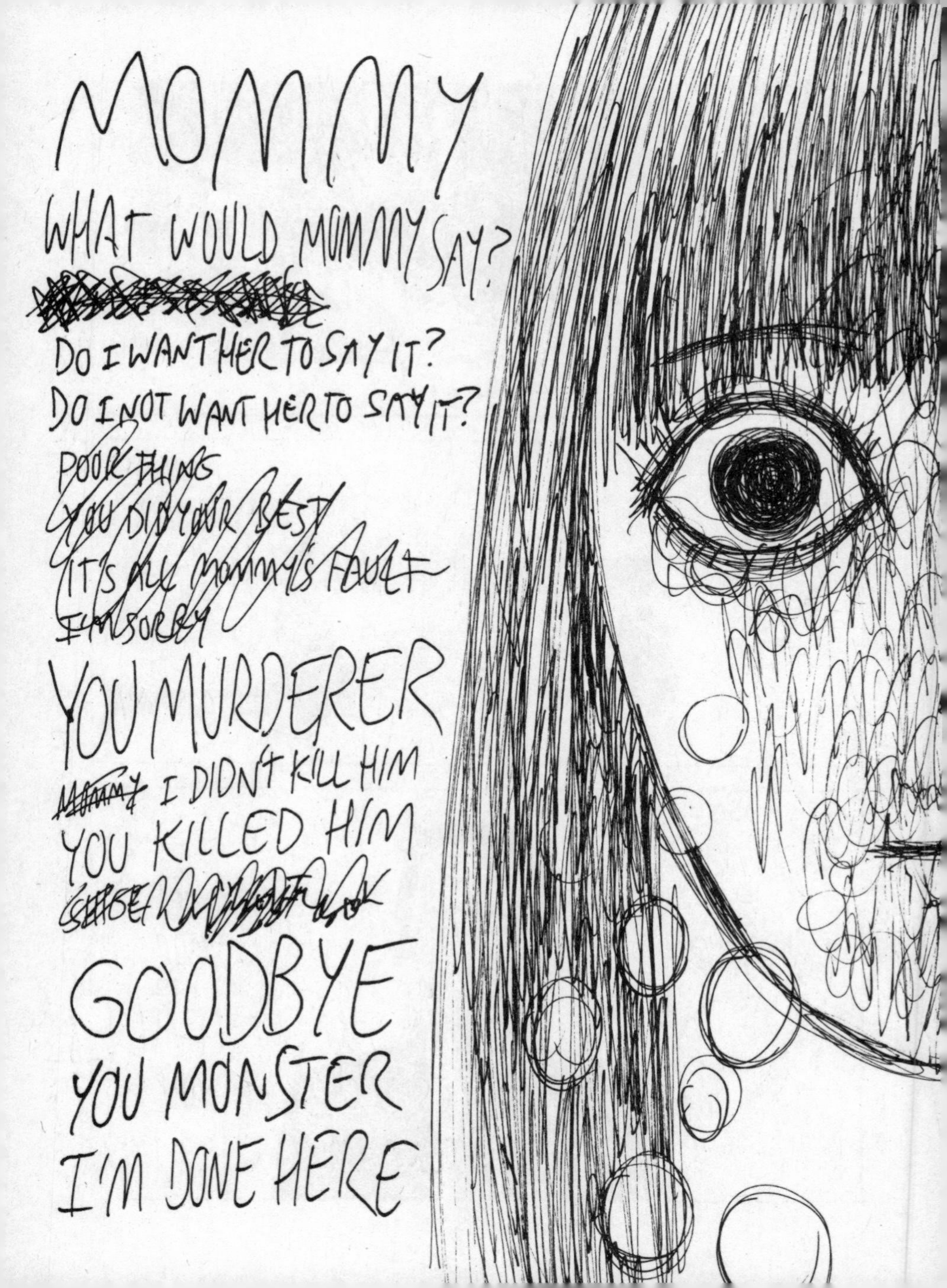
MOMMY
WHAT WOULD MOMMY SAY?
DO I WANT HER TO SAY IT?
DO I NOT WANT HER TO SAY IT?
POOR THING
YOU DID YOUR BEST
IT'S ALL MOMMY'S FAULT
I'M SORRY
YOU MURDERER
MOMMY I DIDN'T KILL HIM
YOU KILLED HIM
GOODBYE
YOU MONSTER
I'M DONE HERE

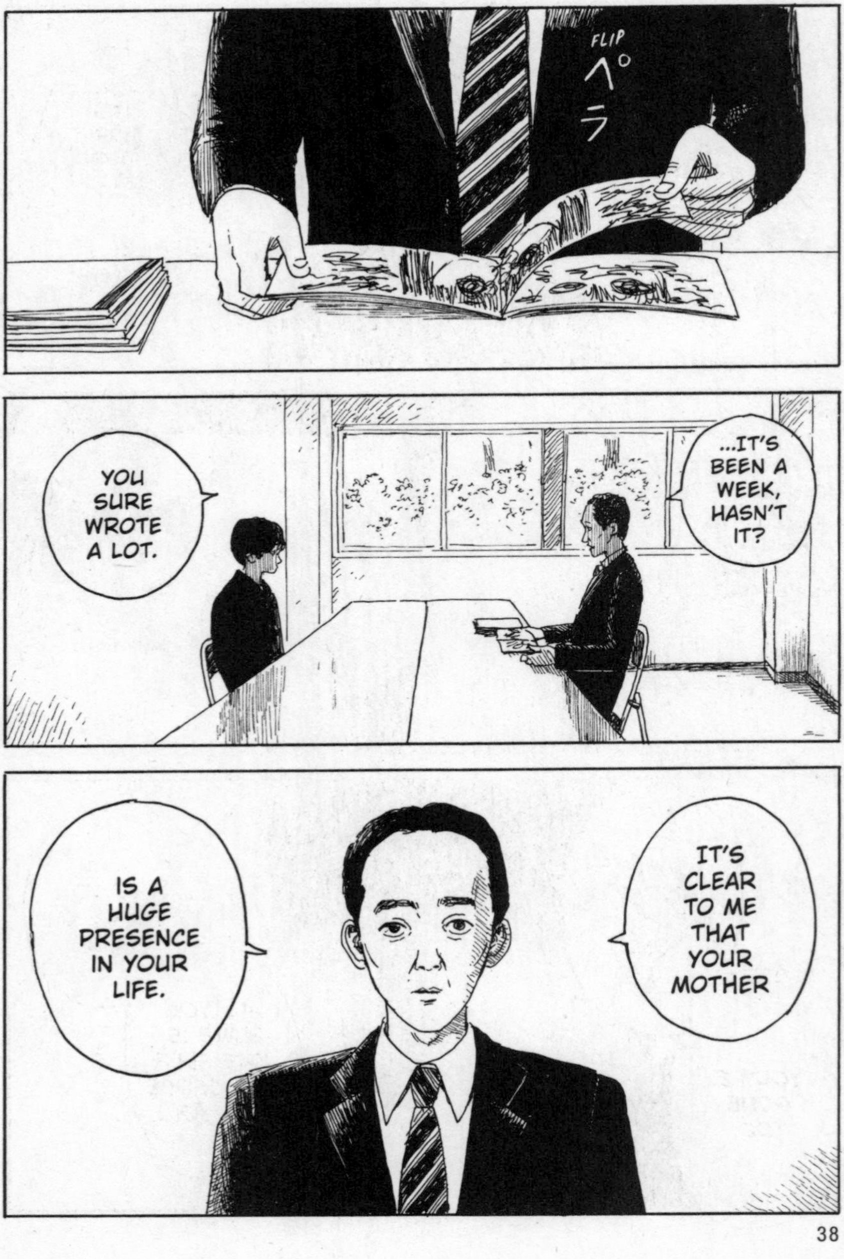
FLIP
ペラ
...IT'S BEEN A WEEK, HASN'T IT?
YOU SURE WROTE A LOT.
IT'S CLEAR TO ME THAT YOUR MOTHER
IS A HUGE PRESENCE IN YOUR LIFE.

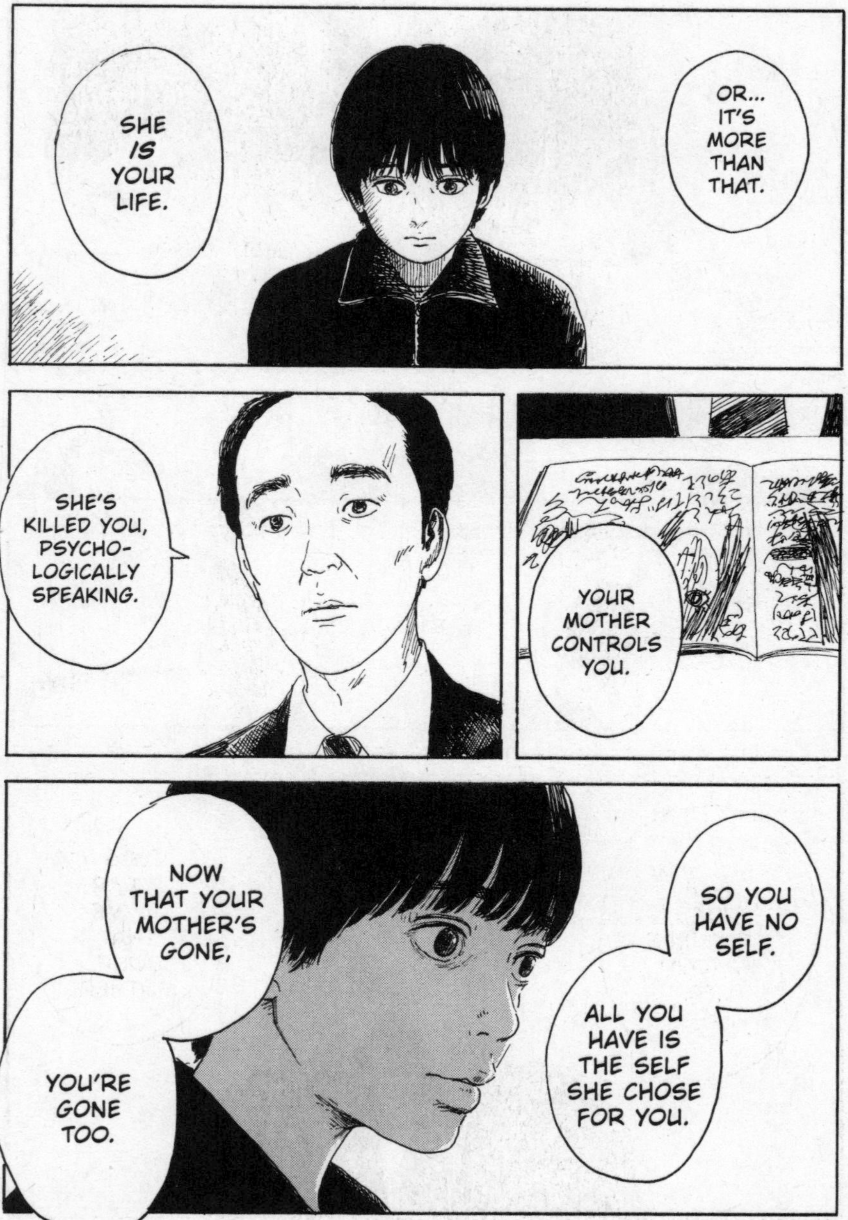
SHE *IS* YOUR LIFE.
OR... IT'S MORE THAN THAT.
SHE'S KILLED YOU, PSYCHO-LOGICALLY SPEAKING.
YOUR MOTHER CONTROLS YOU.
NOW THAT YOUR MOTHER'S GONE,
YOU'RE GONE TOO.
SO YOU HAVE NO SELF.
ALL YOU HAVE IS THE SELF SHE CHOSE FOR YOU.

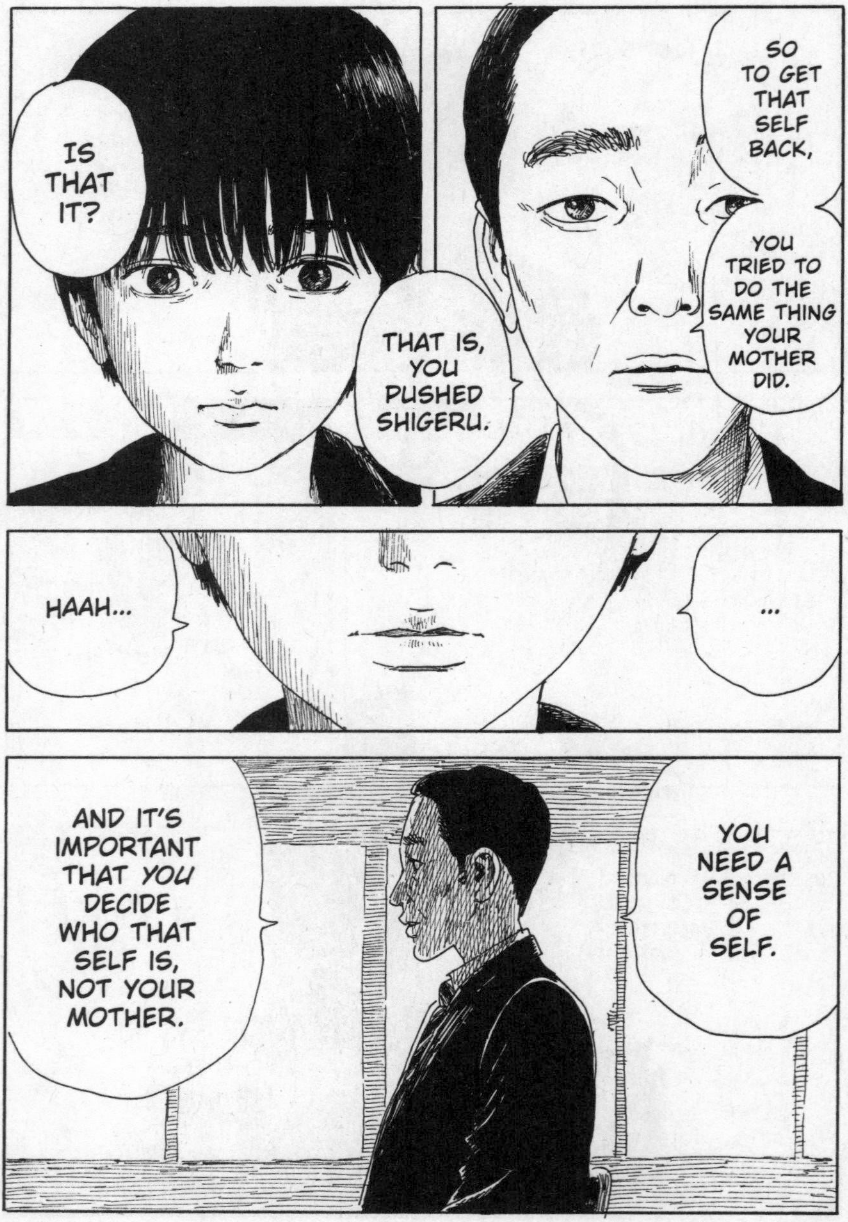
SO TO GET THAT SELF BACK,
YOU TRIED TO DO THE SAME THING YOUR MOTHER DID.
THAT IS, YOU PUSHED SHIGERU.
IS THAT IT?
...
HAAH...
YOU NEED A SENSE OF SELF.
AND IT'S IMPORTANT THAT *YOU* DECIDE WHO THAT SELF IS, NOT YOUR MOTHER.

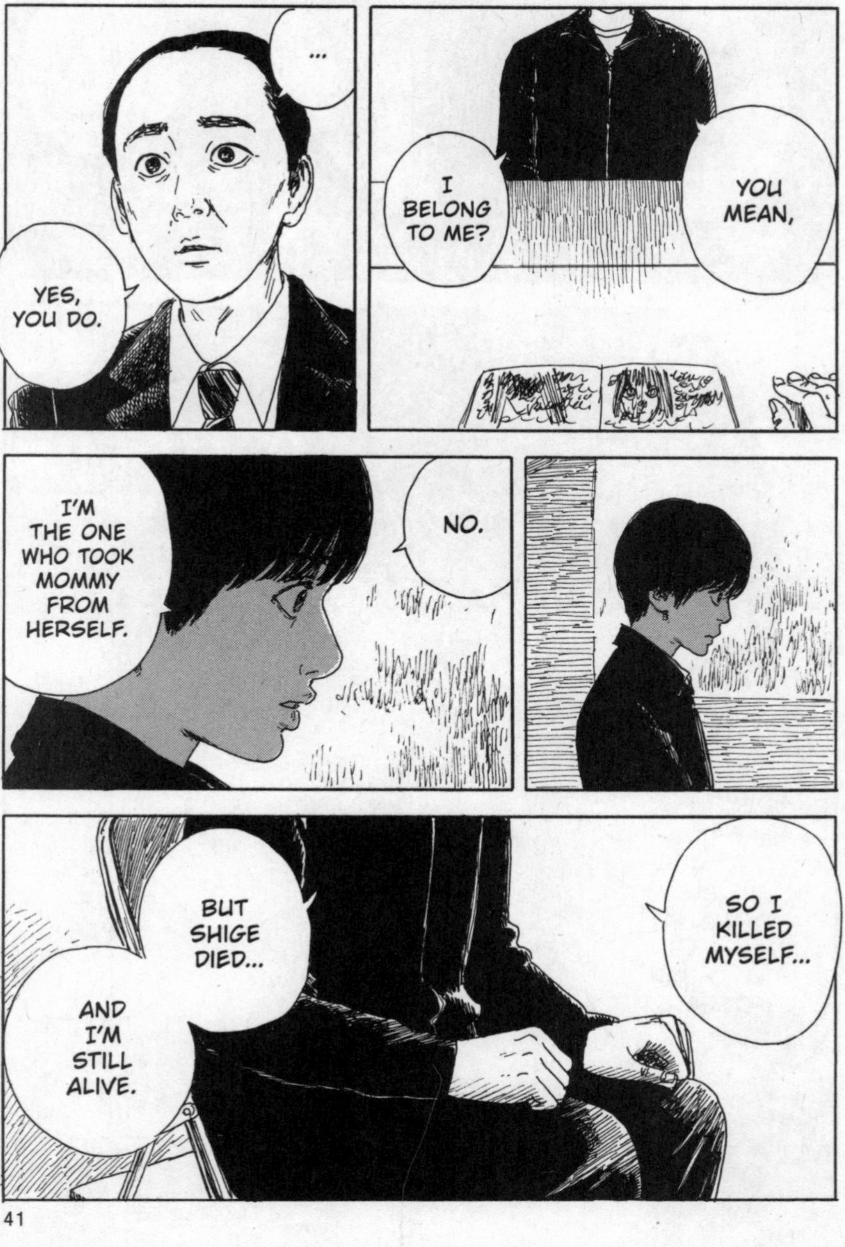
YOU MEAN,
I BELONG TO ME?
...
YES, YOU DO.
NO.
I'M THE ONE WHO TOOK MOMMY FROM HERSELF.
SO I KILLED MYSELF...
BUT SHIGE DIED...
AND I'M STILL ALIVE.

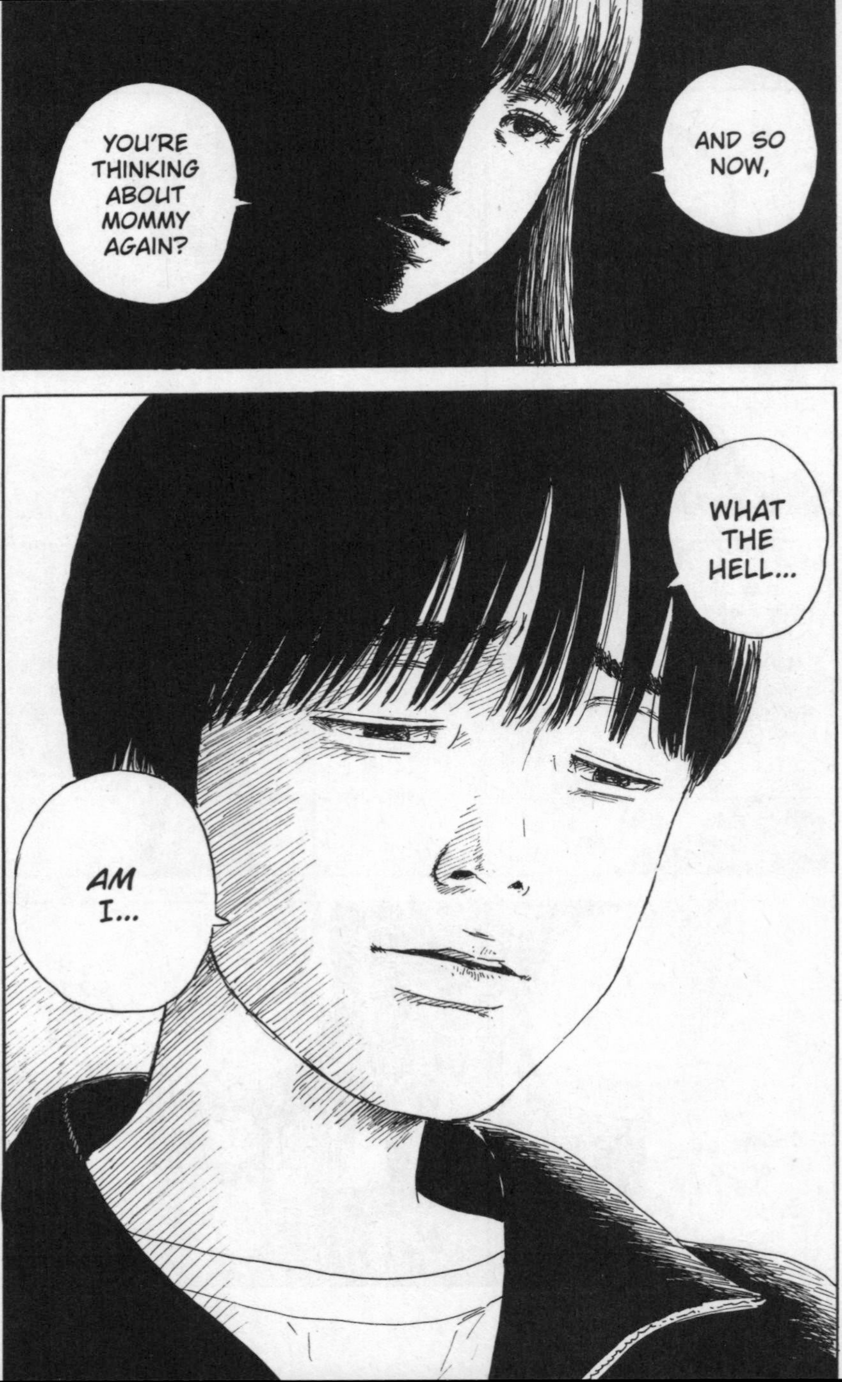
AND SO NOW,
YOU'RE THINKING ABOUT MOMMY AGAIN?
WHAT THE HELL...
AM I...

WHY DID SHIGERU COME TO YOUR HOUSE IN THE MIDDLE OF THE NIGHT?

YOU MUST HAVE CALLED HIM OR SOMETHING, RIGHT?

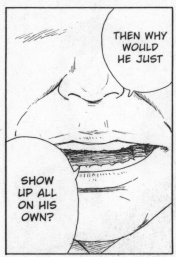

THEN WHY WOULD HE JUST

SHOW UP ALL ON HIS OWN?

...NO...

I DIDN'T.

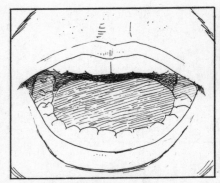

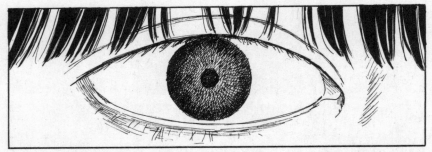

HOW'S IT GOING?
YOU SLEEPING OKAY?
SO, ABOUT SHIGERU.
WHAT DO YOU THINK? ANY NEW IDEAS?

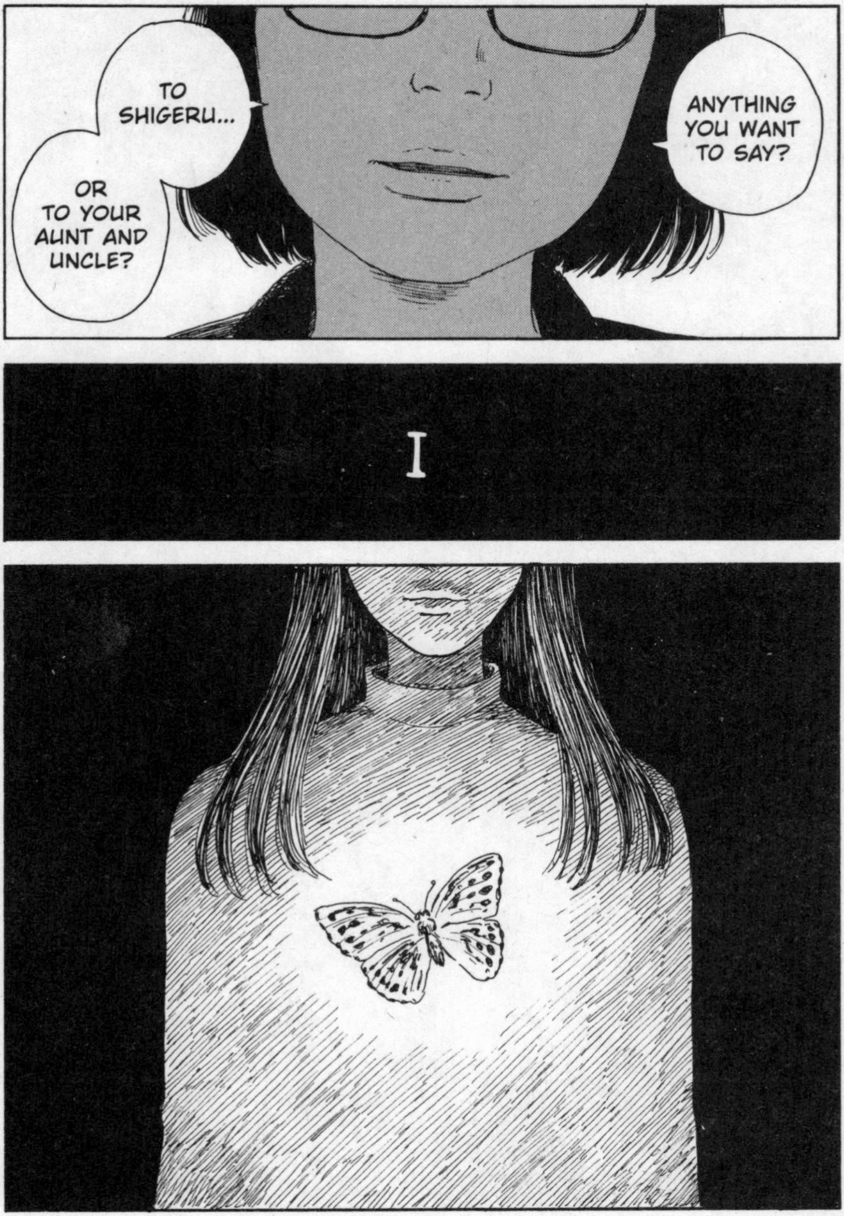
ANYTHING YOU WANT TO SAY?
TO SHIGERU...
OR TO YOUR AUNT AND UNCLE?
I

I

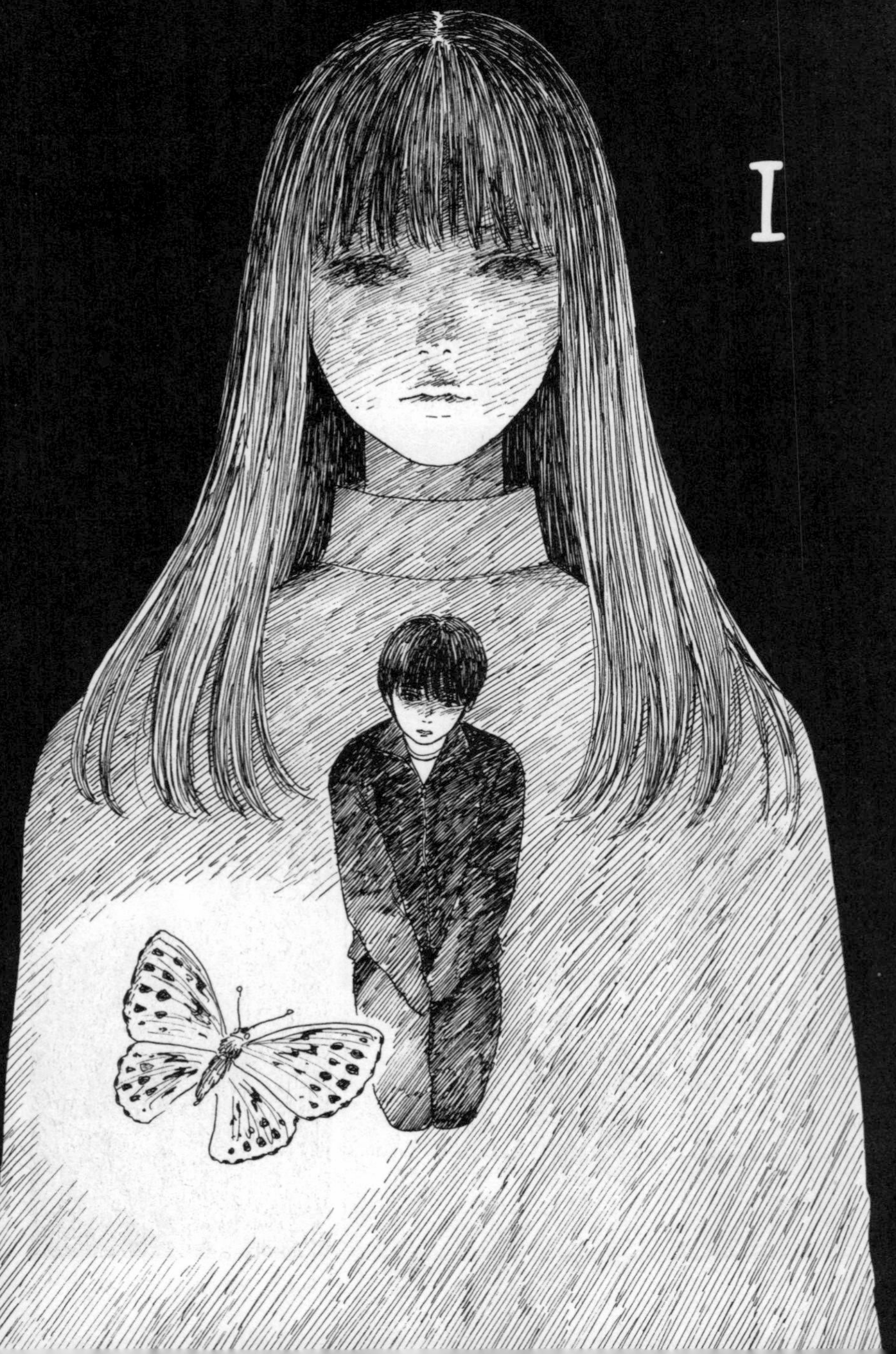

ROOM 14!

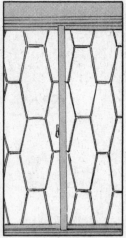

THEY WANT TO TALK TO YOU.

COME WITH US.

47

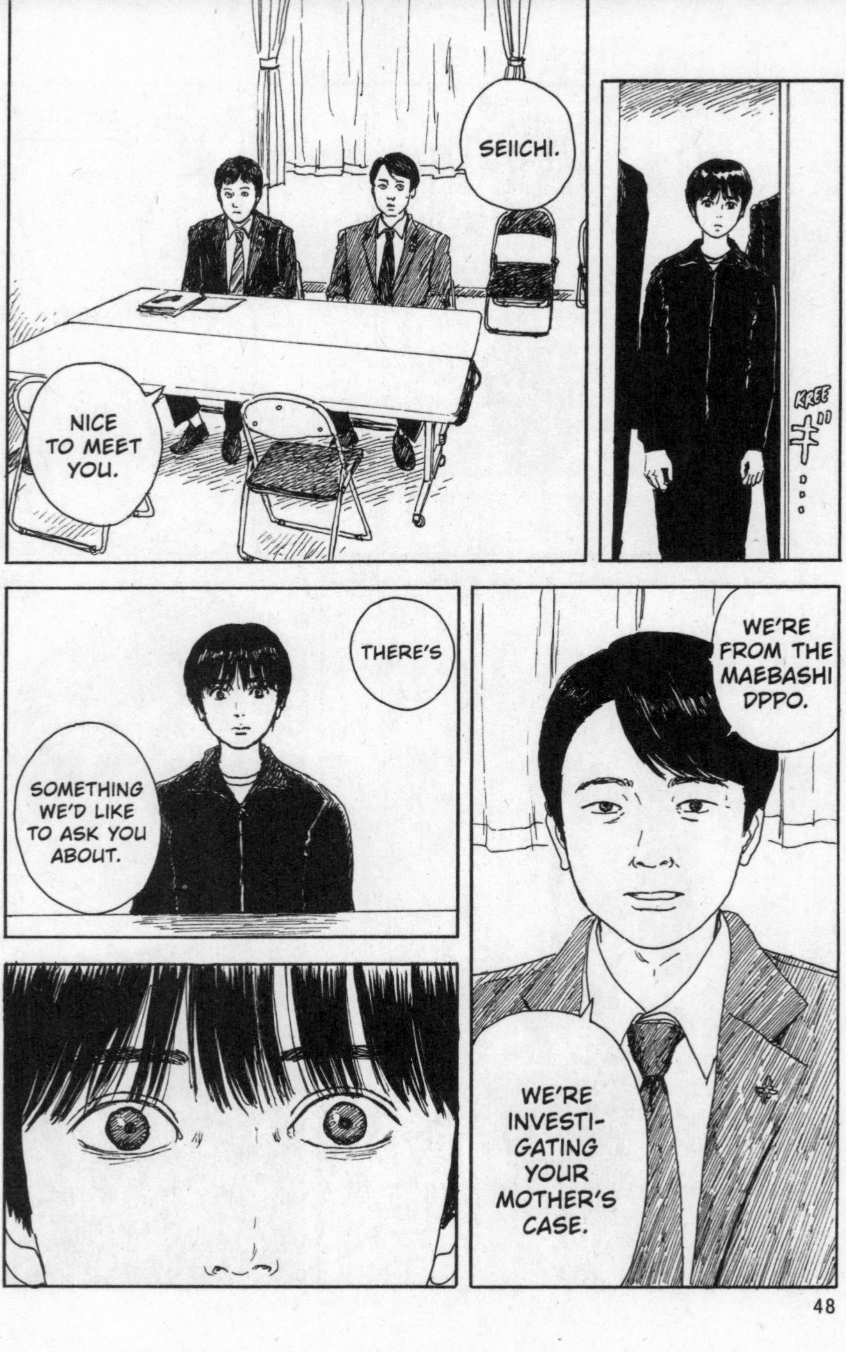
KREE
SEIICHI.
NICE TO MEET YOU.
WE'RE FROM THE MAEBASHI DPPO.
WE'RE INVESTIGATING YOUR MOTHER'S CASE.
THERE'S
SOMETHING WE'D LIKE TO ASK YOU ABOUT.

YOUR MOTHER'S PSYCHIATRIC EVALUATION IS FINISHED.
SHE WAS FOUND FIT TO STAND TRIAL,
SO NOW SHE'S UNDER EXAMINATION BY THE PROSECUTOR.
IN HER PRIOR INTERVIEWS WITH POLICE...
SHE'D ADMITTED TO THE ALLEGATIONS,
AND AGREED THAT THINGS WERE JUST AS YOU TESTIFIED.

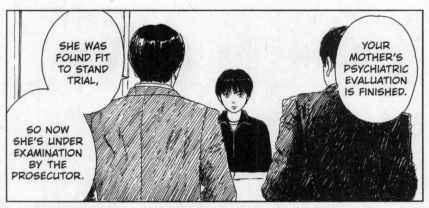

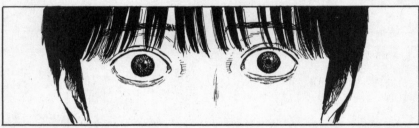

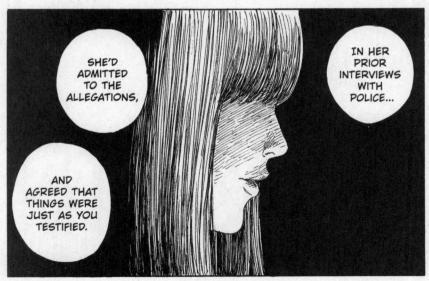

THE THING IS,
NOW SHE'S CHANGED HER STORY.
SHE'S SAYING
SHE DIDN'T DO IT.

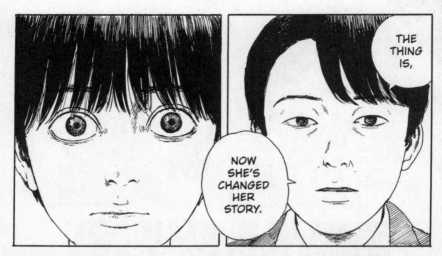

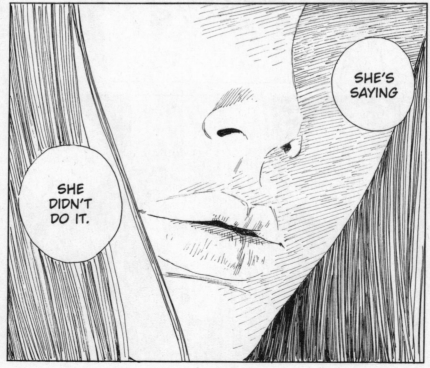

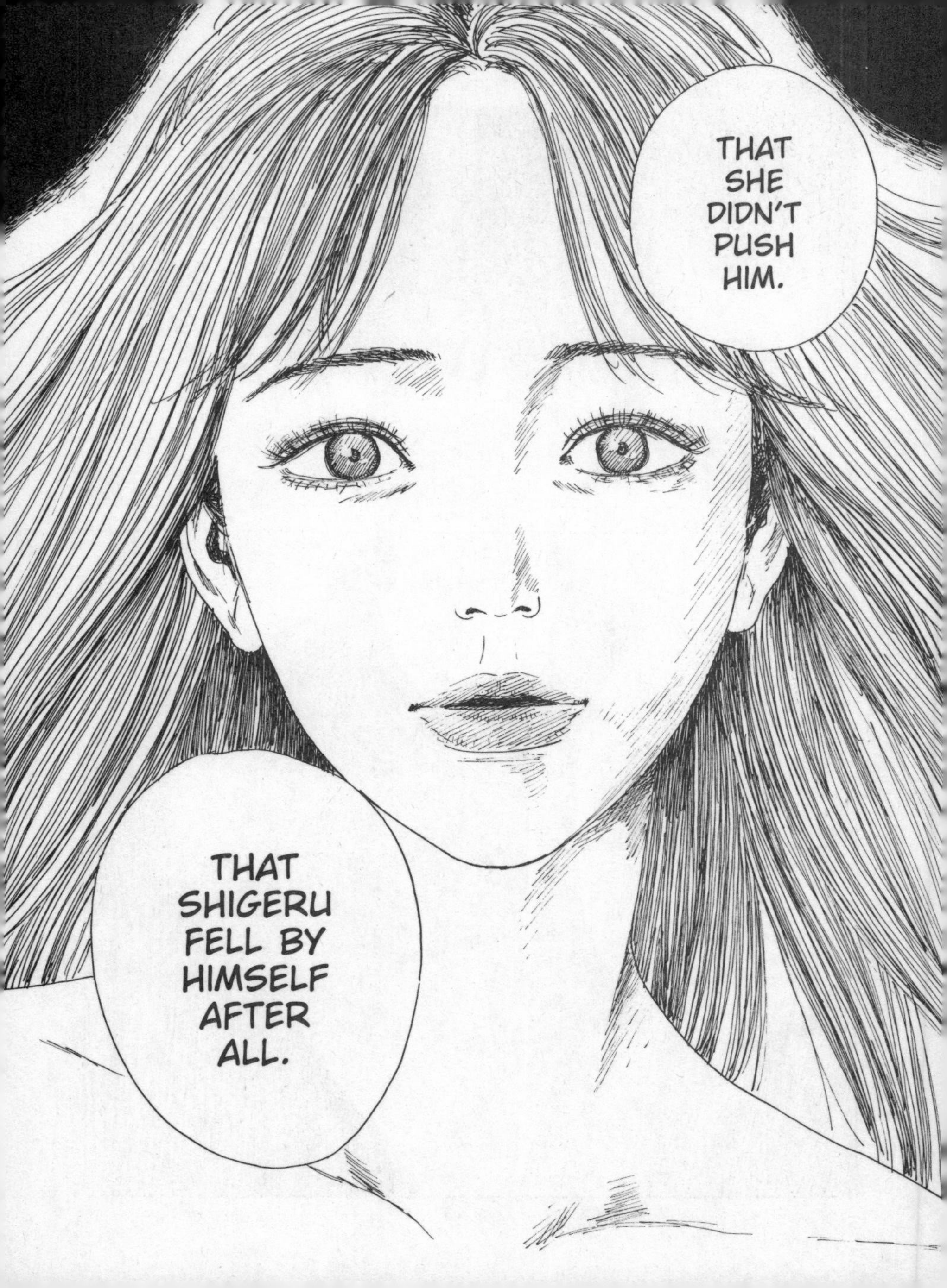
THAT SHE DIDN'T PUSH HIM.
THAT SHIGERU FELL BY HIMSELF AFTER ALL.

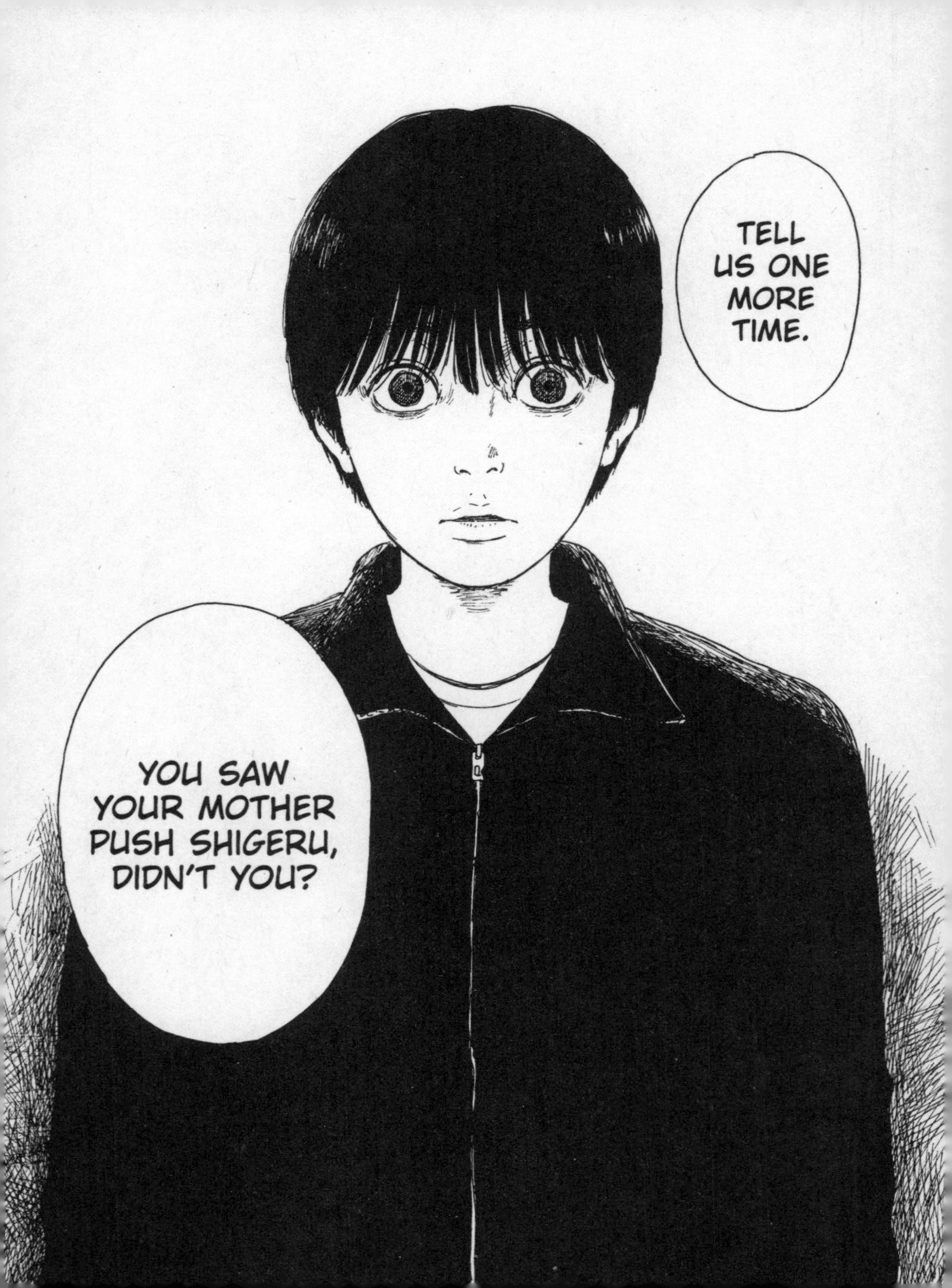
TELL US ONE MORE TIME.
YOU SAW YOUR MOTHER PUSH SHIGERU, DIDN'T YOU?

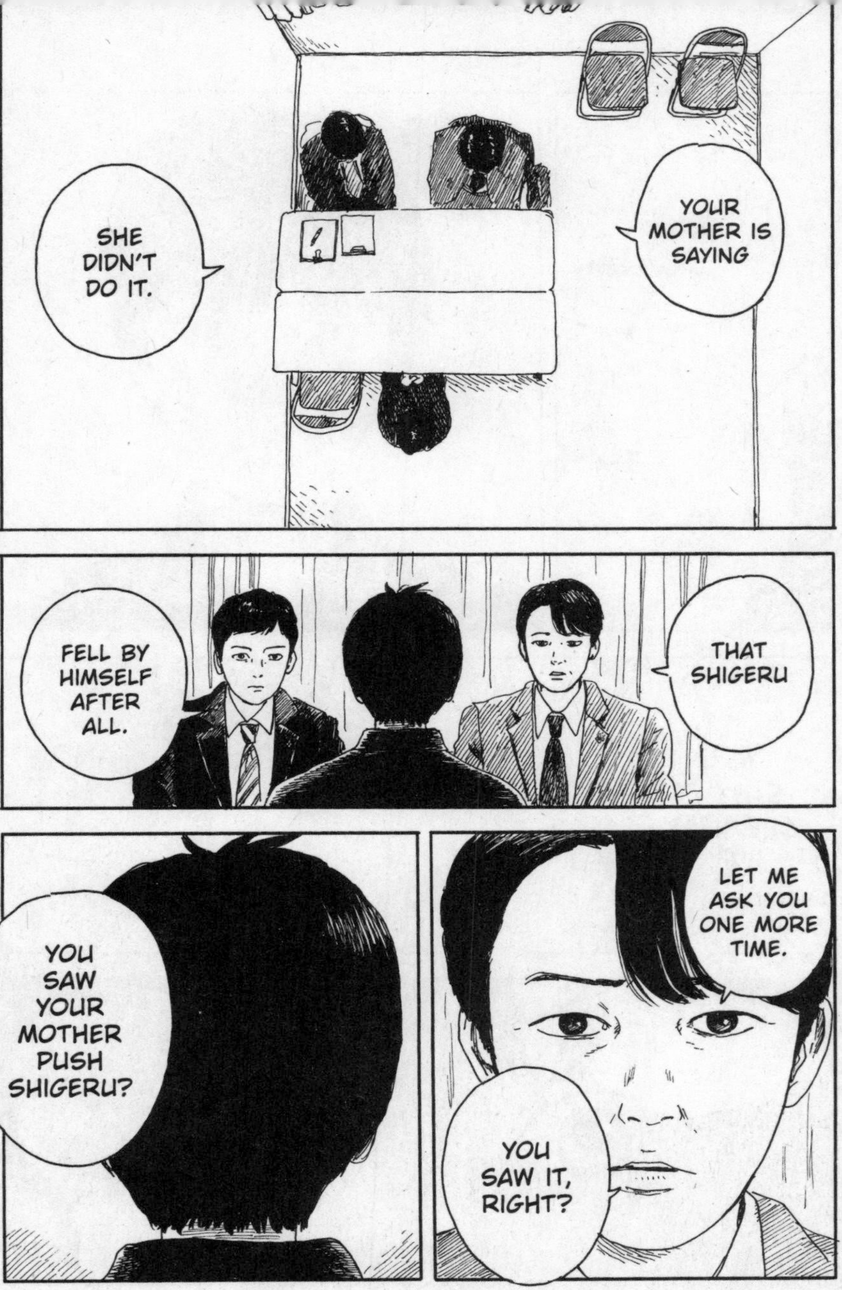
YOUR MOTHER IS SAYING
SHE DIDN'T DO IT.
THAT SHIGERU
FELL BY HIMSELF AFTER ALL.
LET ME ASK YOU ONE MORE TIME.
YOU SAW IT, RIGHT?
YOU SAW YOUR MOTHER PUSH SHIGERU?

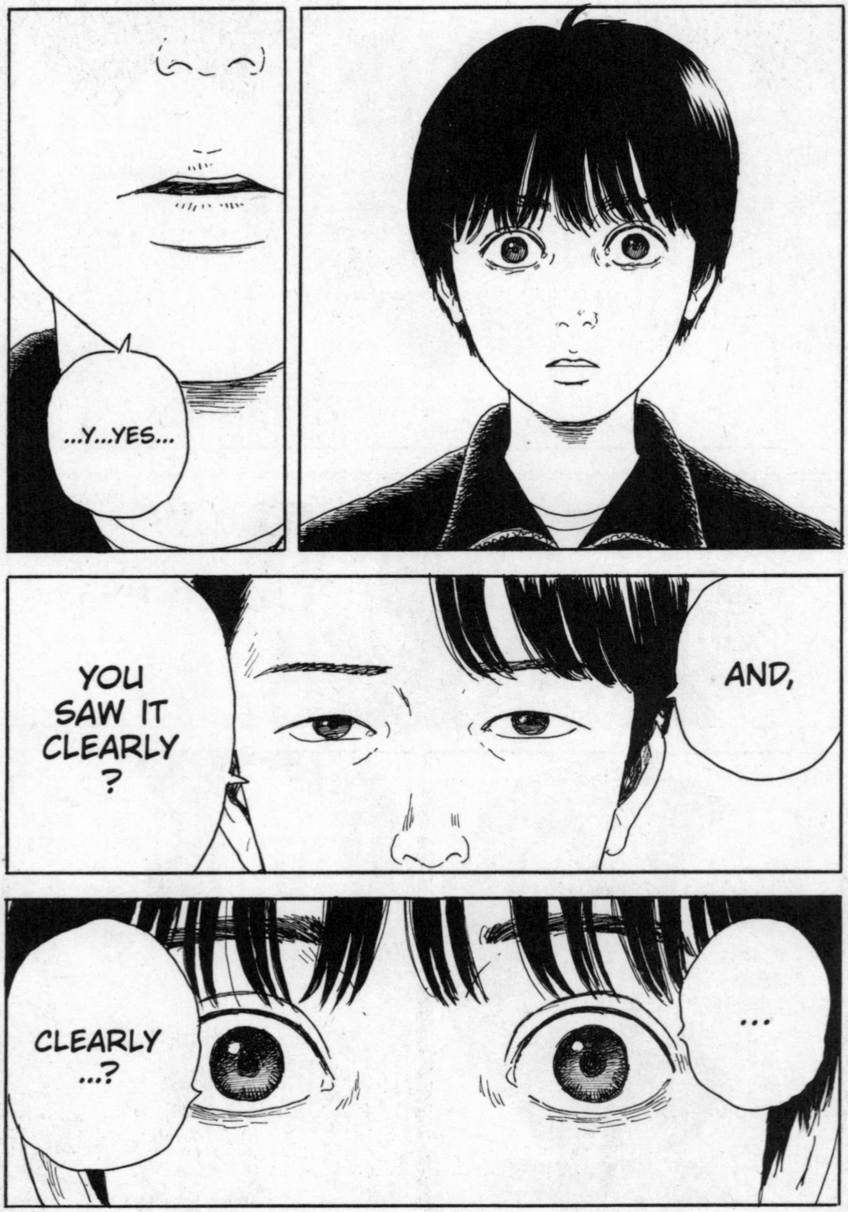
...Y...YES...
AND,
YOU SAW IT CLEARLY?
...
CLEARLY ...?

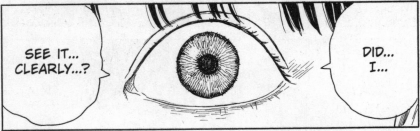

SEE IT...
CLEARLY...?

DID...
I...

Awhh?

Oh,
shut
up!

IT...
LOOKED
LIKE IT...

BUT...
IT
COULD
BE...

THAT...
I WAS
THINKING...

...NO...
I KNOW
I WAS
THINKING...

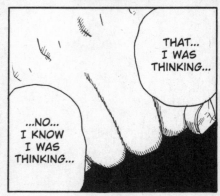

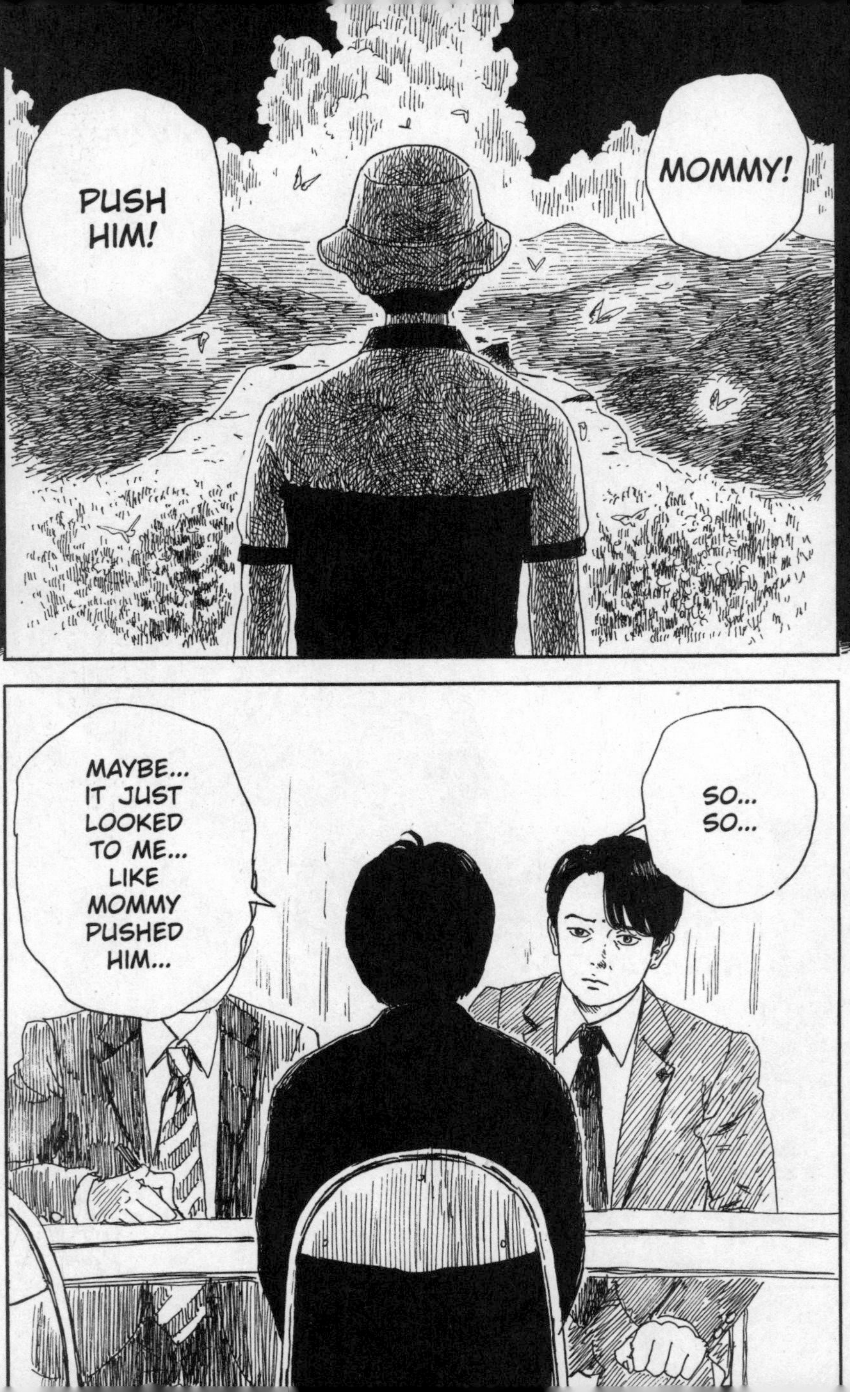
MOMMY!
PUSH HIM!
SO... SO...
MAYBE... IT JUST LOOKED TO ME... LIKE MOMMY PUSHED HIM...

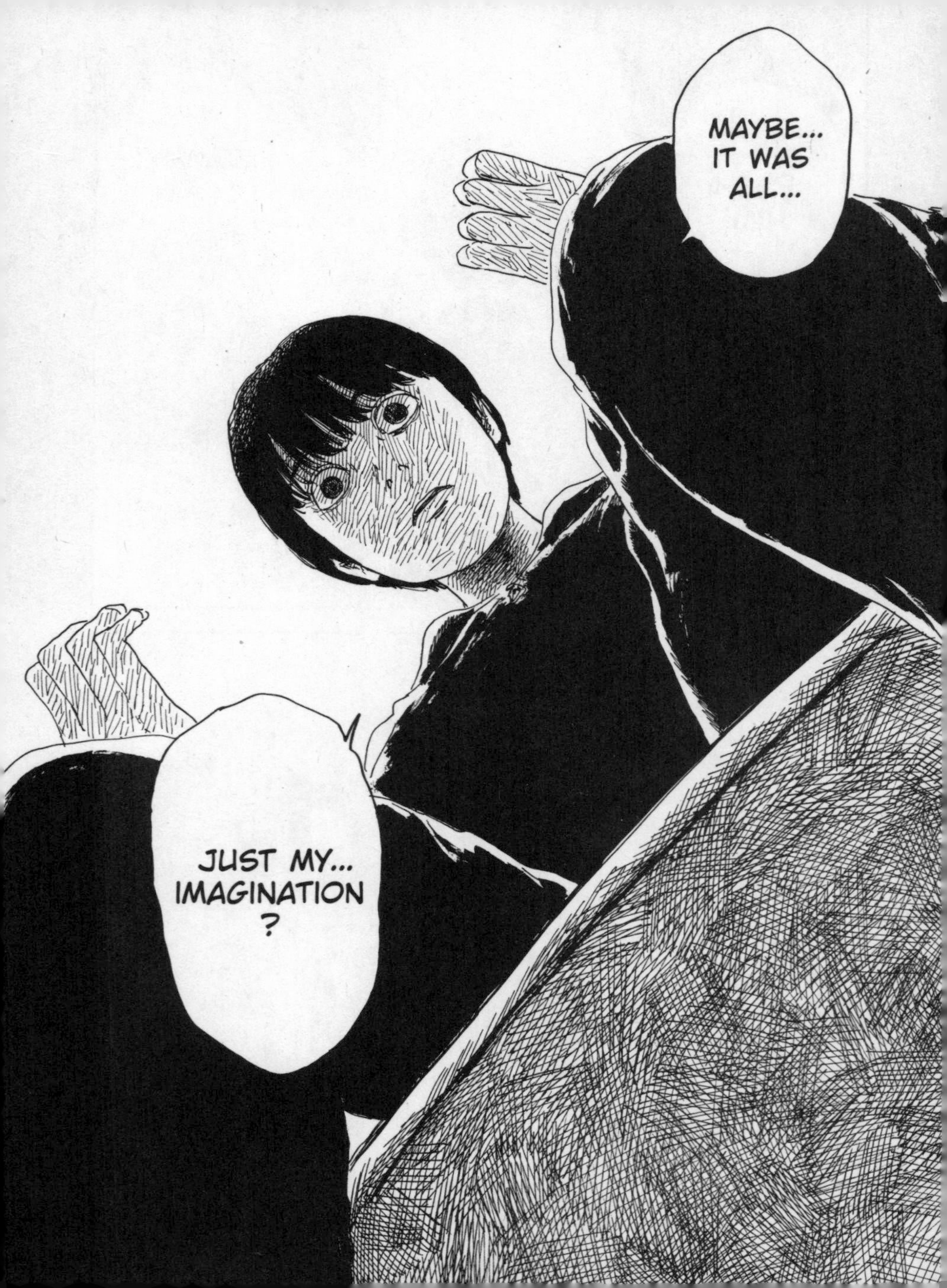
MAYBE... IT WAS ALL...
JUST MY... IMAGINATION ?

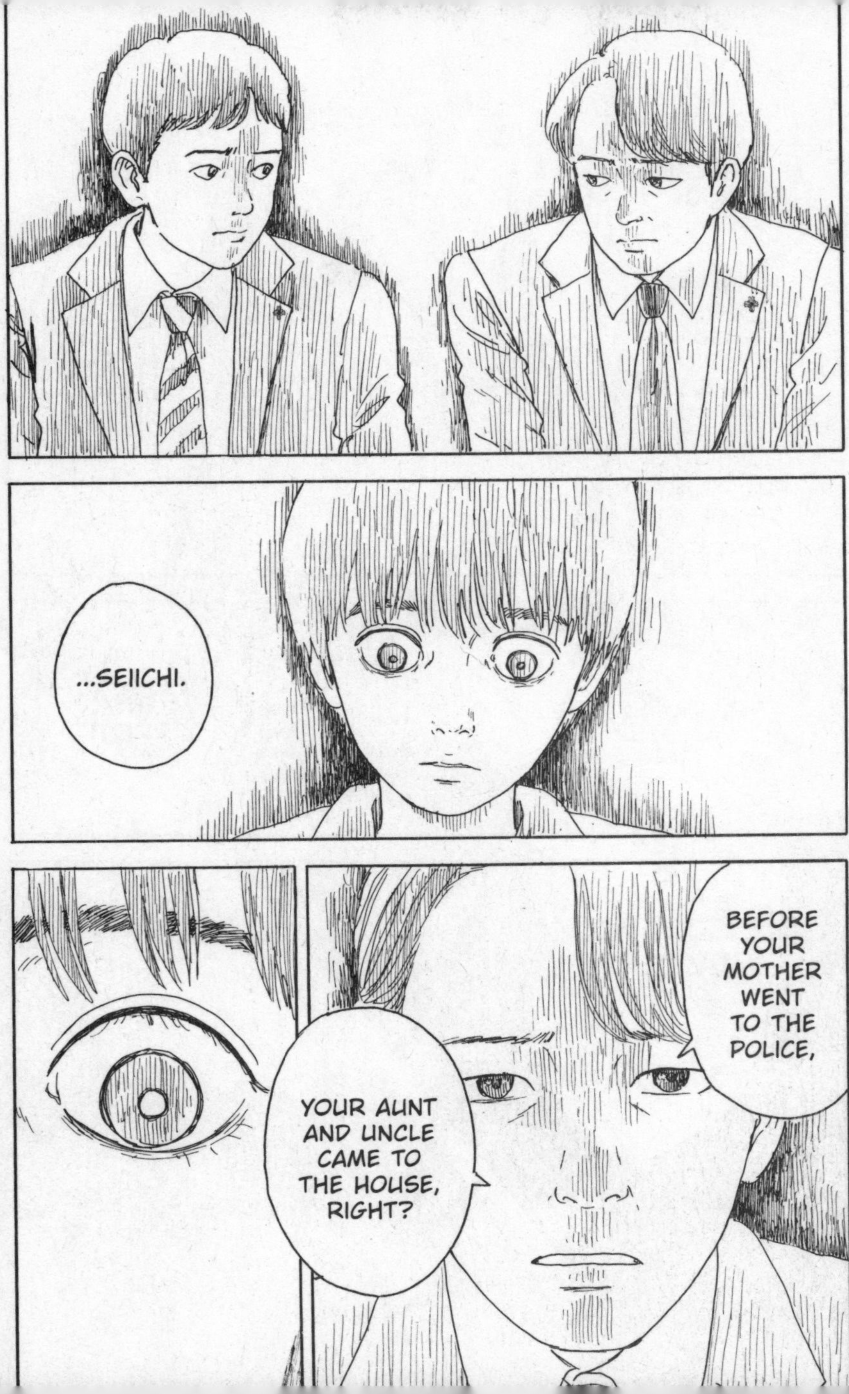
...SEIICHI.
BEFORE YOUR MOTHER WENT TO THE POLICE,
YOUR AUNT AND UNCLE CAME TO THE HOUSE, RIGHT?

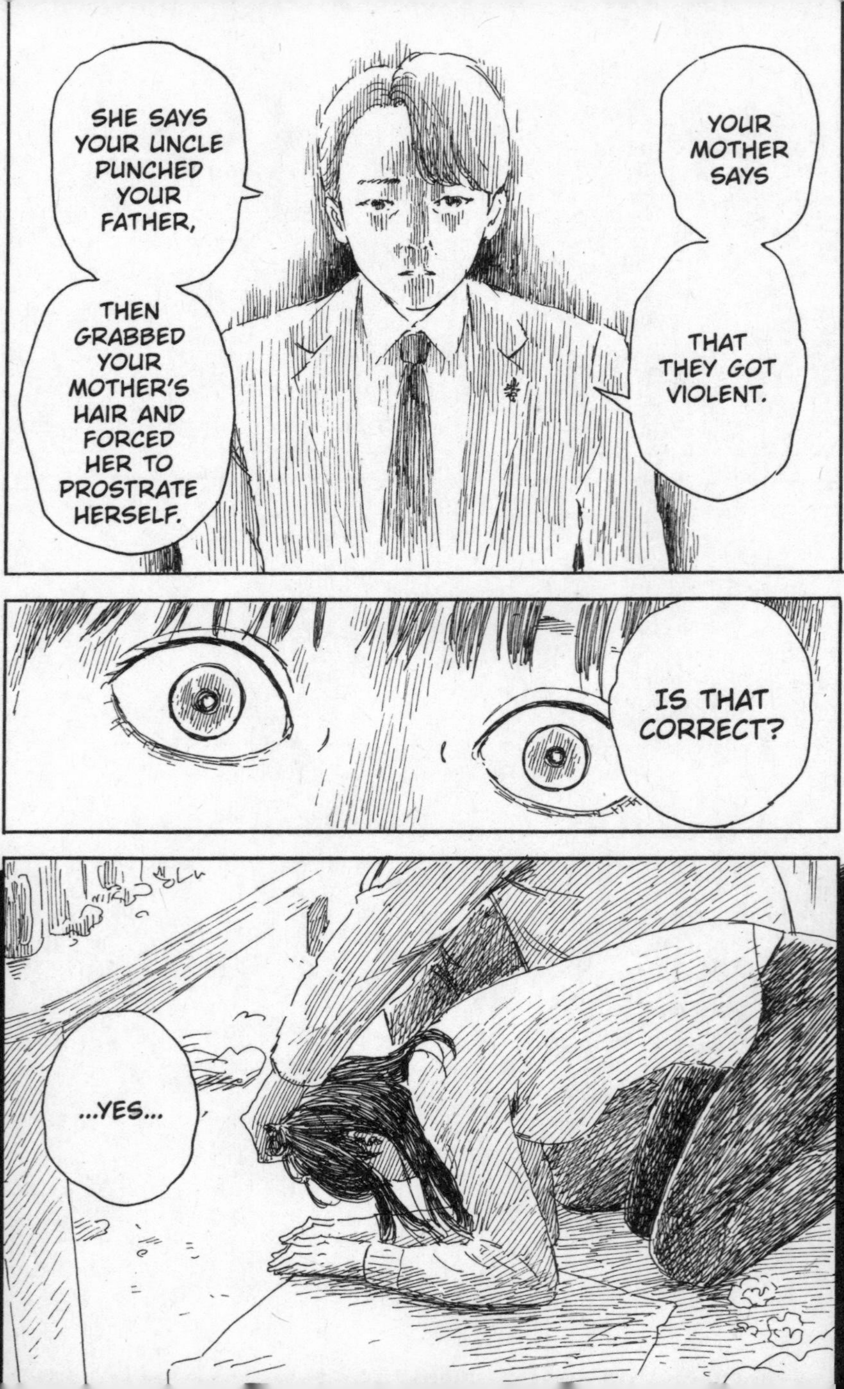
YOUR MOTHER SAYS
THAT THEY GOT VIOLENT.
SHE SAYS YOUR UNCLE PUNCHED YOUR FATHER,
THEN GRABBED YOUR MOTHER'S HAIR AND FORCED HER TO PROSTRATE HERSELF.
IS THAT CORRECT?
...YES...

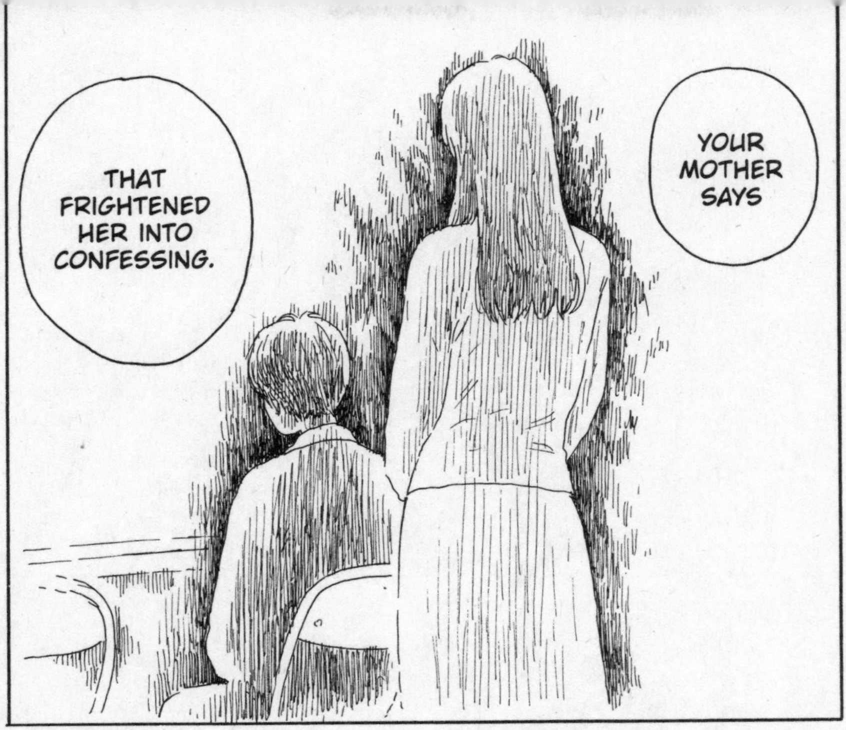
YOUR MOTHER SAYS
THAT FRIGHTENED HER INTO CONFESSING.

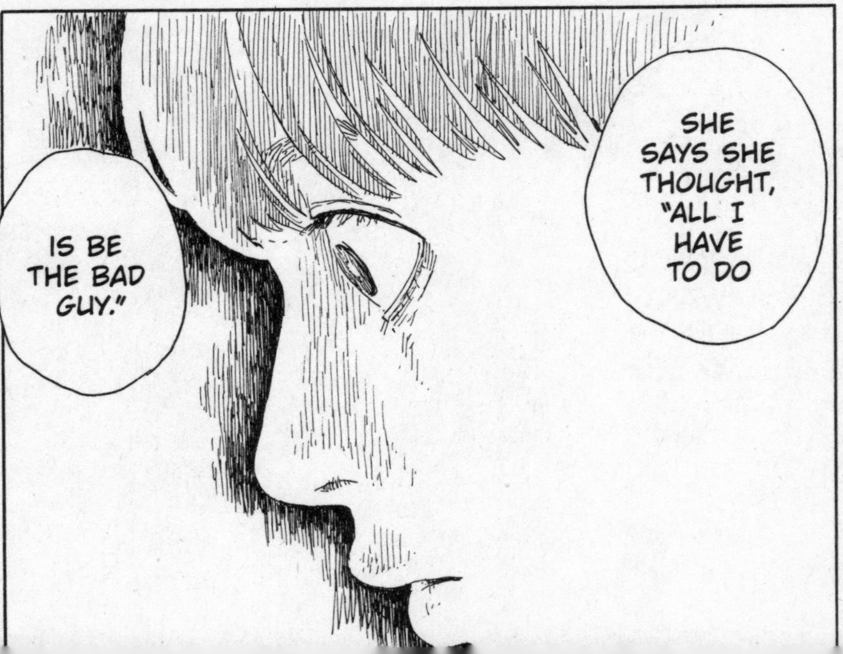
SHE SAYS SHE THOUGHT, "ALL I HAVE TO DO
IS BE THE BAD GUY."

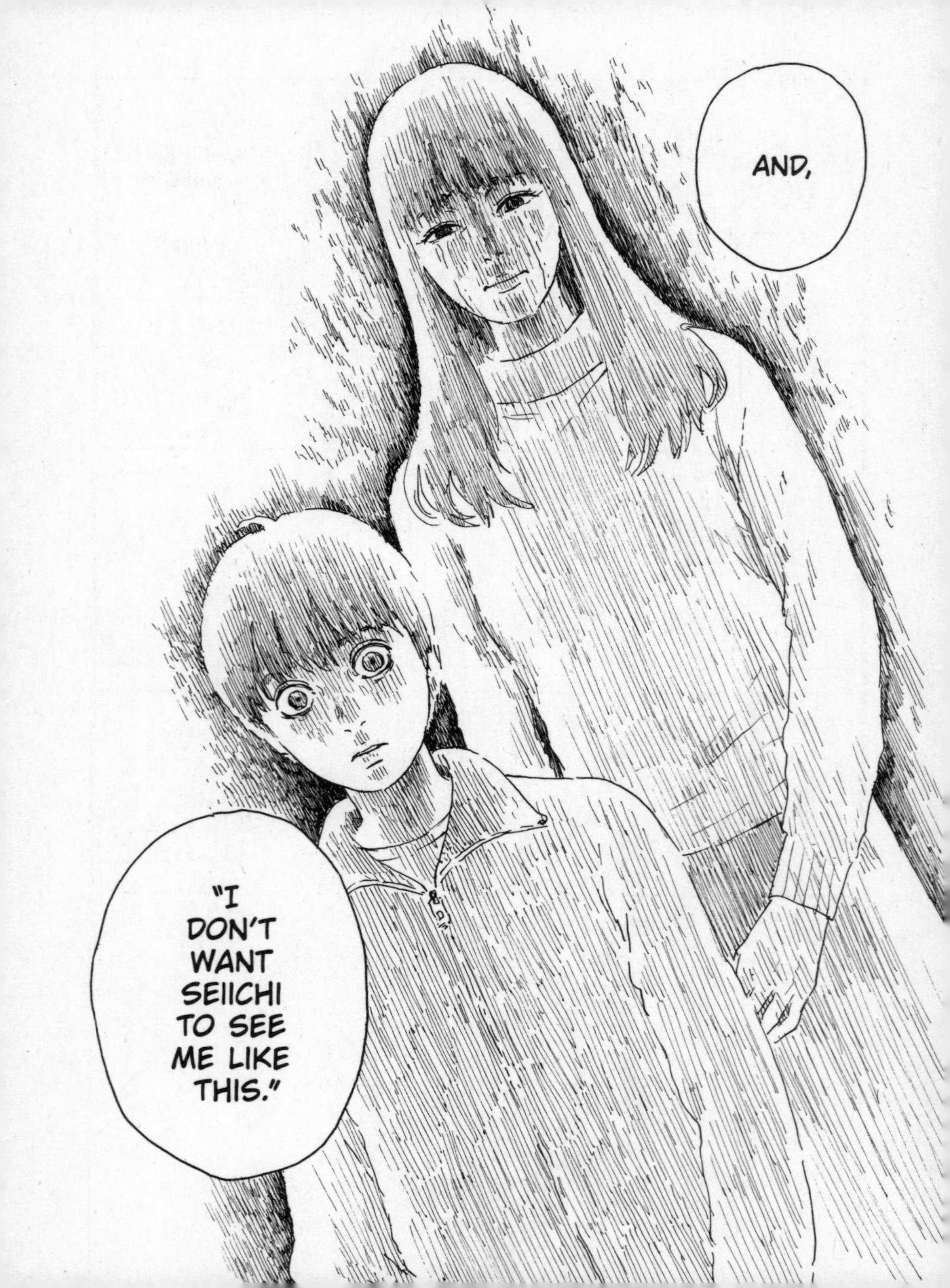
AND,
"I DON'T WANT SEIICHI TO SEE ME LIKE THIS."

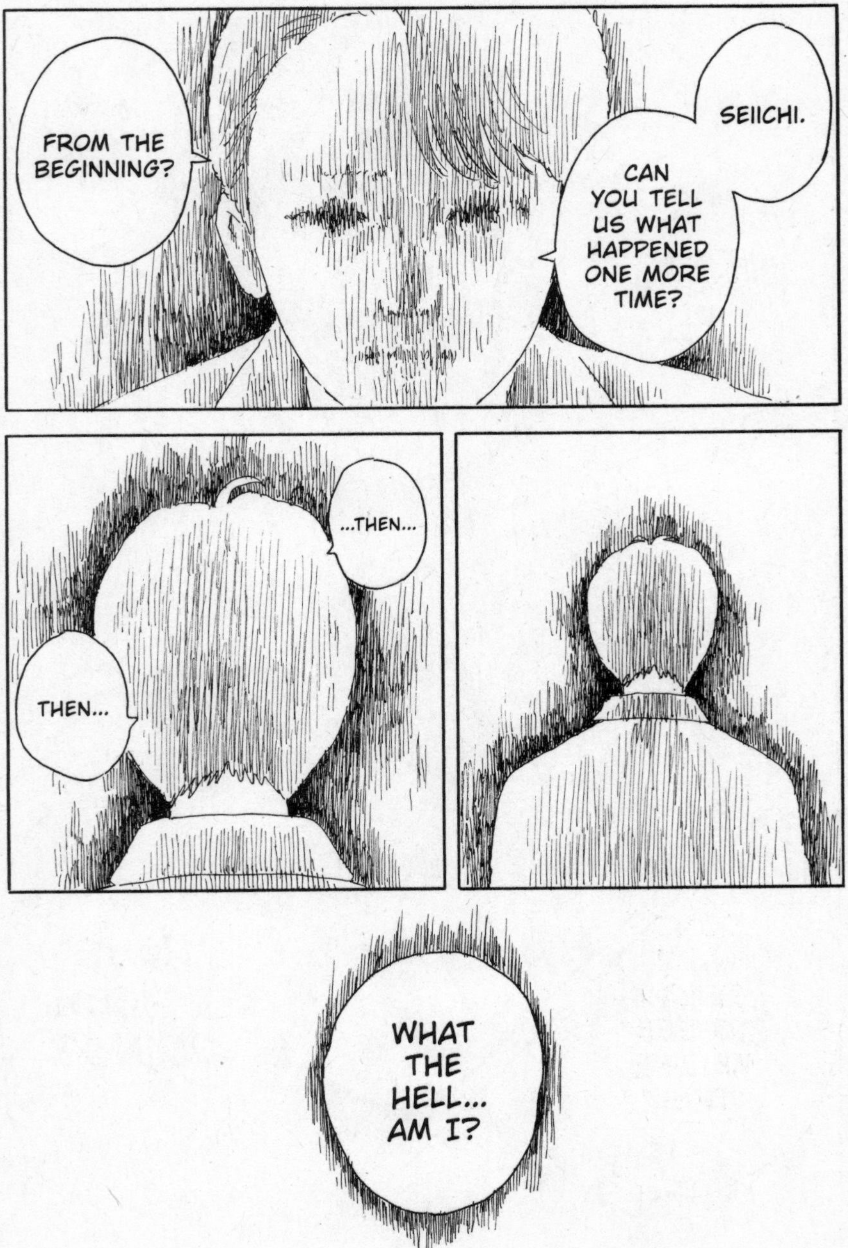
SEIICHI.
CAN YOU TELL US WHAT HAPPENED ONE MORE TIME?
FROM THE BEGINNING?
...THEN...
THEN...
WHAT THE HELL... AM I?

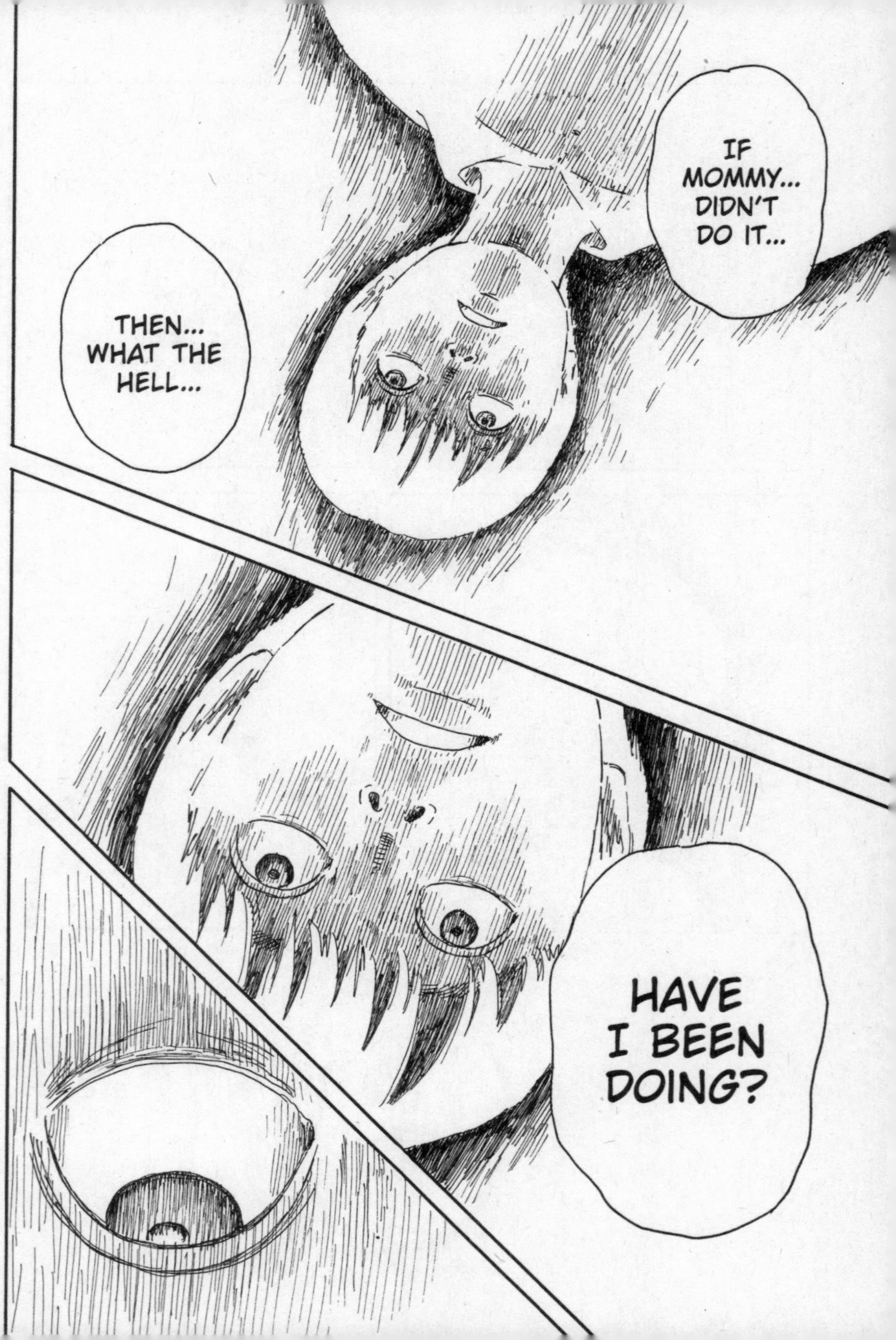
IF MOMMY... DIDN'T DO IT...
THEN... WHAT THE HELL...
HAVE I BEEN DOING?

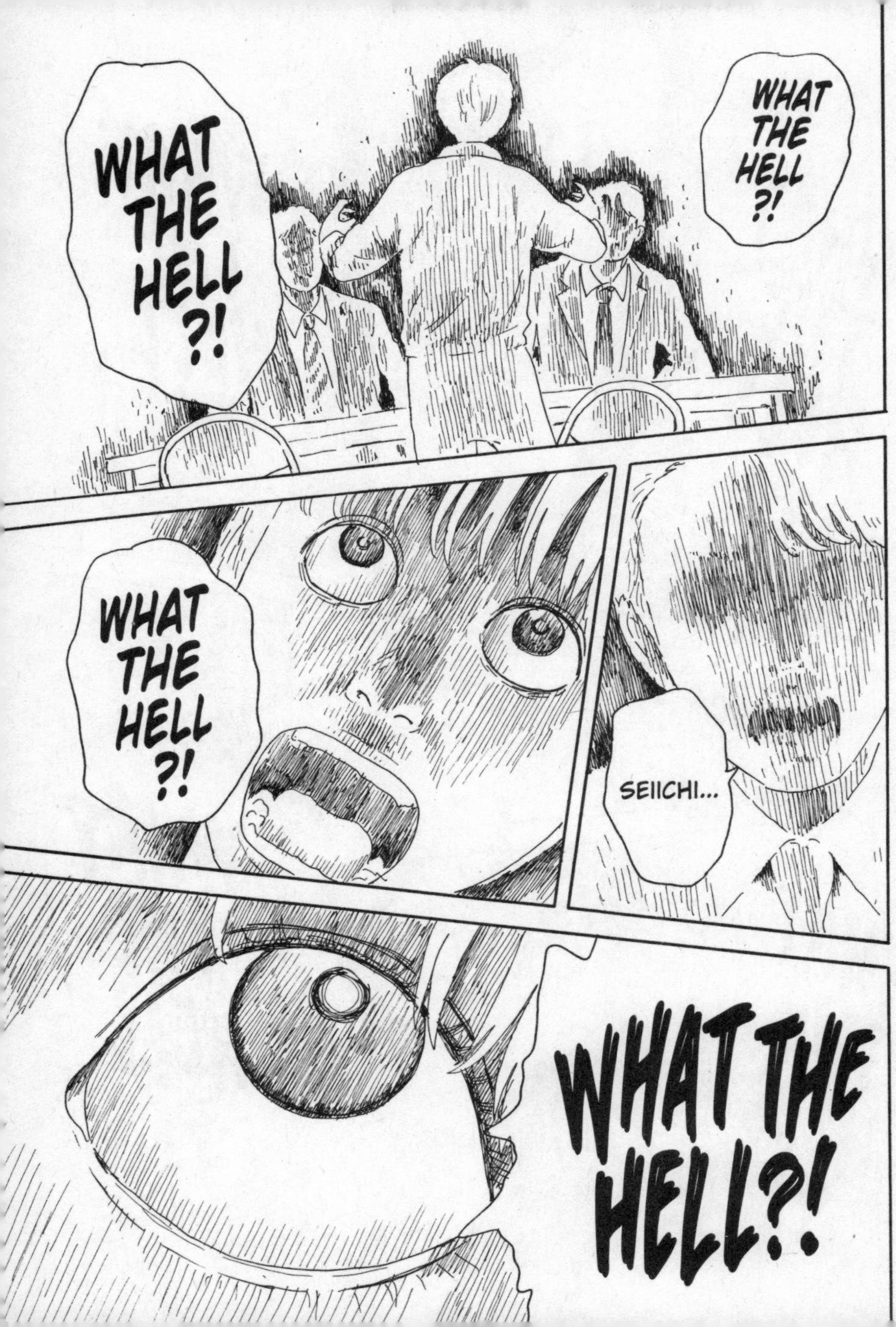
WHAT THE HELL?!
WHAT THE HELL?!
SEIICHI...
WHAT THE HELL?!
WHAT THE HELL?!

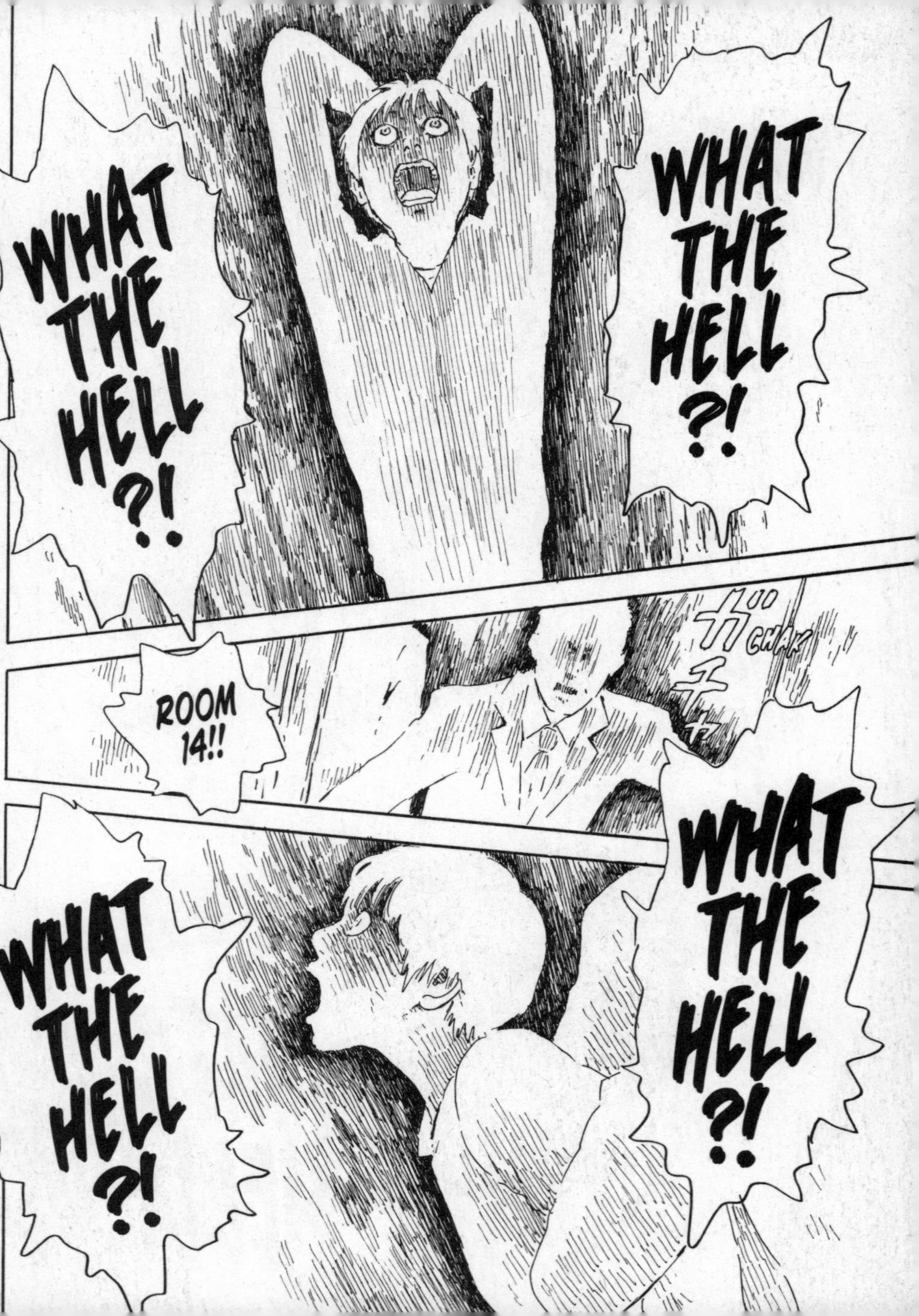
WHAT THE HELL ?!
WHAT THE HELL ?!
ガチャ
CHAK
ROOM 14!!
WHAT THE HELL ?!
WHAT THE HELL ?!

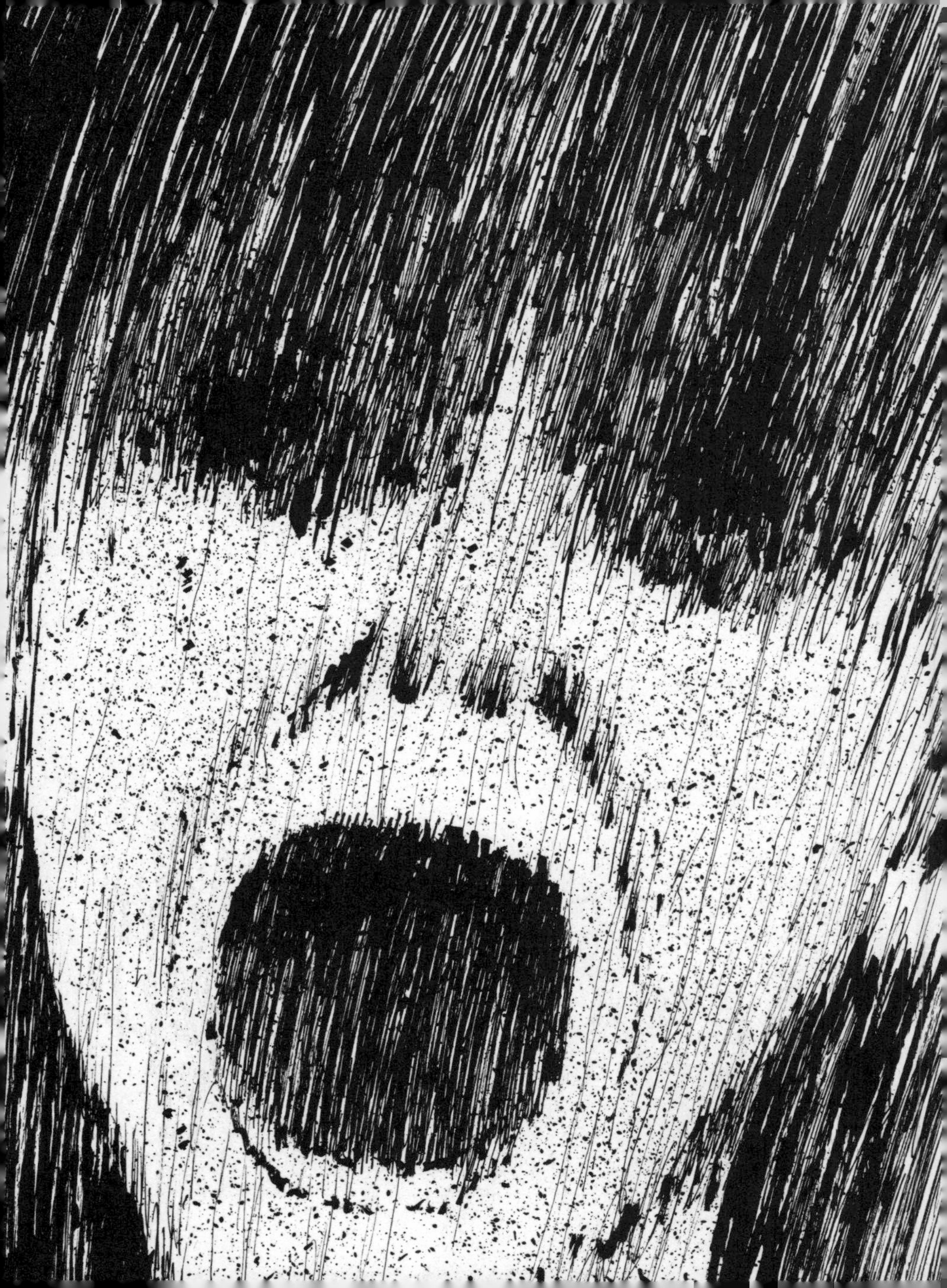

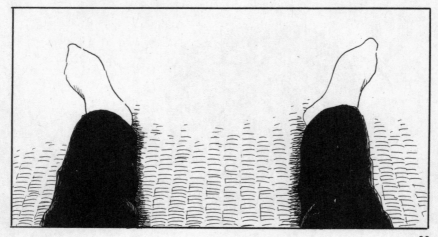

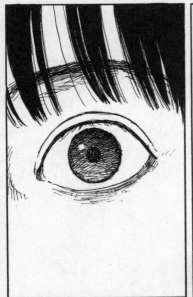

HEY,
SEI.

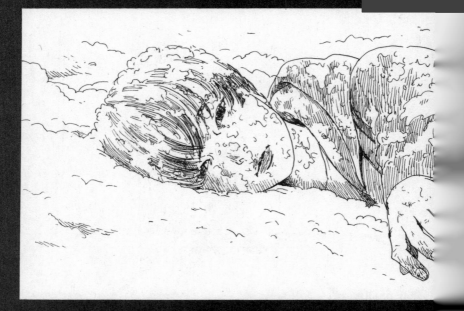

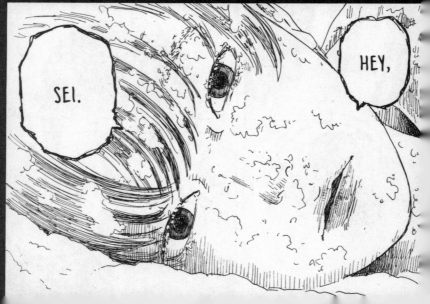

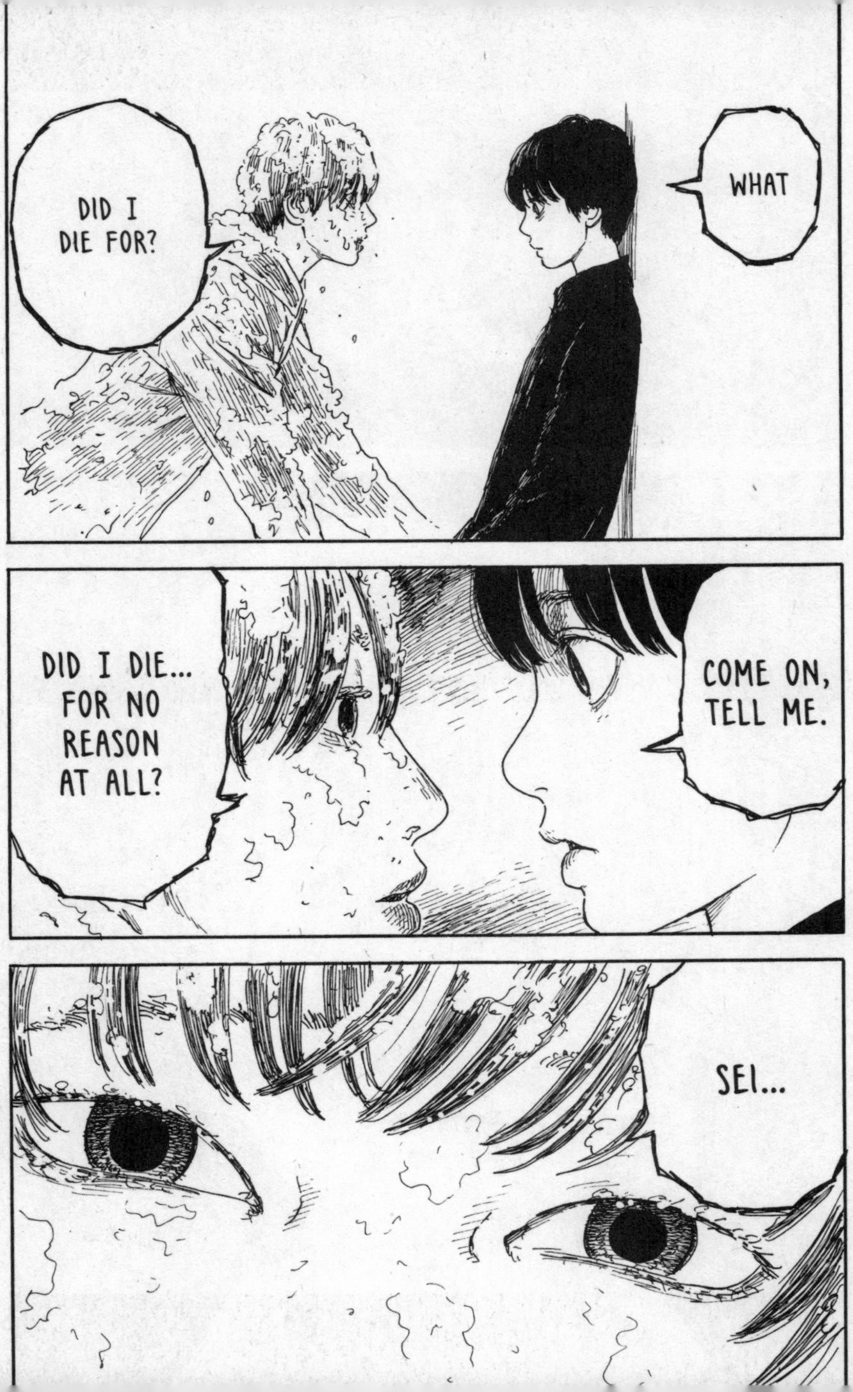
WHAT
DID I DIE FOR?
COME ON, TELL ME.
DID I DIE... FOR NO REASON AT ALL?
SEI...

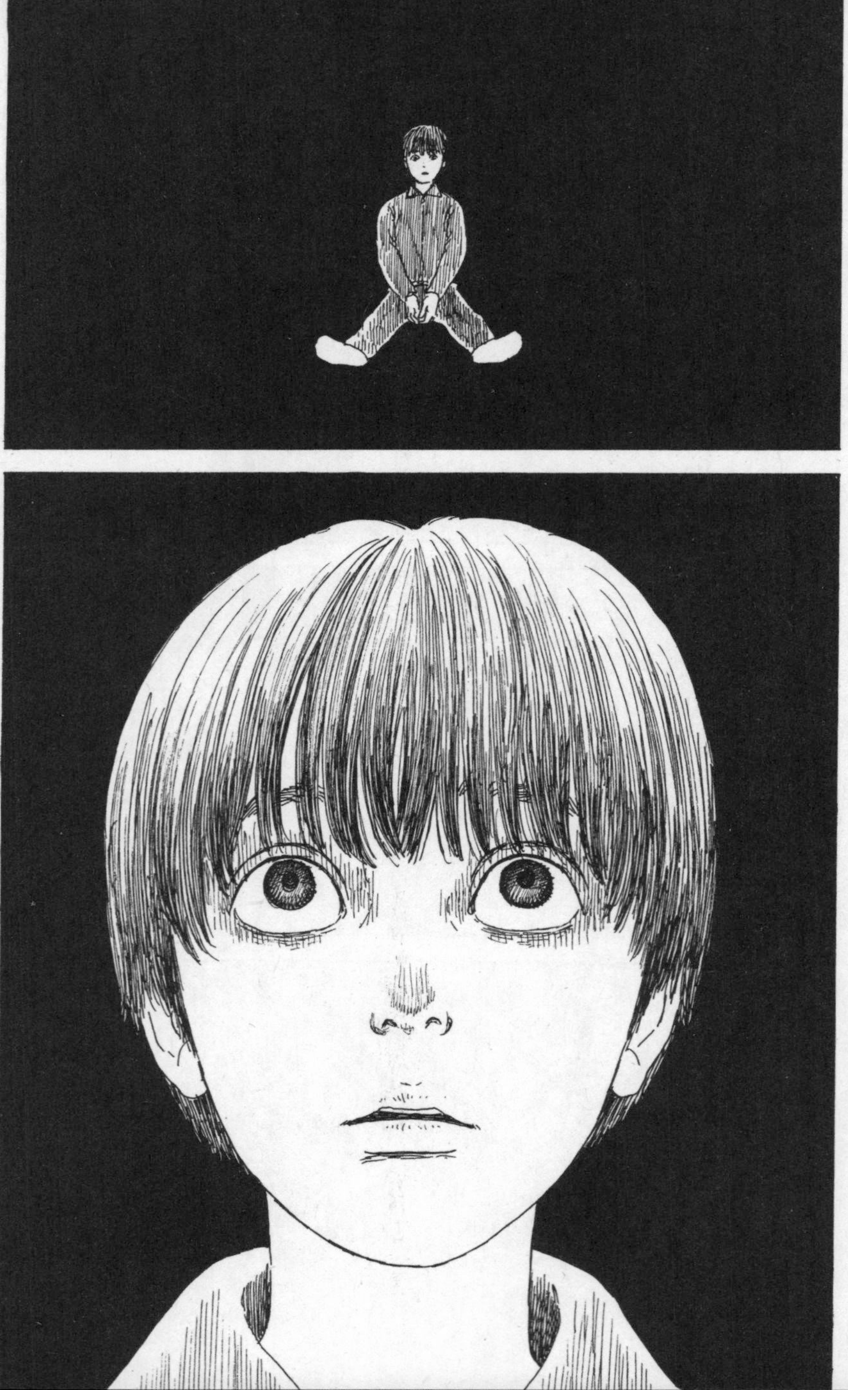

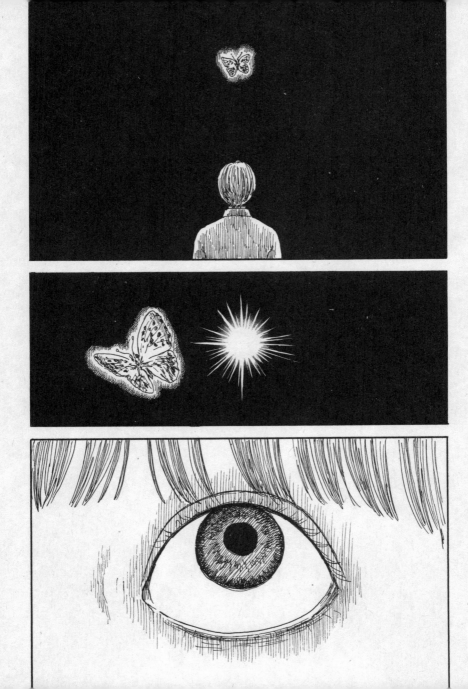

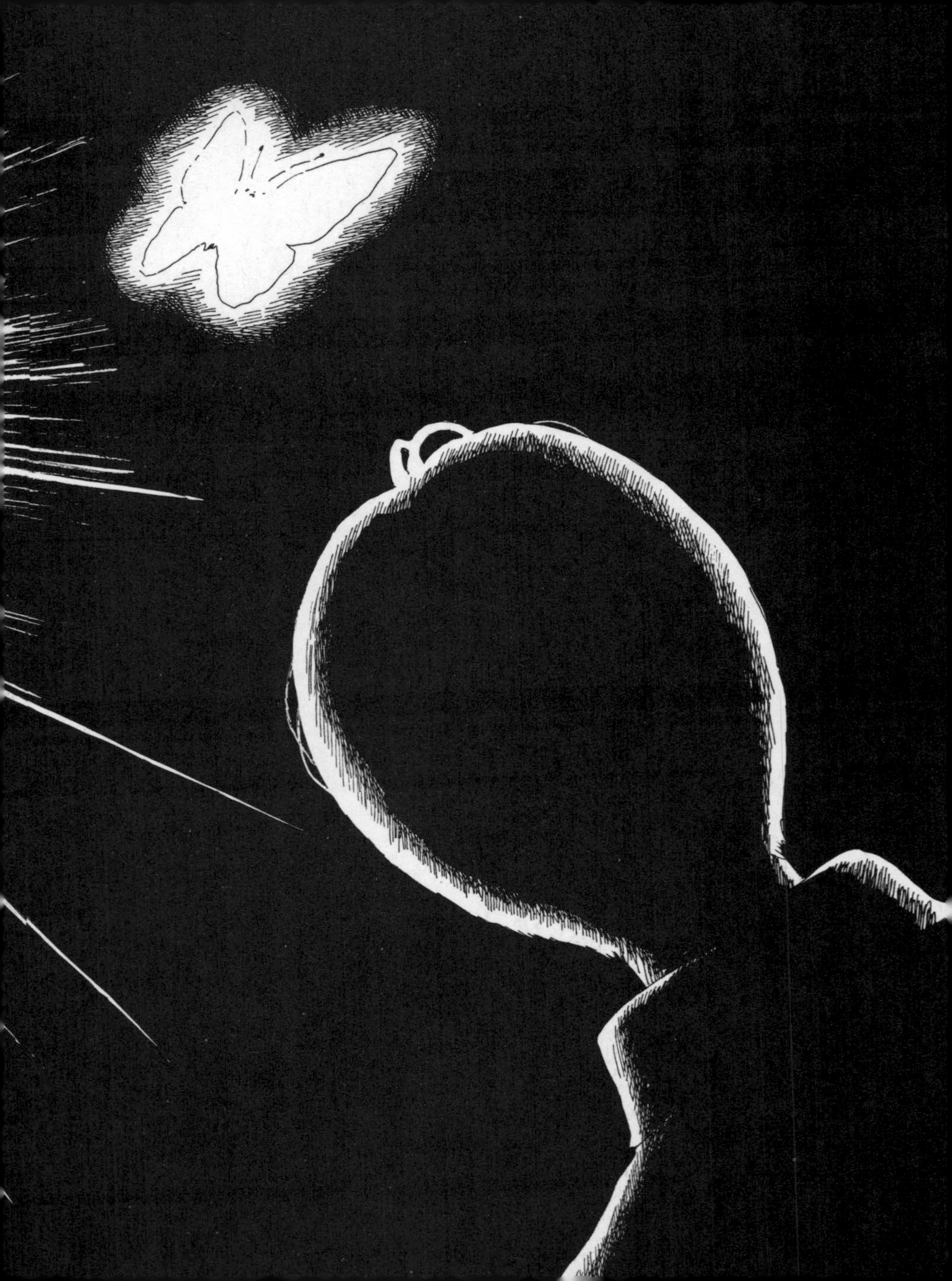

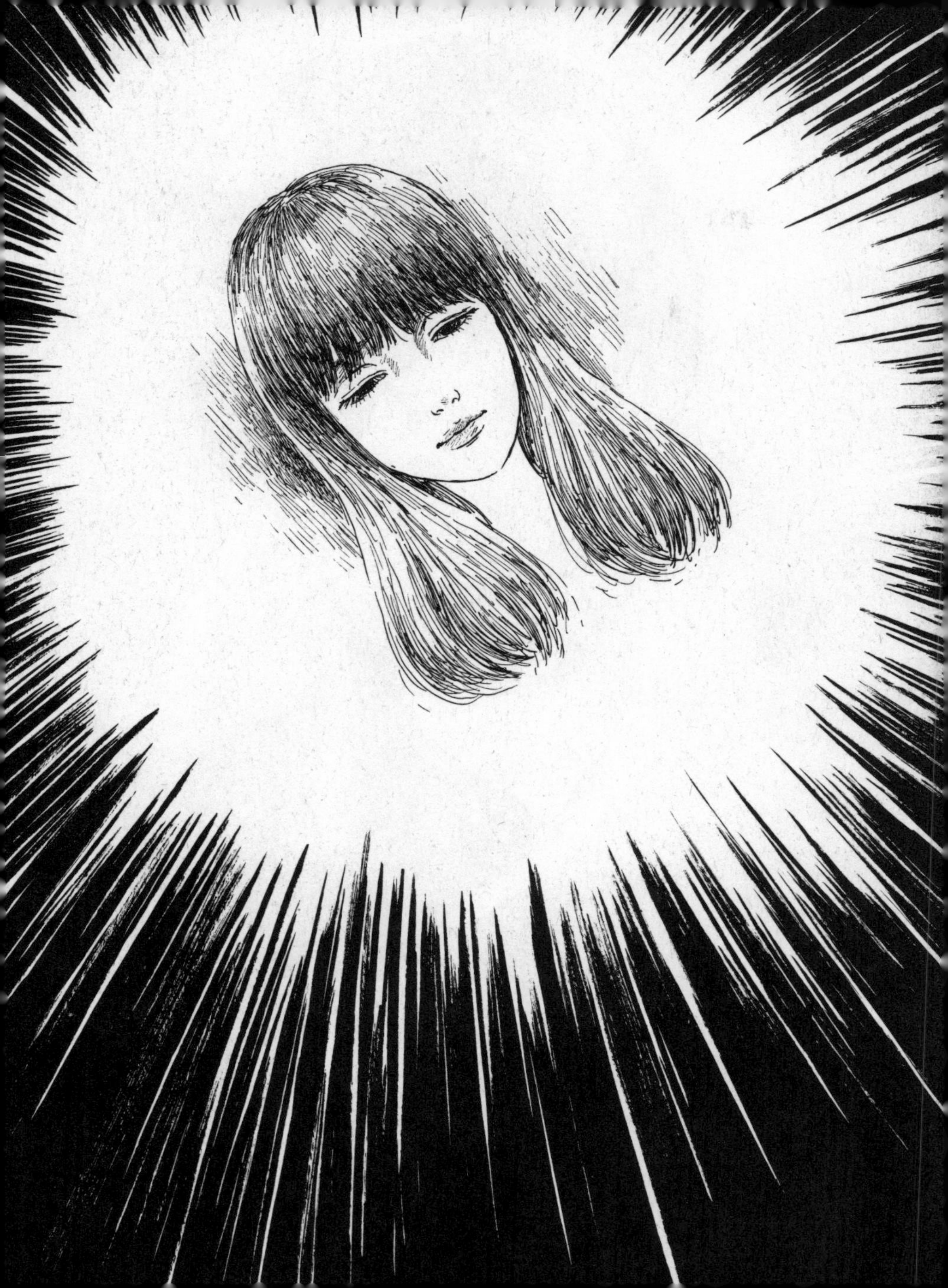

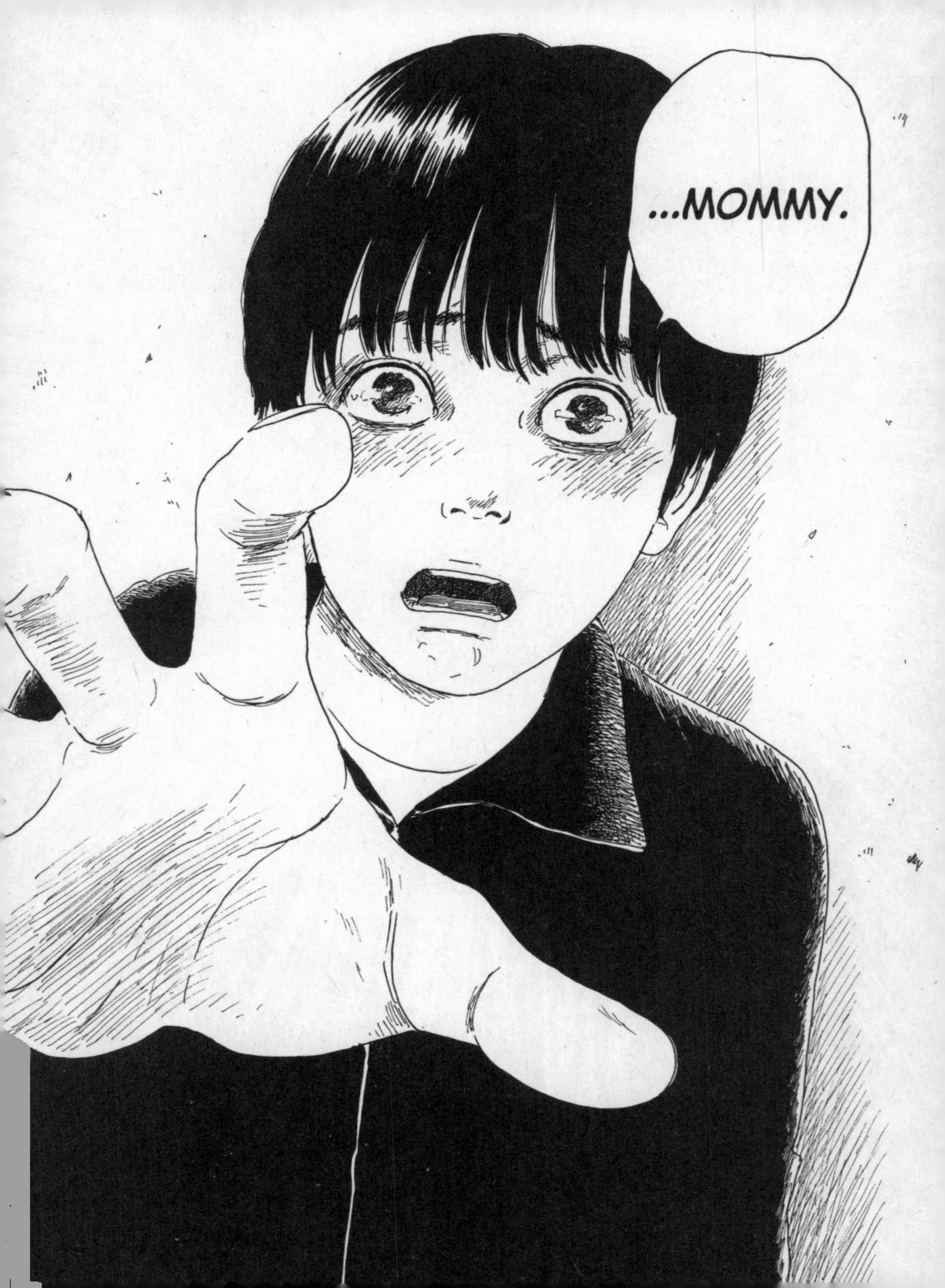
...MOMMY.

CHAPTER 102 Good News

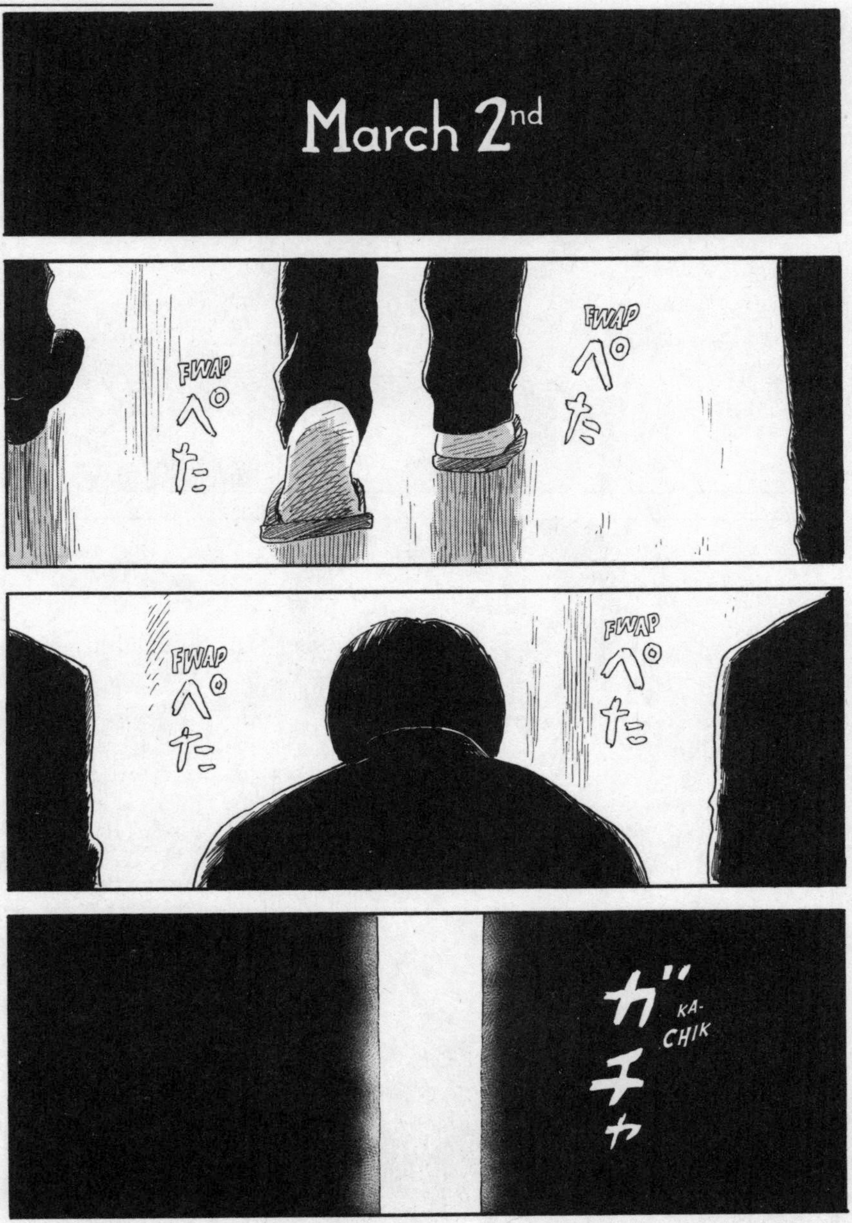
March 2nd
FWAP
ぺた
FWAP
ぺた
FWAP
ぺた
FWAP
ぺた
ガチャ
KA-CHIK

SEIICHI...

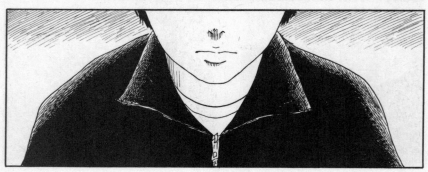

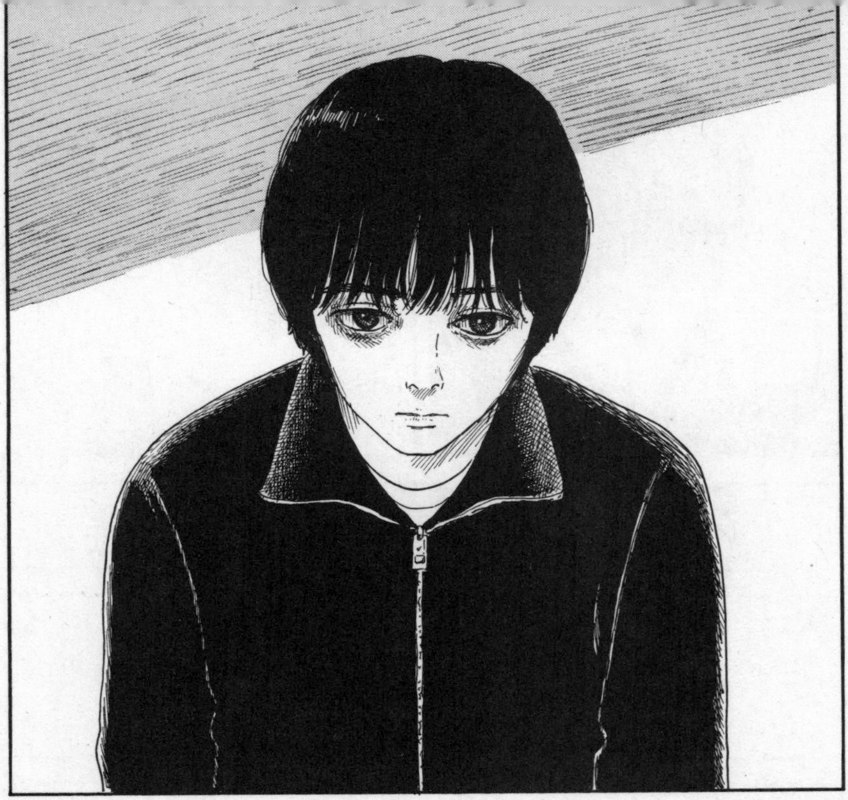

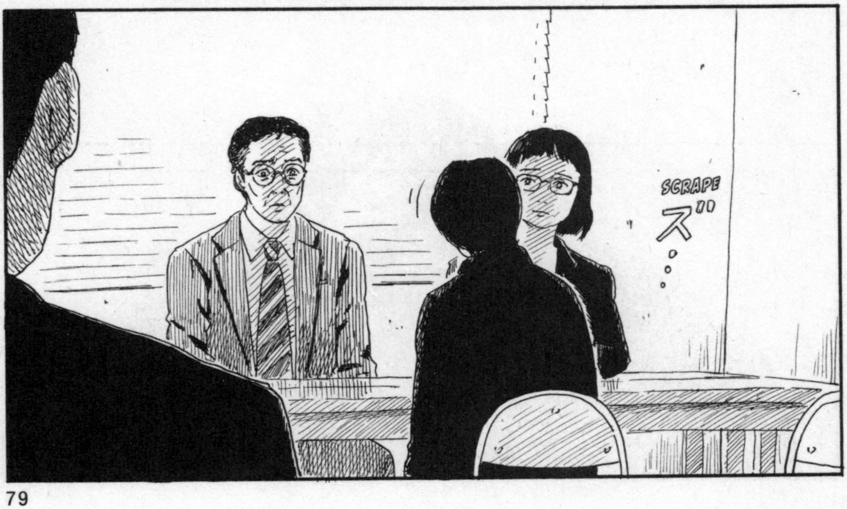
SCRAPE
ズ

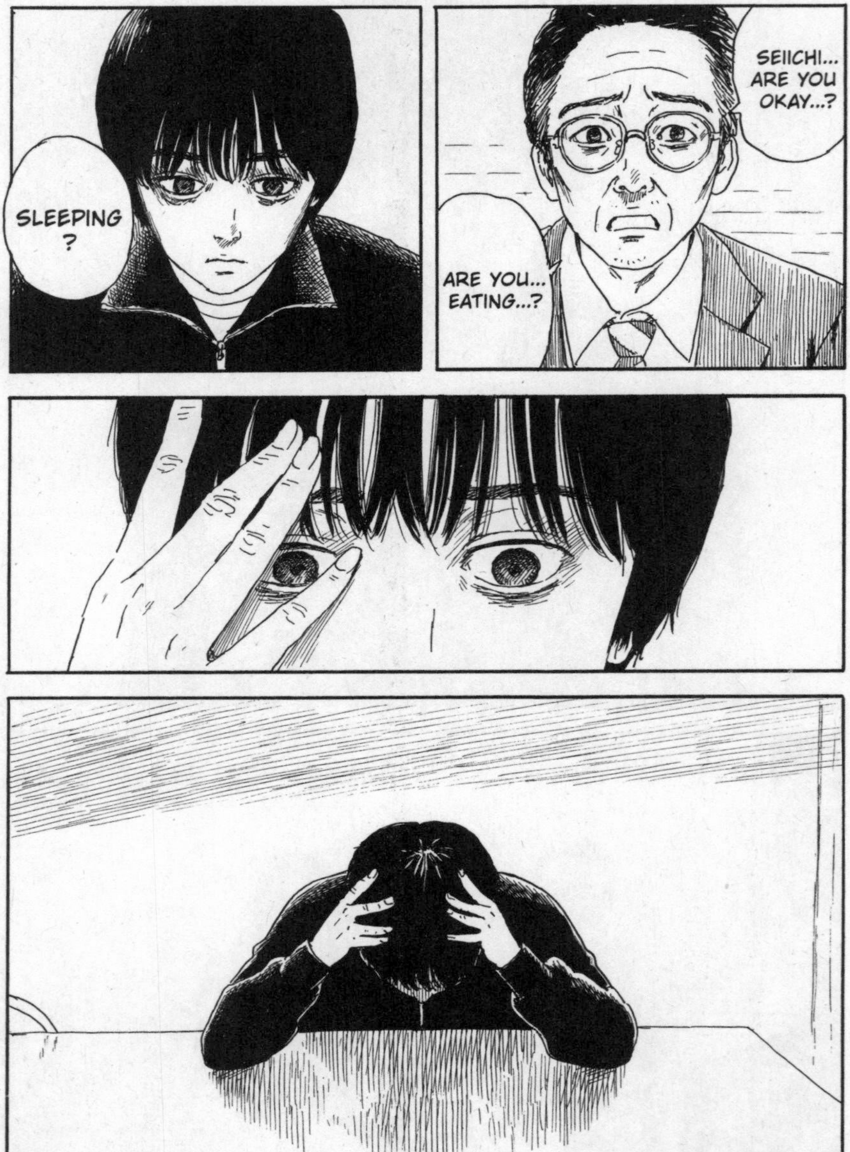
SEIICHI... ARE YOU OKAY...?
ARE YOU... EATING...?
SLEEPING ?

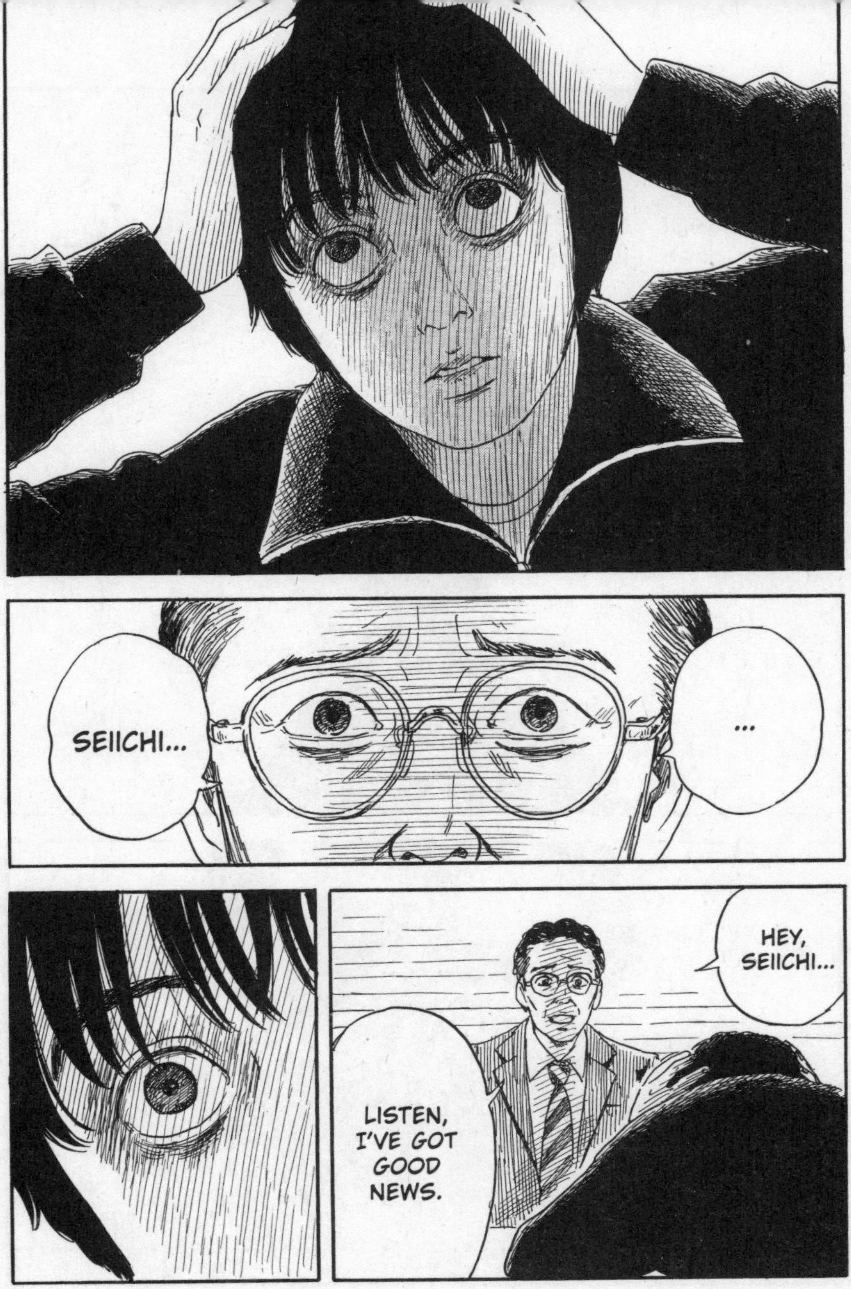
...
SEIICHI...
HEY, SEIICHI...
LISTEN, I'VE GOT GOOD NEWS.

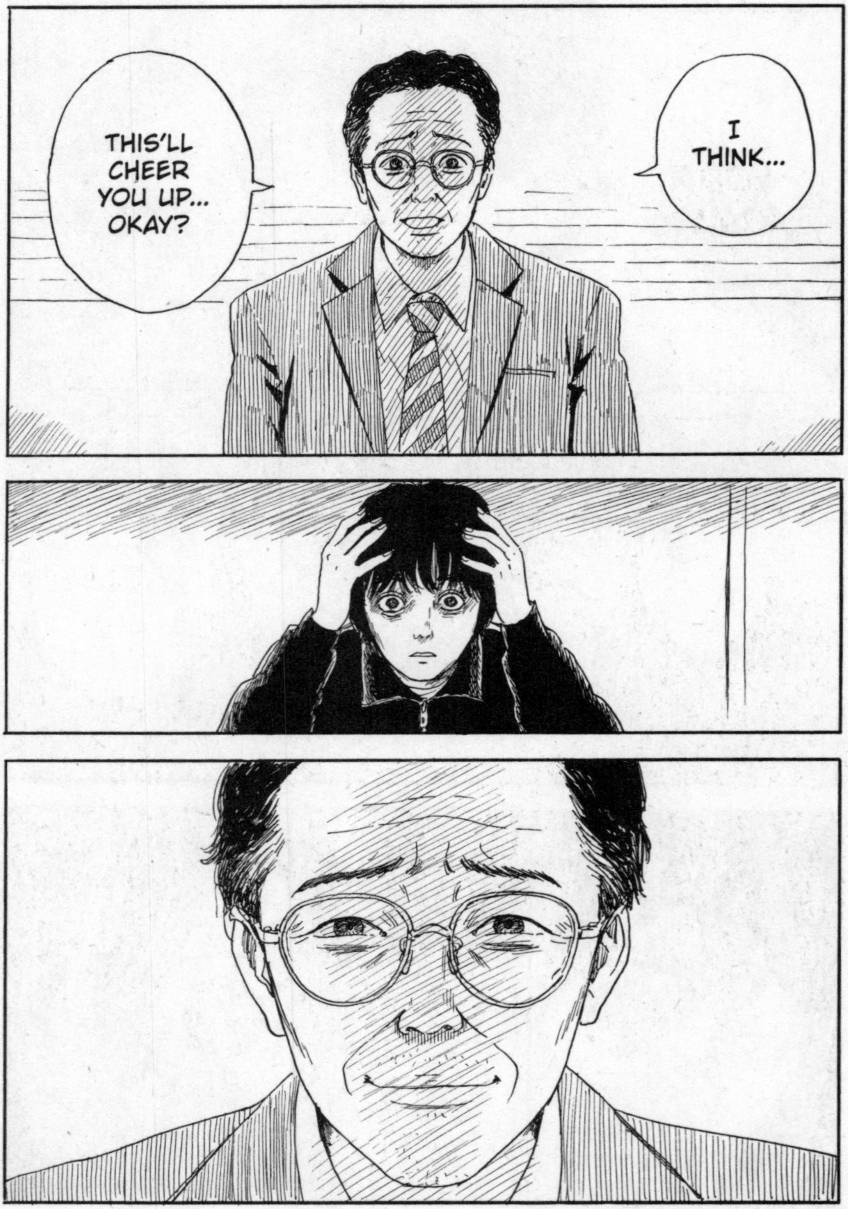
I THINK...
THIS'LL CHEER YOU UP... OKAY?

YOUR MOMMY...
WELL,

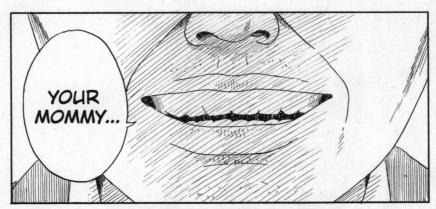

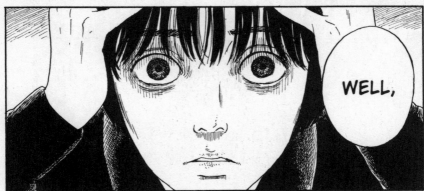

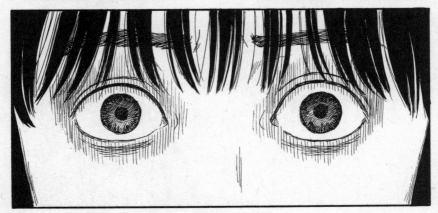

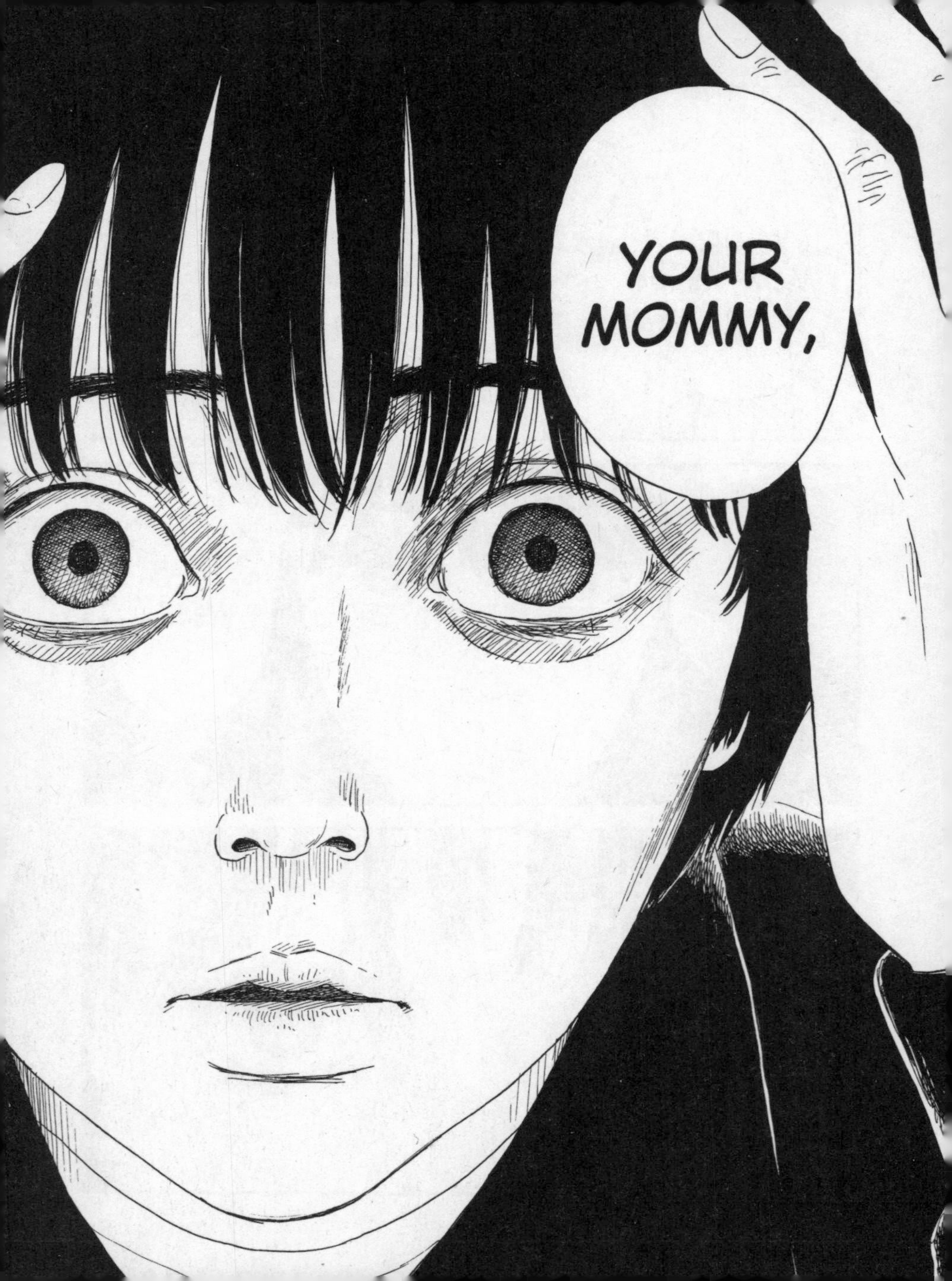
YOUR MOMMY,

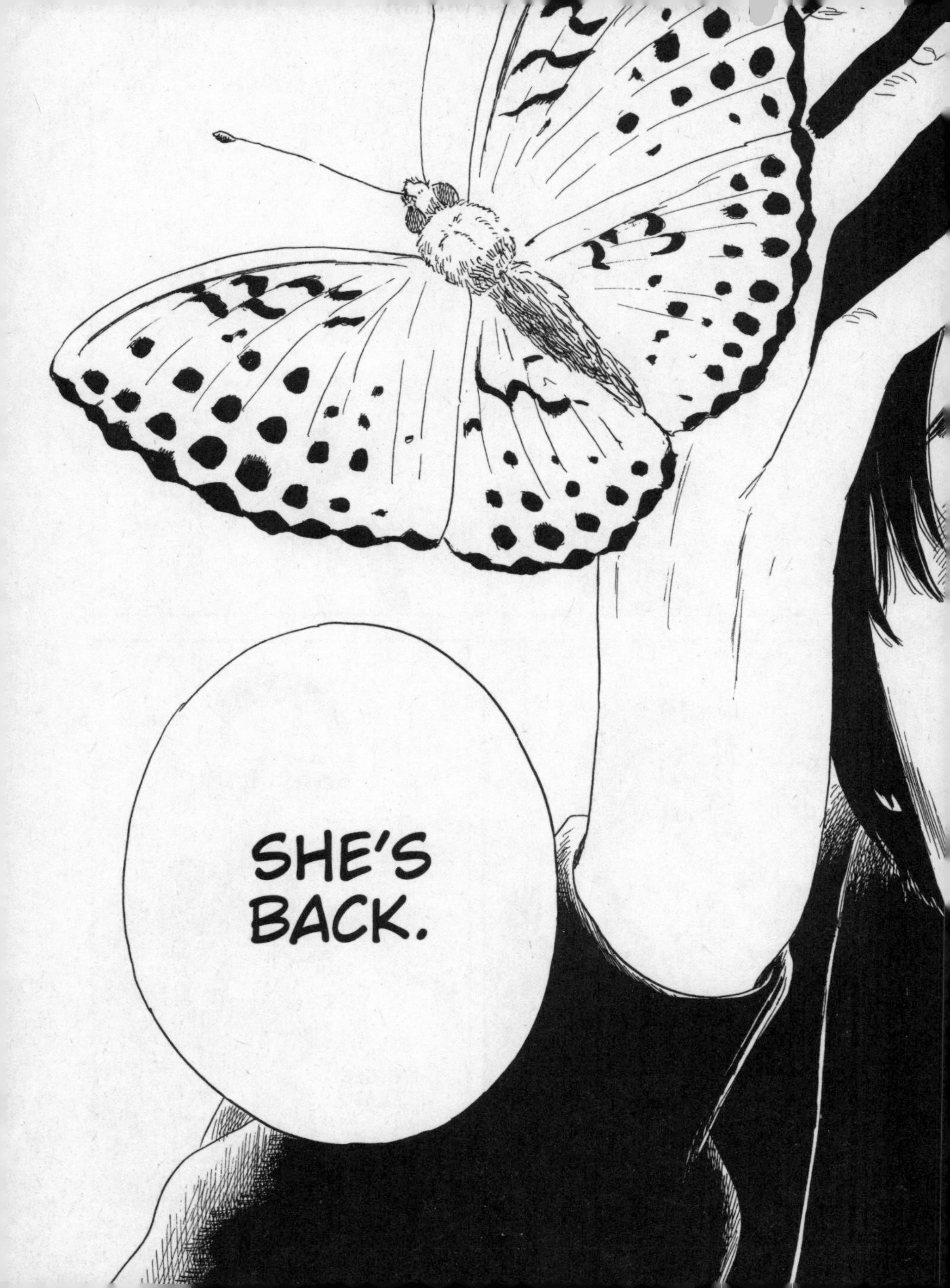
SHE'S BACK.

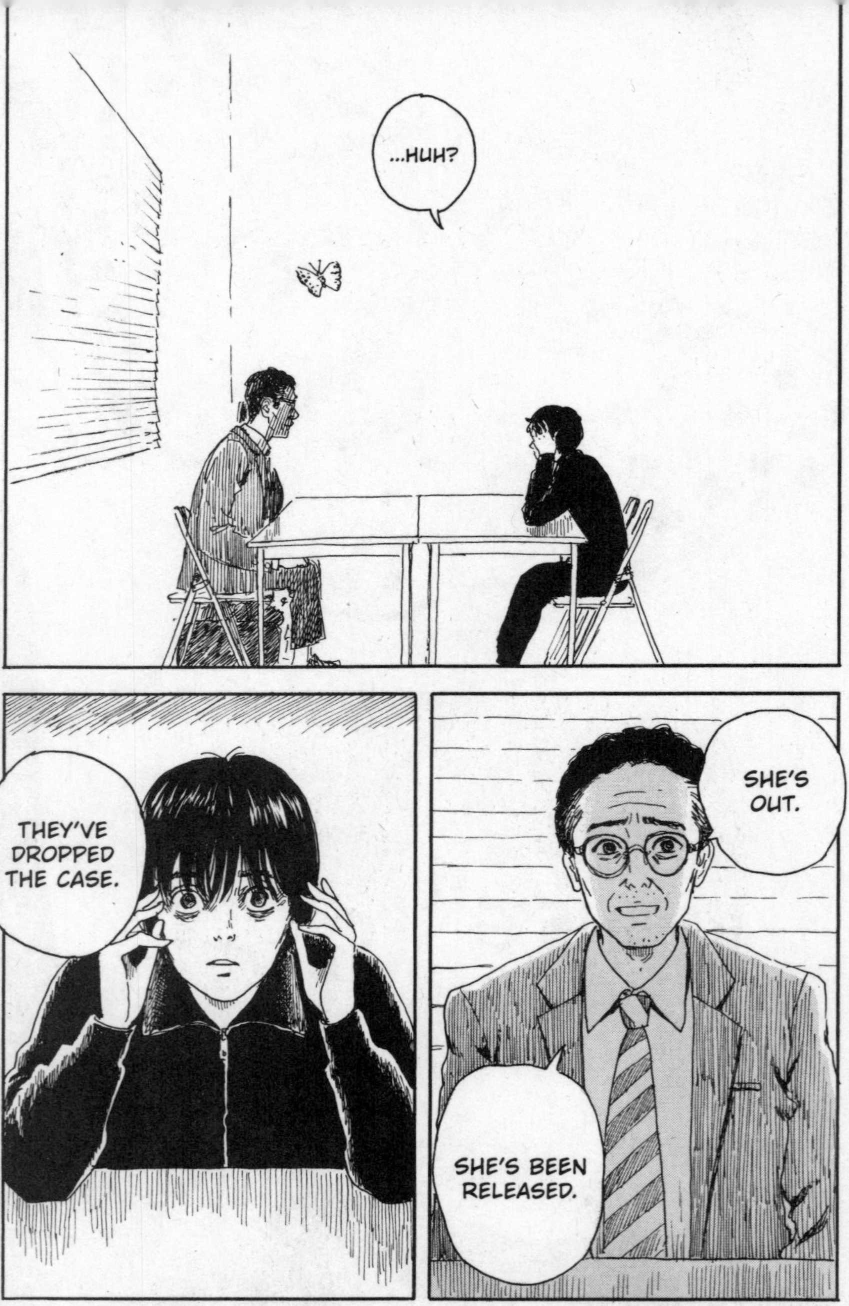
...HUH?
SHE'S OUT.
SHE'S BEEN RELEASED.
THEY'VE DROPPED THE CASE.

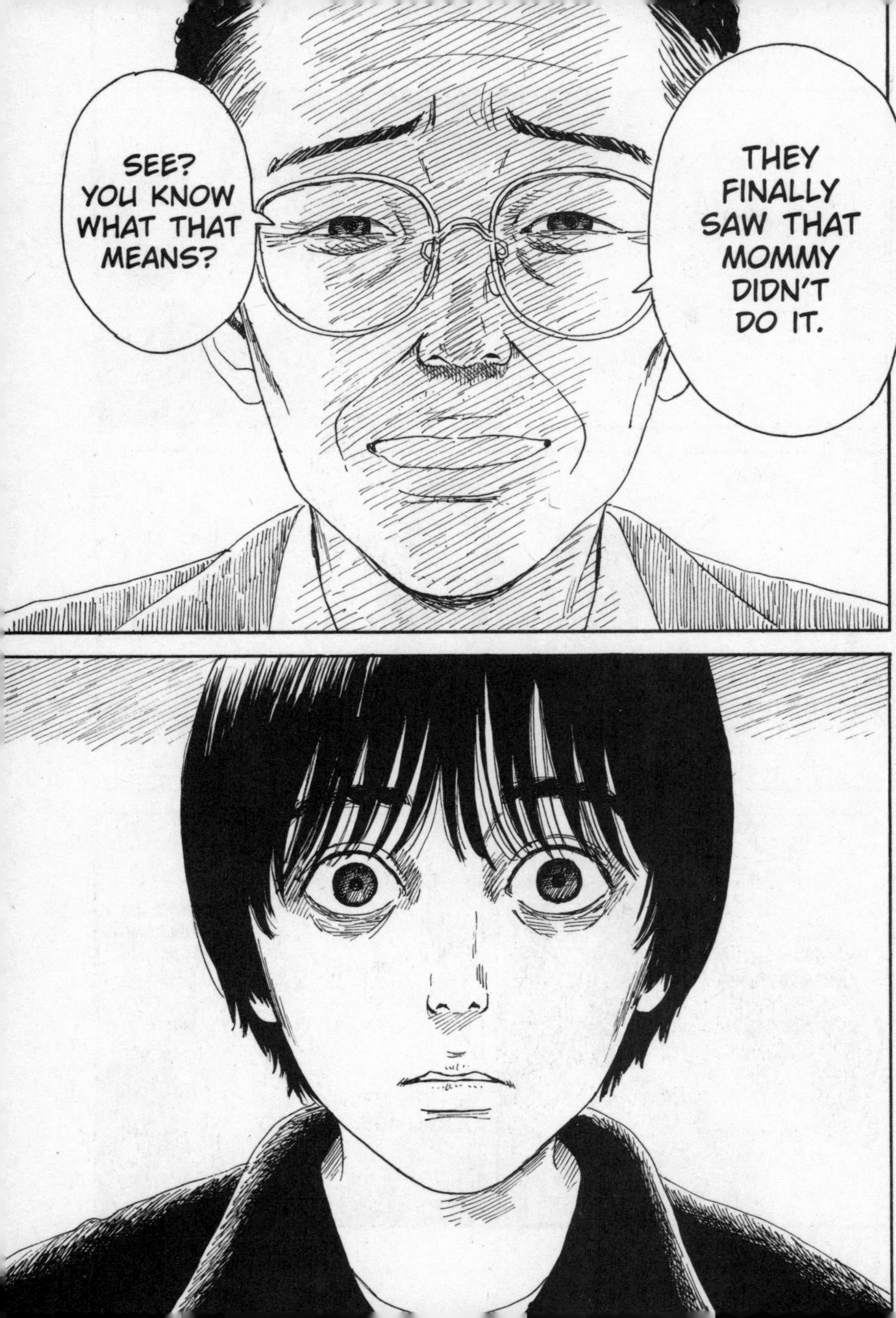
THEY FINALLY SAW THAT MOMMY DIDN'T DO IT.
SEE? YOU KNOW WHAT THAT MEANS?

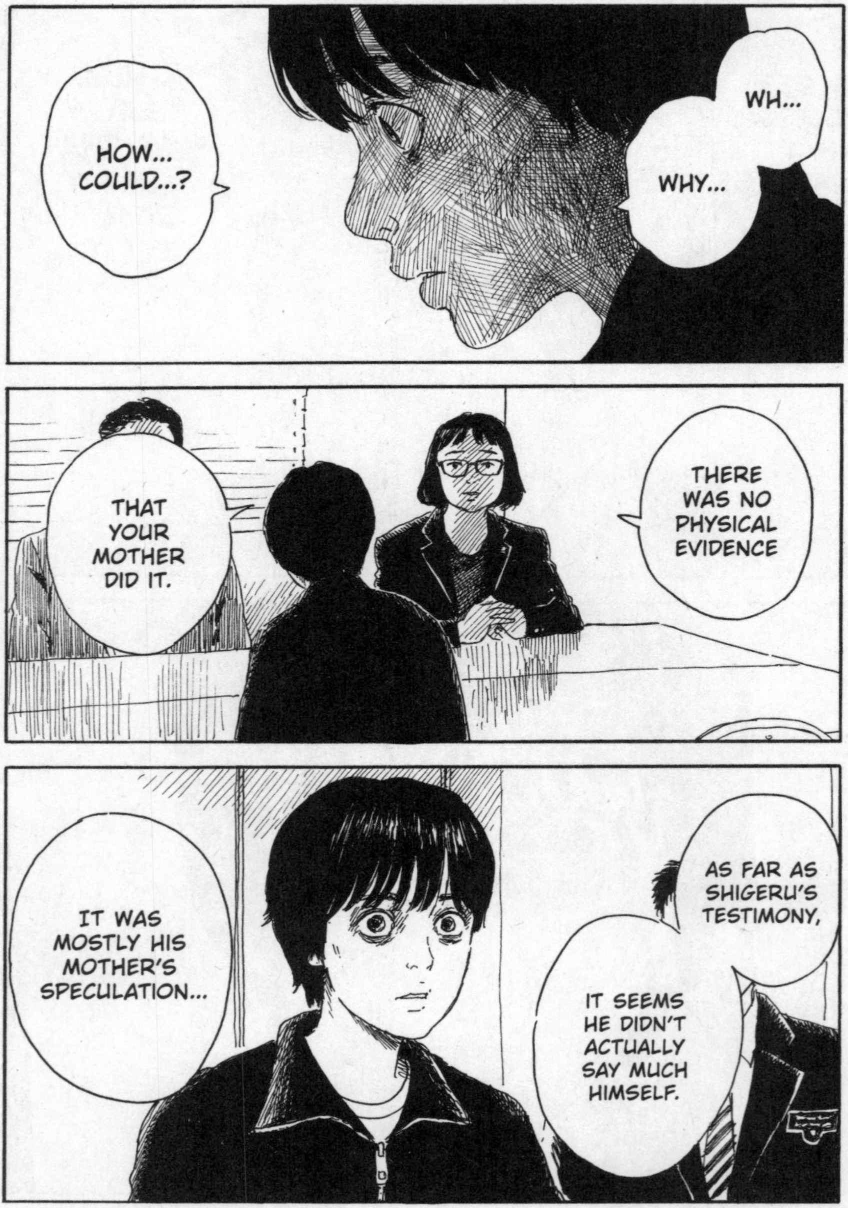
WH...
WHY...
HOW... COULD...?
THERE WAS NO PHYSICAL EVIDENCE
THAT YOUR MOTHER DID IT.
AS FAR AS SHIGERU'S TESTIMONY,
IT SEEMS HE DIDN'T ACTUALLY SAY MUCH HIMSELF.
IT WAS MOSTLY HIS MOTHER'S SPECULATION...

SEIICHI?

...ISN'T THAT GREAT,

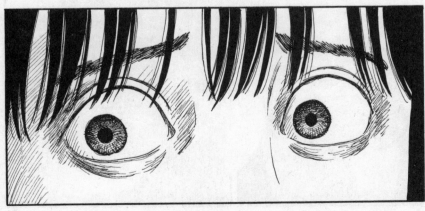

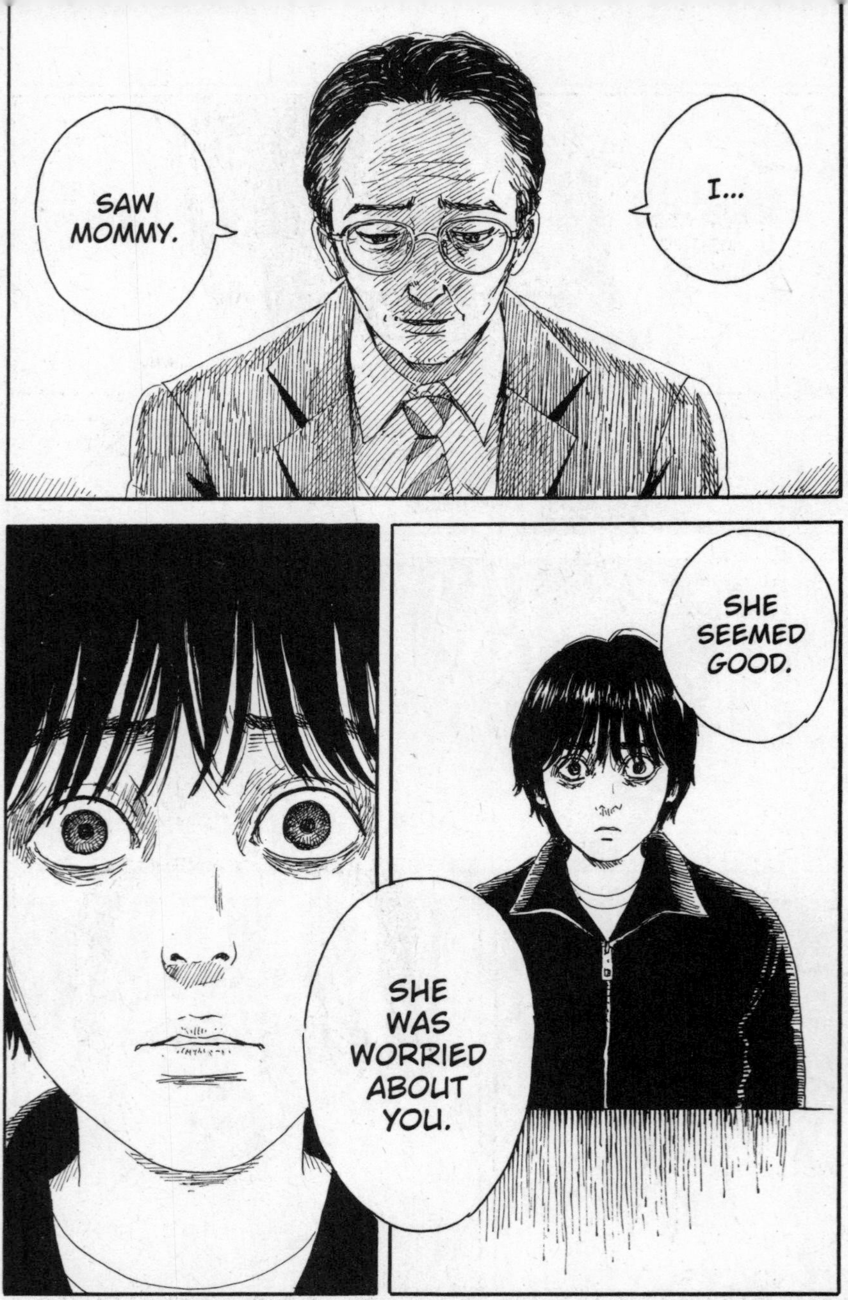
I...
SAW MOMMY.
SHE SEEMED GOOD.
SHE WAS WORRIED ABOUT YOU.

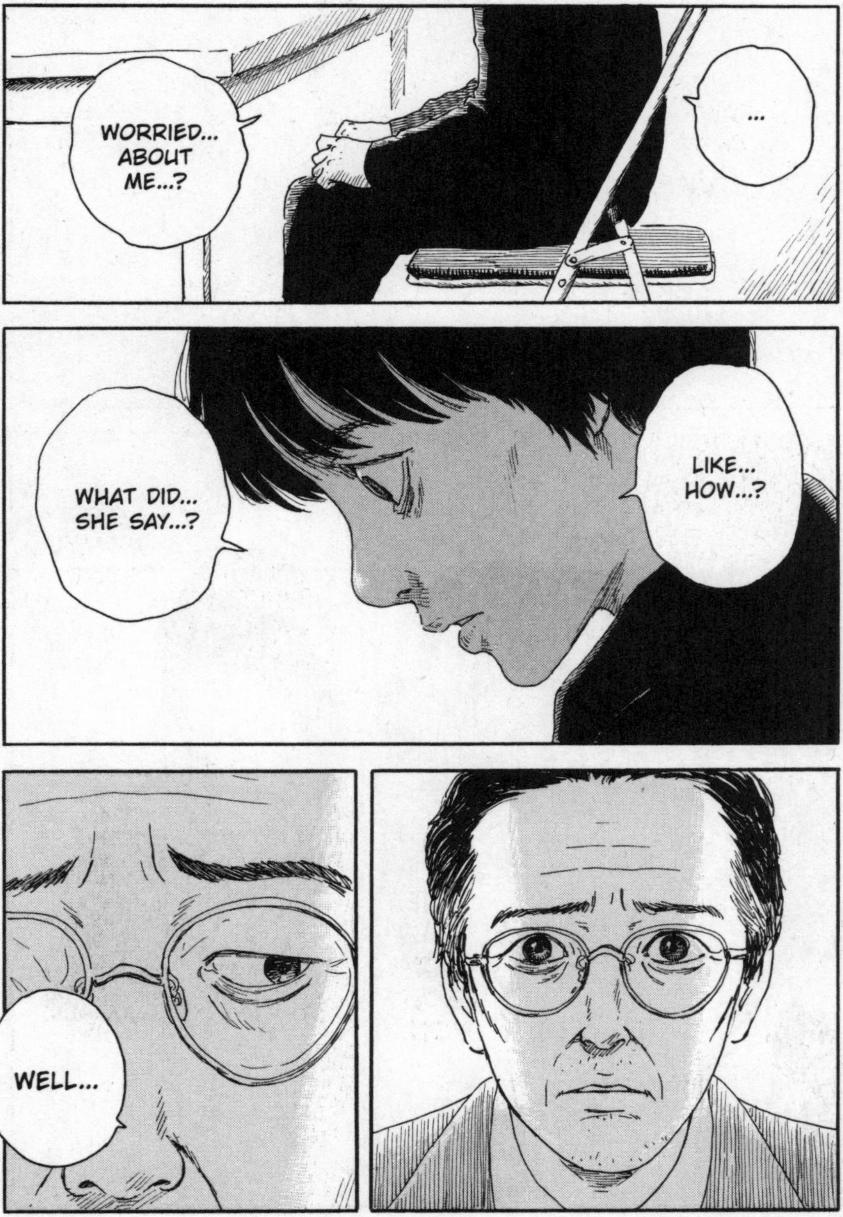
...
WORRIED... ABOUT ME...?
LIKE... HOW...?
WHAT DID... SHE SAY...?
WELL...

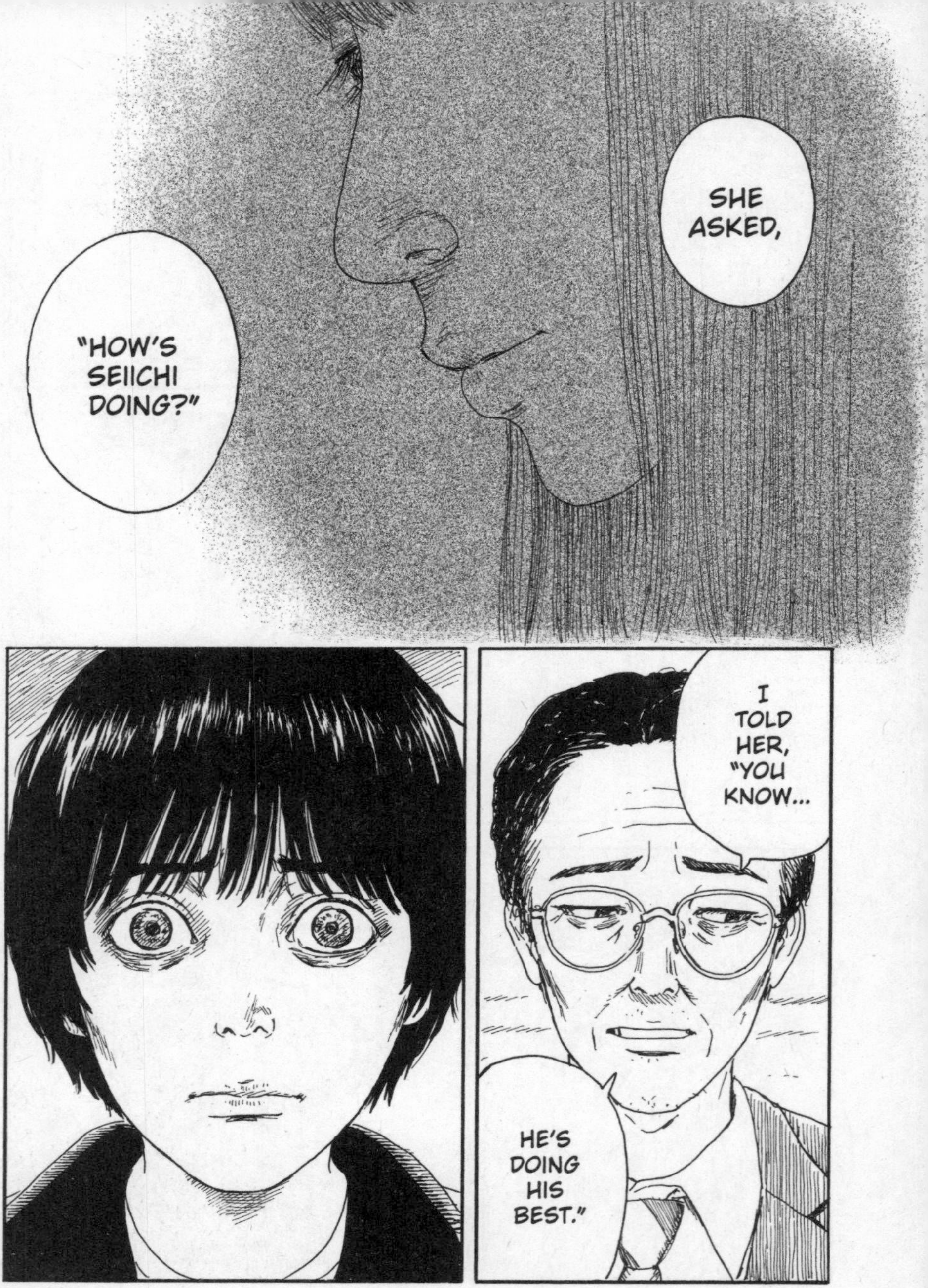
SHE ASKED,
"HOW'S SEIICHI DOING?"
I TOLD HER, "YOU KNOW...
HE'S DOING HIS BEST."

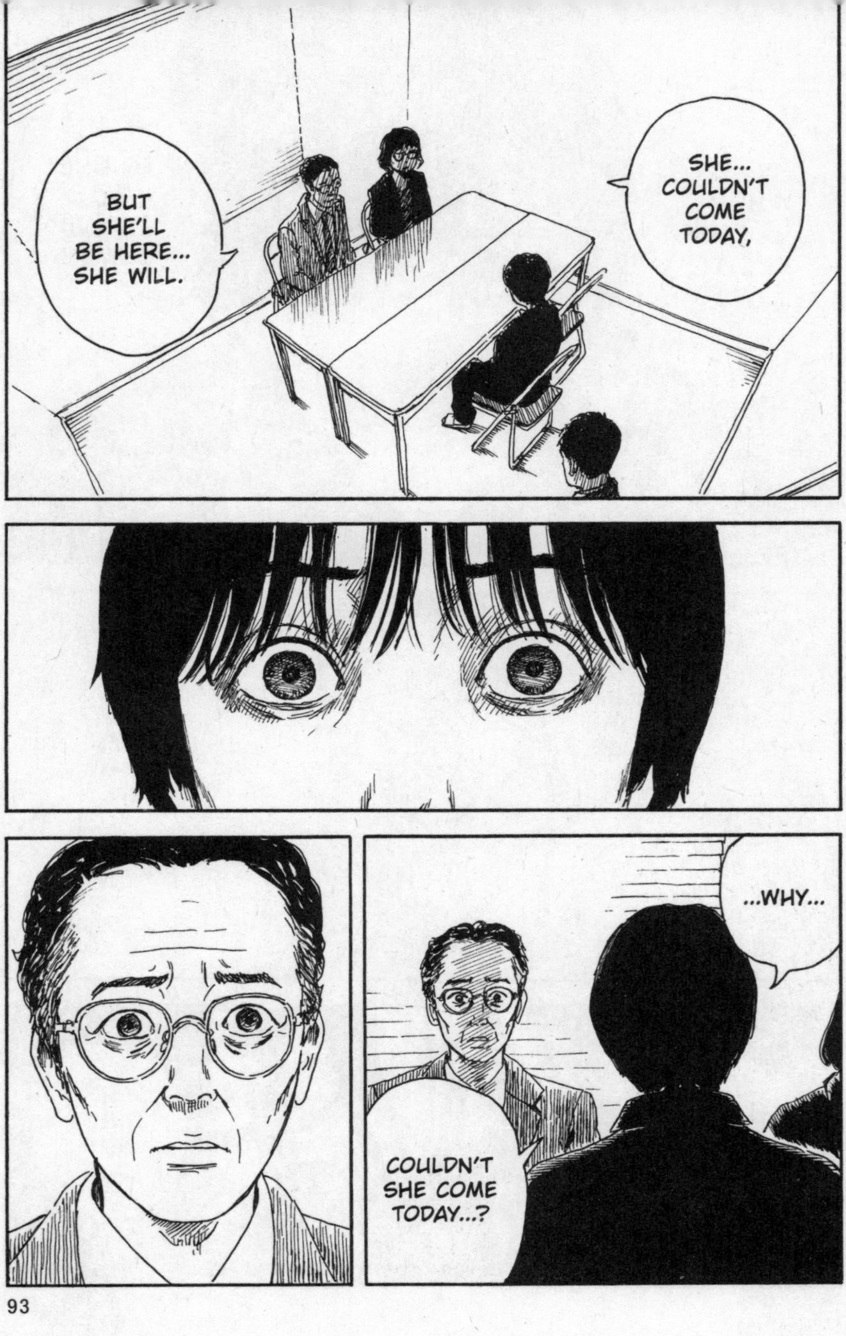
SHE... COULDN'T COME TODAY,
BUT SHE'LL BE HERE... SHE WILL.
...WHY...
COULDN'T SHE COME TODAY...?

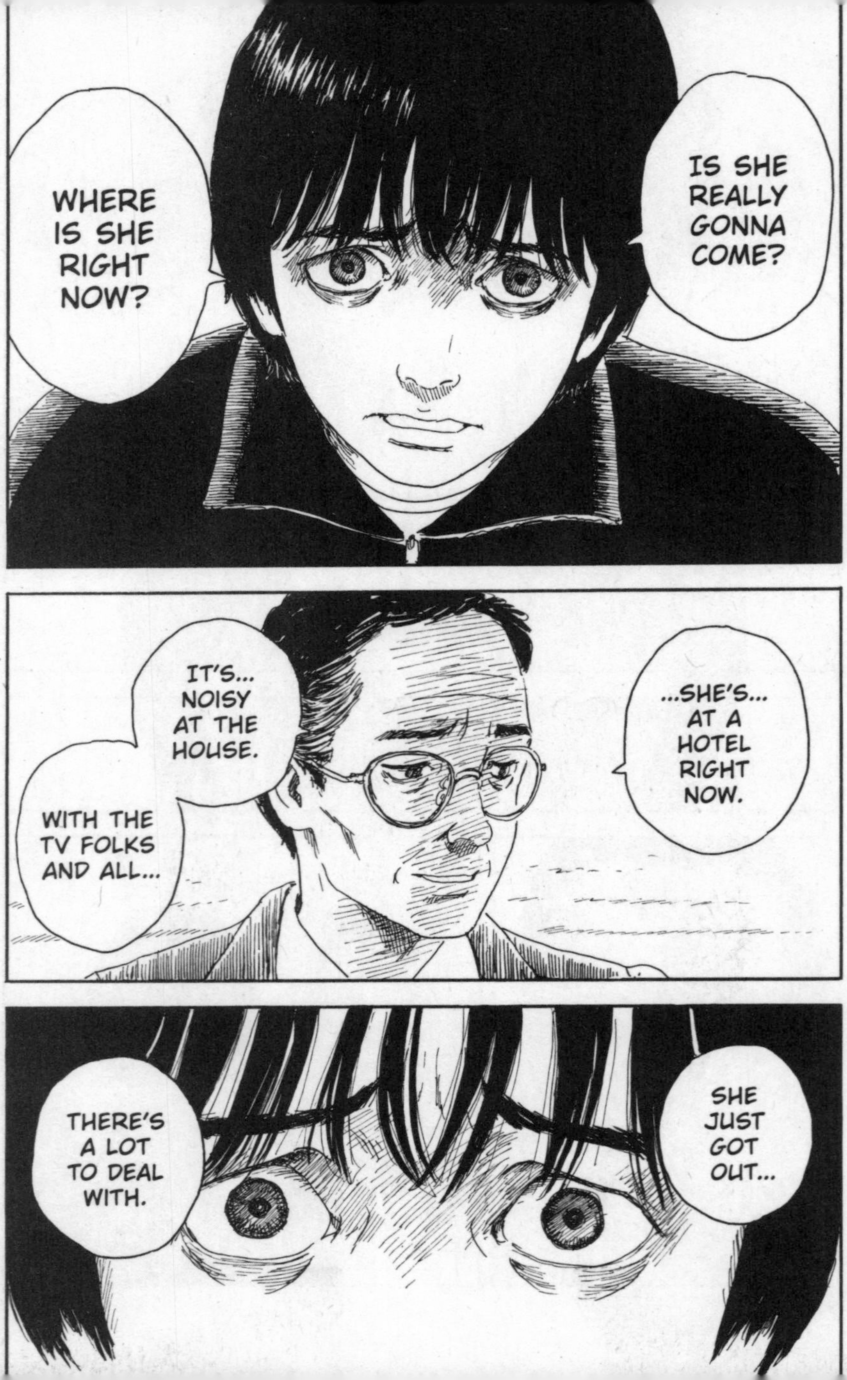
IS SHE REALLY GONNA COME?
WHERE IS SHE RIGHT NOW?
...SHE'S... AT A HOTEL RIGHT NOW.
IT'S... NOISY AT THE HOUSE.
WITH THE TV FOLKS AND ALL...
SHE JUST GOT OUT...
THERE'S A LOT TO DEAL WITH.

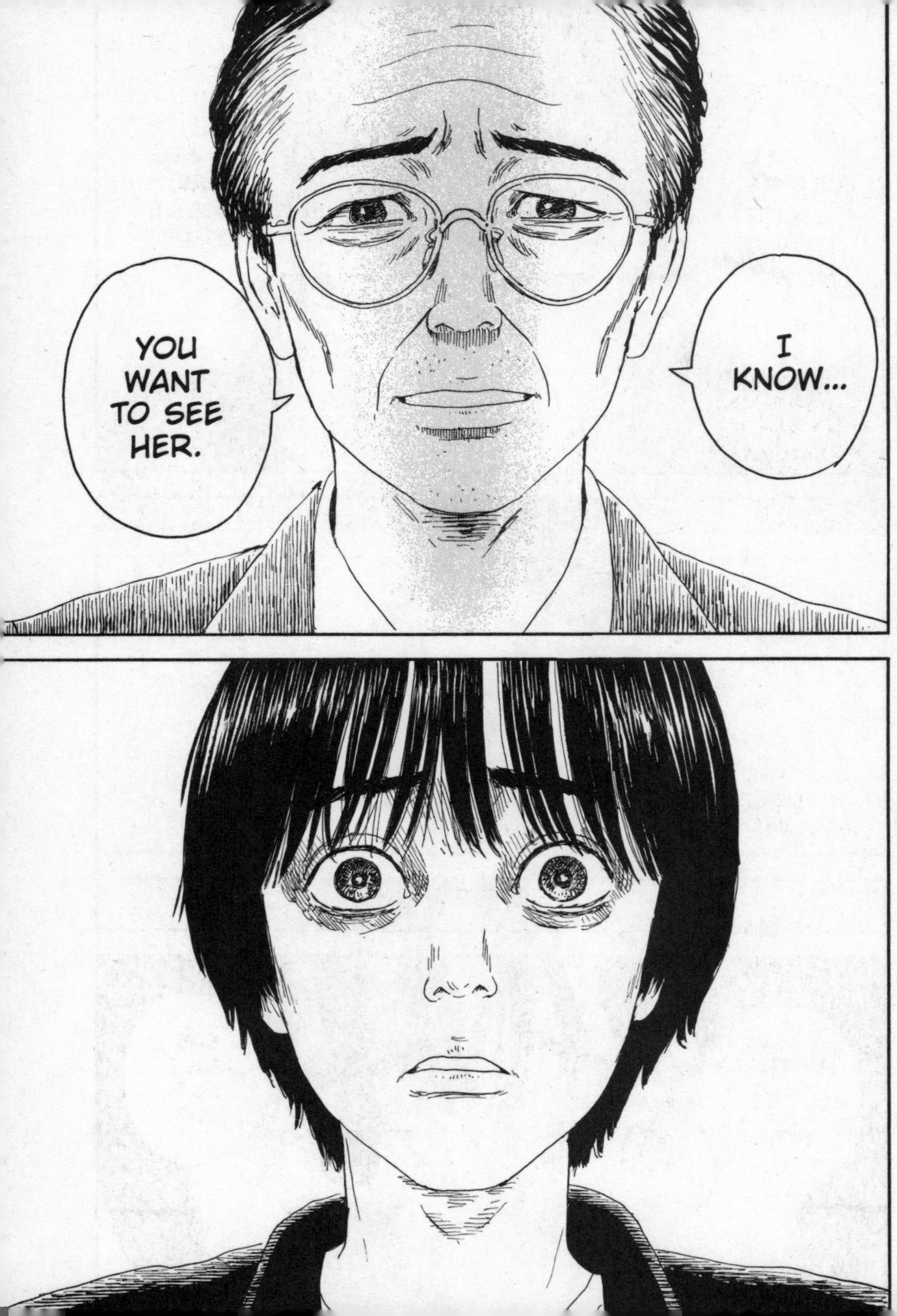
I KNOW...
YOU WANT TO SEE HER.

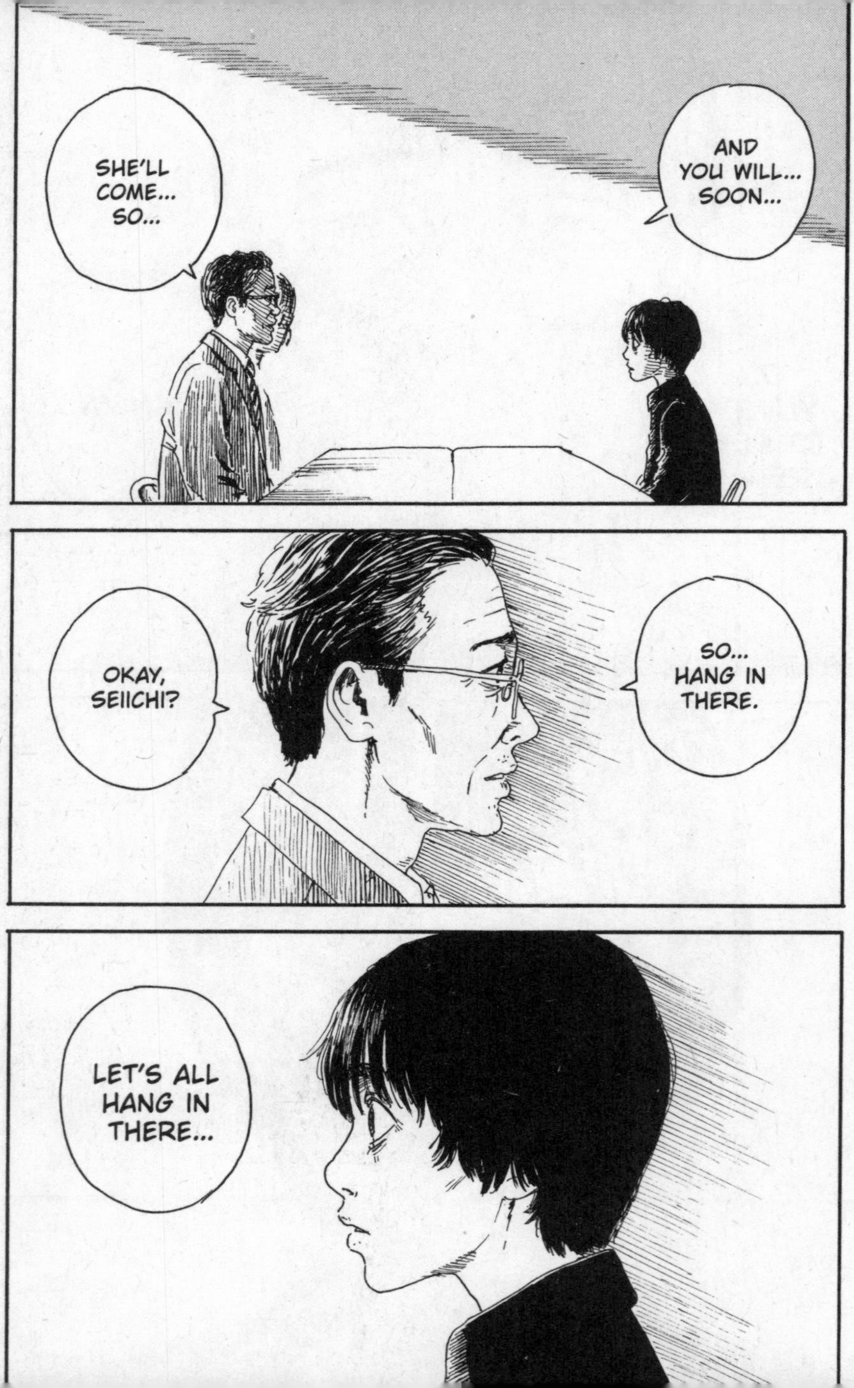
AND YOU WILL... SOON...
SHE'LL COME... SO...
SO... HANG IN THERE.
OKAY, SEIICHI?
LET'S ALL HANG IN THERE...

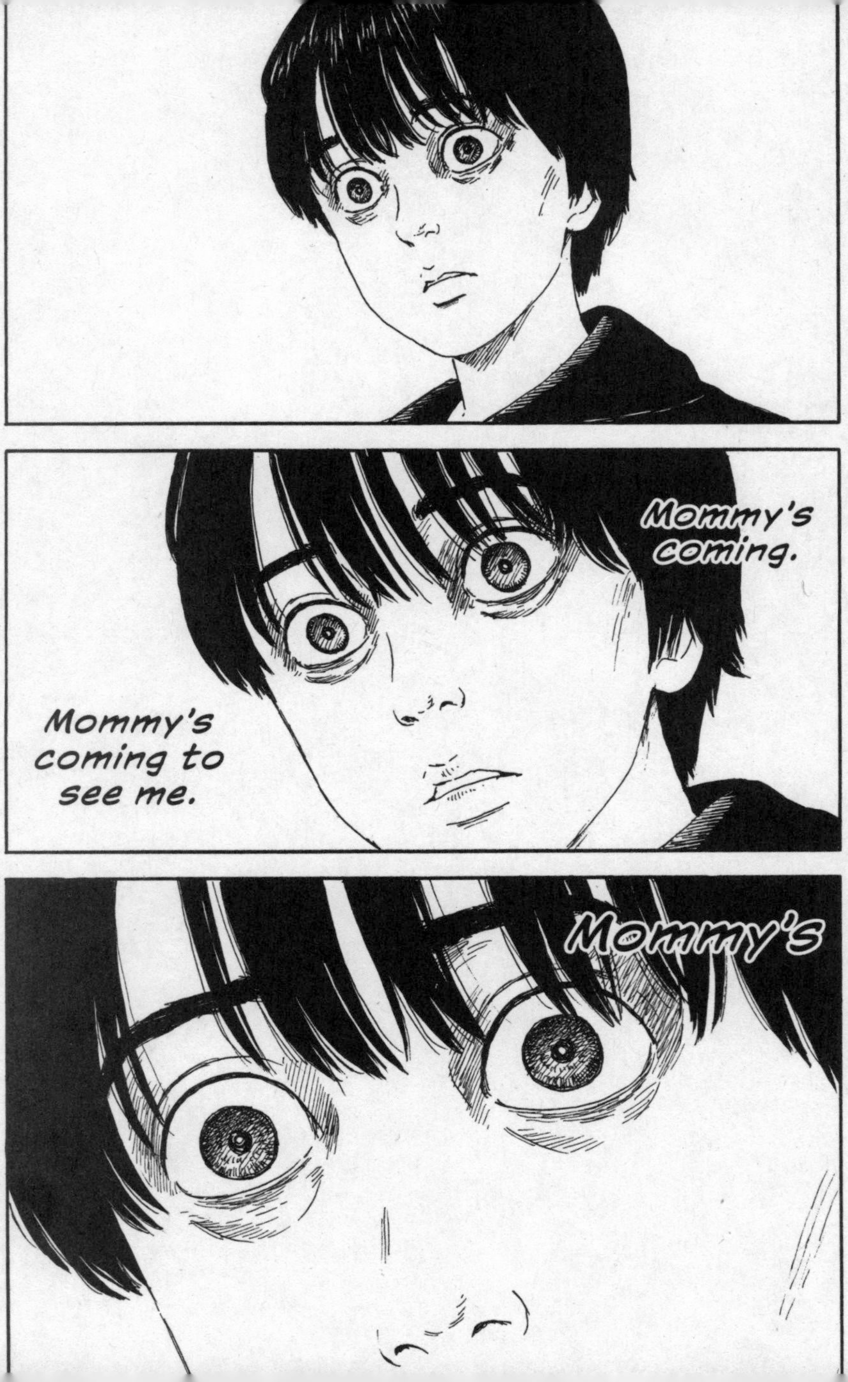
Mommy's coming.
Mommy's coming to see me.
Mommy's

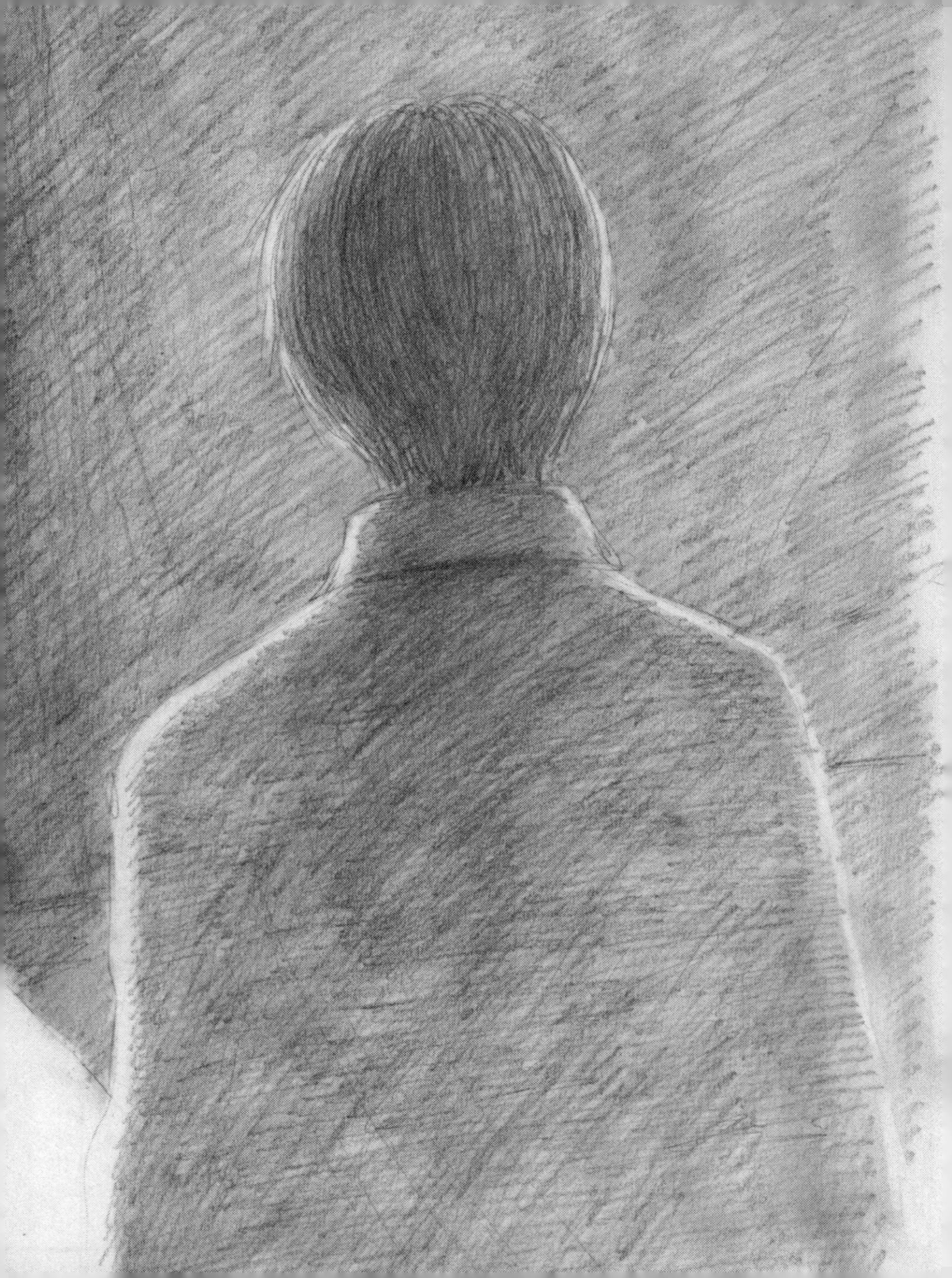

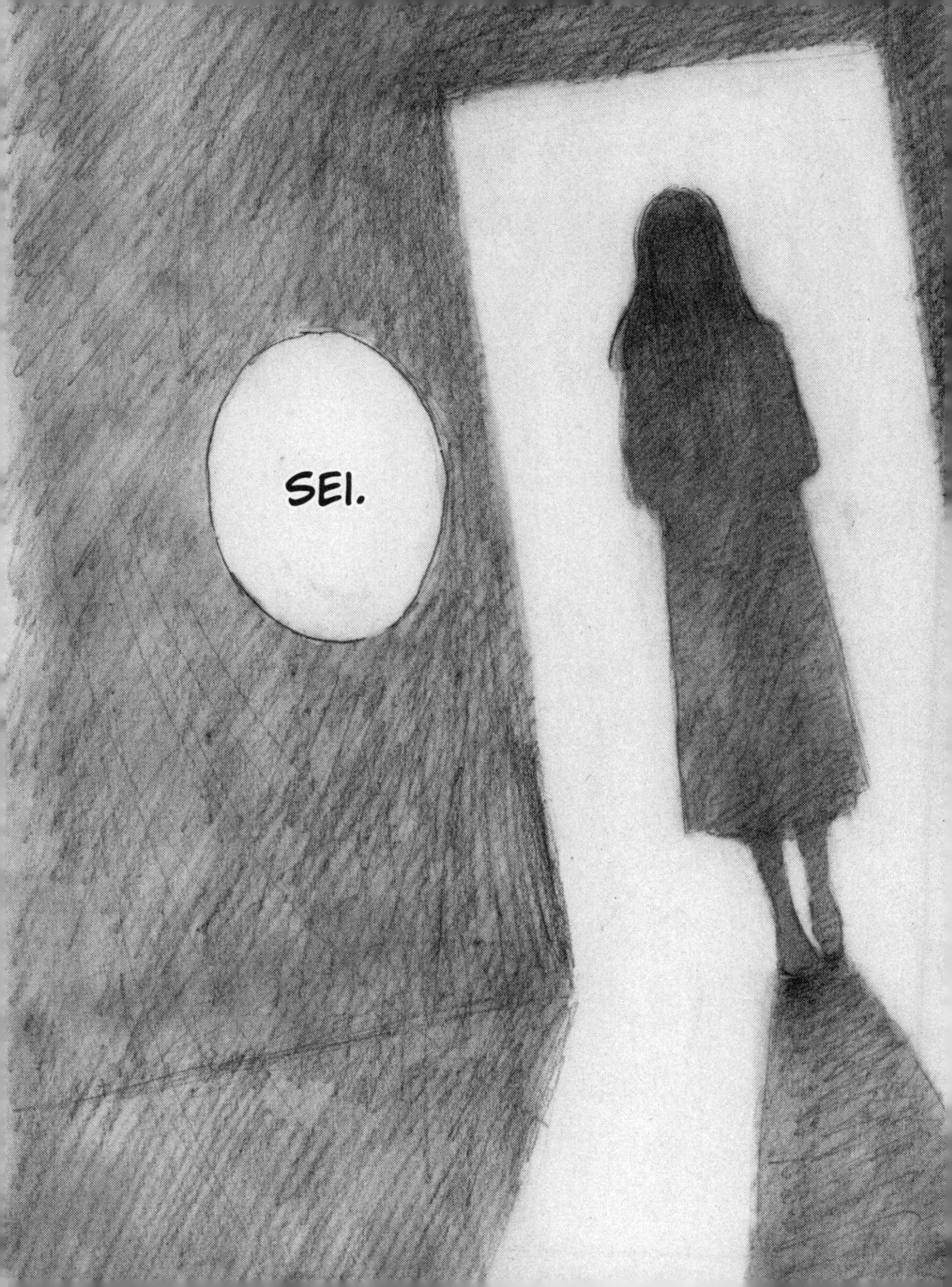
SEI.

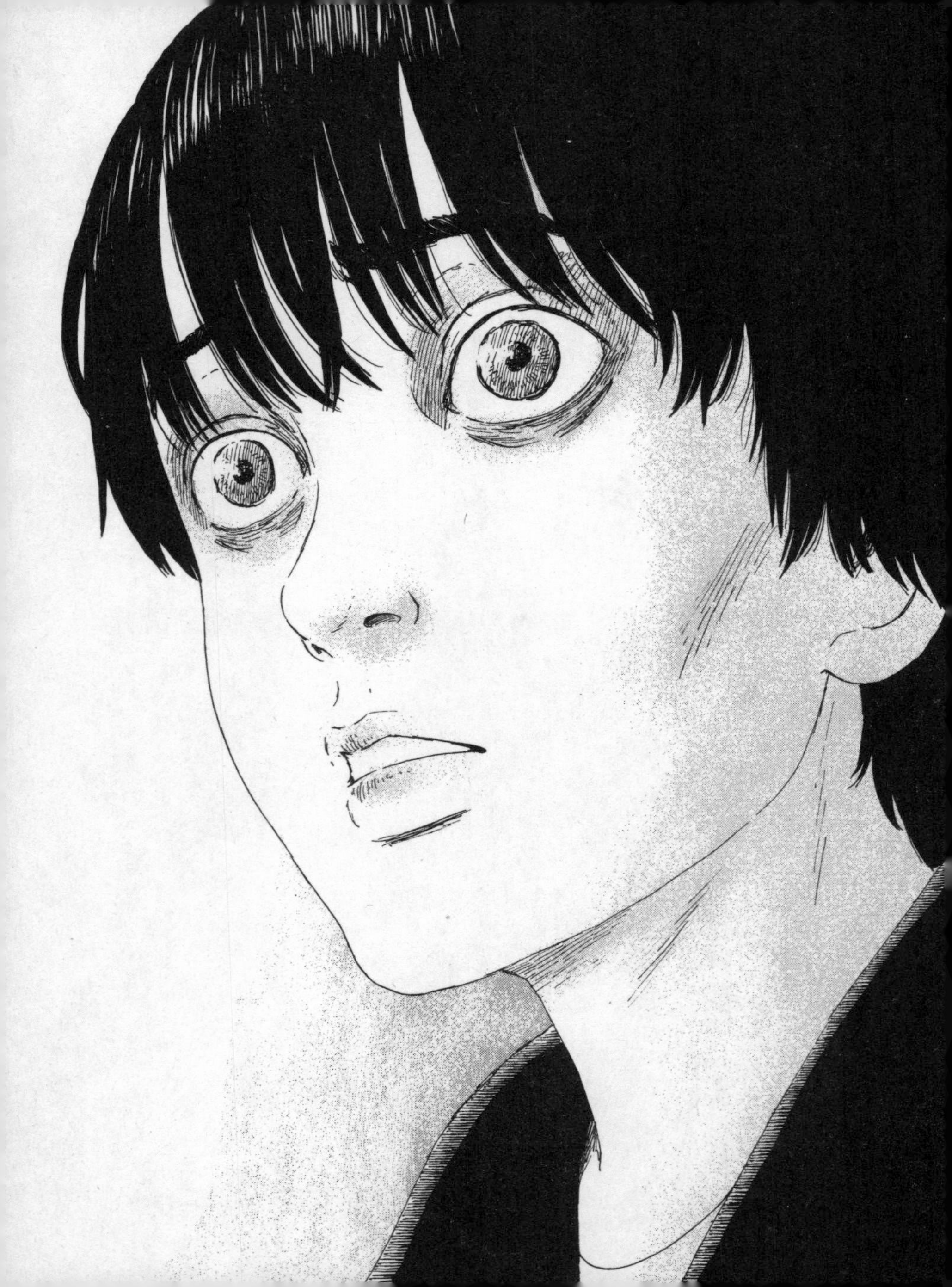

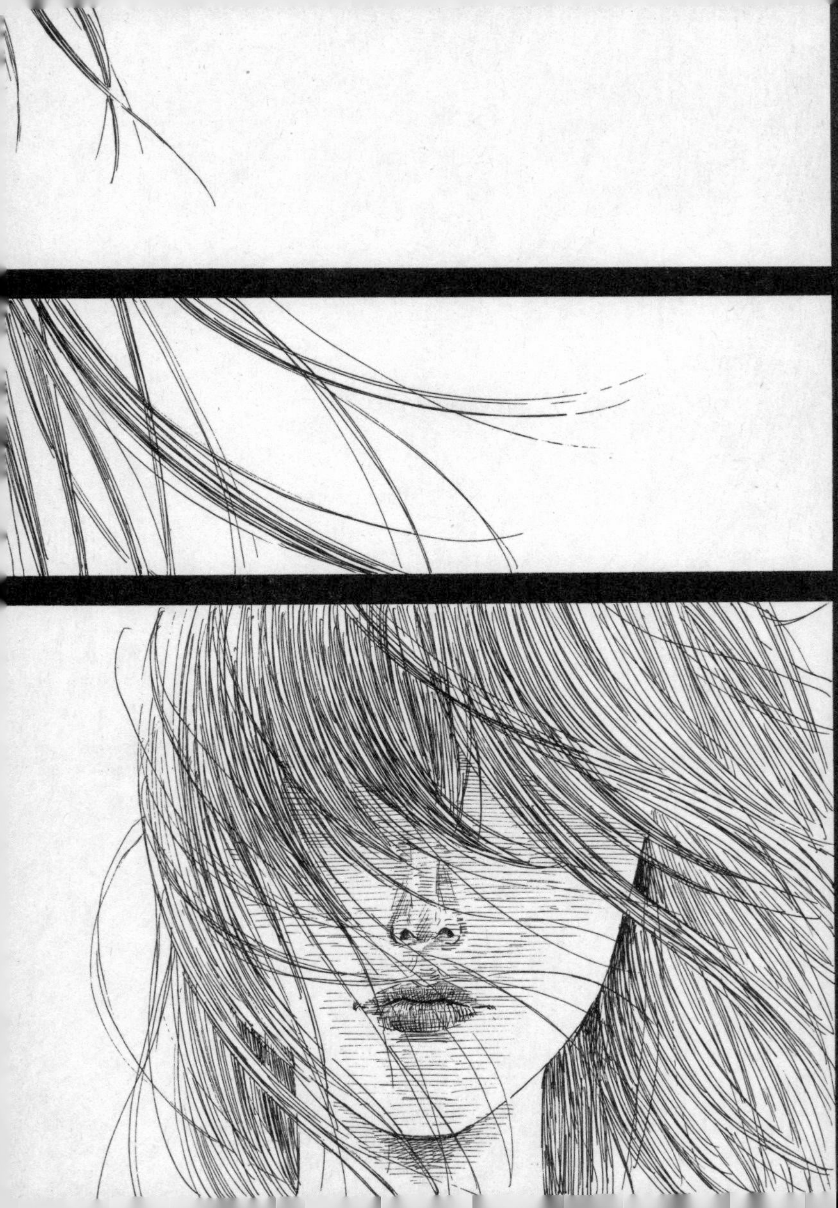

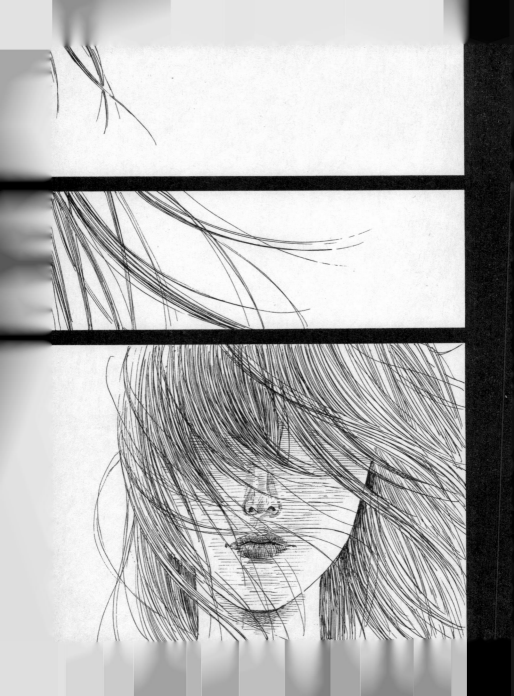

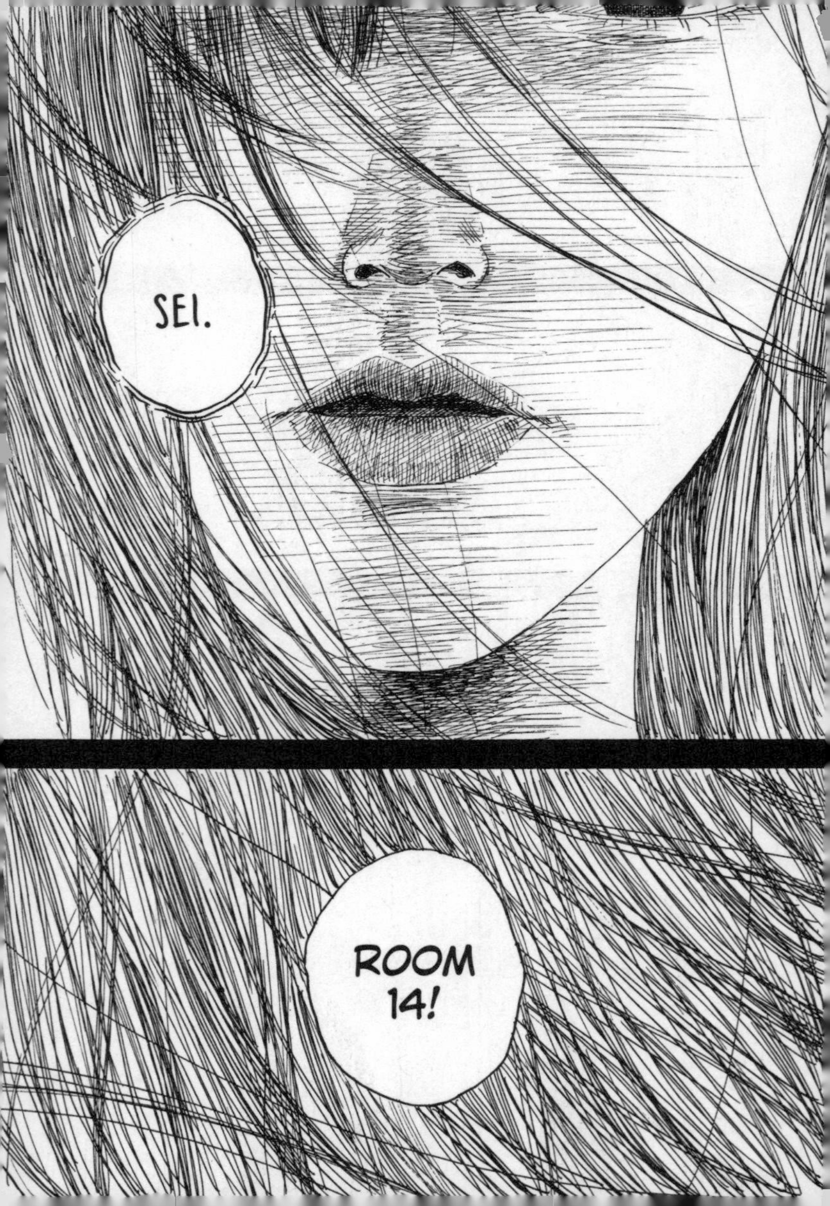
SEI.
ROOM 14!

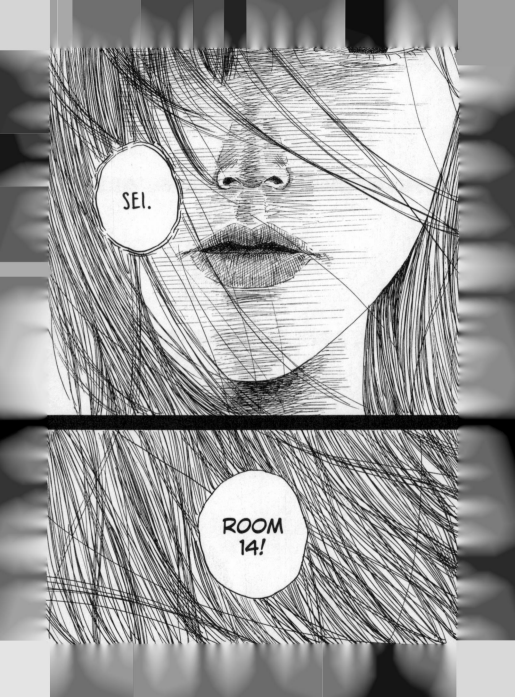

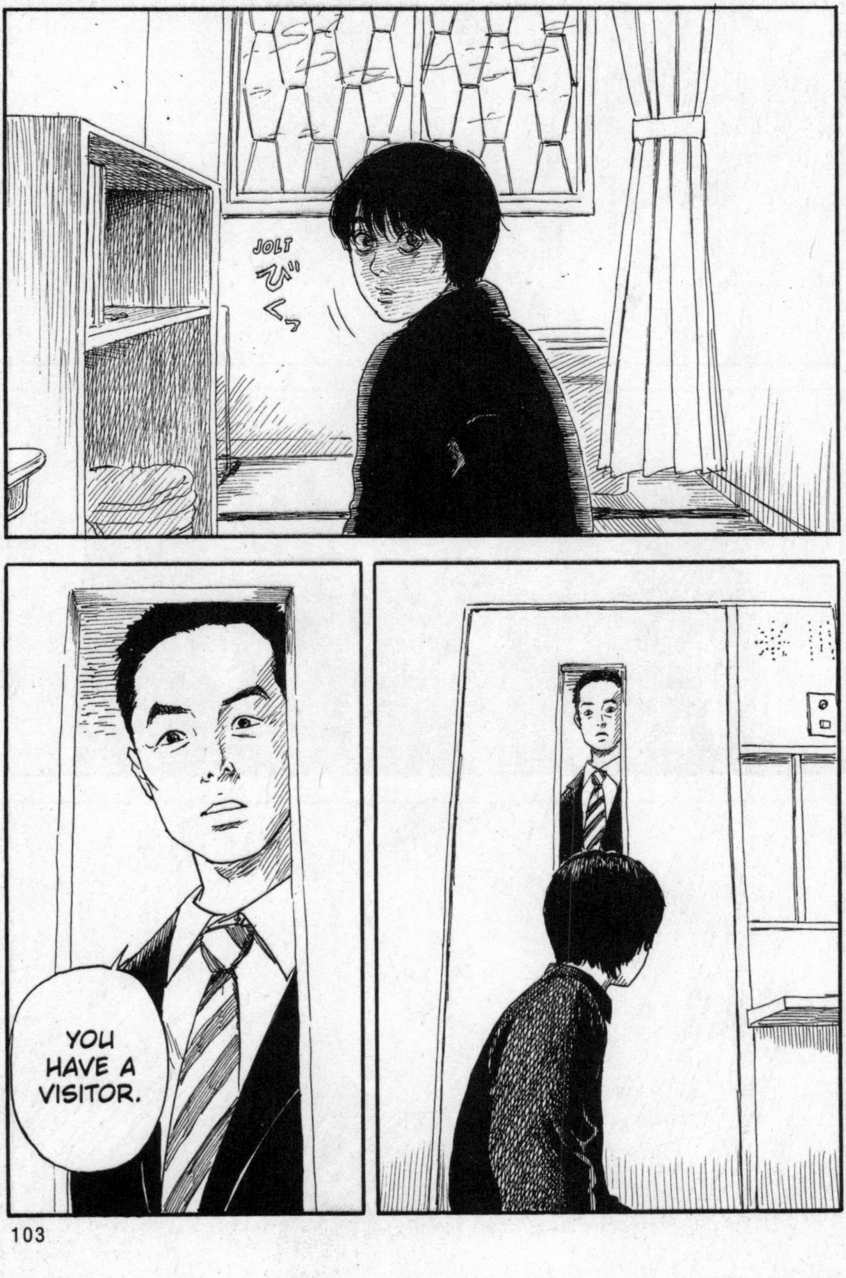
JOLT
びくっ
YOU HAVE A VISITOR.

ガ
チ
ャ
KA-
CHIK

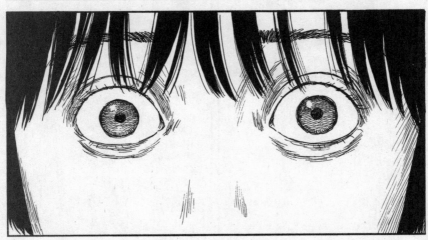

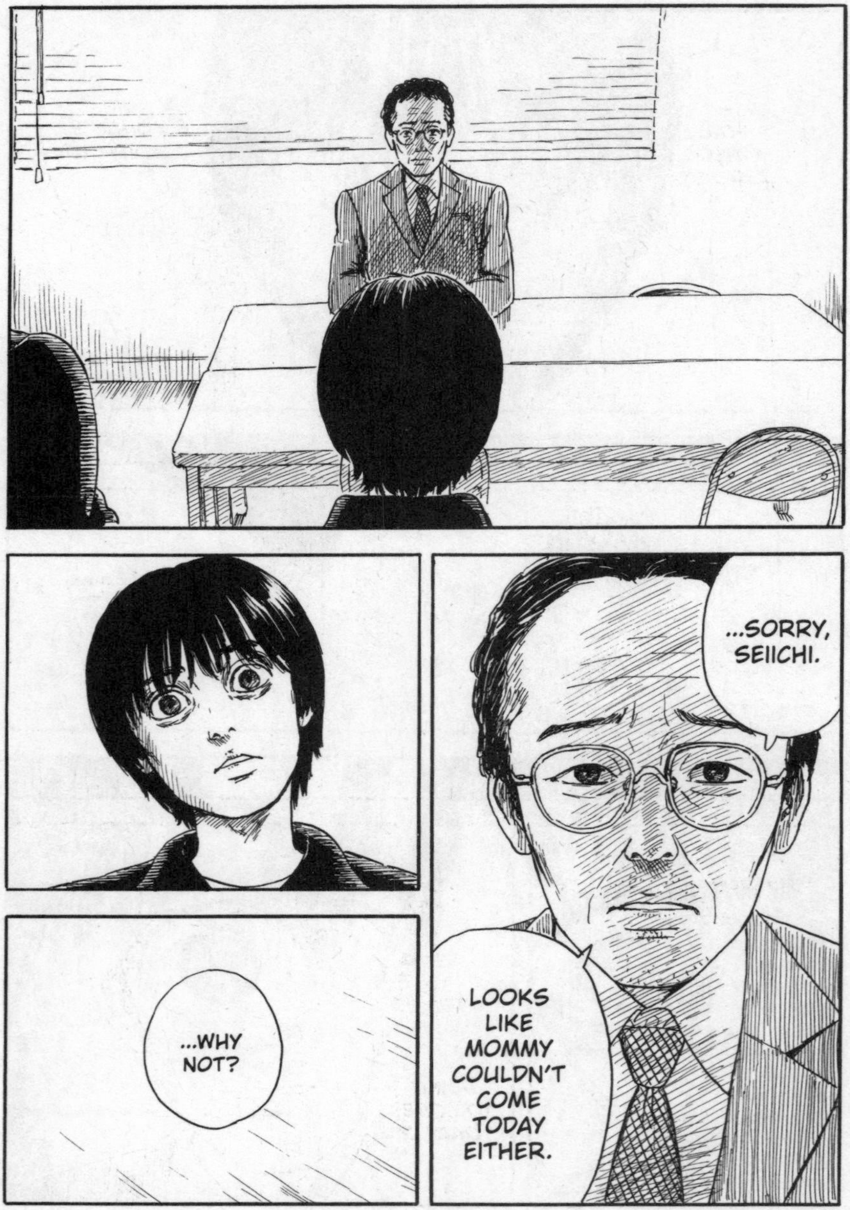
...SORRY, SEIICHI.
LOOKS LIKE MOMMY COULDN'T COME TODAY EITHER.
...WHY NOT?

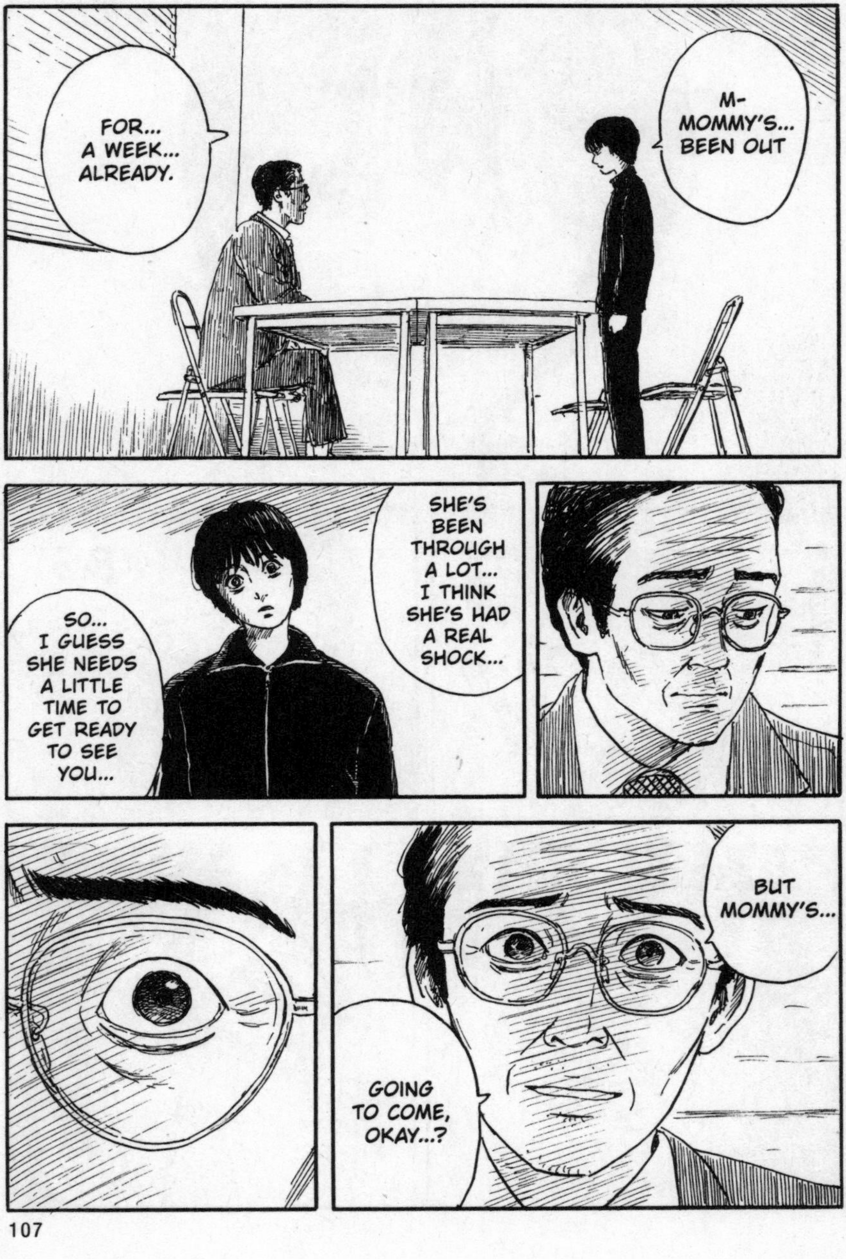
M- MOMMY'S... BEEN OUT
FOR... A WEEK... ALREADY.
SHE'S BEEN THROUGH A LOT... I THINK SHE'S HAD A REAL SHOCK...
SO... I GUESS SHE NEEDS A LITTLE TIME TO GET READY TO SEE YOU...
BUT MOMMY'S...
GOING TO COME, OKAY...?

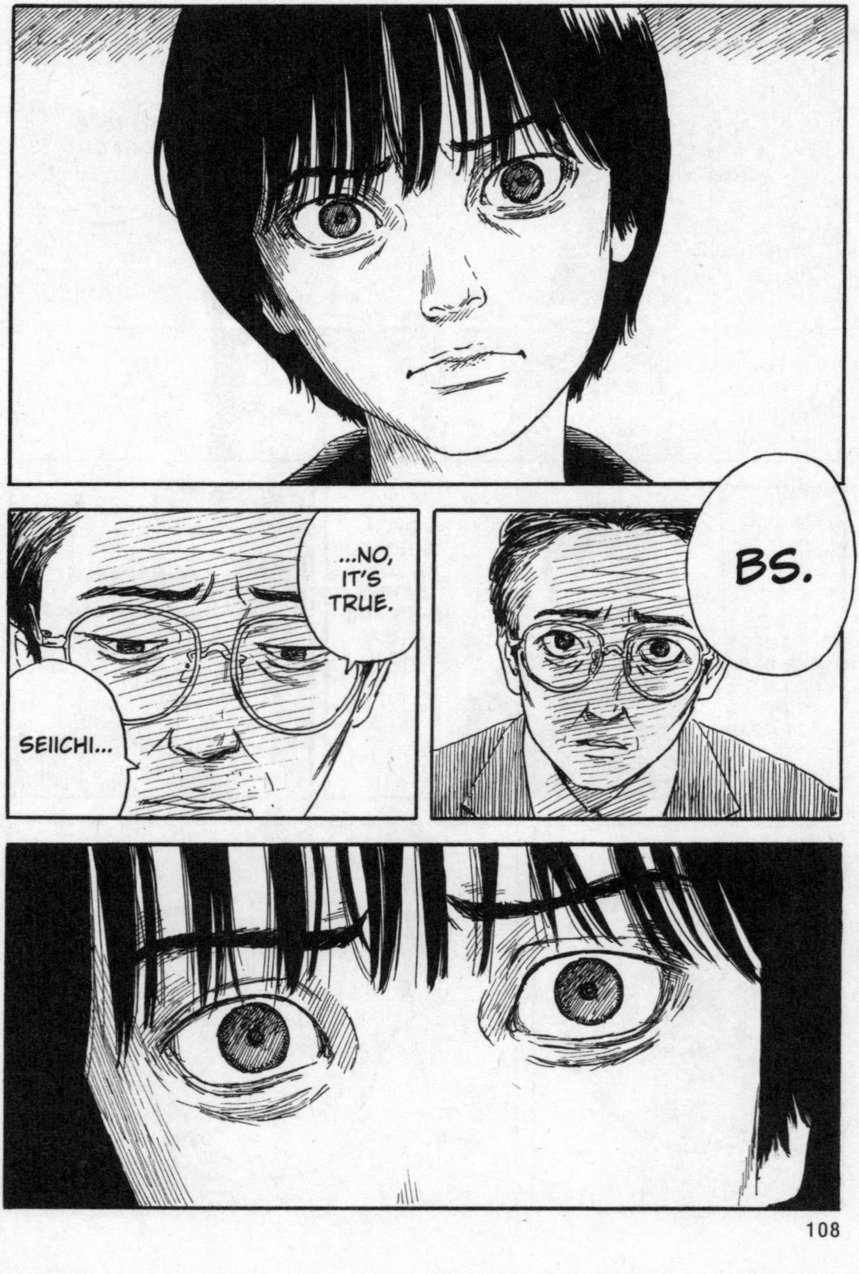
BS.
...NO, IT'S TRUE.
SEIICHI...

MOMMY'S...
GOING TO
COME.

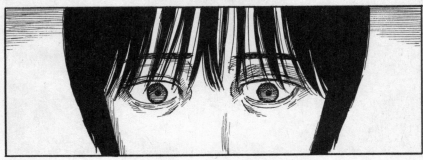

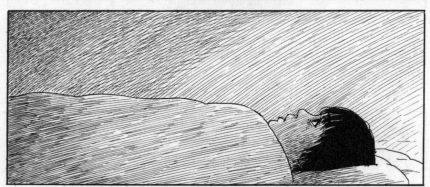

She didn't come today either.

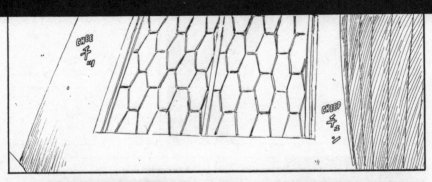

GOOD
MORNING
...

GOOD
MORNING!

Will she

come today?

ROOM 14!

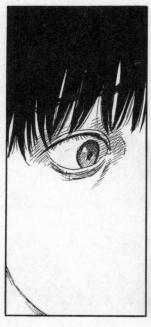

THE INVESTI-GATOR WANTS TO SEE YOU.

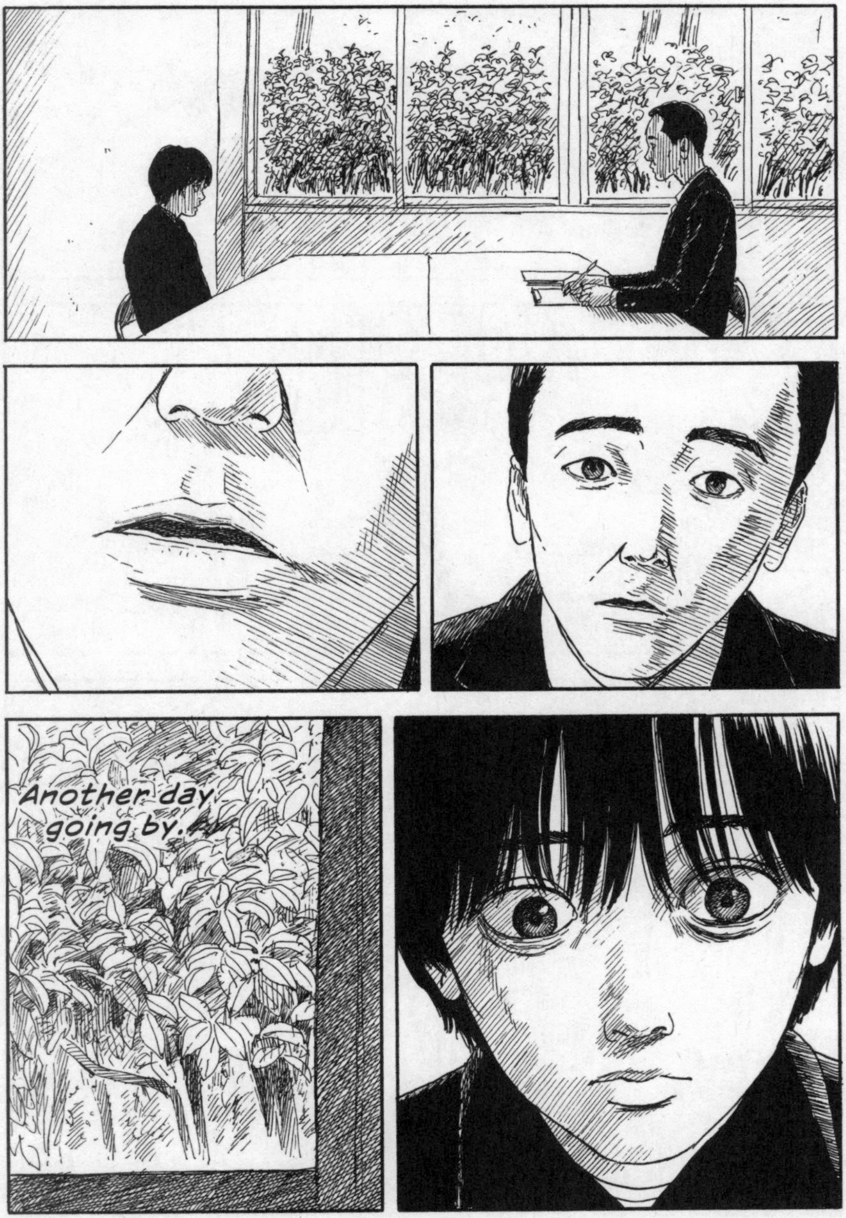
Another day going by...

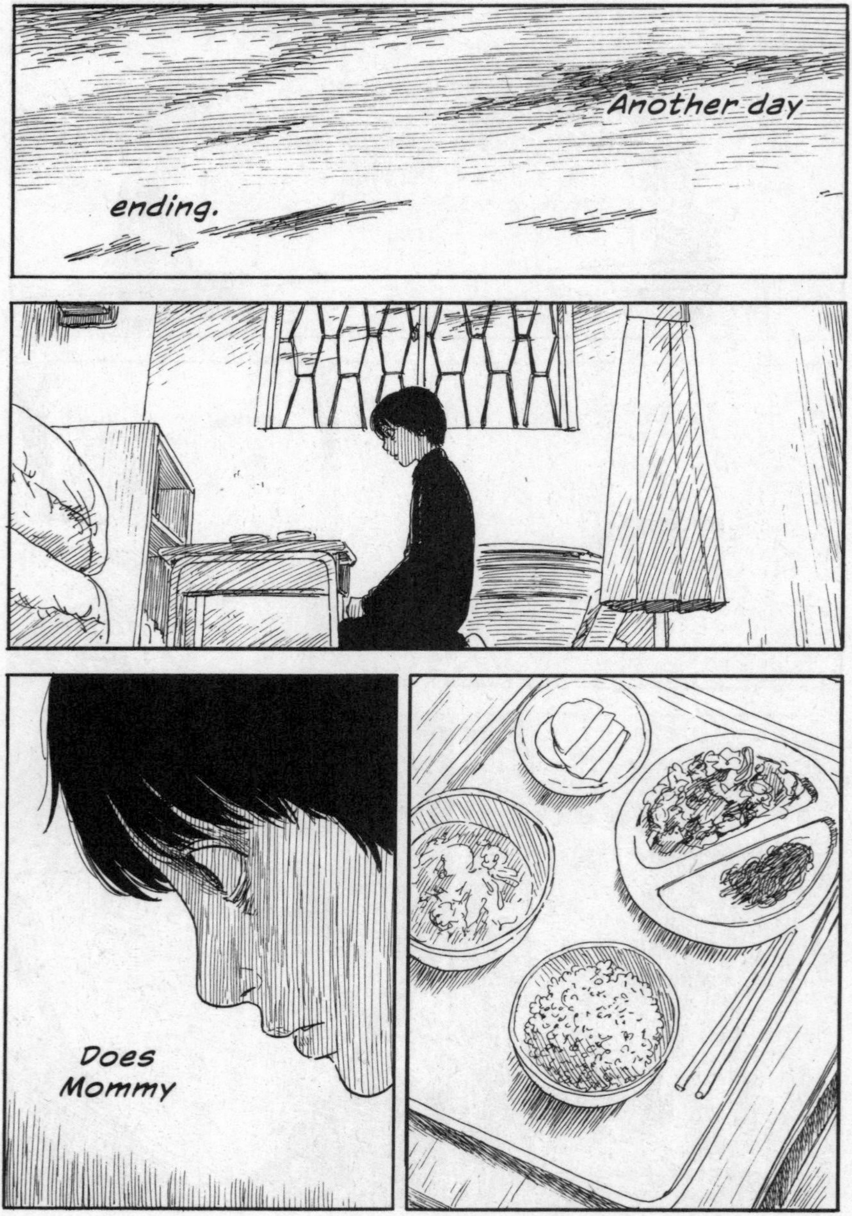
Another day
ending.
Does
Mommy

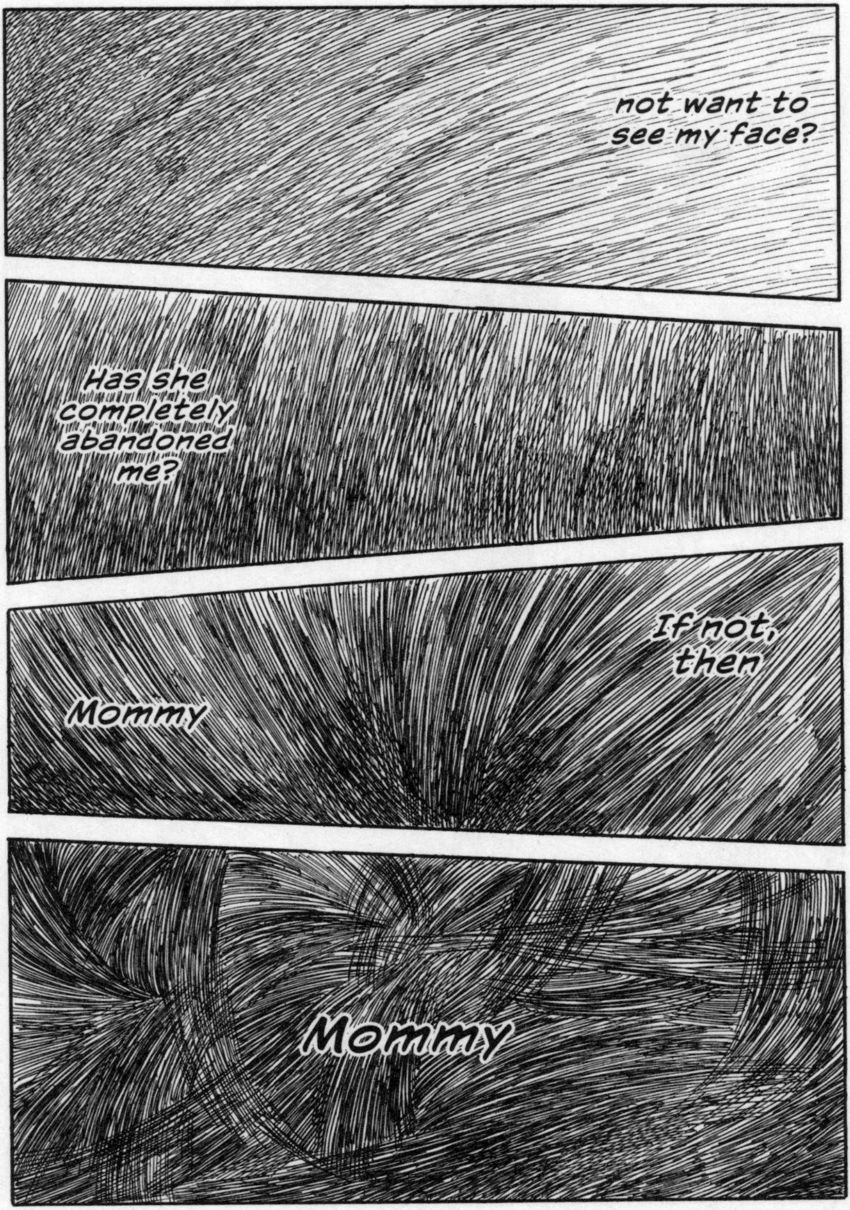
not want to
see my face?
Has she completely abandoned me?
If not, then
Mommy
Mommy

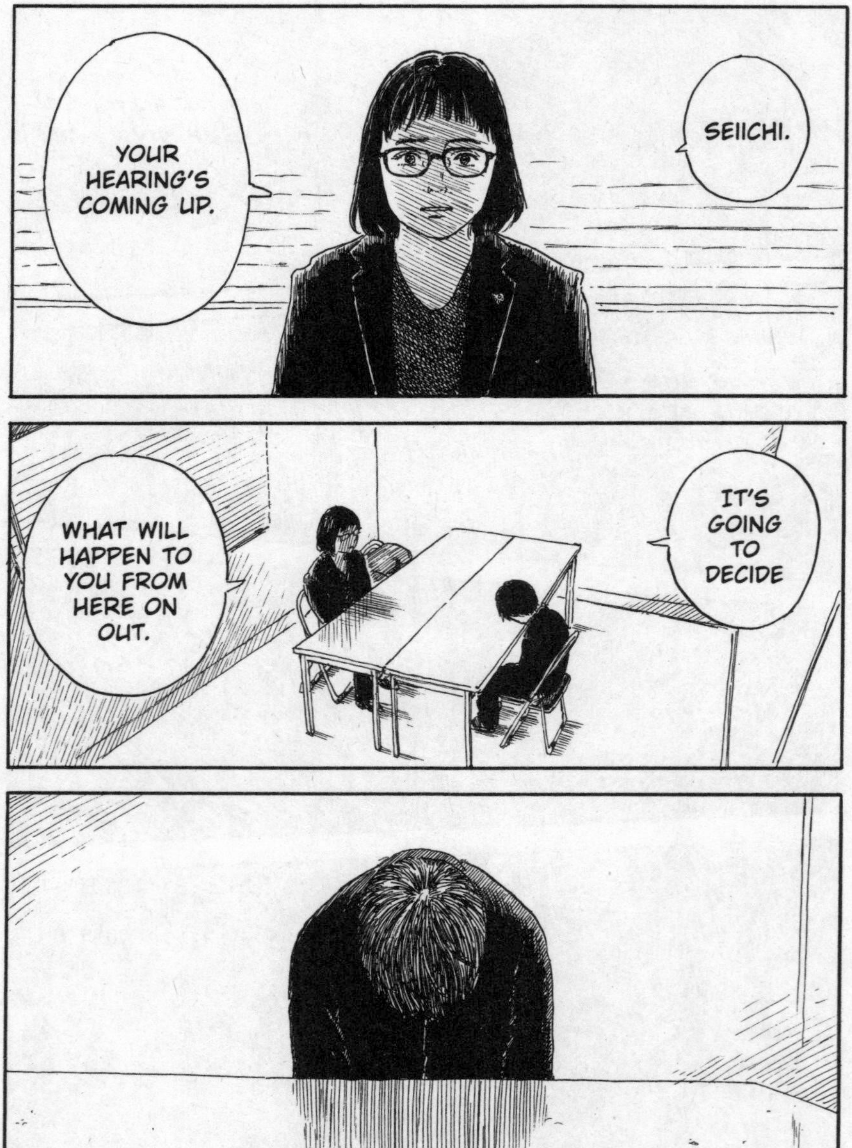
SEIICHI.
YOUR HEARING'S COMING UP.
IT'S GOING TO DECIDE
WHAT WILL HAPPEN TO YOU FROM HERE ON OUT.

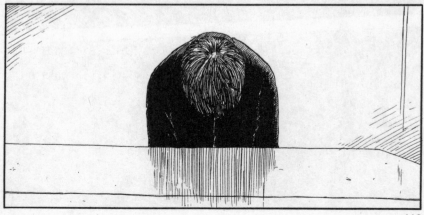

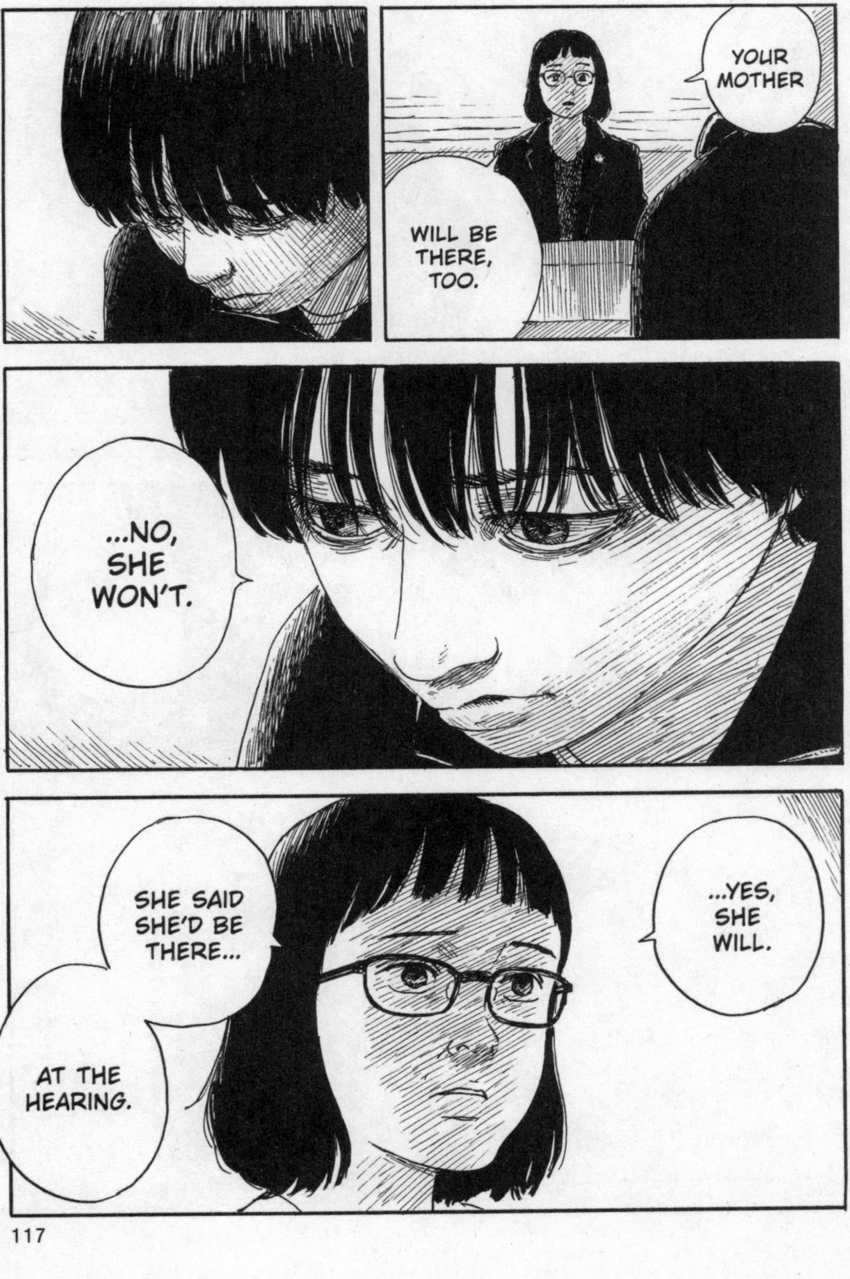
YOUR MOTHER
WILL BE THERE, TOO.
...NO, SHE WON'T.
...YES, SHE WILL.
SHE SAID SHE'D BE THERE...
AT THE HEARING.

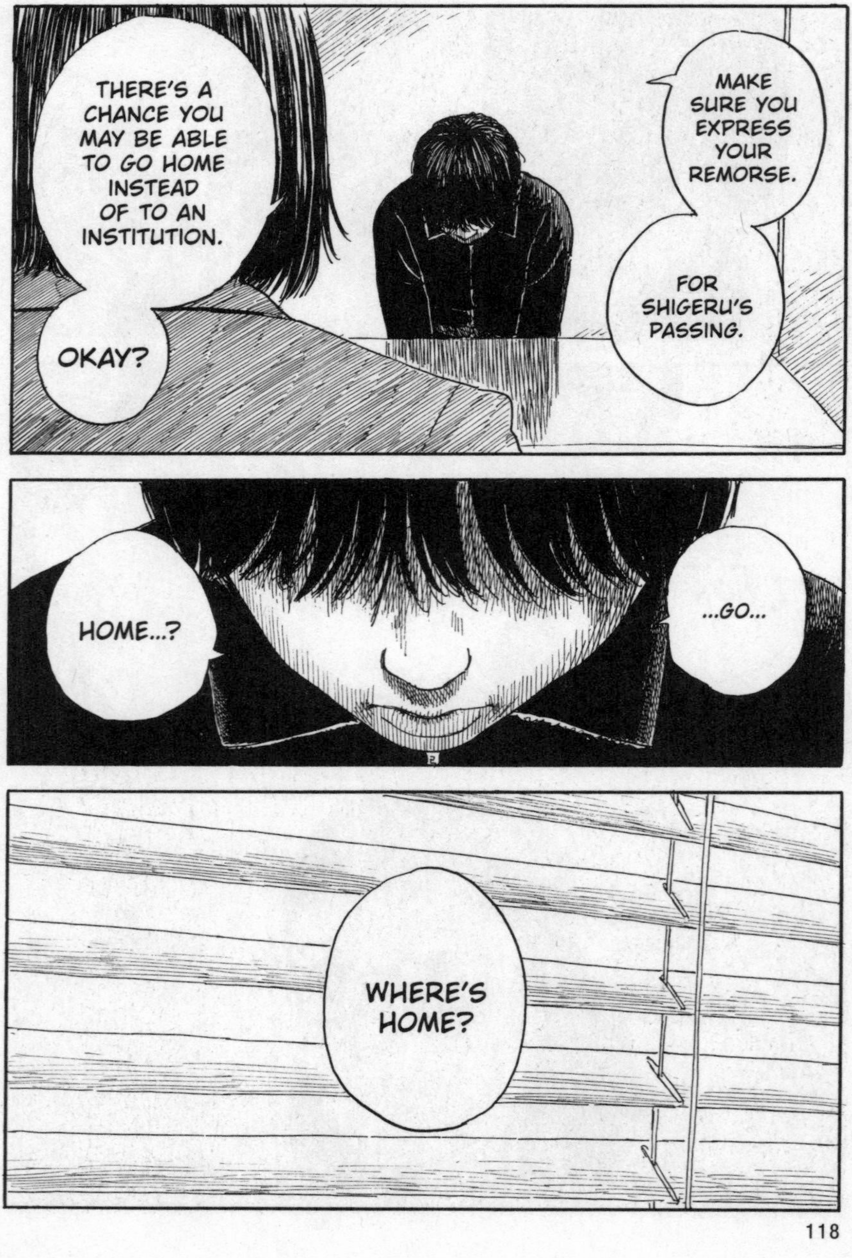
MAKE SURE YOU EXPRESS YOUR REMORSE.
FOR SHIGERU'S PASSING.
THERE'S A CHANCE YOU MAY BE ABLE TO GO HOME INSTEAD OF TO AN INSTITUTION.
OKAY?
...GO...
HOME...?
WHERE'S HOME?

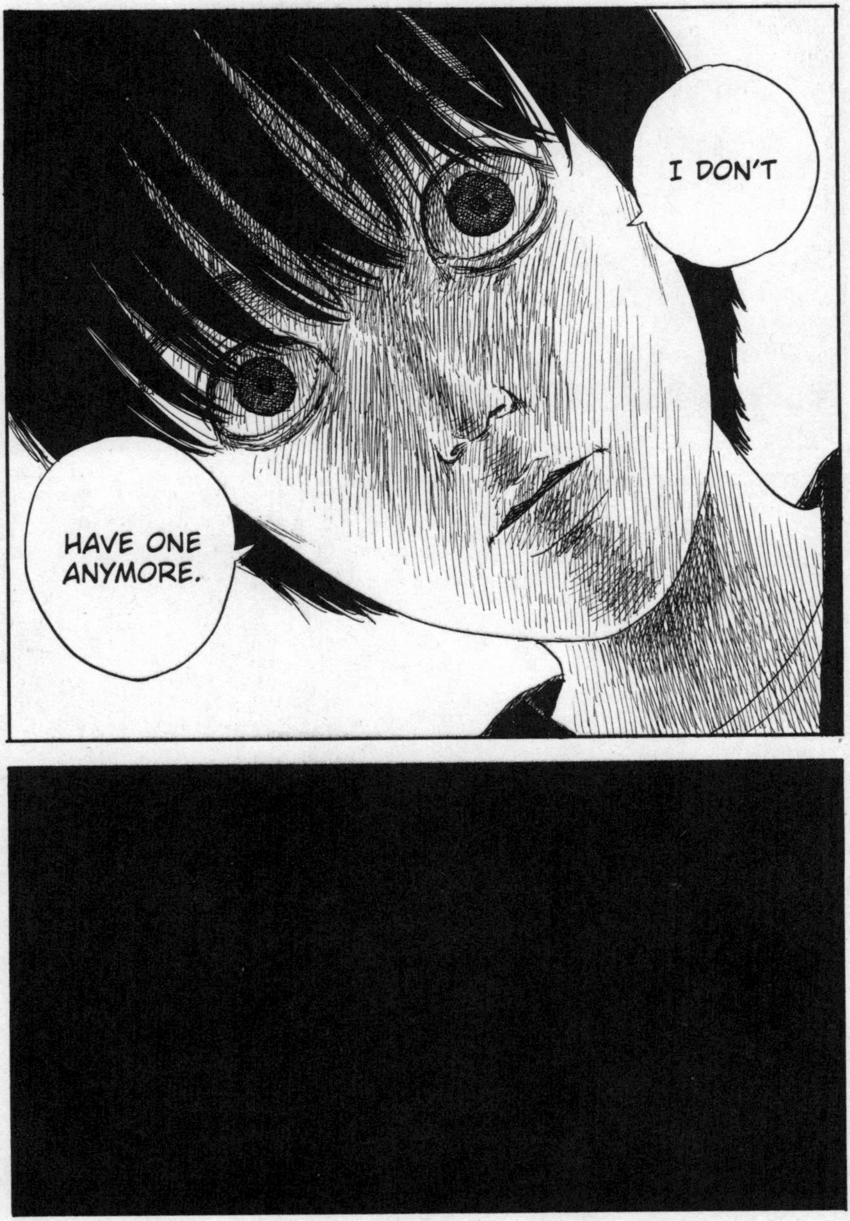
I DON'T
HAVE ONE ANYMORE.

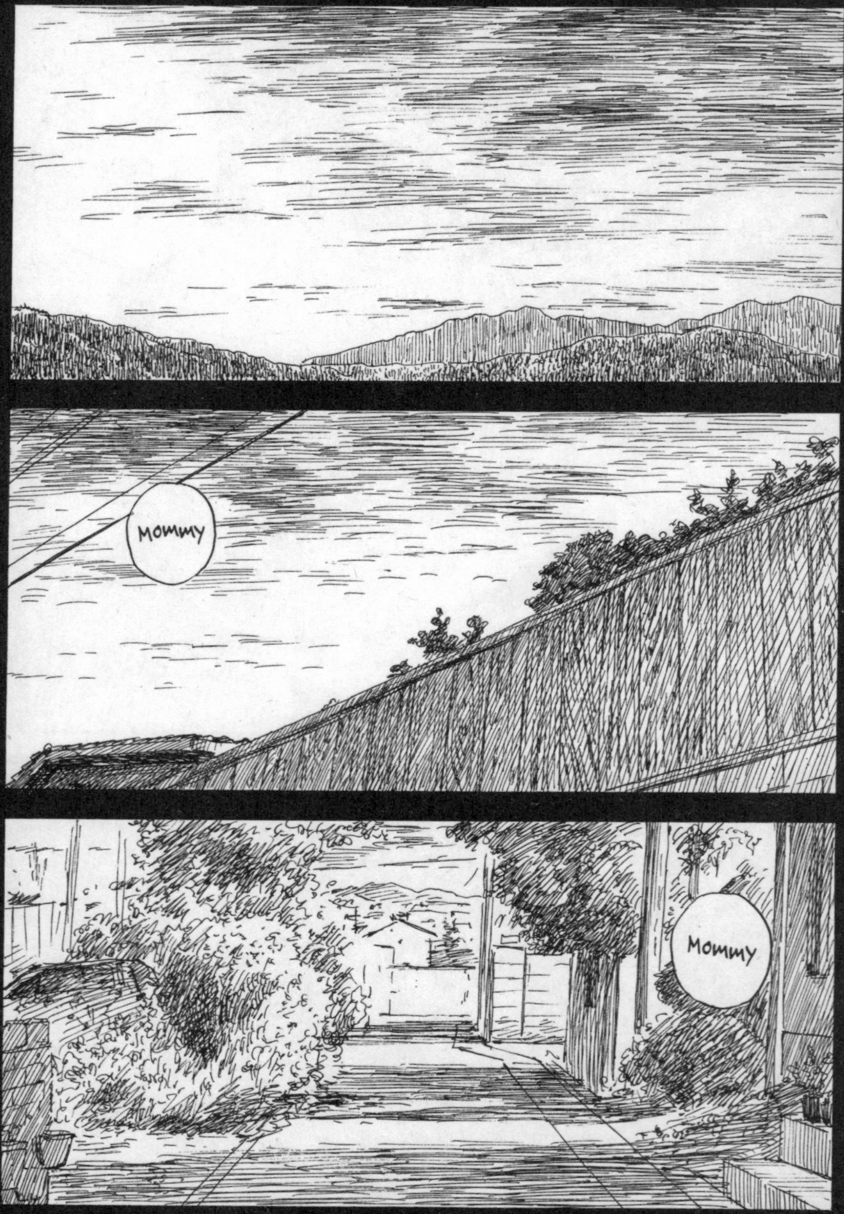
Mommy
Mommy

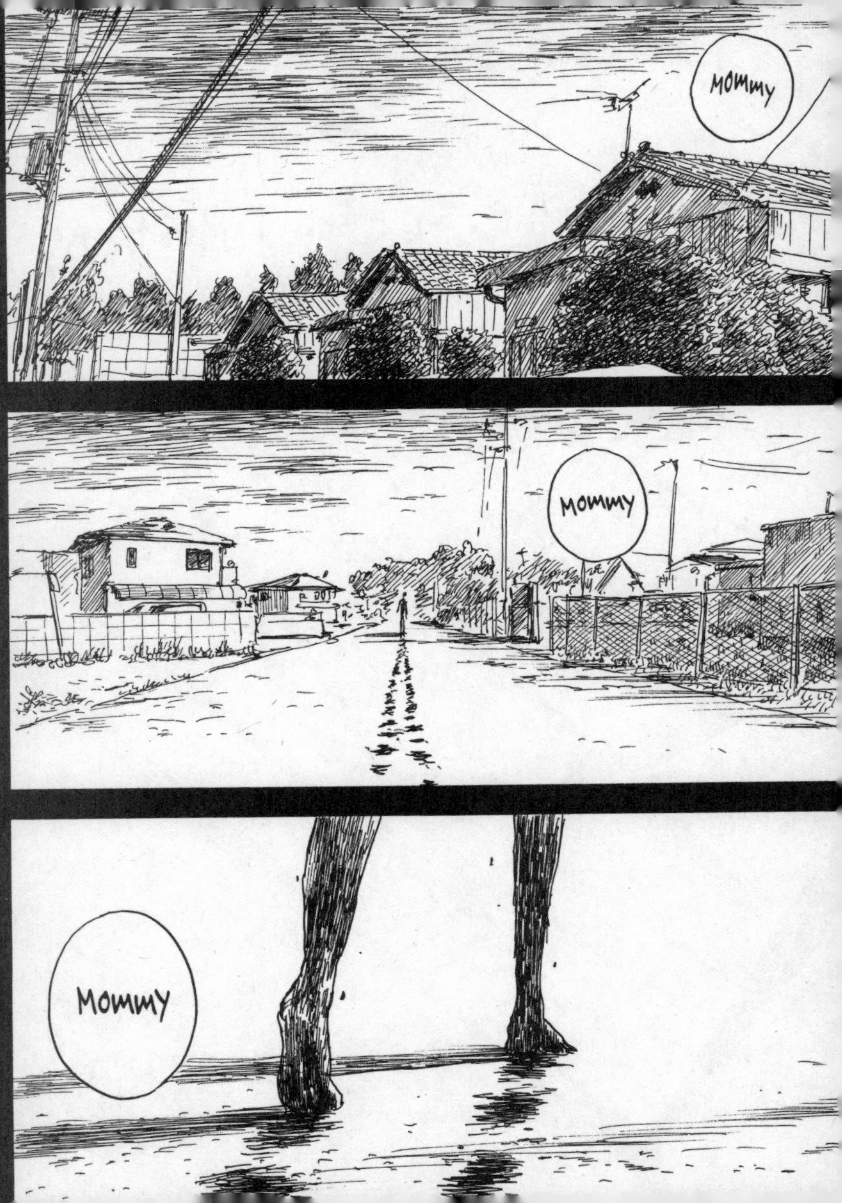
MOMMY
MOMMY
MOMMY

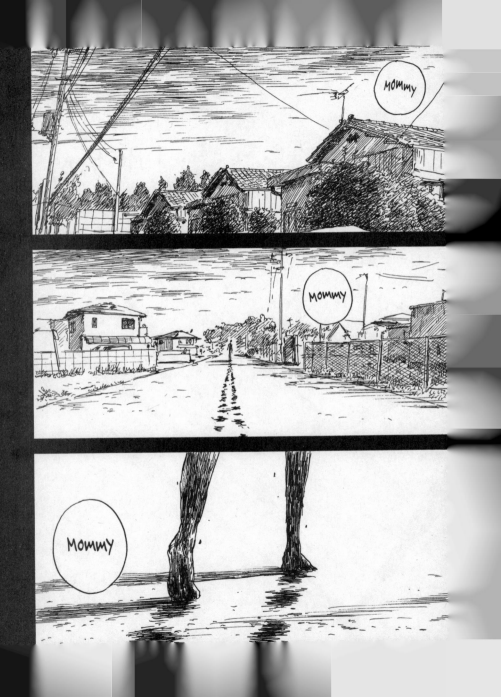

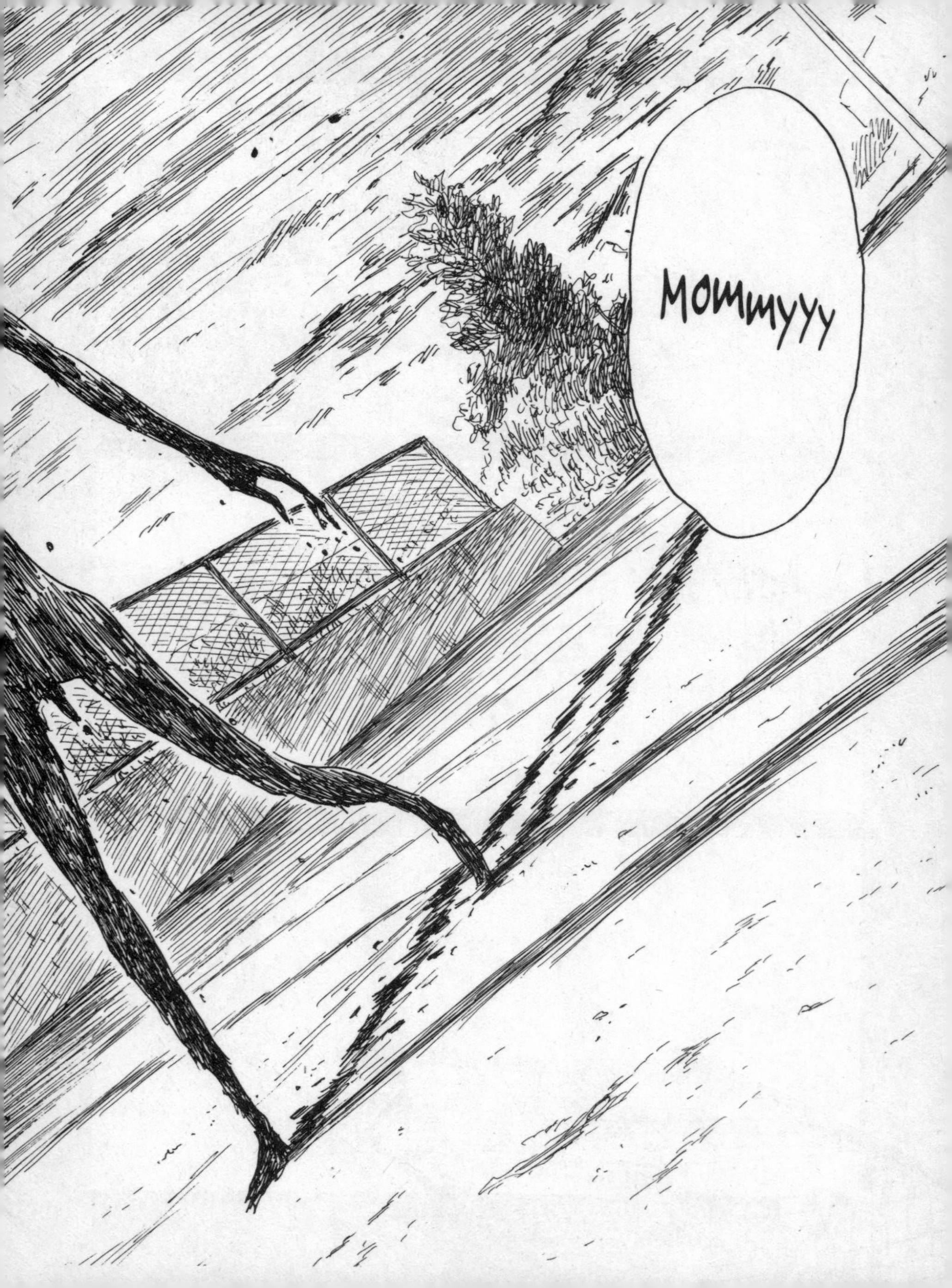
MOMMYYY

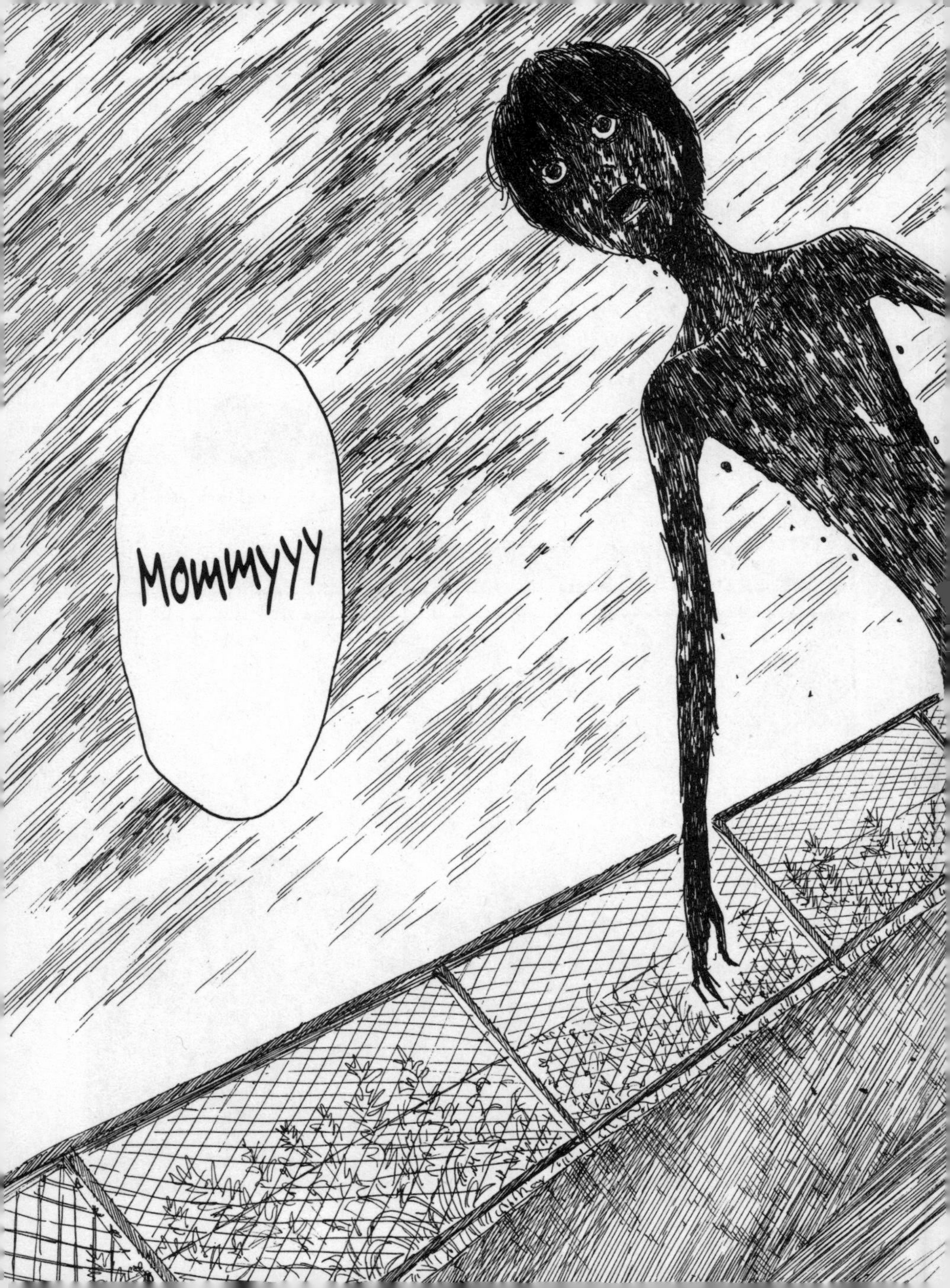
MOMMYYY

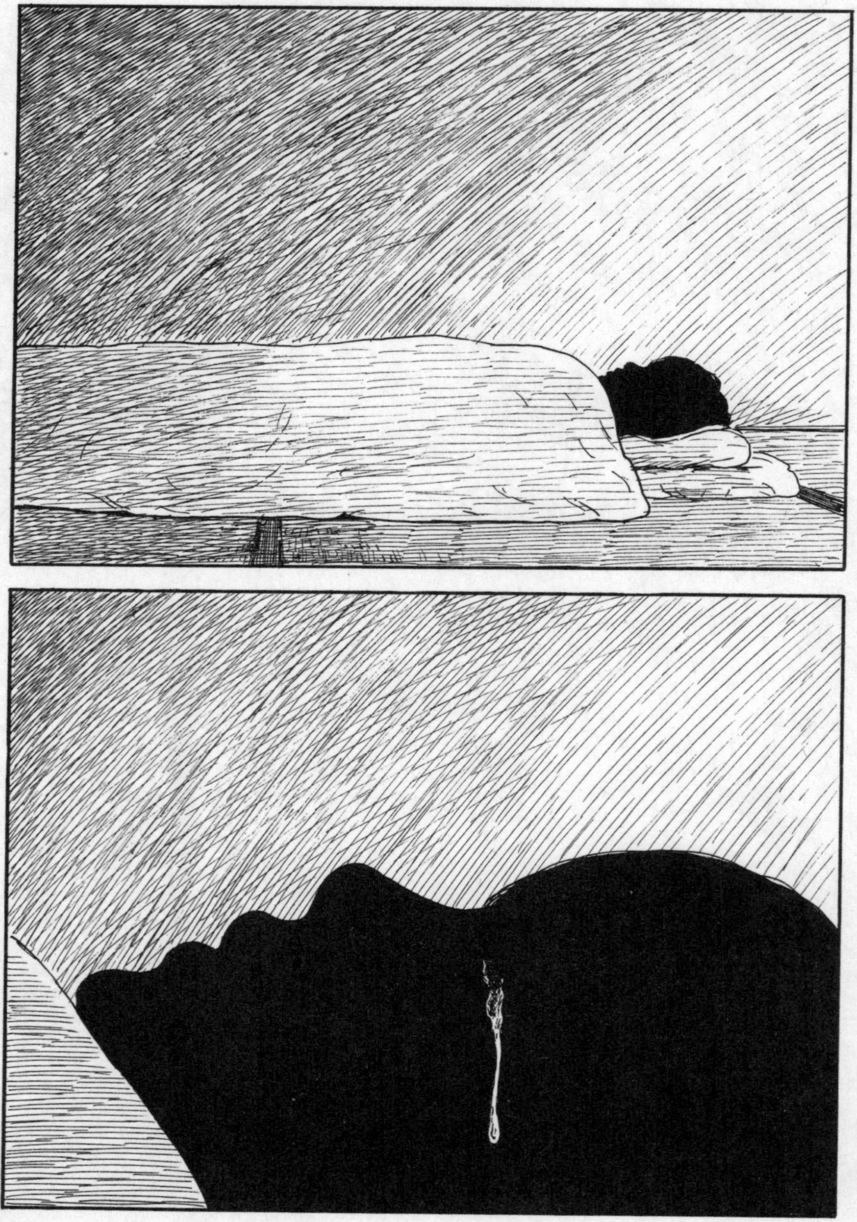

March 14th

CHAPTER 104 Judgment

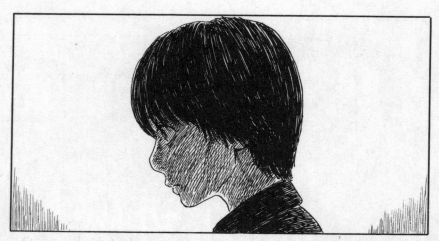

ROOM 14!

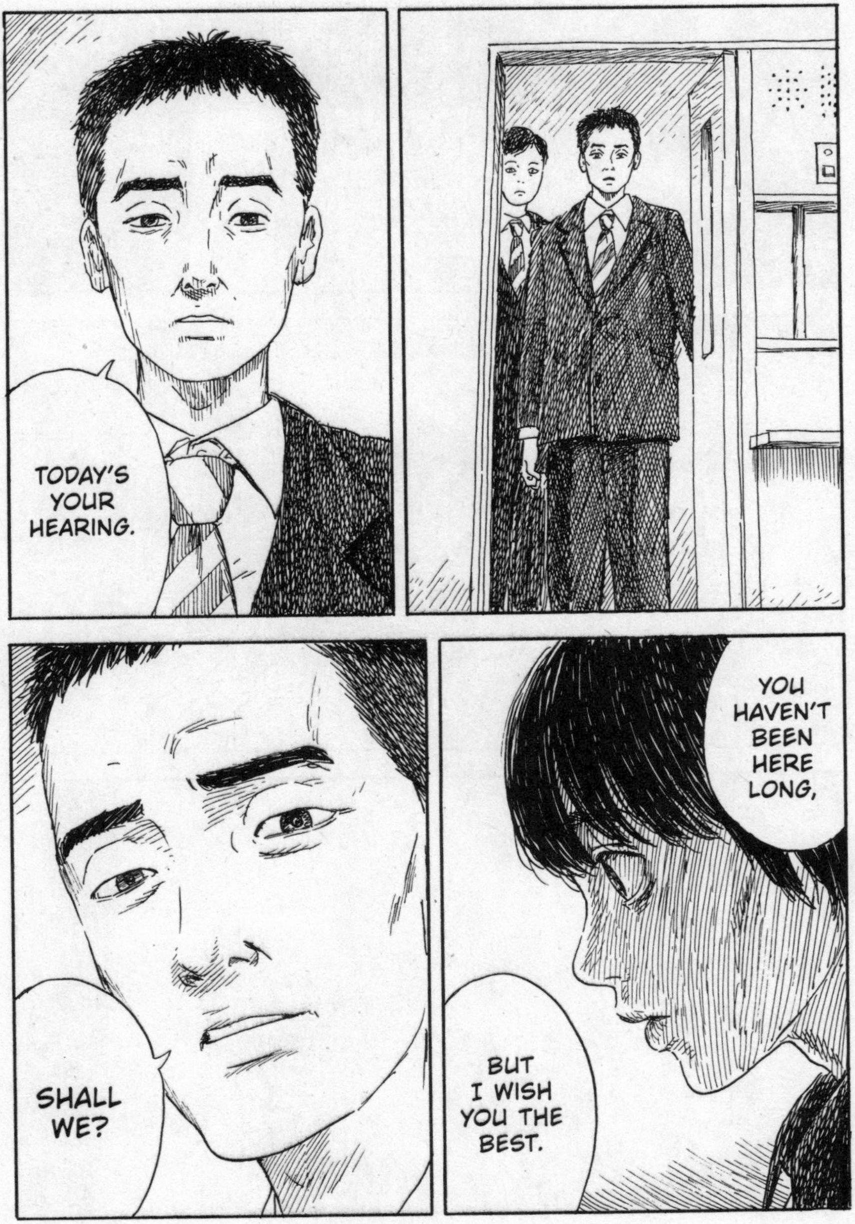
TODAY'S YOUR HEARING.
YOU HAVEN'T BEEN HERE LONG,
BUT I WISH YOU THE BEST.
SHALL WE?

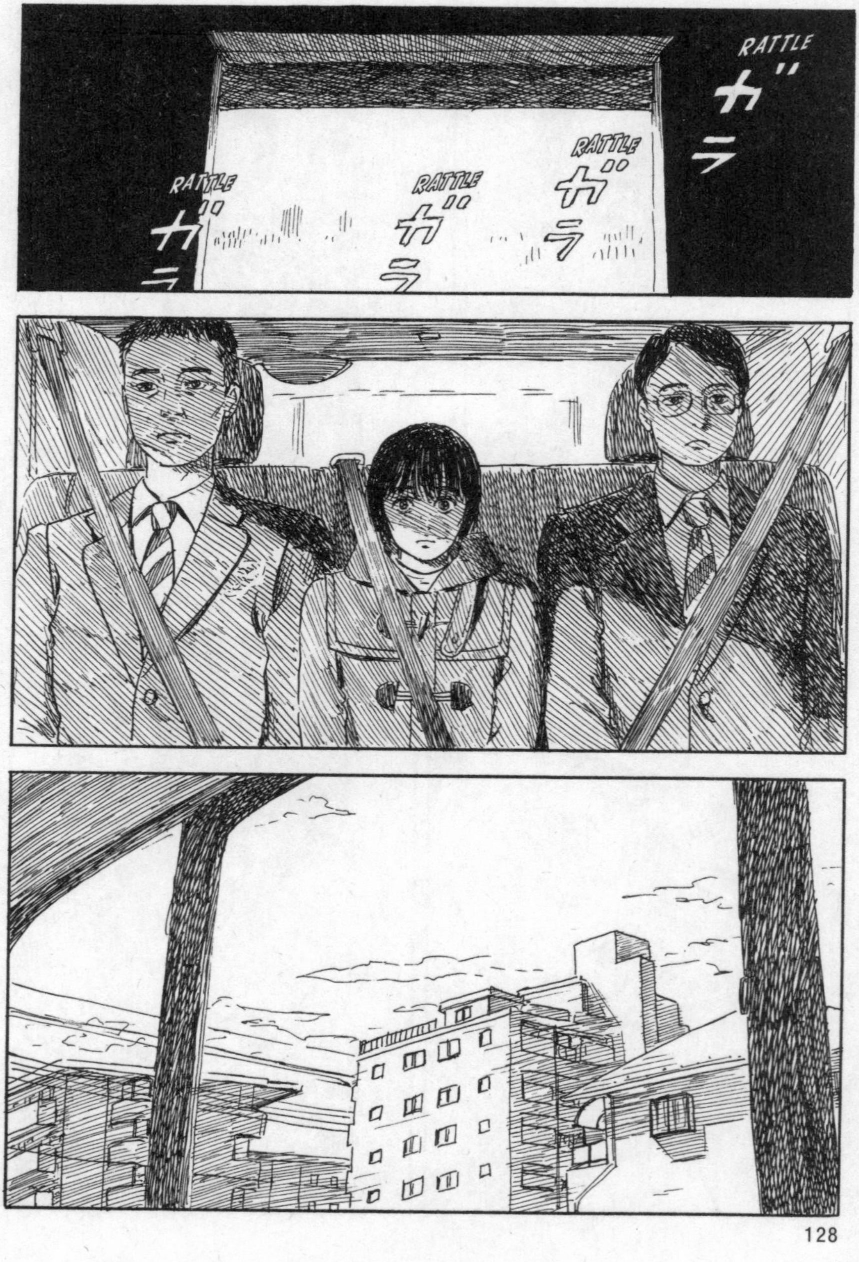
RATTLE
ガラ
RATTLE
ガラ
RATTLE
ガラ
RATTLE
ガラ

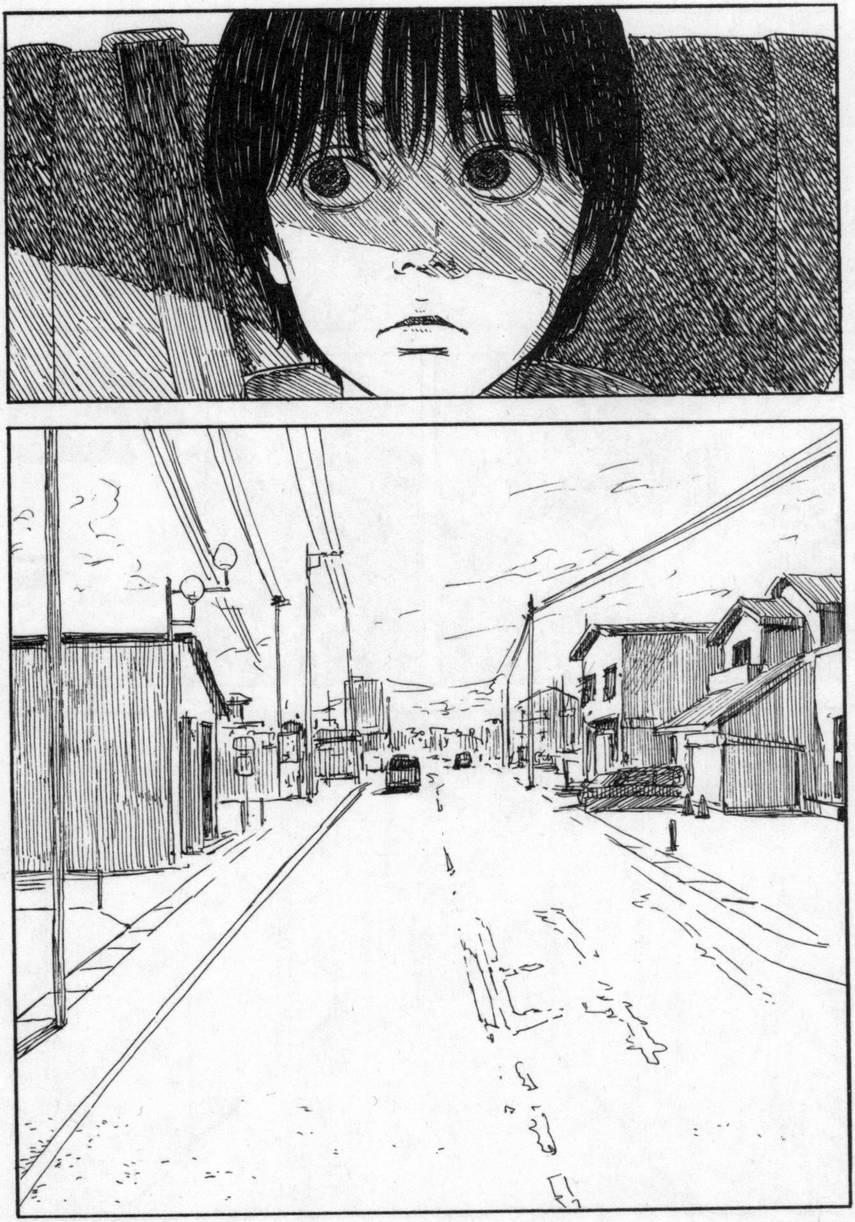

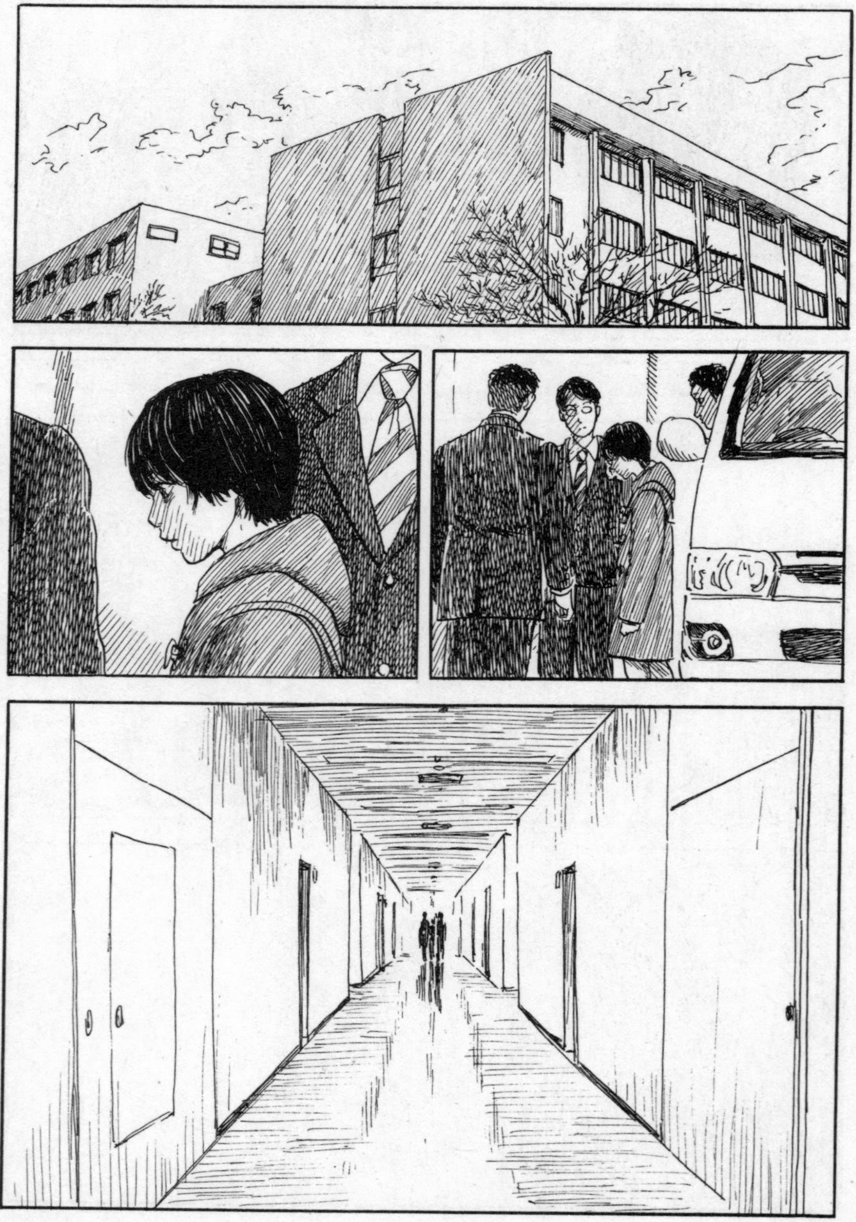

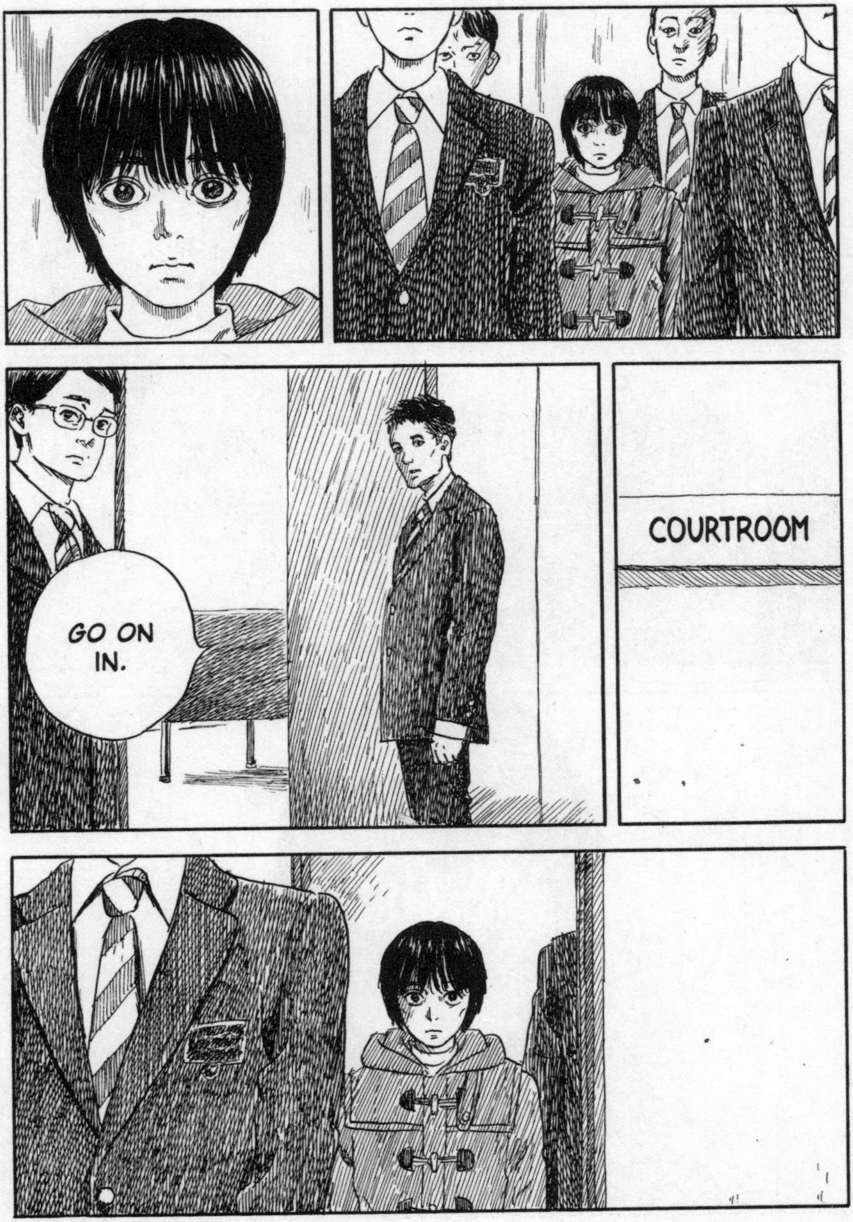
COURTROOM
GO ON IN.

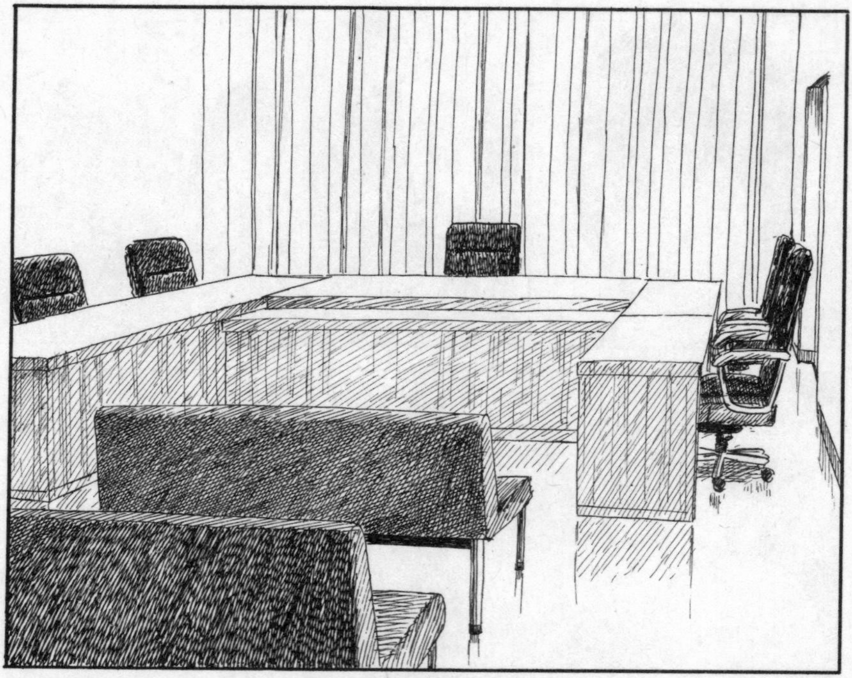

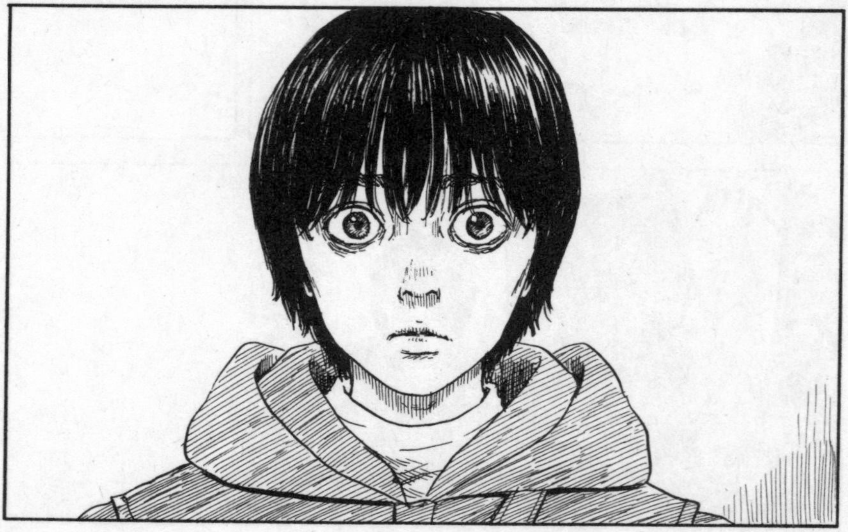

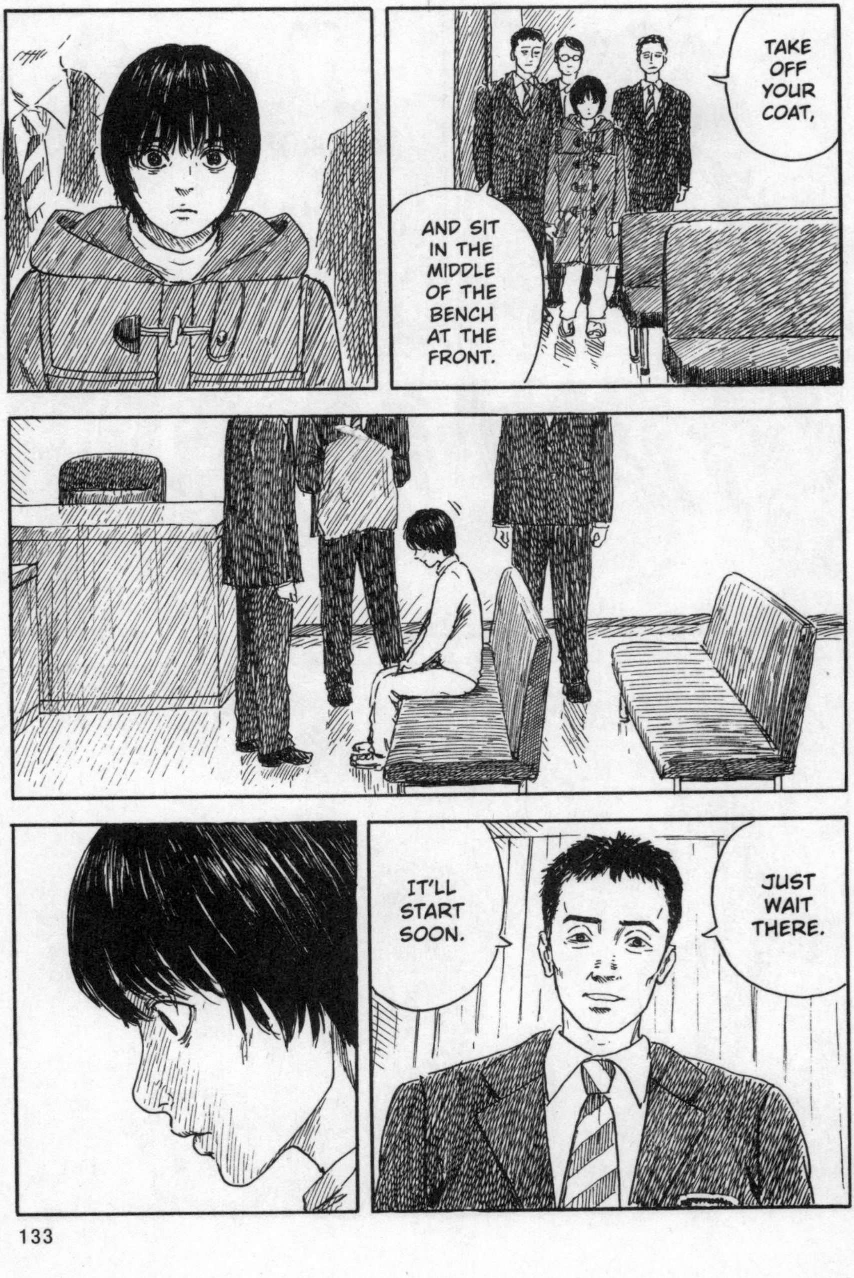
TAKE OFF YOUR COAT,
AND SIT IN THE MIDDLE OF THE BENCH AT THE FRONT.
JUST WAIT THERE.
IT'LL START SOON.

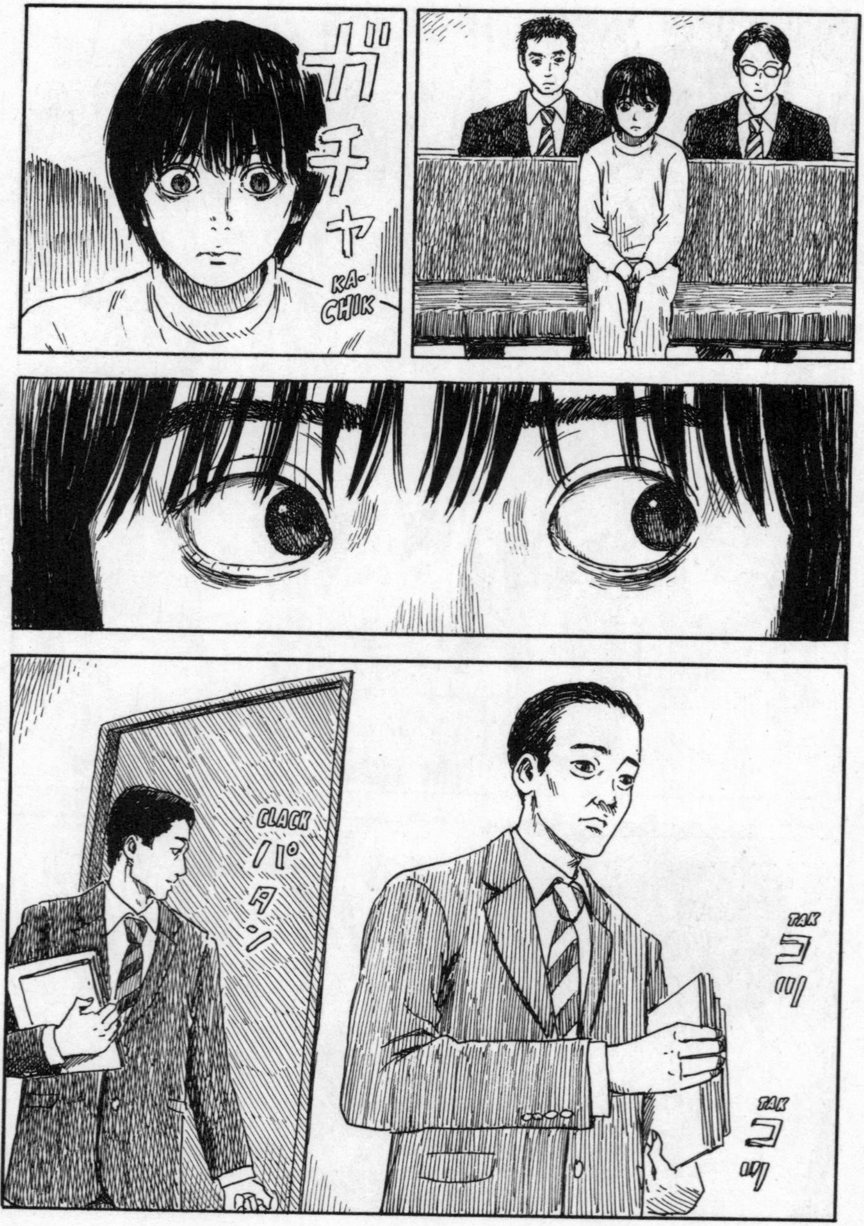
ガチャ
KA-CHIK
TAK
コッ
TAK
コッ
CLACK
パタン

KA-
CHIK

ガチャ

CREAK
ぎし

CREAK
ぎ

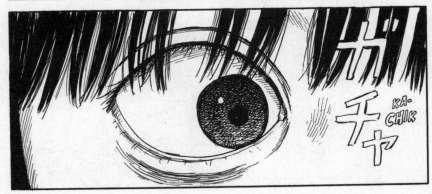

ガチャ

KA-
CHIK

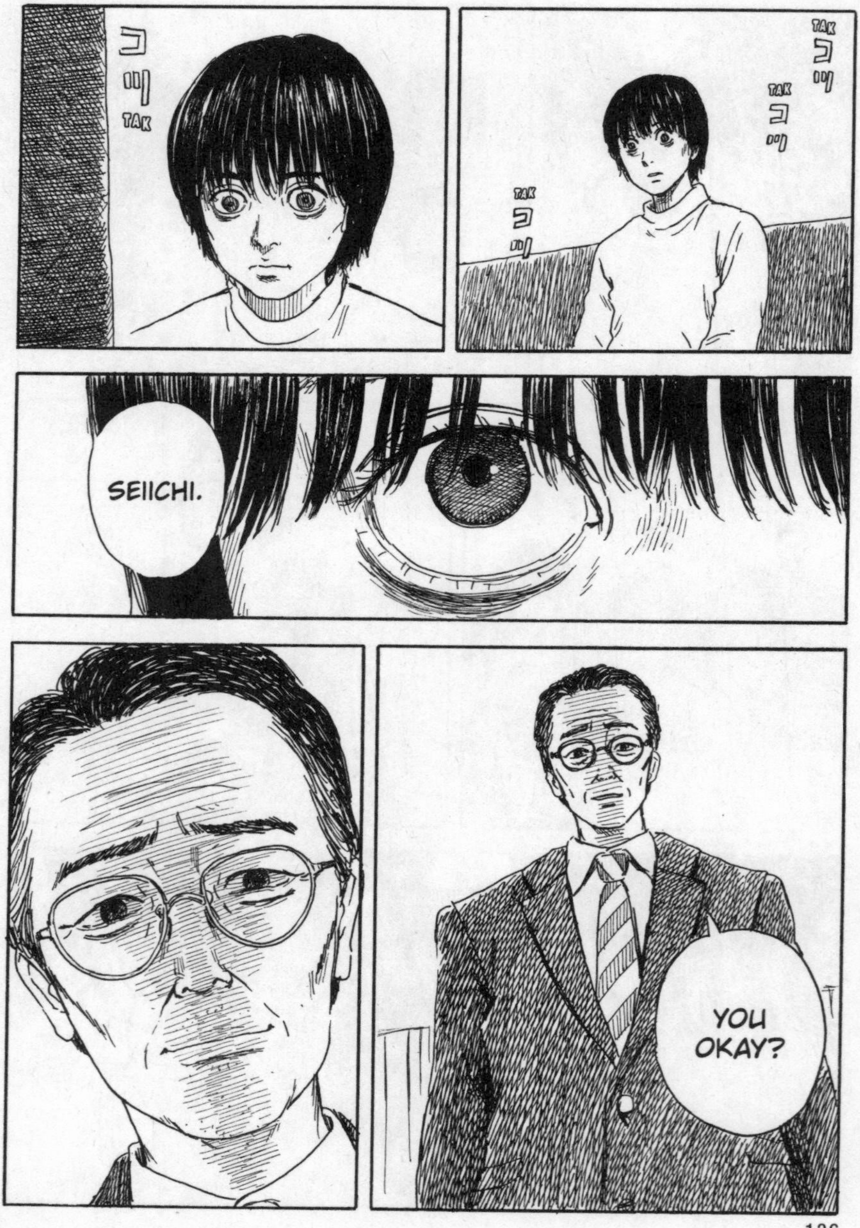
TAK コツ
TAK コツ
TAK コツ
コツ TAK
SEIICHI.
YOU OKAY?

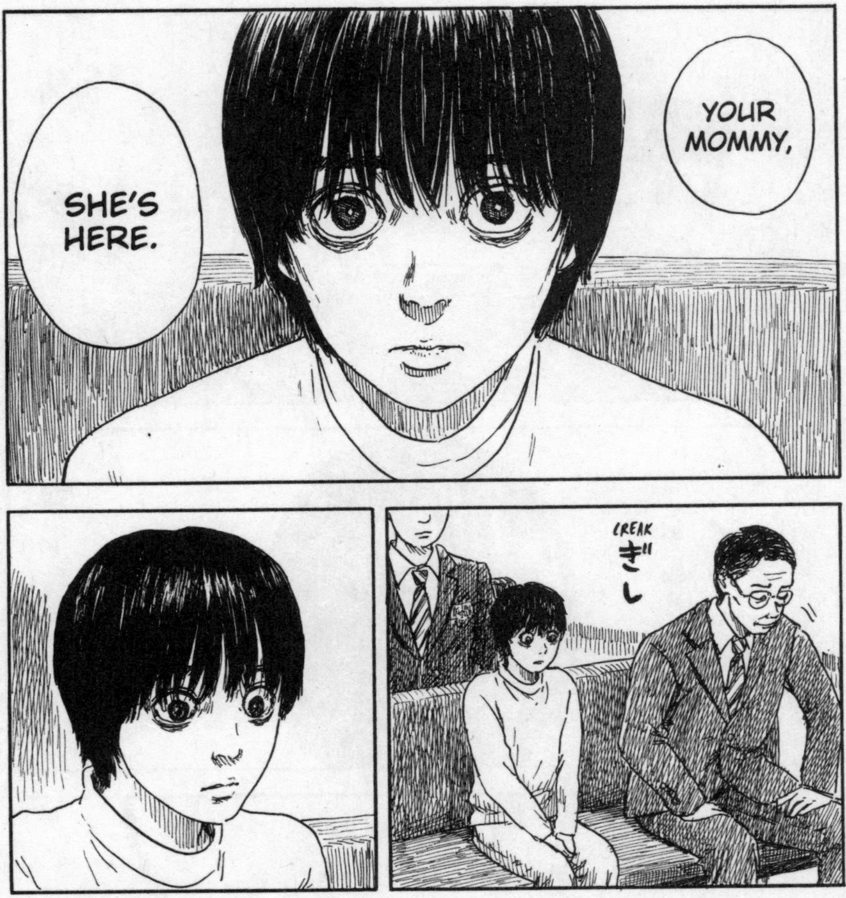
YOUR MOMMY,
SHE'S HERE.
CREAK ぎし
TAK コツ

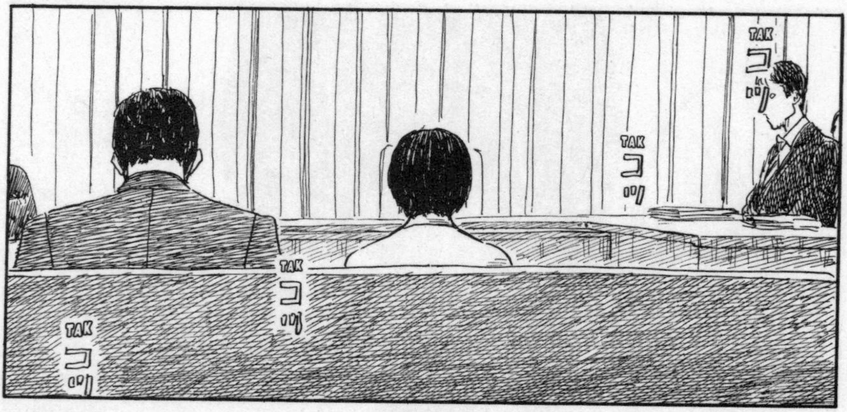
TAK
コッ
TAK
コッ
TAK
コッ
TAK
コッ

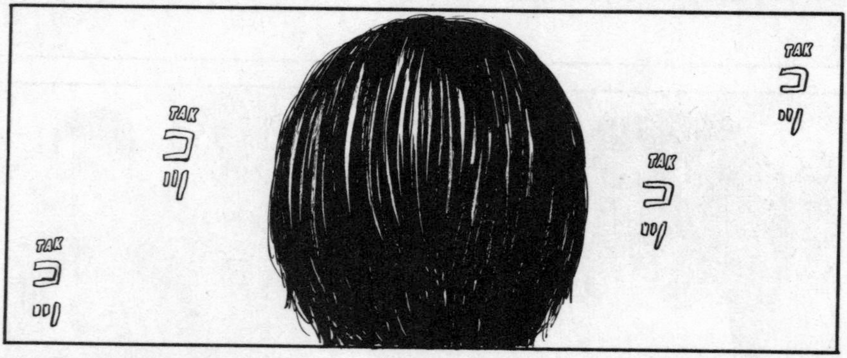
TAK
コッ
TAK
コッ
TAK
コッ
TAK
コッ

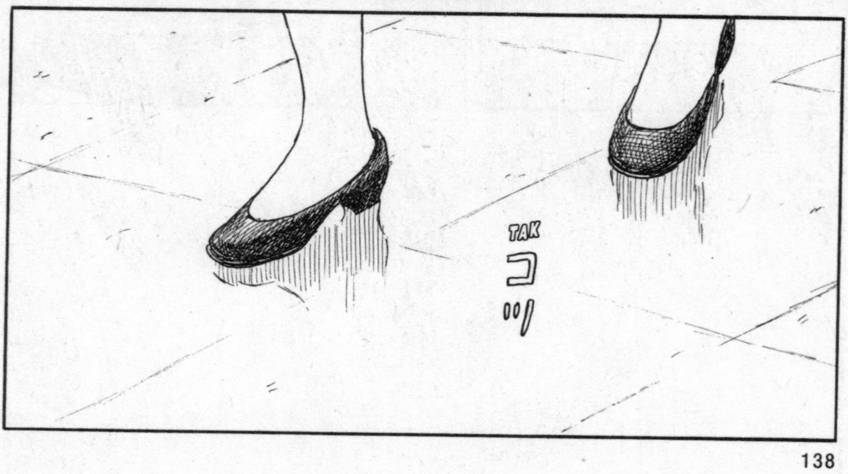
TAK
コッ

CREAK
ぎし

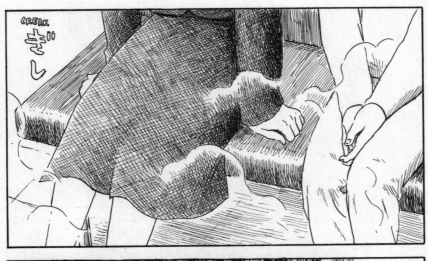

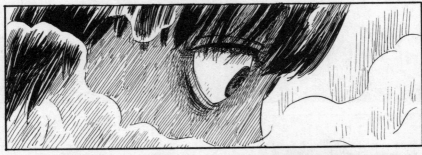

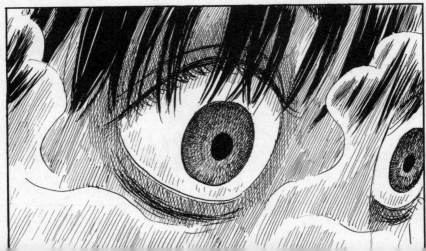

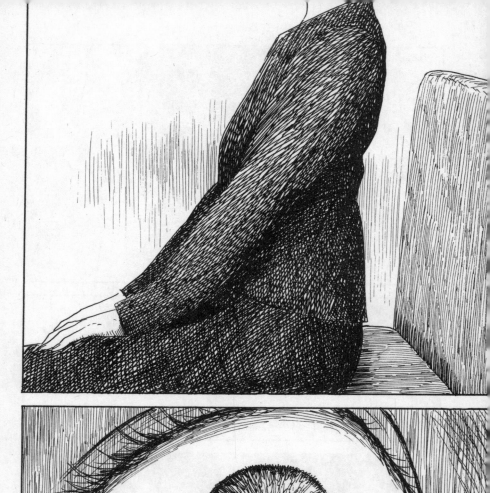
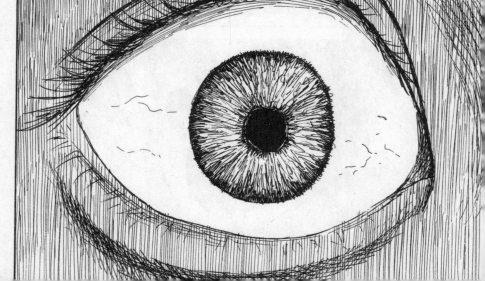

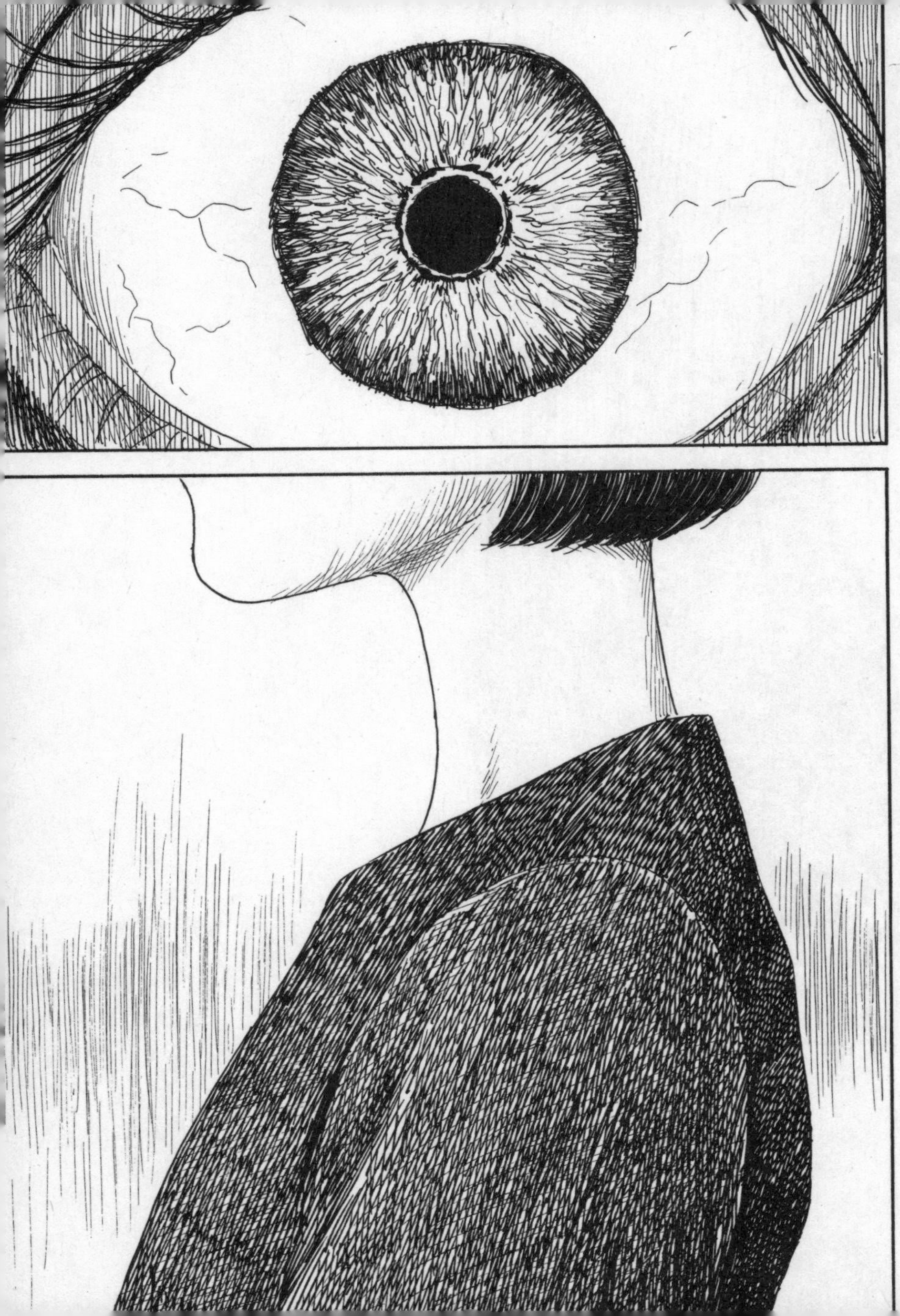

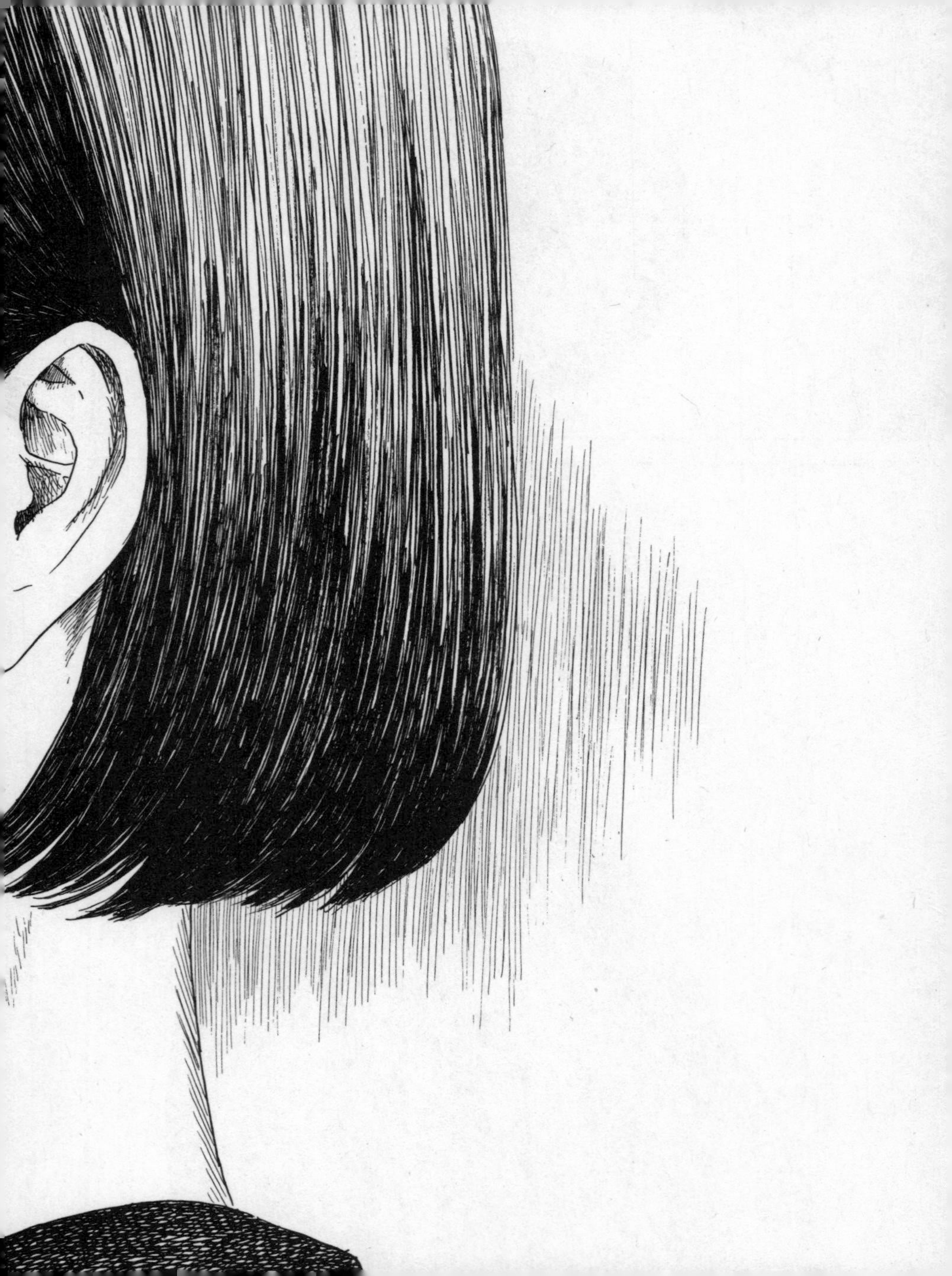

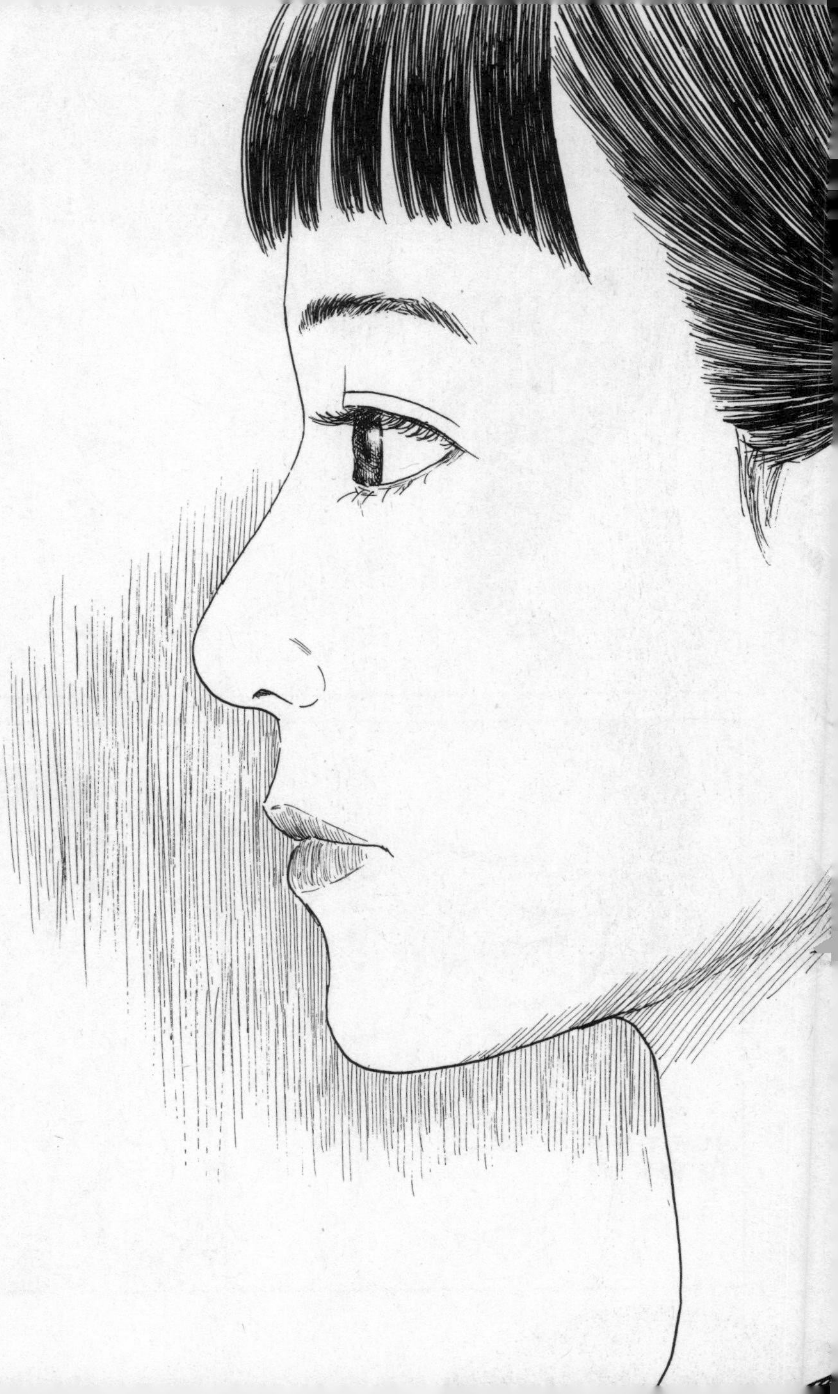

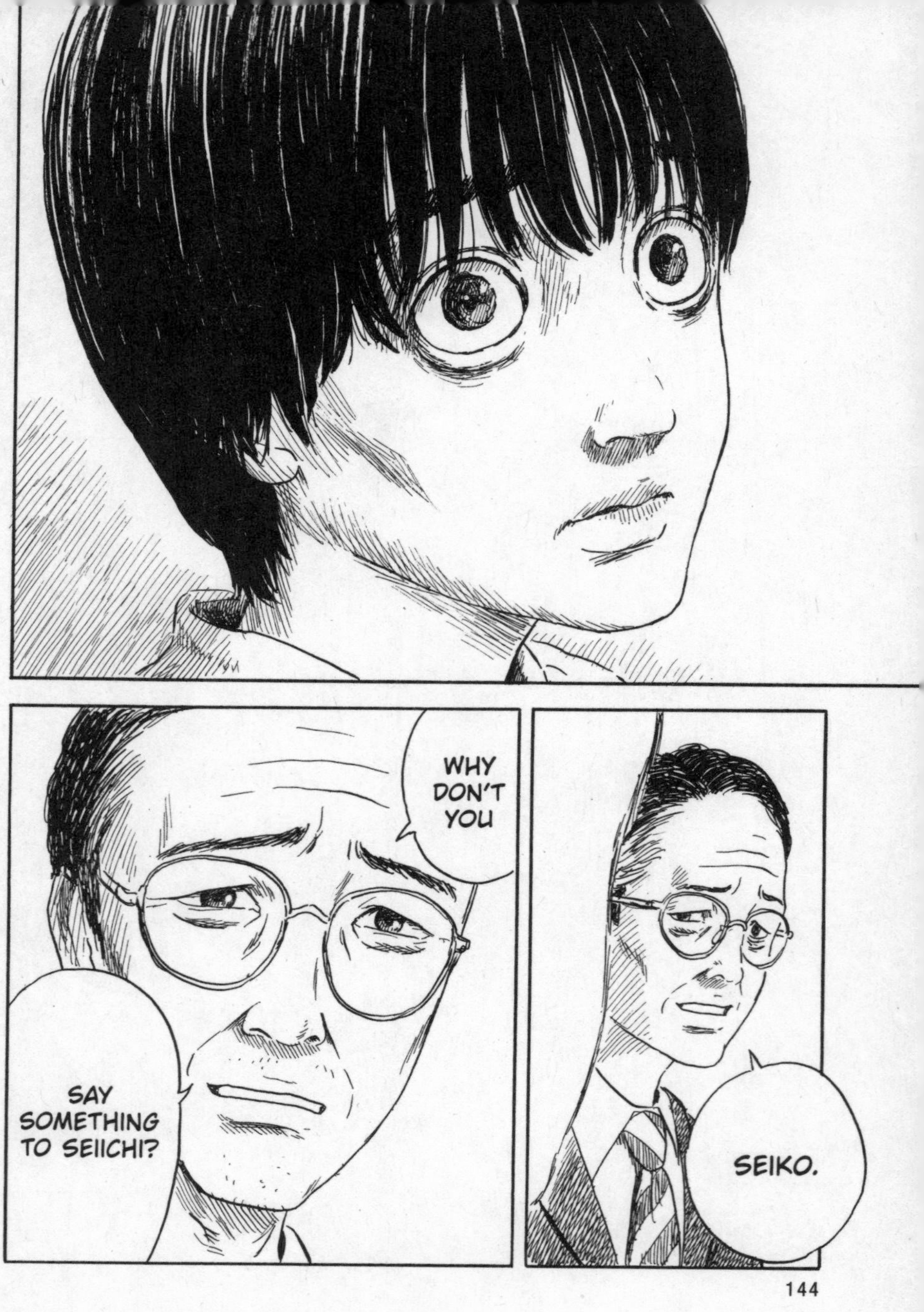
SEIKO.
WHY DON'T YOU
SAY SOMETHING TO SEIICHI?

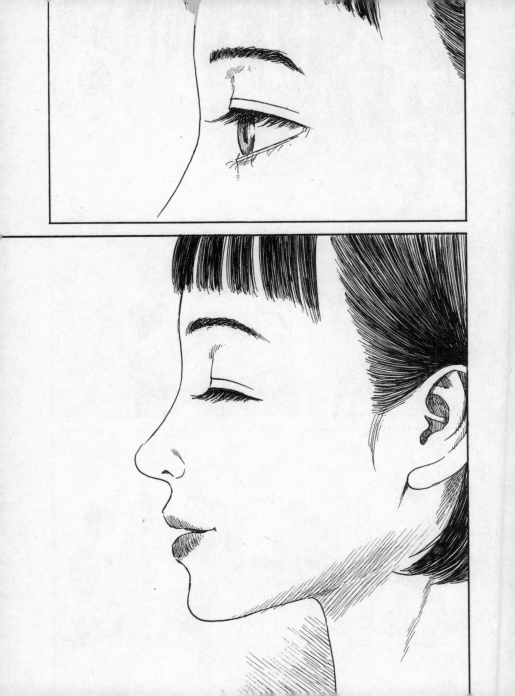

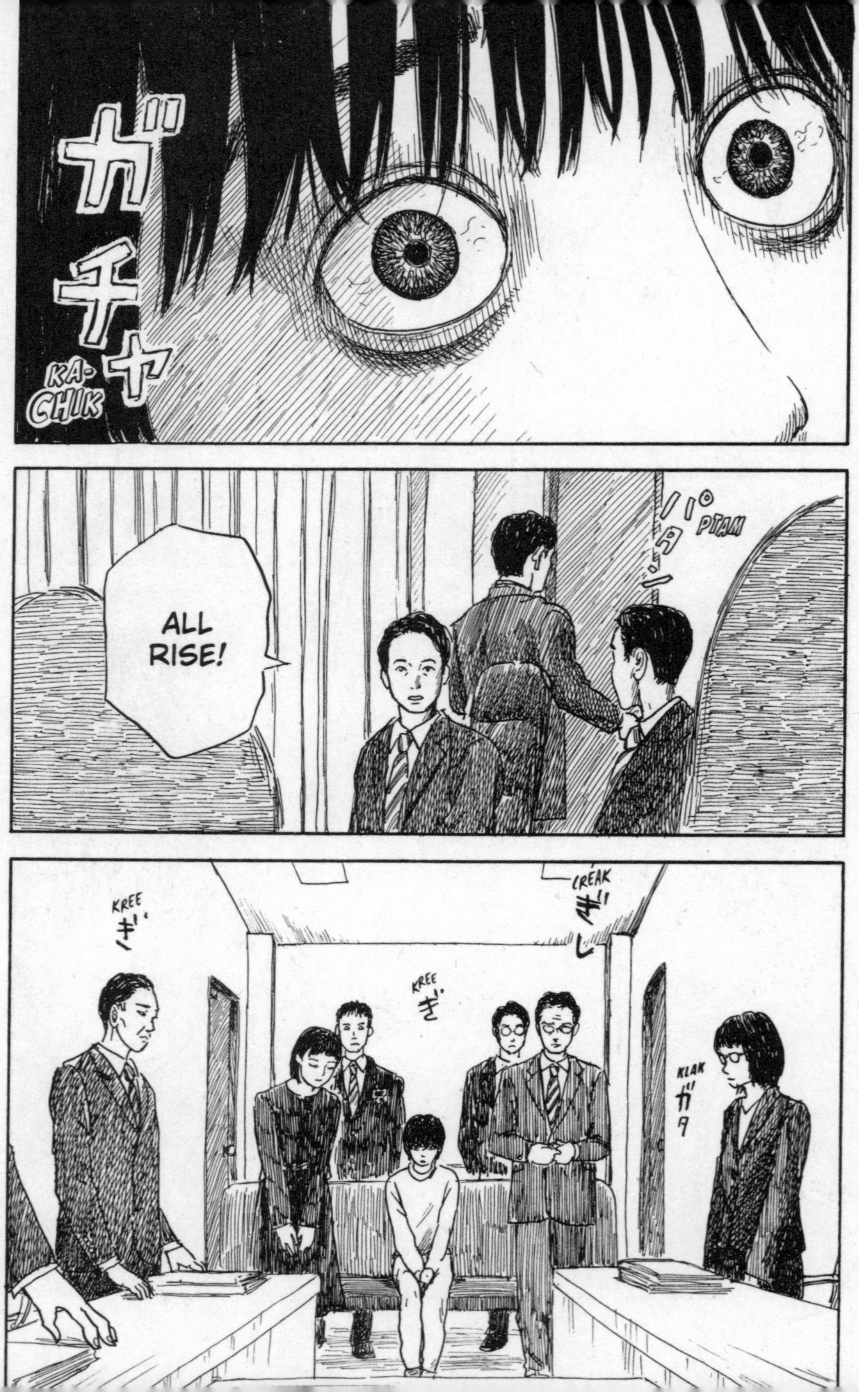
ガチャ
KA-CHIK
パタン
PTAM
ALL RISE!
CREAK
ぎし
KLAK
ガタ
KREE
ぎ
KREE
ぎ

ATTEN-
TION.

BOW!

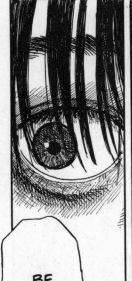

BE
SEATED!

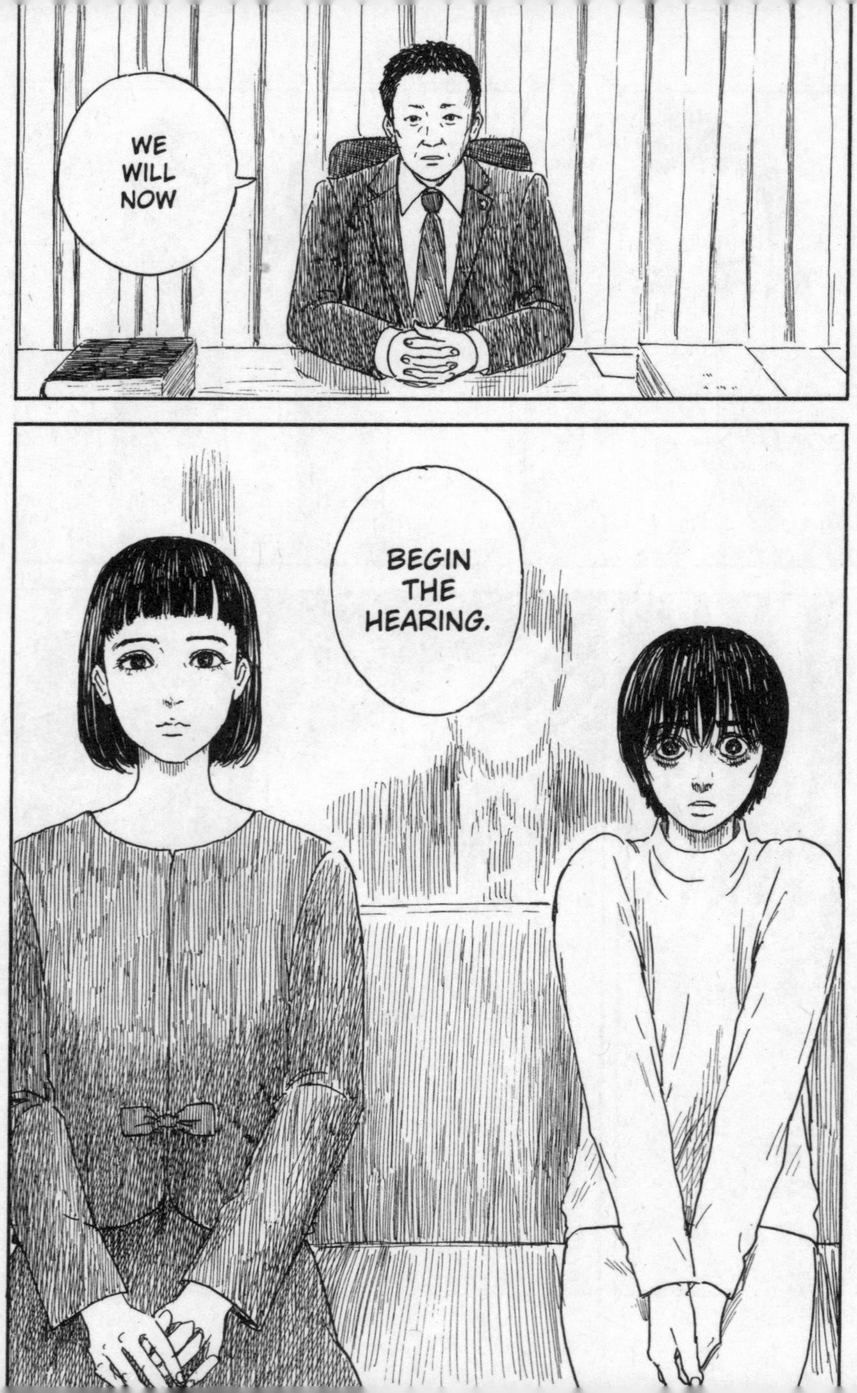
WE WILL NOW
BEGIN THE HEARING.

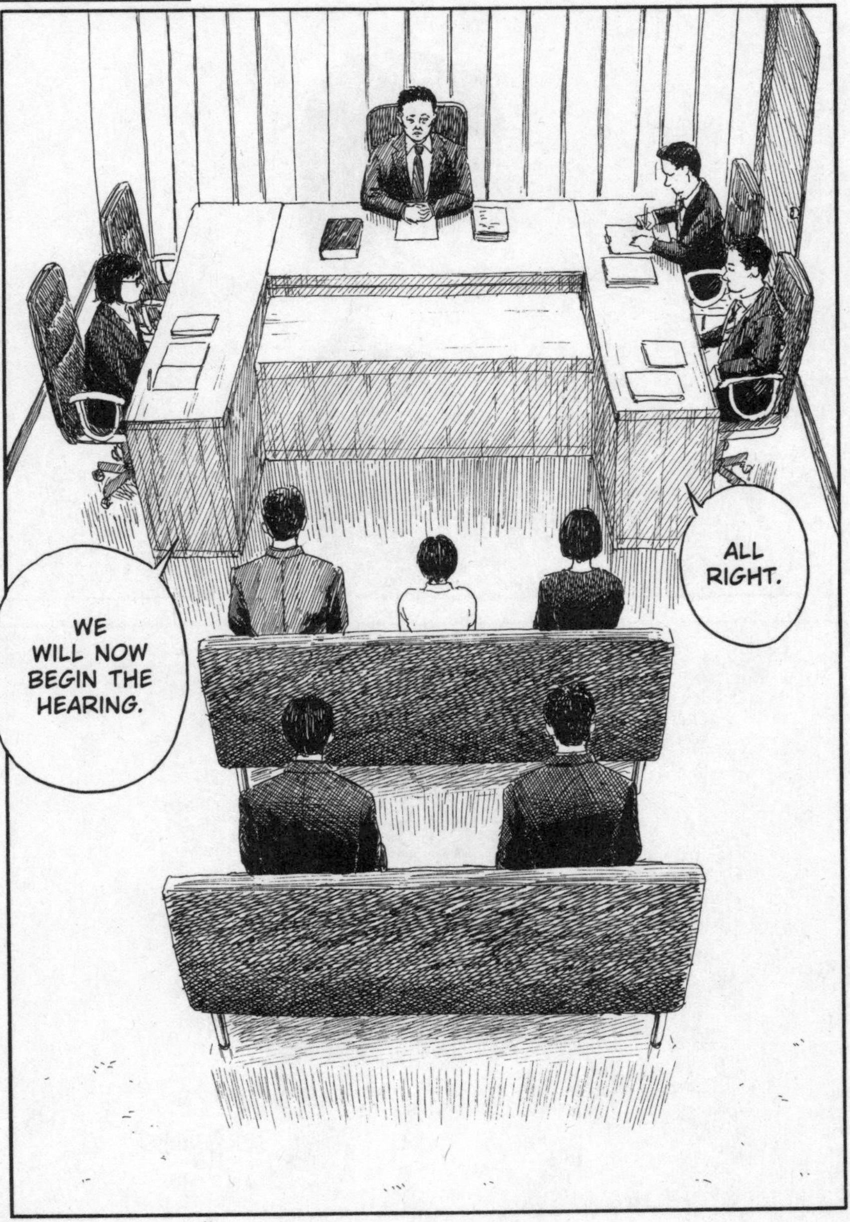
ALL RIGHT.
WE WILL NOW BEGIN THE HEARING.

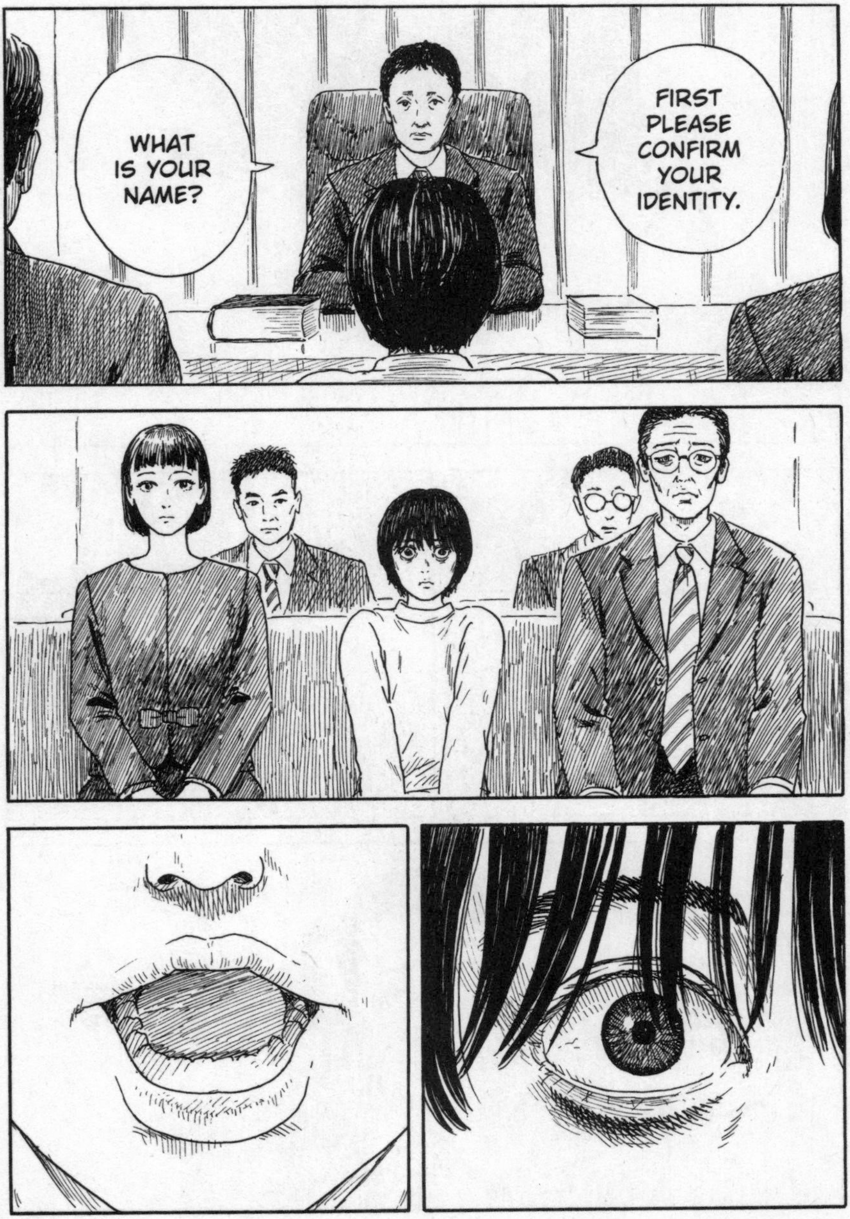
FIRST PLEASE CONFIRM YOUR IDENTITY.
WHAT IS YOUR NAME?

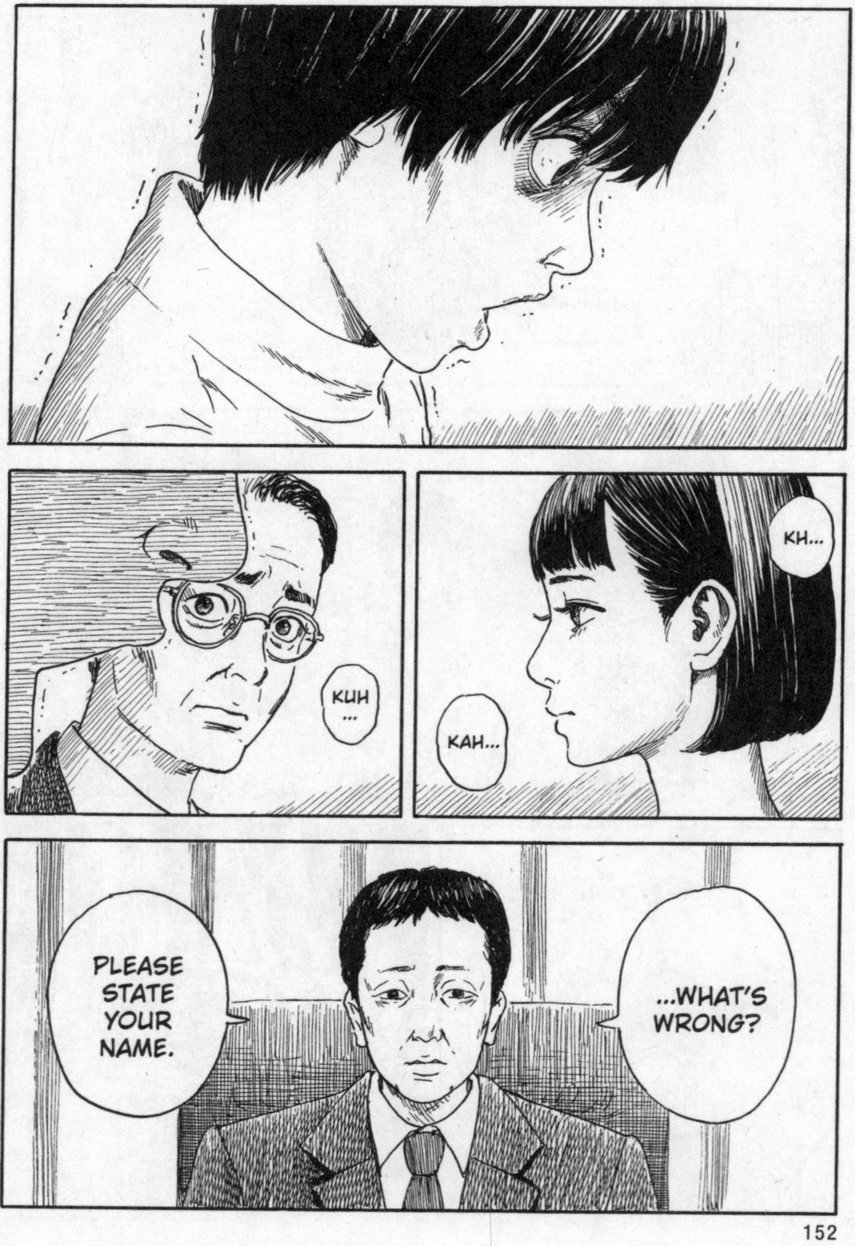
KH...
KAH...
KUH ...
...WHAT'S WRONG?
PLEASE STATE YOUR NAME.

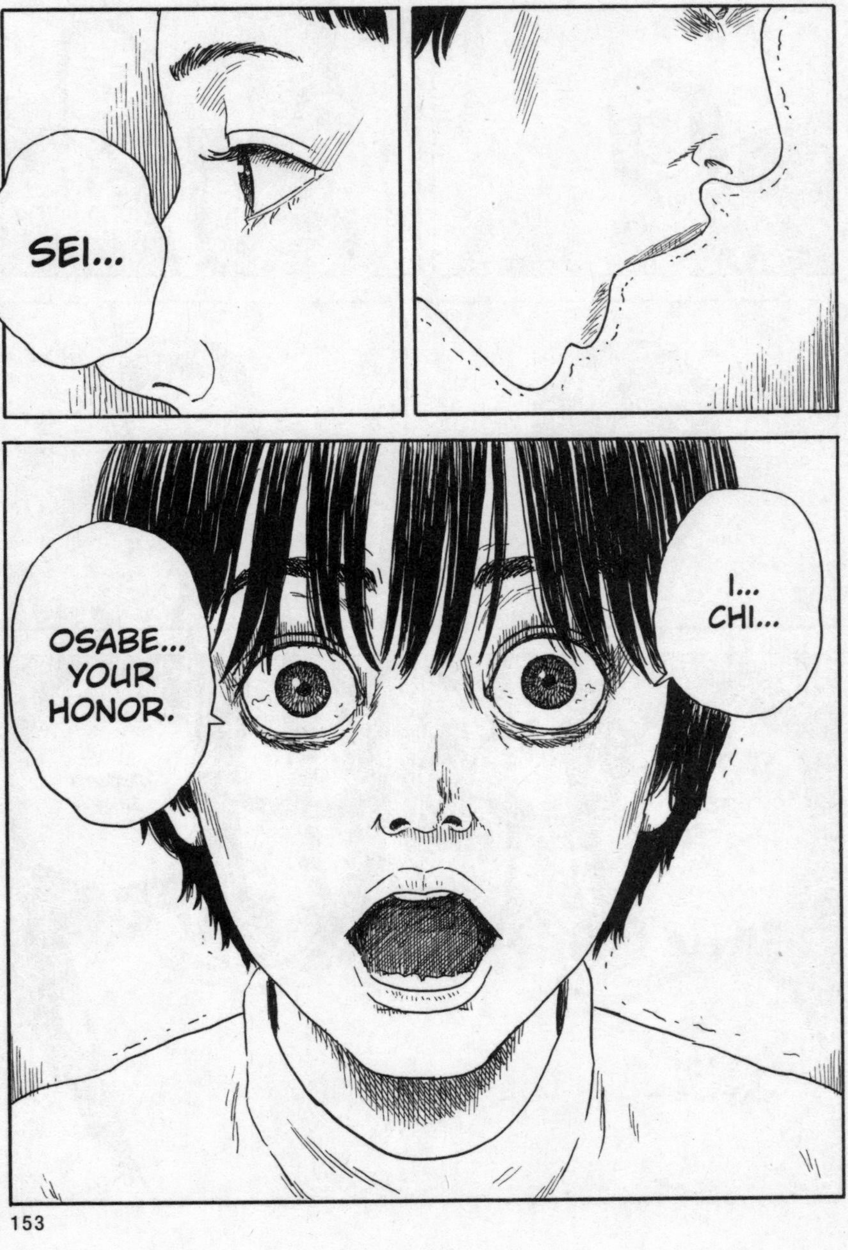
SEI...
I... CHI...
OSABE... YOUR HONOR.

...NOW...

YOUR DATE OF BIRTH...

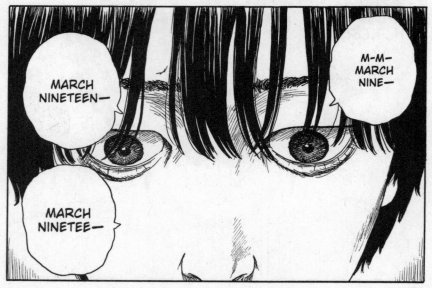

MARCH NINETEEN—

M-M-MARCH NINE—

MARCH NINETEE—

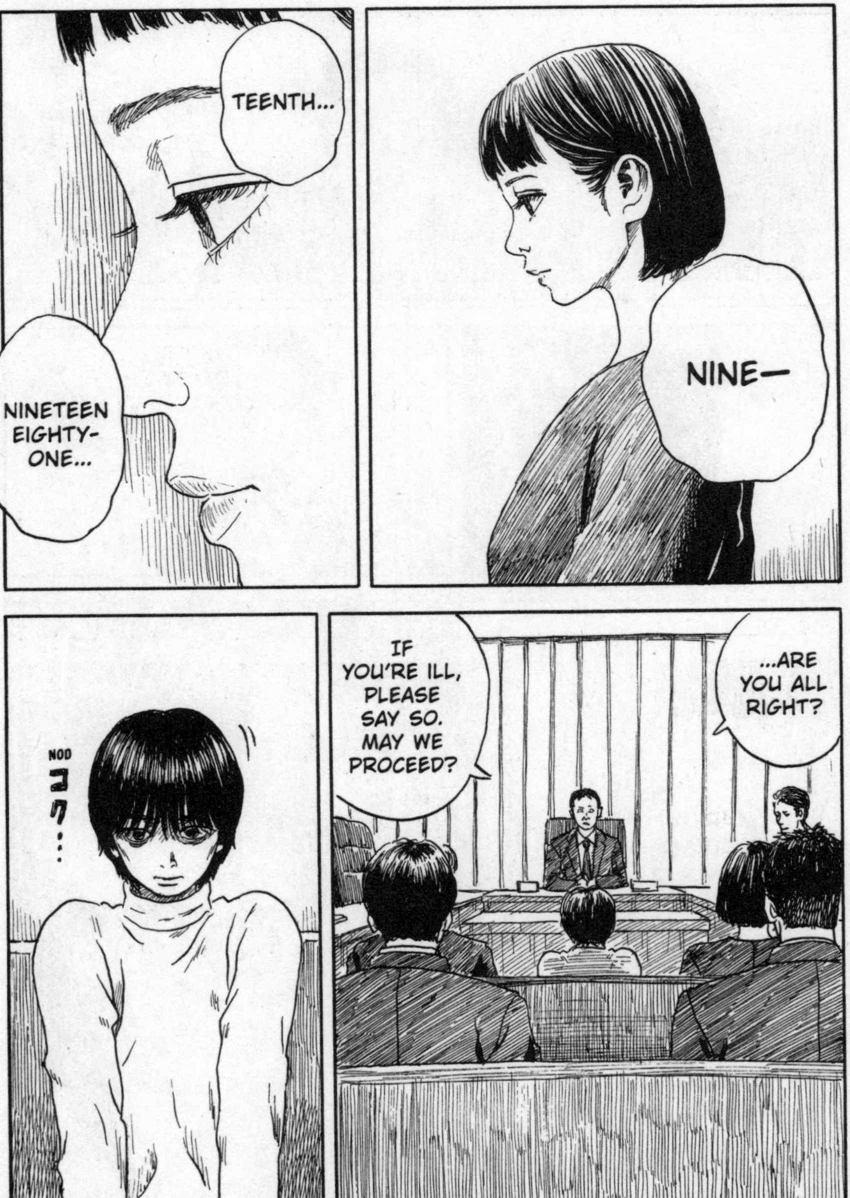
NINE—
TEENTH...
NINETEEN EIGHTY-ONE...
...ARE YOU ALL RIGHT?
IF YOU'RE ILL, PLEASE SAY SO. MAY WE PROCEED?
NOD
コク…

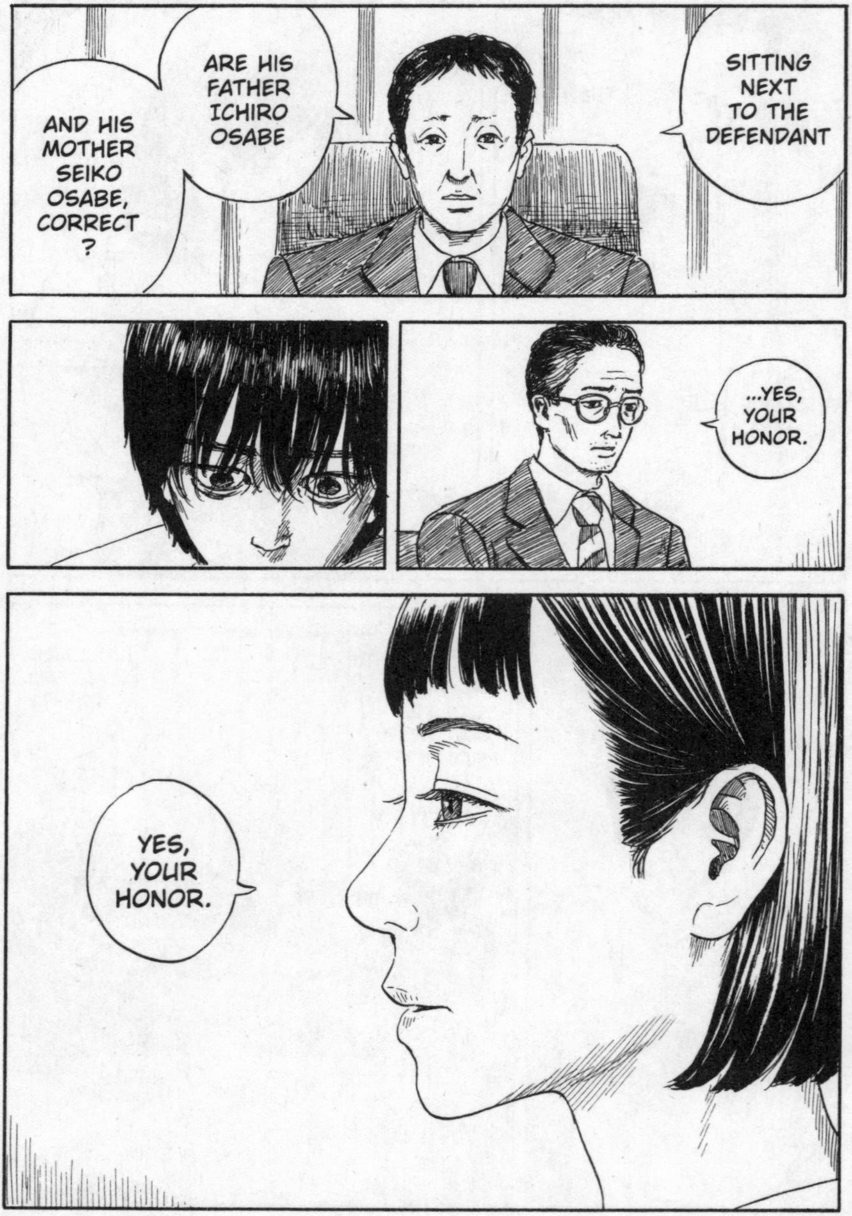
SITTING NEXT TO THE DEFENDANT
ARE HIS FATHER ICHIRO OSABE
AND HIS MOTHER SEIKO OSABE, CORRECT ?
...YES, YOUR HONOR.
YES, YOUR HONOR.

VERY WELL. THE COURT WILL NOW EXAMINE
YOUR INFRINGEMENT OF THE LAW.
I'M GOING TO ASK YOU SOME QUESTIONS,
BUT YOU ARE NOT REQUIRED TO ANSWER.
IF YOU DO ANSWER, HOWEVER, PLEASE DO SO TRUTHFULLY.
DO YOU UNDERSTAND?

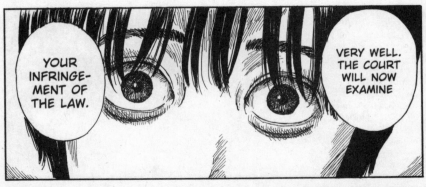

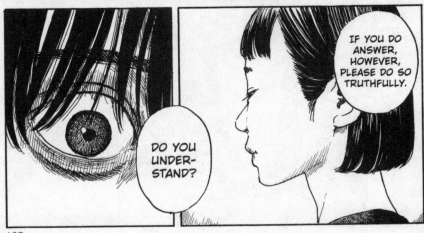

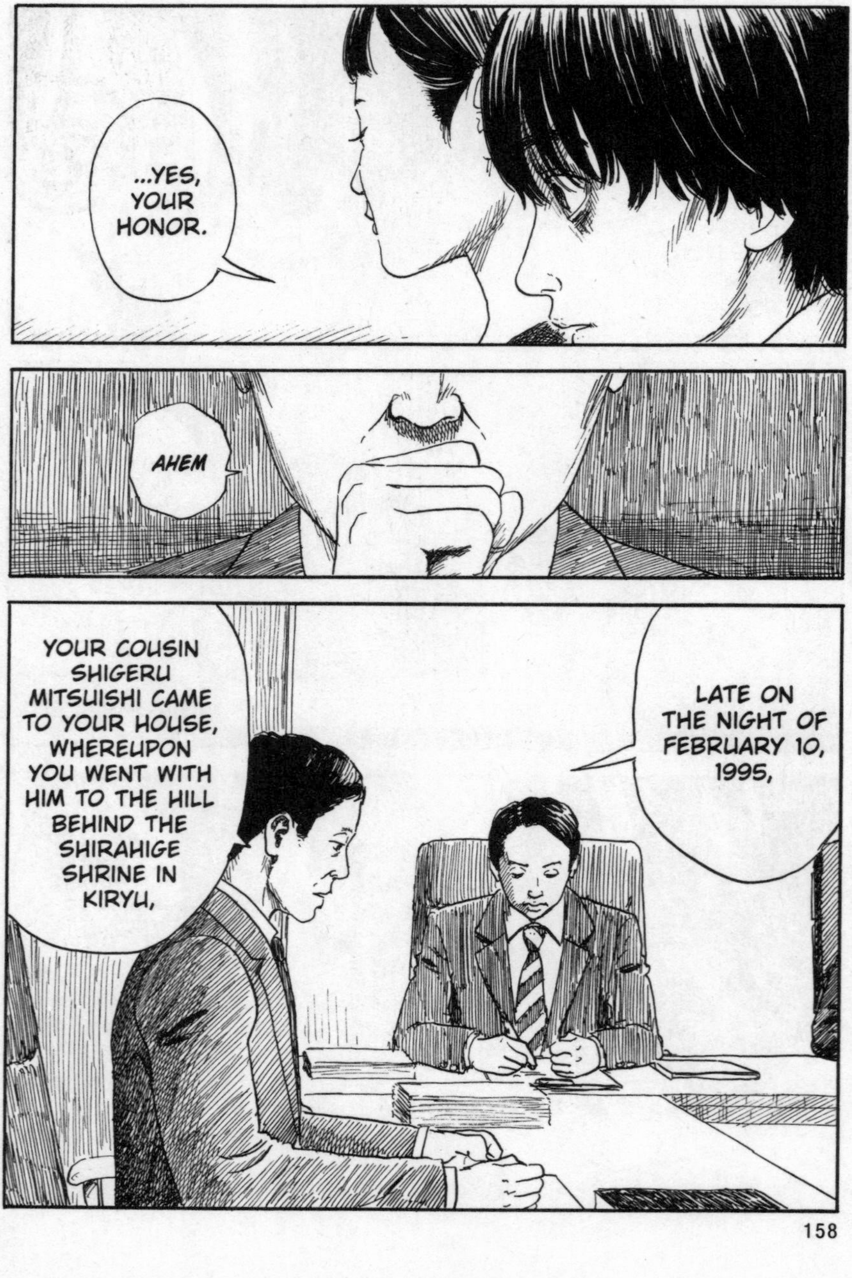
...YES, YOUR HONOR.
AHEM
LATE ON THE NIGHT OF FEBRUARY 10, 1995,
YOUR COUSIN SHIGERU MITSUISHI CAME TO YOUR HOUSE, WHEREUPON YOU WENT WITH HIM TO THE HILL BEHIND THE SHIRAHIGE SHRINE IN KIRYU,

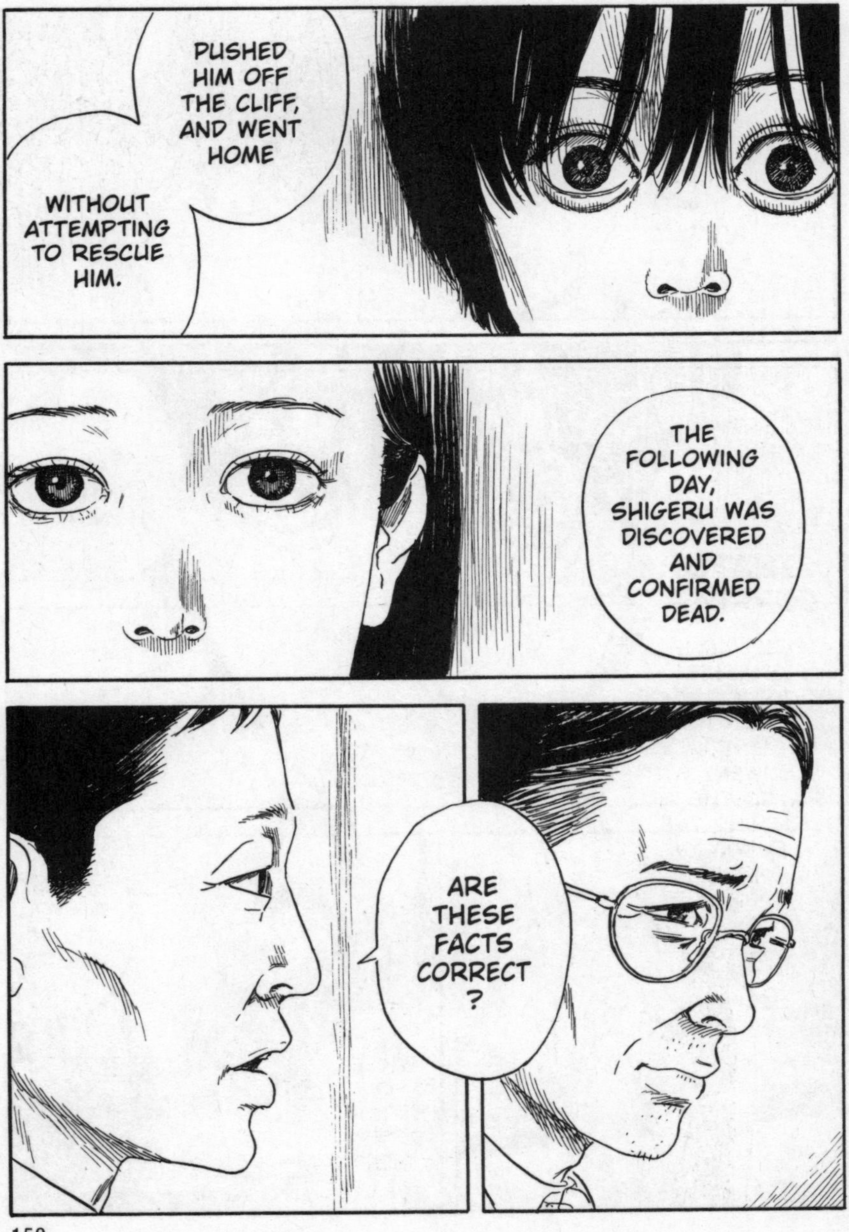
PUSHED HIM OFF THE CLIFF, AND WENT HOME
WITHOUT ATTEMPTING TO RESCUE HIM.
THE FOLLOWING DAY, SHIGERU WAS DISCOVERED AND CONFIRMED DEAD.
ARE THESE FACTS CORRECT?

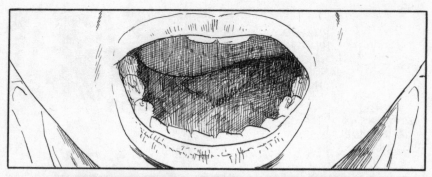

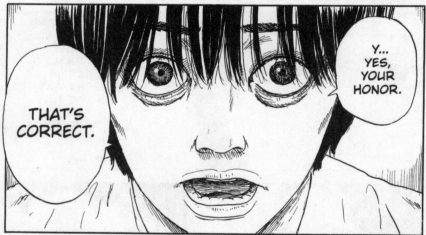

Y... YES, YOUR HONOR.
THAT'S CORRECT.
...WHAT DID YOU THINK ABOUT
WHILE YOU WERE IN DETEN- TION?

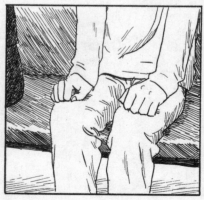

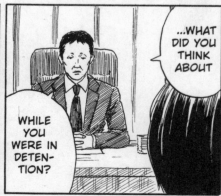

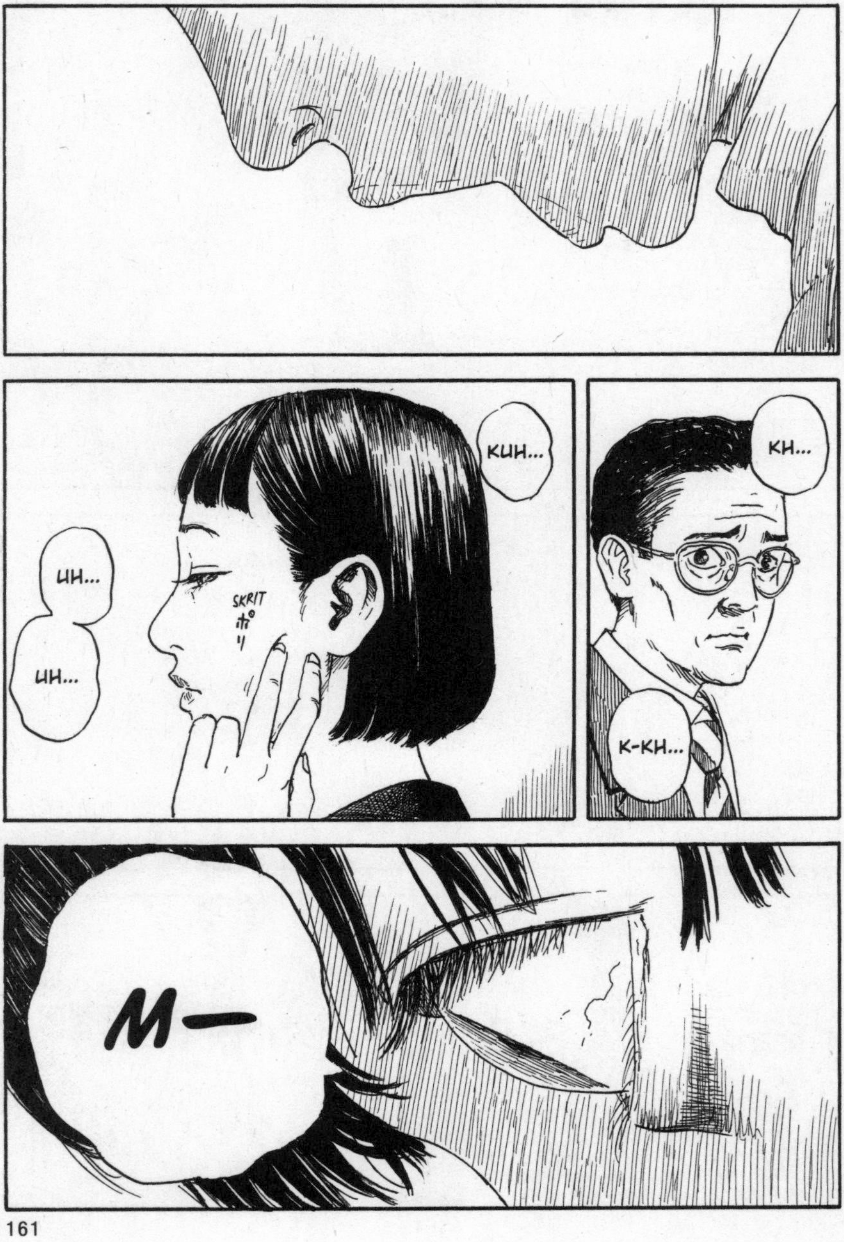
KH...
K-KH...
KUH...
UH...
UH...
SKRIT
ポリ
M—

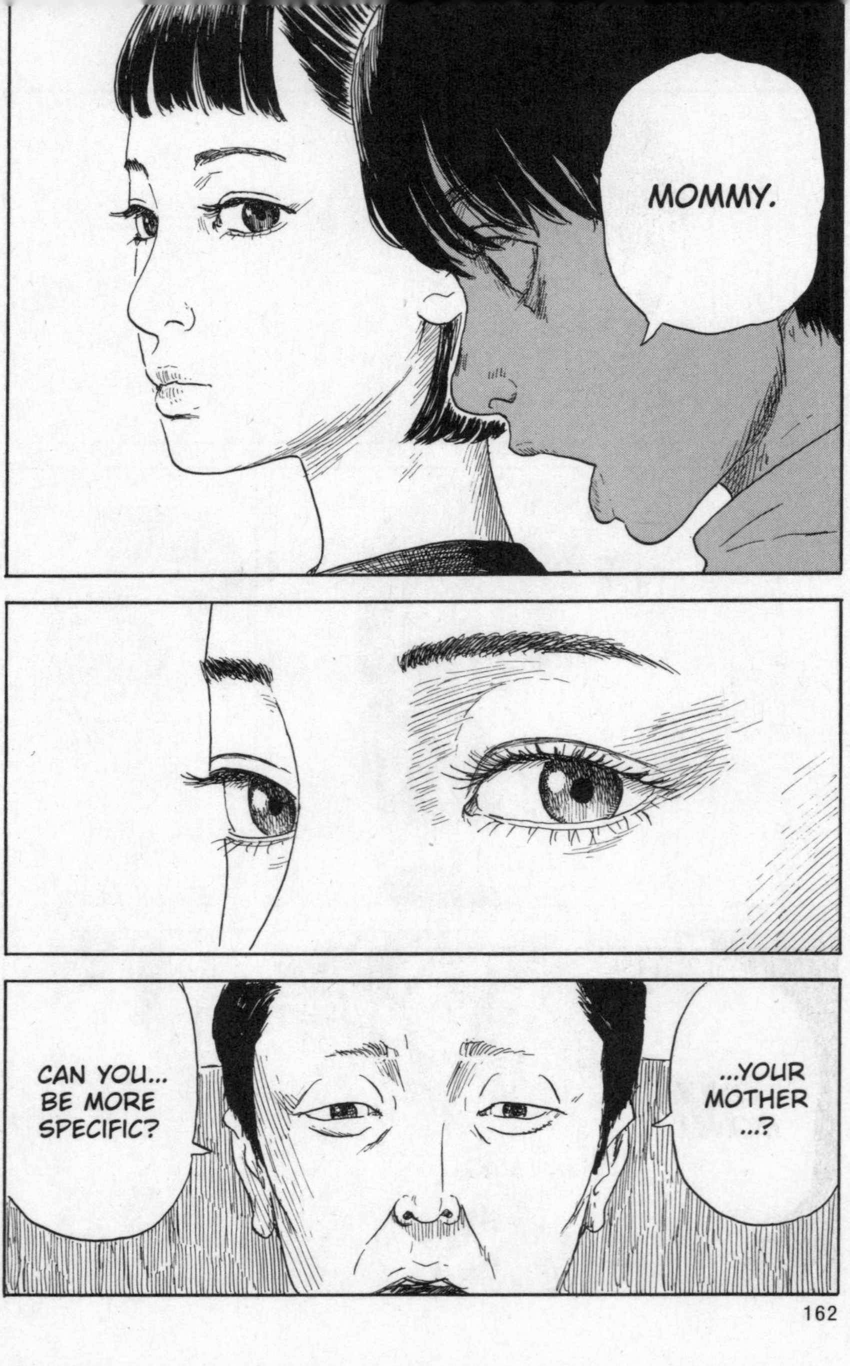
MOMMY.
...YOUR MOTHER ...?
CAN YOU... BE MORE SPECIFIC?

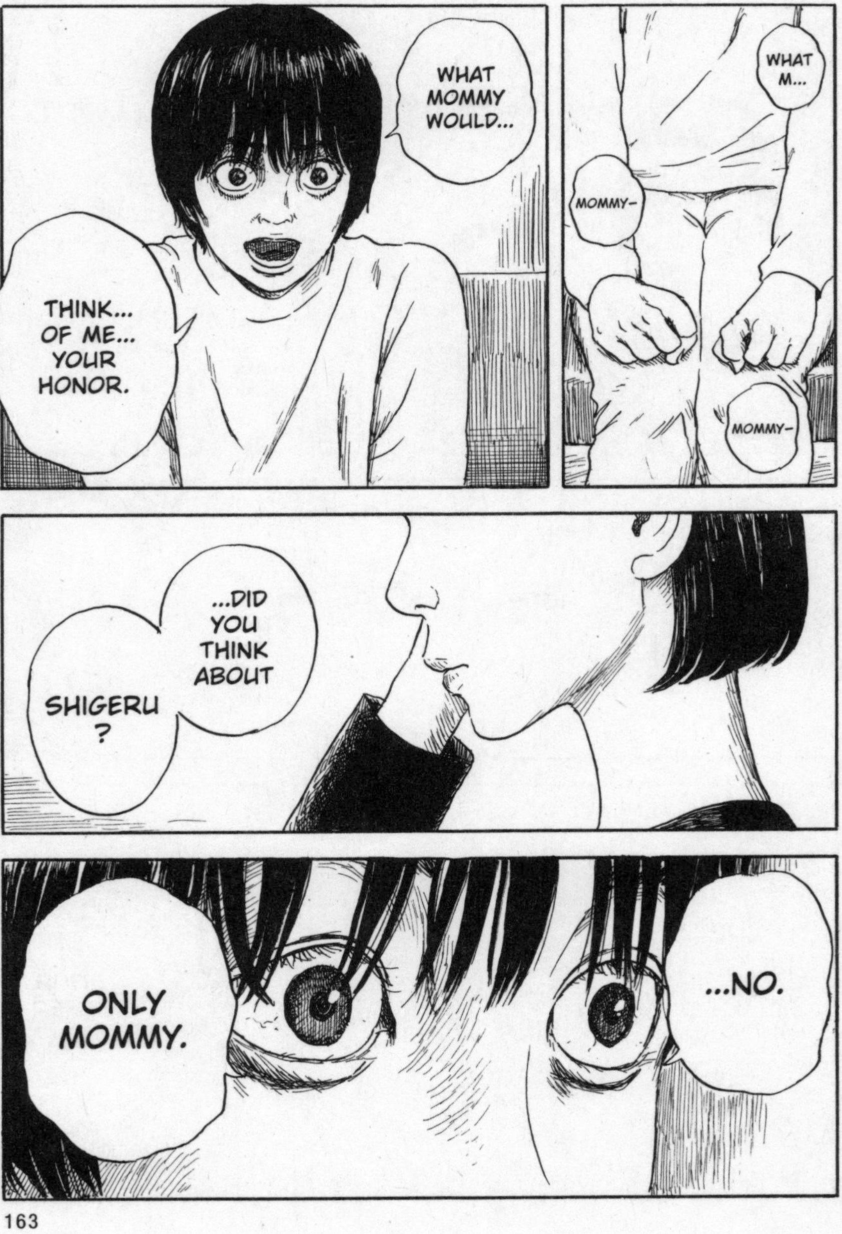
WHAT M...
MOMMY-
MOMMY-
WHAT MOMMY WOULD...
THINK... OF ME... YOUR HONOR.
...DID YOU THINK ABOUT SHIGERU ?
...NO.
ONLY MOMMY.

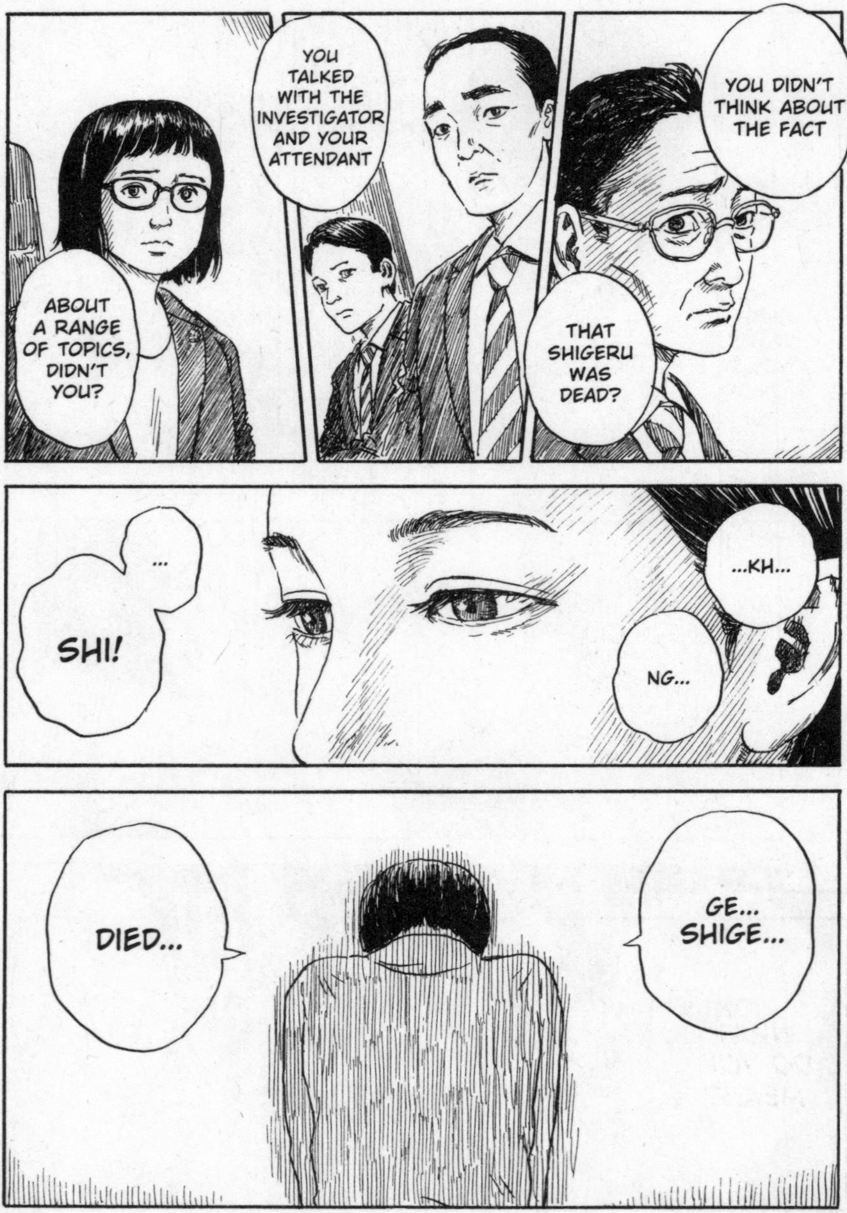
YOU DIDN'T THINK ABOUT THE FACT
THAT SHIGERU WAS DEAD?
YOU TALKED WITH THE INVESTIGATOR AND YOUR ATTENDANT
ABOUT A RANGE OF TOPICS, DIDN'T YOU?
...KH...
NG...
... SHI!
GE... SHIGE...
DIED...

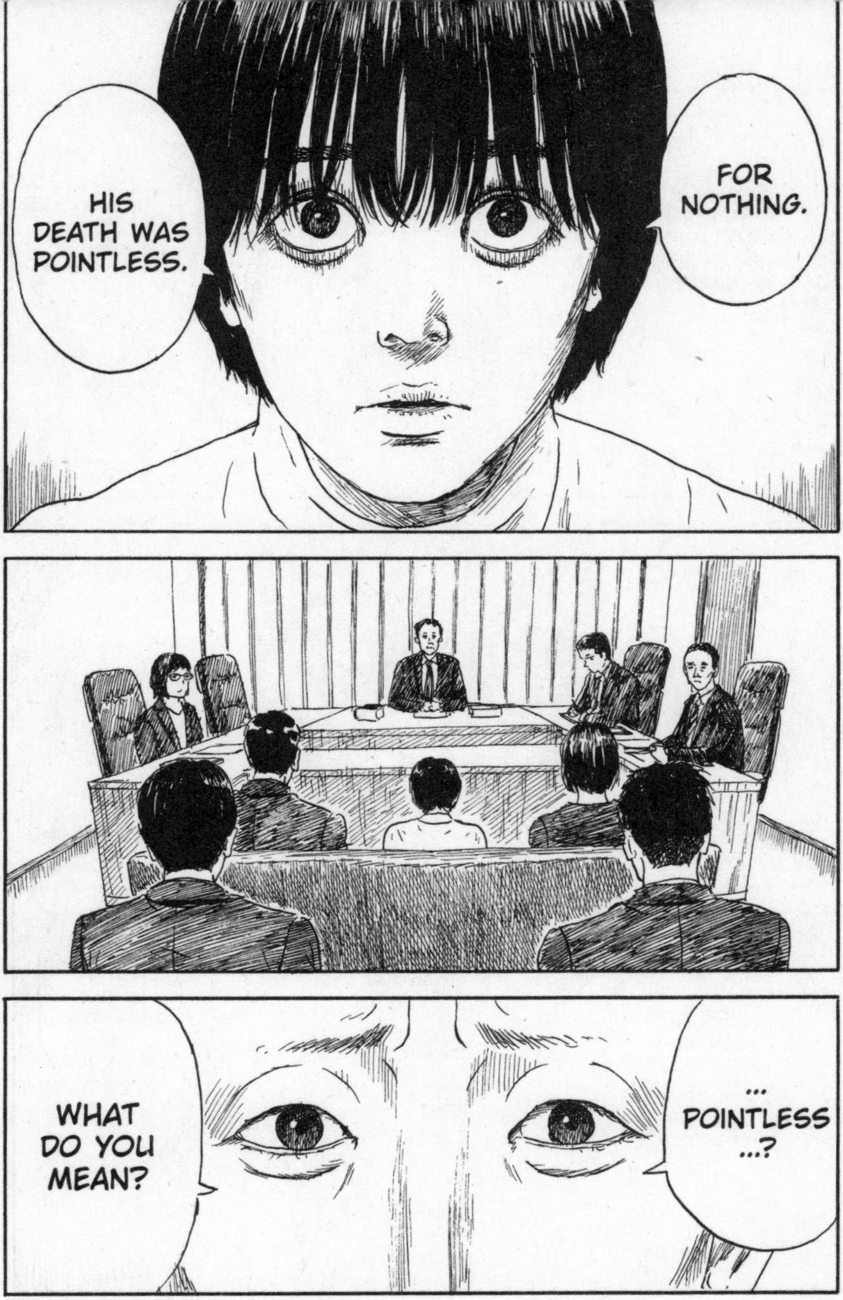
FOR NOTHING.
HIS DEATH WAS POINTLESS.
... POINTLESS ...?
WHAT DO YOU MEAN?

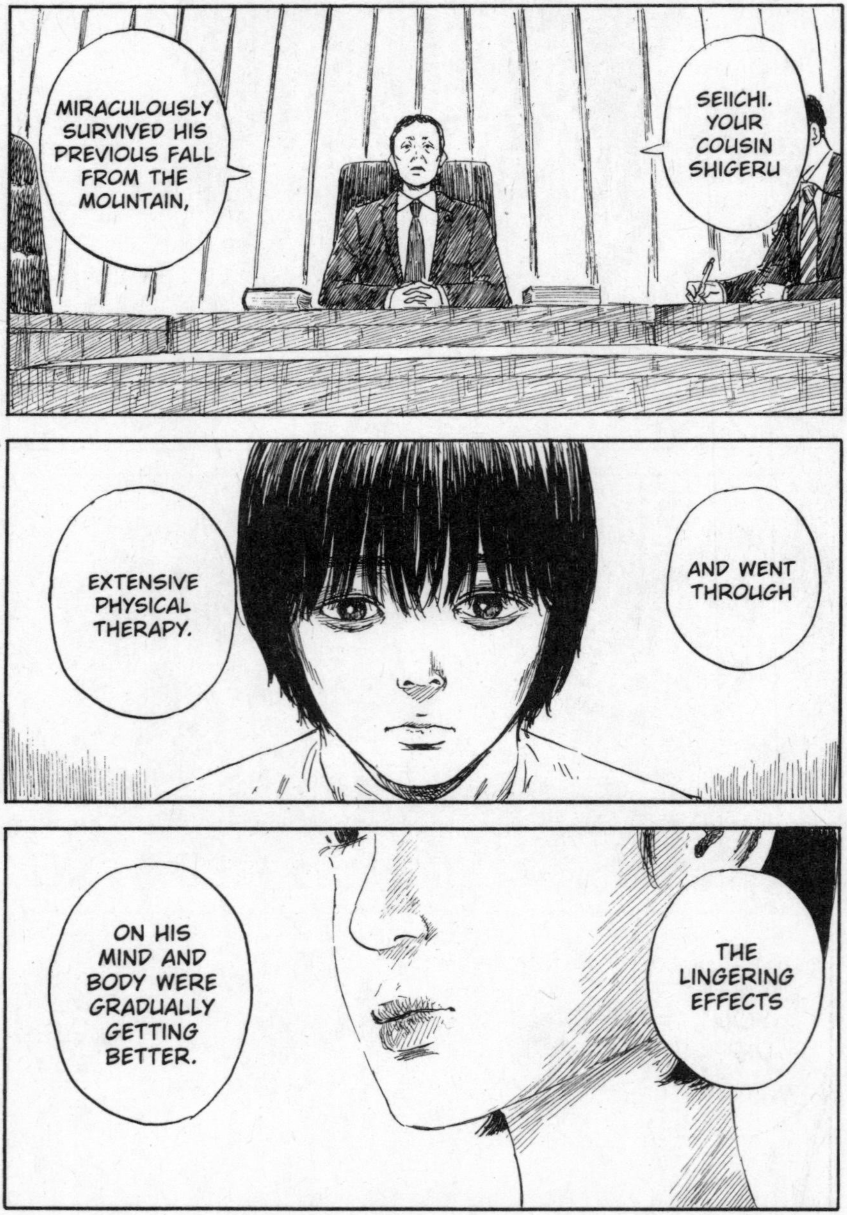
SEIICHI. YOUR COUSIN SHIGERU
MIRACULOUSLY SURVIVED HIS PREVIOUS FALL FROM THE MOUNTAIN,
AND WENT THROUGH
EXTENSIVE PHYSICAL THERAPY.
THE LINGERING EFFECTS
ON HIS MIND AND BODY WERE GRADUALLY GETTING BETTER.

DO YOU UNDERSTAND THE GRIEF
YOUR AUNT AND UNCLE MUST FEEL?
...
YES, YOUR HONOR.
THEN WHAT DO YOU THINK
OF WHAT YOU DID?

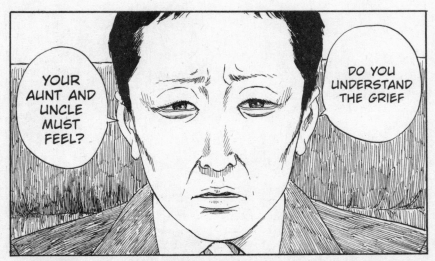

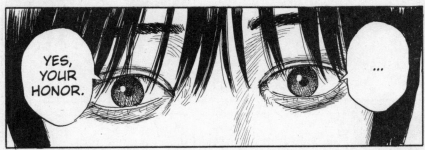

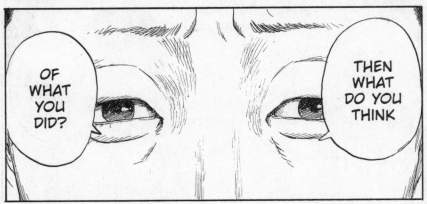

...SEIICHI.

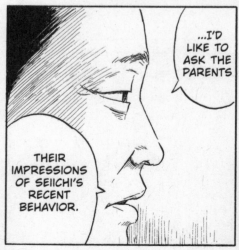

...I'D LIKE TO ASK THE PARENTS

THEIR IMPRESSIONS OF SEIICHI'S RECENT BEHAVIOR.

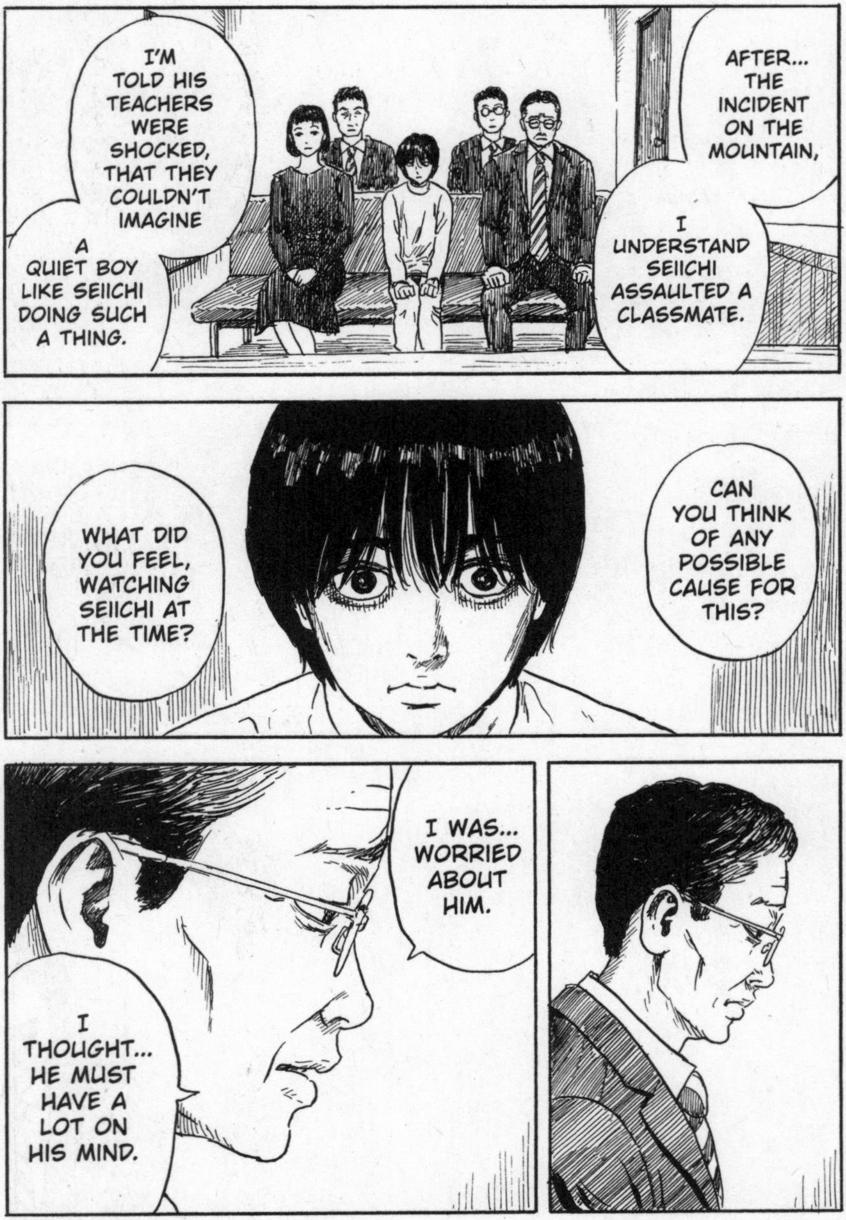
AFTER... THE INCIDENT ON THE MOUNTAIN,
I UNDERSTAND SEIICHI ASSAULTED A CLASSMATE.
I'M TOLD HIS TEACHERS WERE SHOCKED, THAT THEY COULDN'T IMAGINE
A QUIET BOY LIKE SEIICHI DOING SUCH A THING.
CAN YOU THINK OF ANY POSSIBLE CAUSE FOR THIS?
WHAT DID YOU FEEL, WATCHING SEIICHI AT THE TIME?
I WAS... WORRIED ABOUT HIM.
I THOUGHT... HE MUST HAVE A LOT ON HIS MIND.

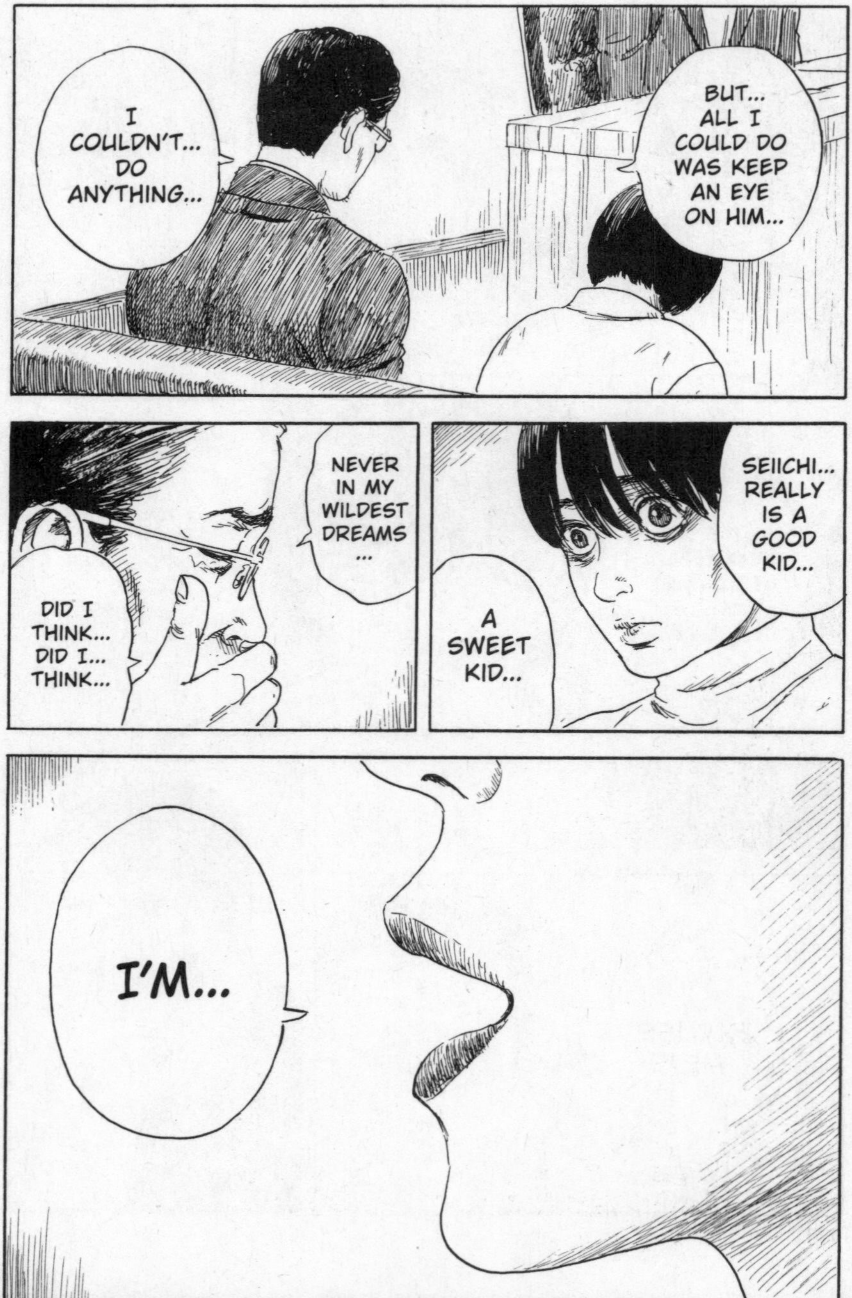
BUT... ALL I COULD DO WAS KEEP AN EYE ON HIM...
I COULDN'T... DO ANYTHING...
SEIICHI... REALLY IS A GOOD KID...
A SWEET KID...
NEVER IN MY WILDEST DREAMS ...
DID I THINK... DID I... THINK...
I'M...

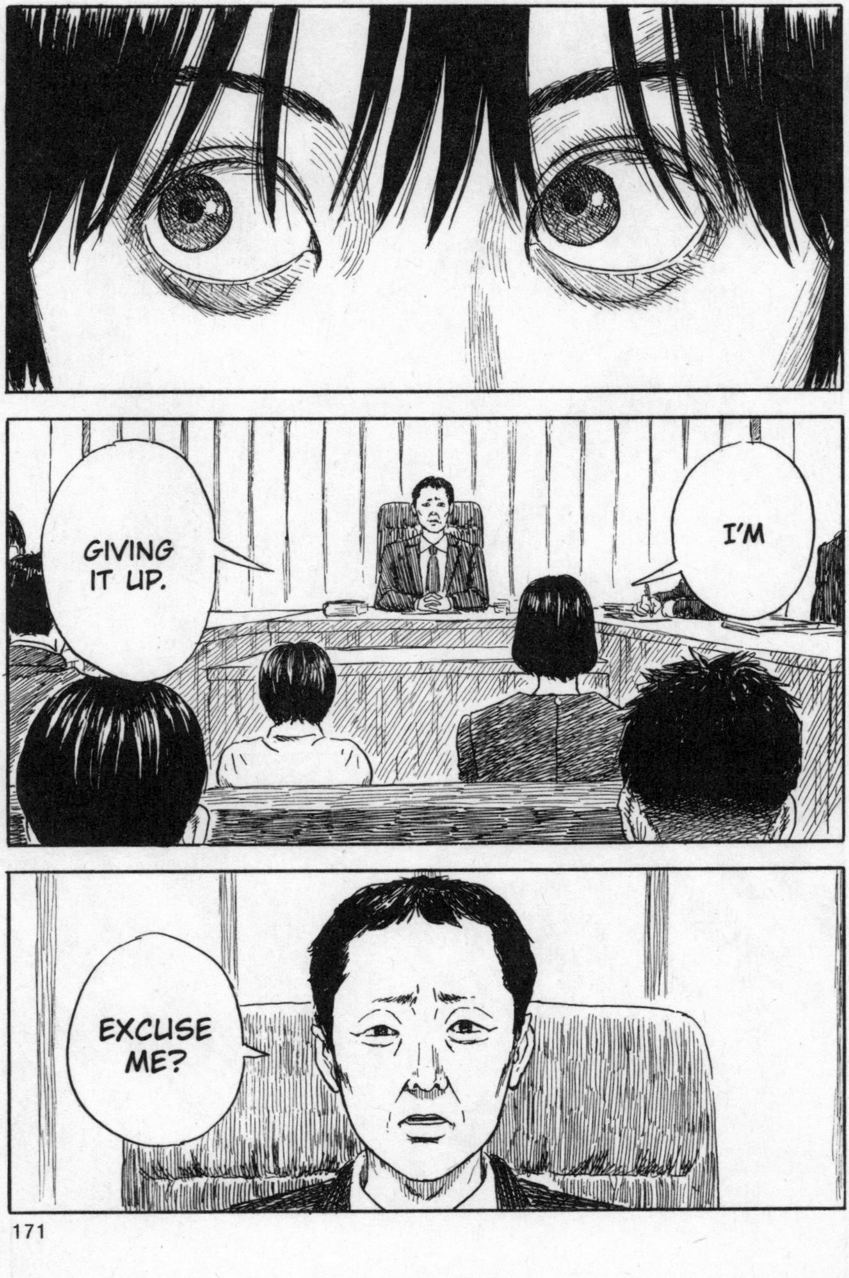
I'M
GIVING IT UP.
EXCUSE ME?

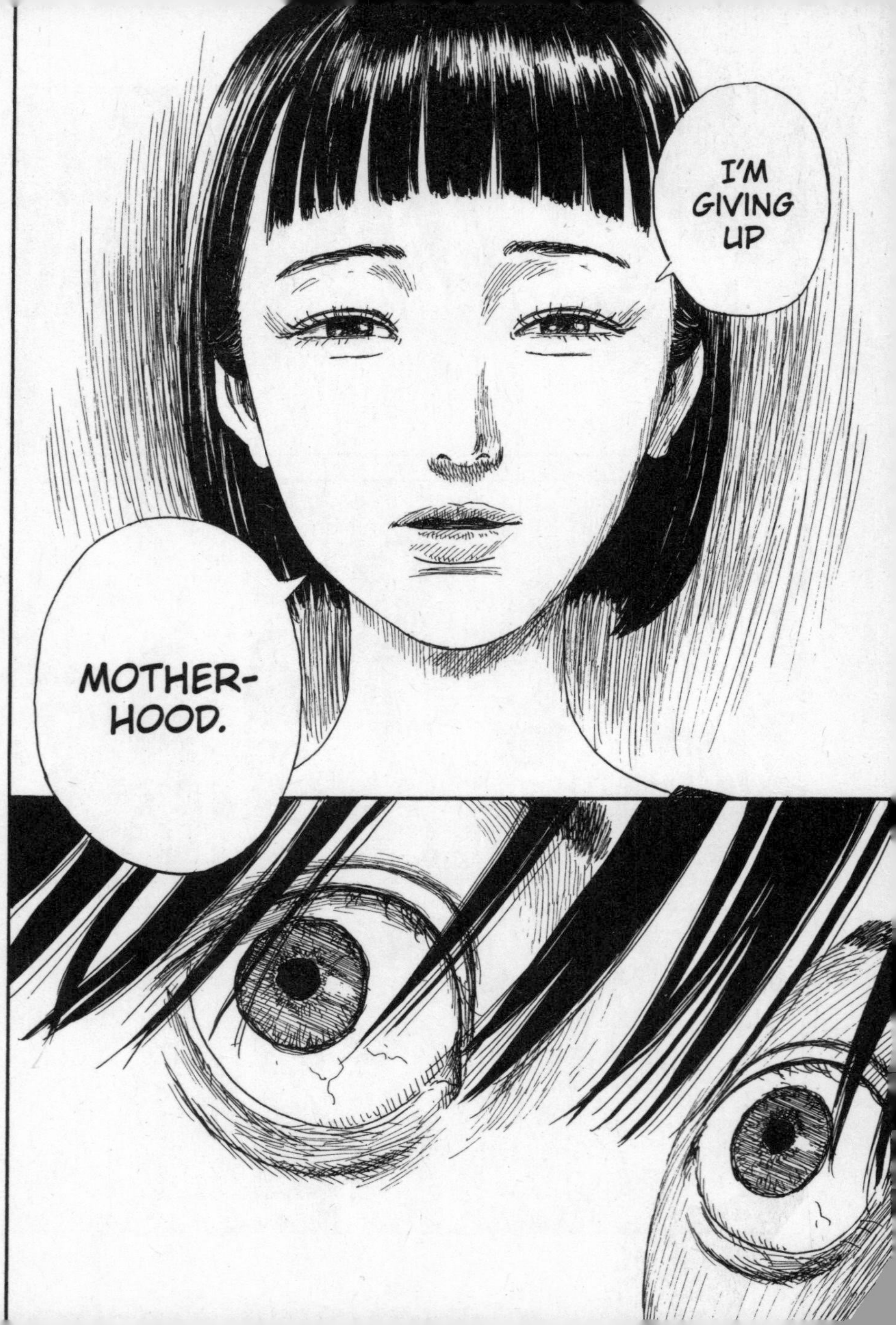
I'M GIVING UP
MOTHER-HOOD.

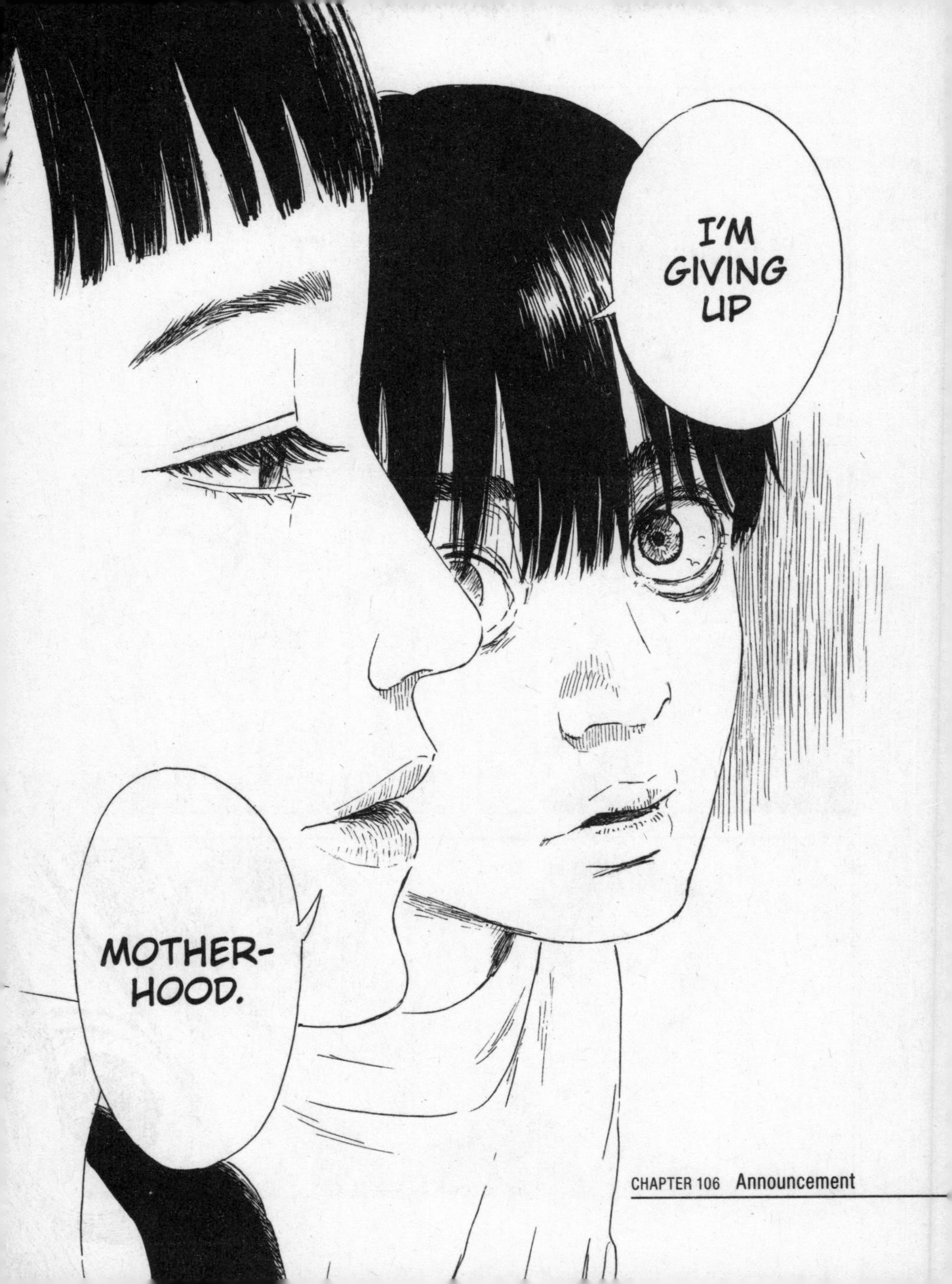
I'M GIVING UP
MOTHER-HOOD.

CHAPTER 106 Announcement

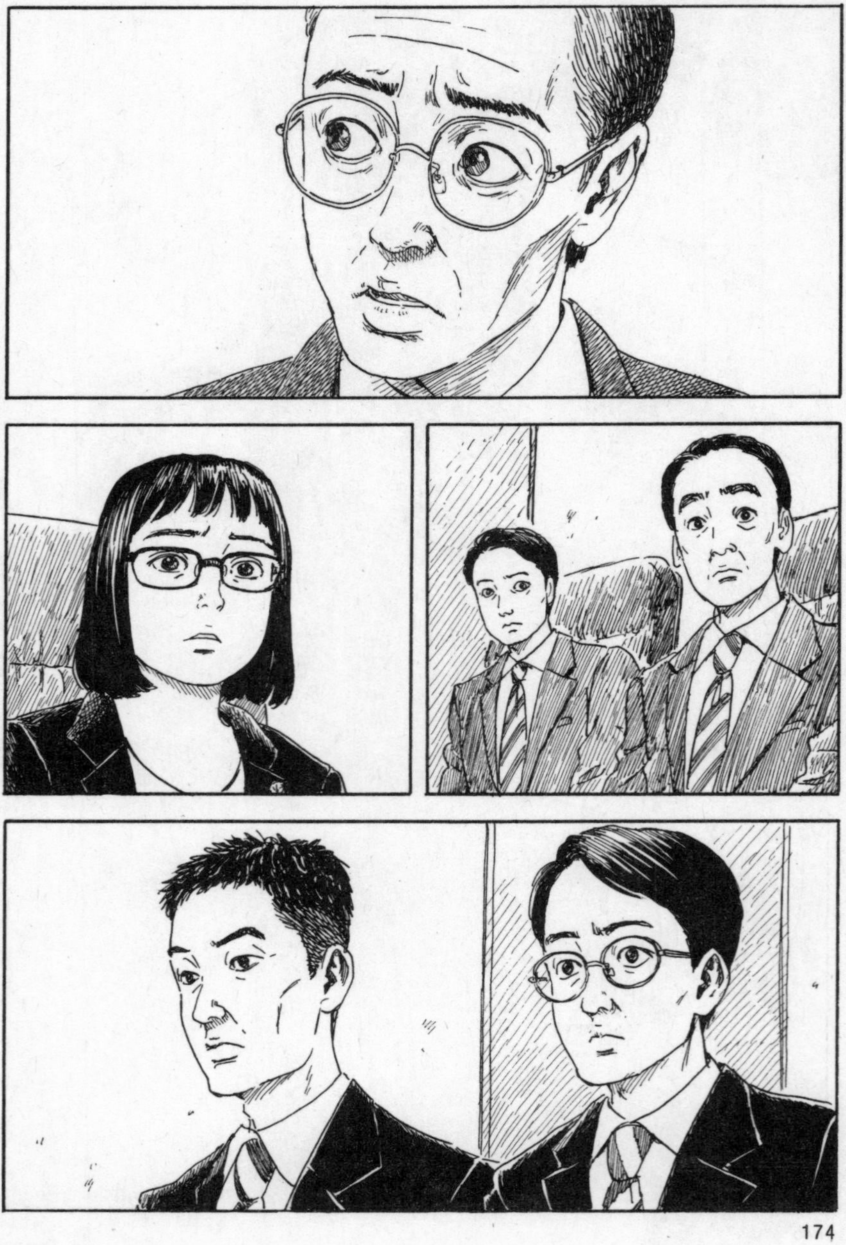

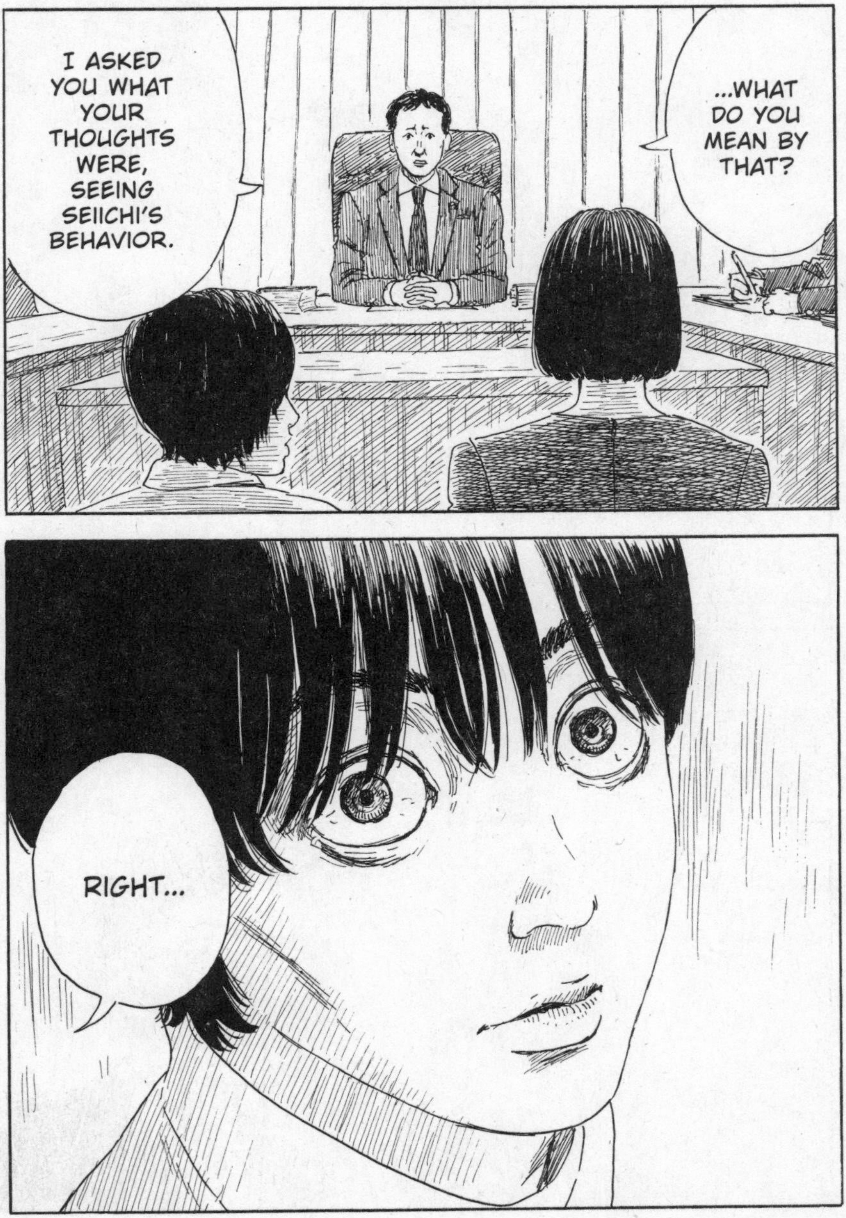
...WHAT DO YOU MEAN BY THAT?
I ASKED YOU WHAT YOUR THOUGHTS WERE, SEEING SEIICHI'S BEHAVIOR.
RIGHT...

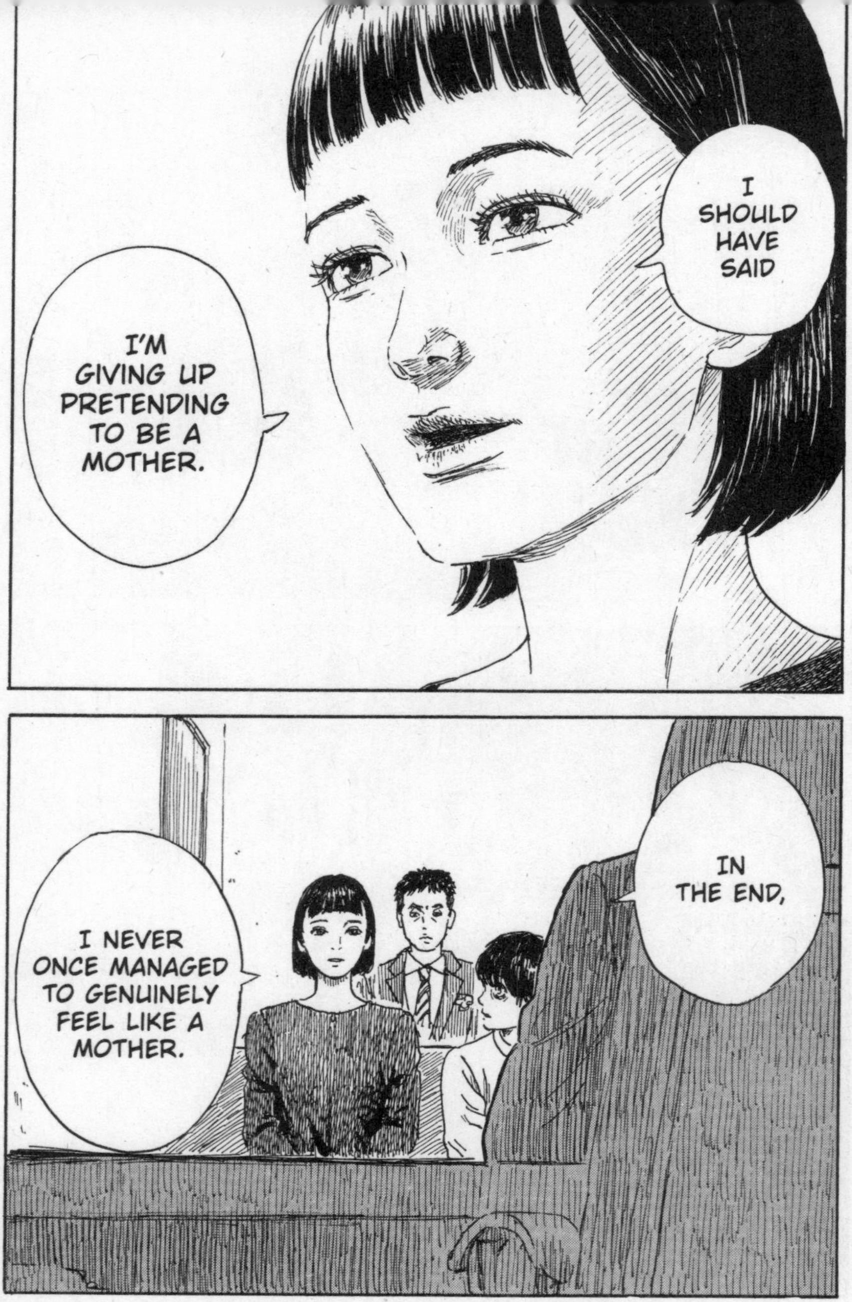
I SHOULD HAVE SAID
I'M GIVING UP PRETENDING TO BE A MOTHER.
IN THE END,
I NEVER ONCE MANAGED TO GENUINELY FEEL LIKE A MOTHER.

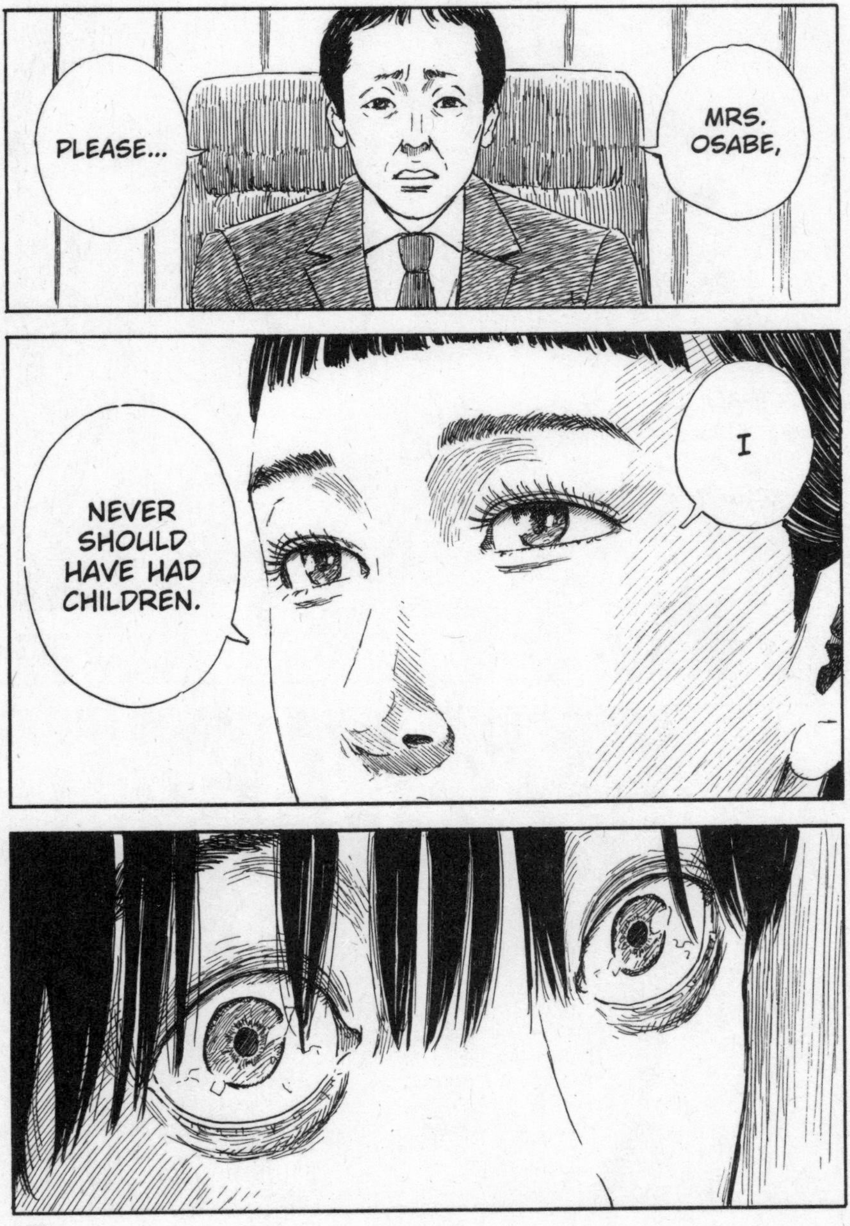
MRS. OSABE,
PLEASE...
I
NEVER SHOULD HAVE HAD CHILDREN.

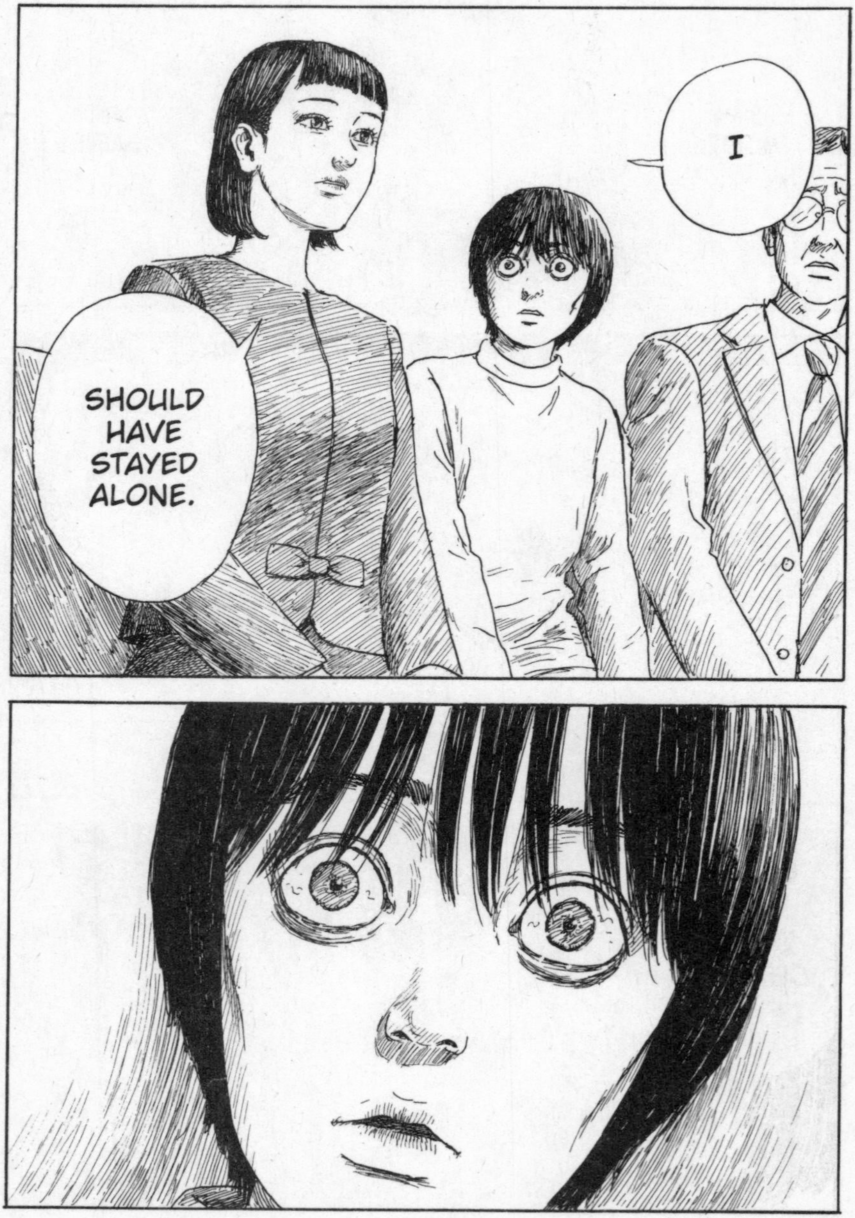
I
SHOULD HAVE STAYED ALONE.

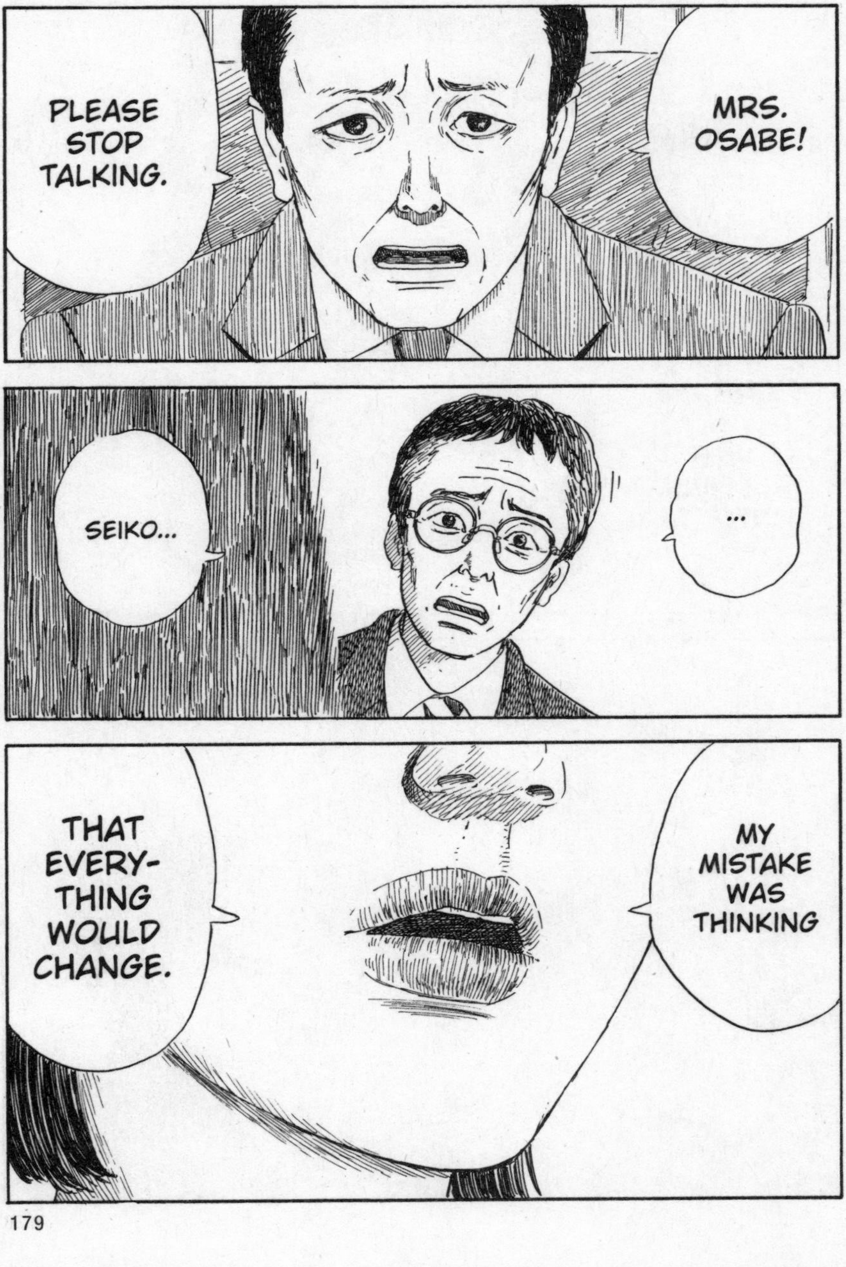
MRS. OSABE!
PLEASE STOP TALKING.
...
SEIKO...
MY MISTAKE WAS THINKING
THAT EVERY-THING WOULD CHANGE.

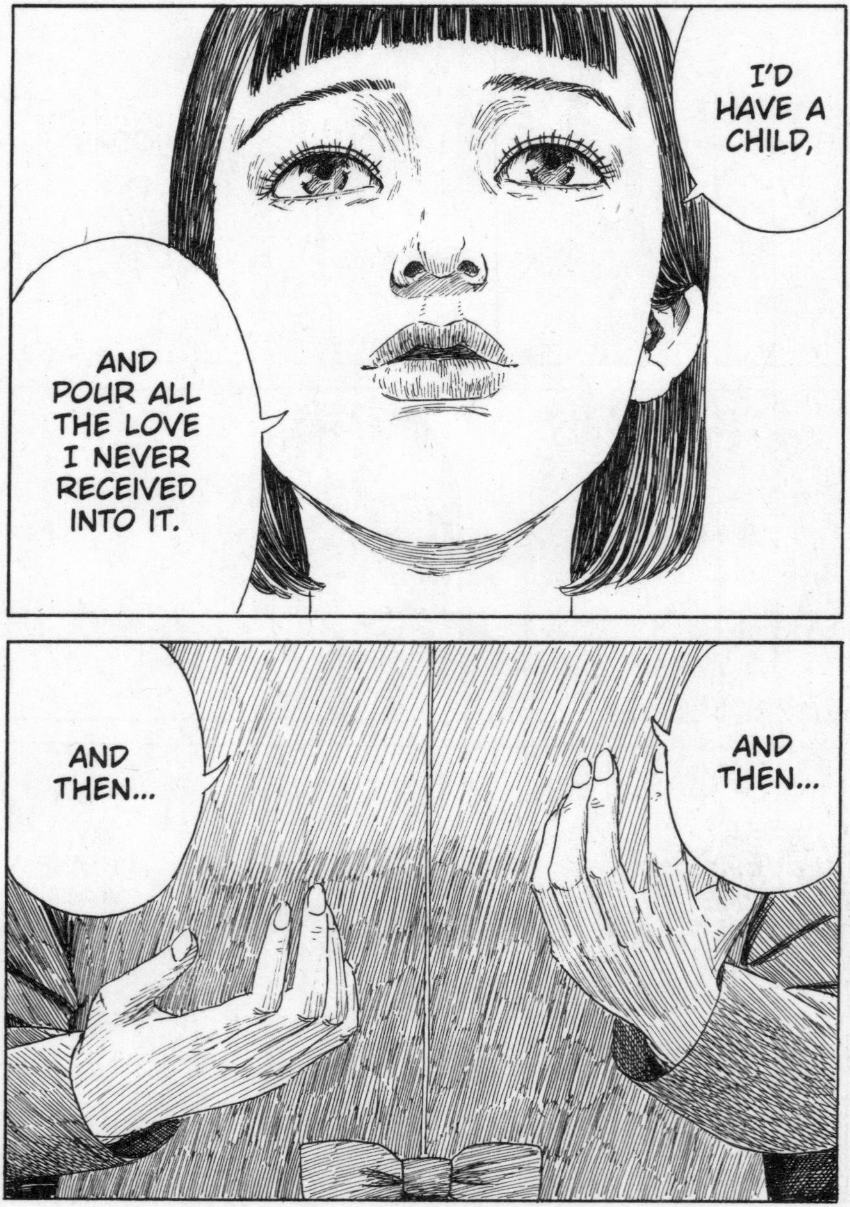
I'D HAVE A CHILD,
AND POUR ALL THE LOVE I NEVER RECEIVED INTO IT.
AND THEN...
AND THEN...

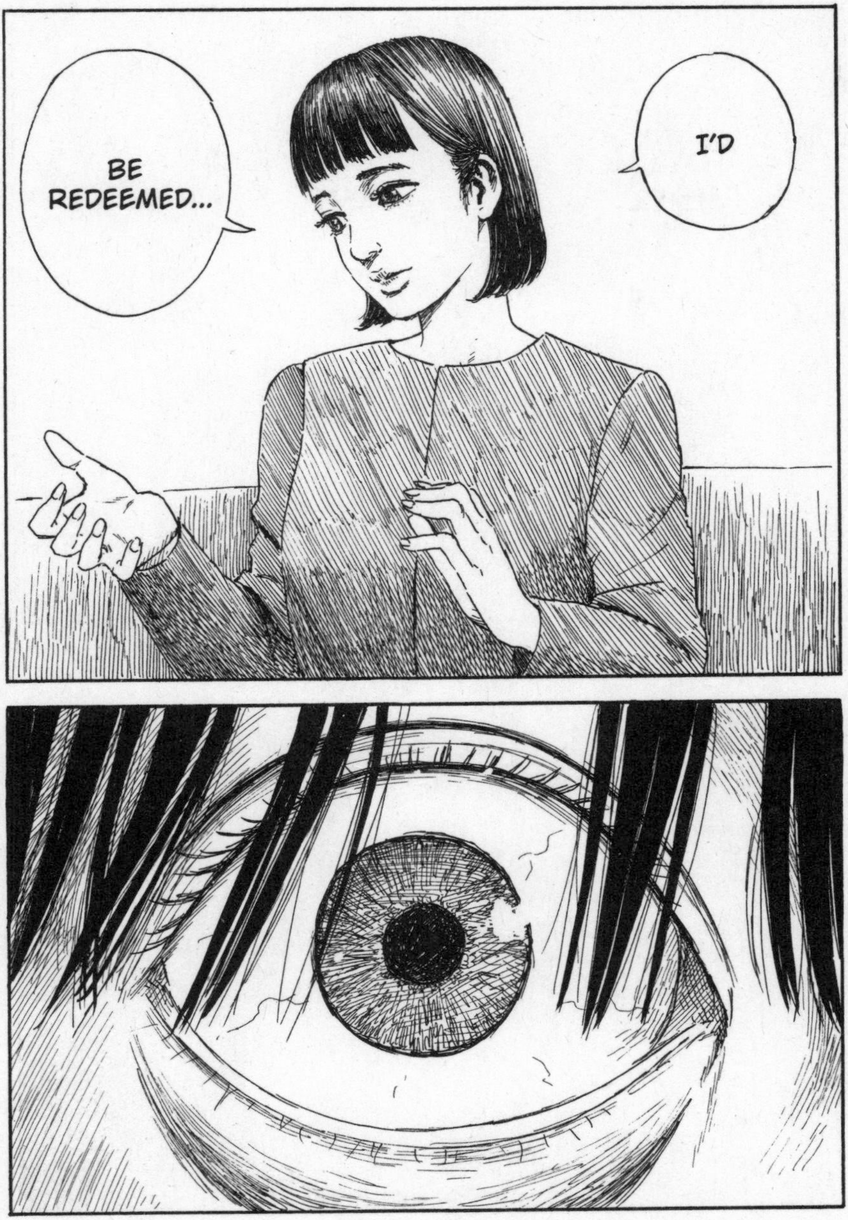
I'D
BE REDEEMED...

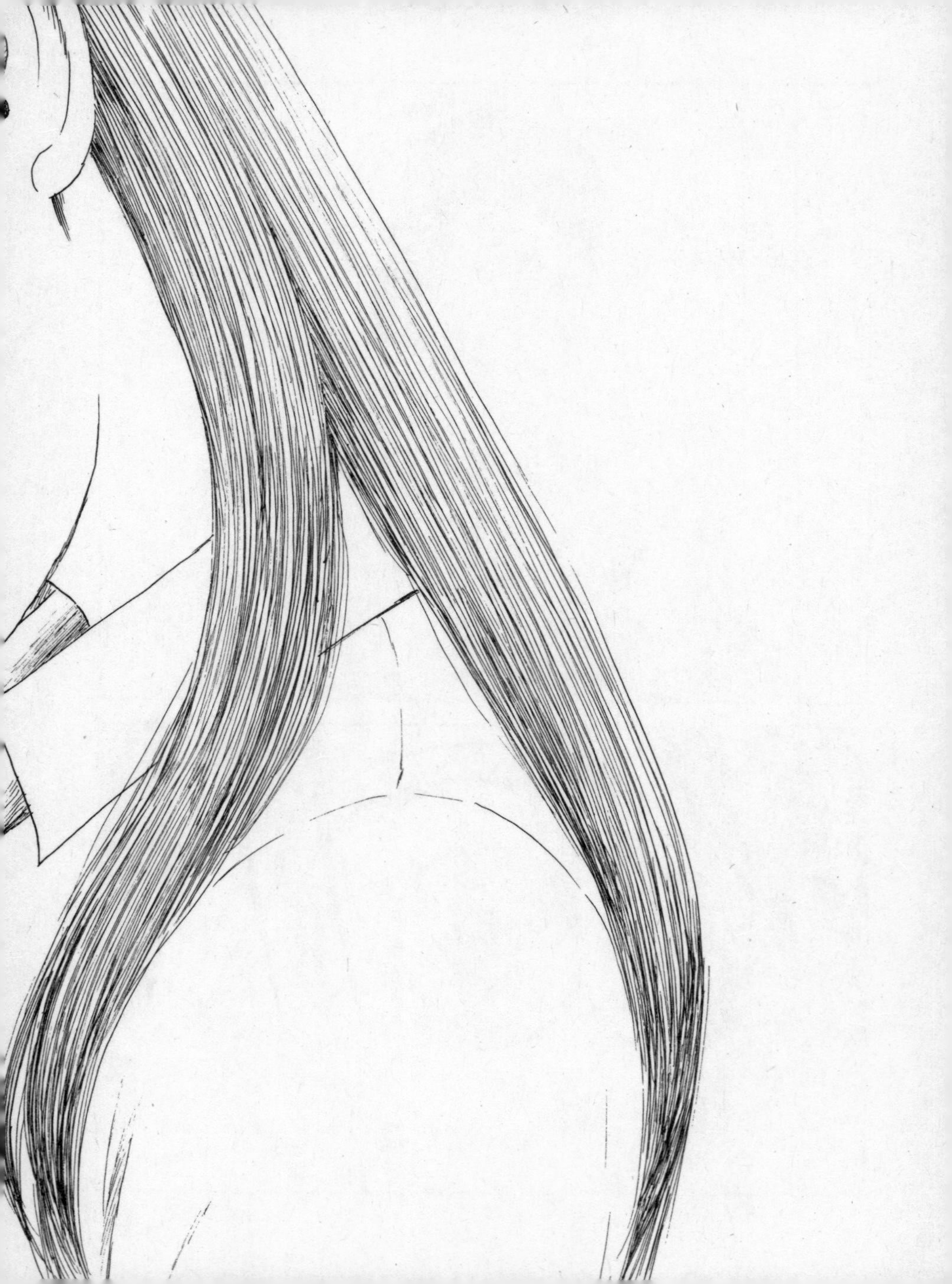

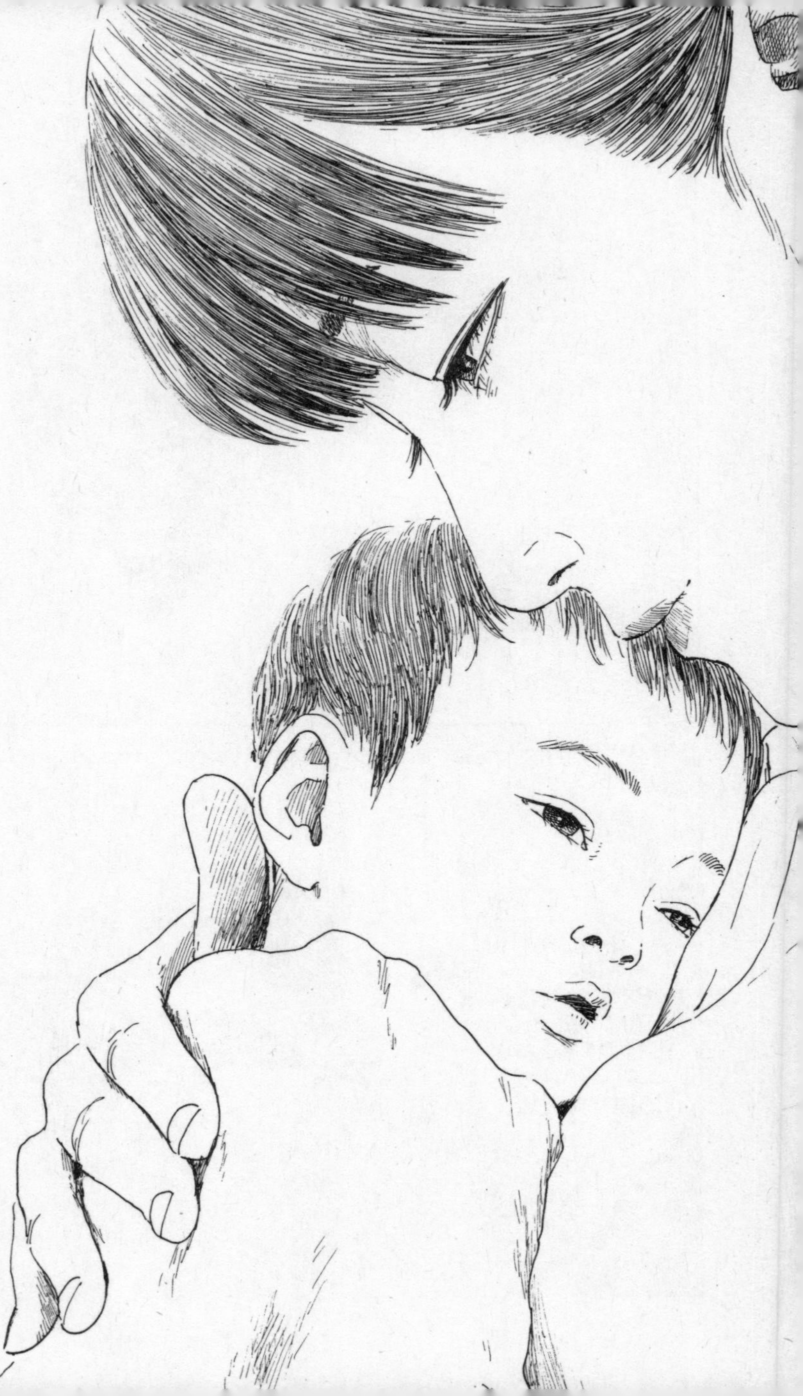

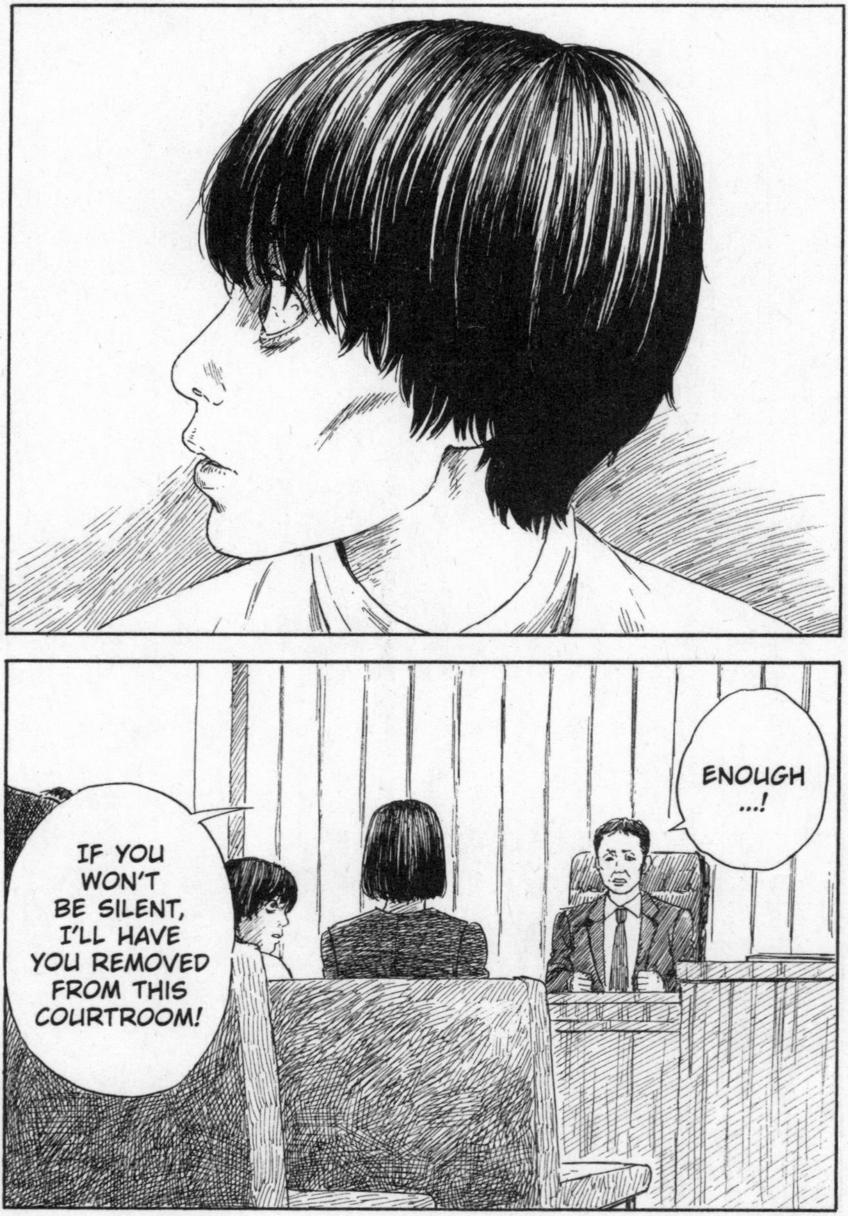
ENOUGH ...!
IF YOU WON'T BE SILENT, I'LL HAVE YOU REMOVED FROM THIS COURTROOM!

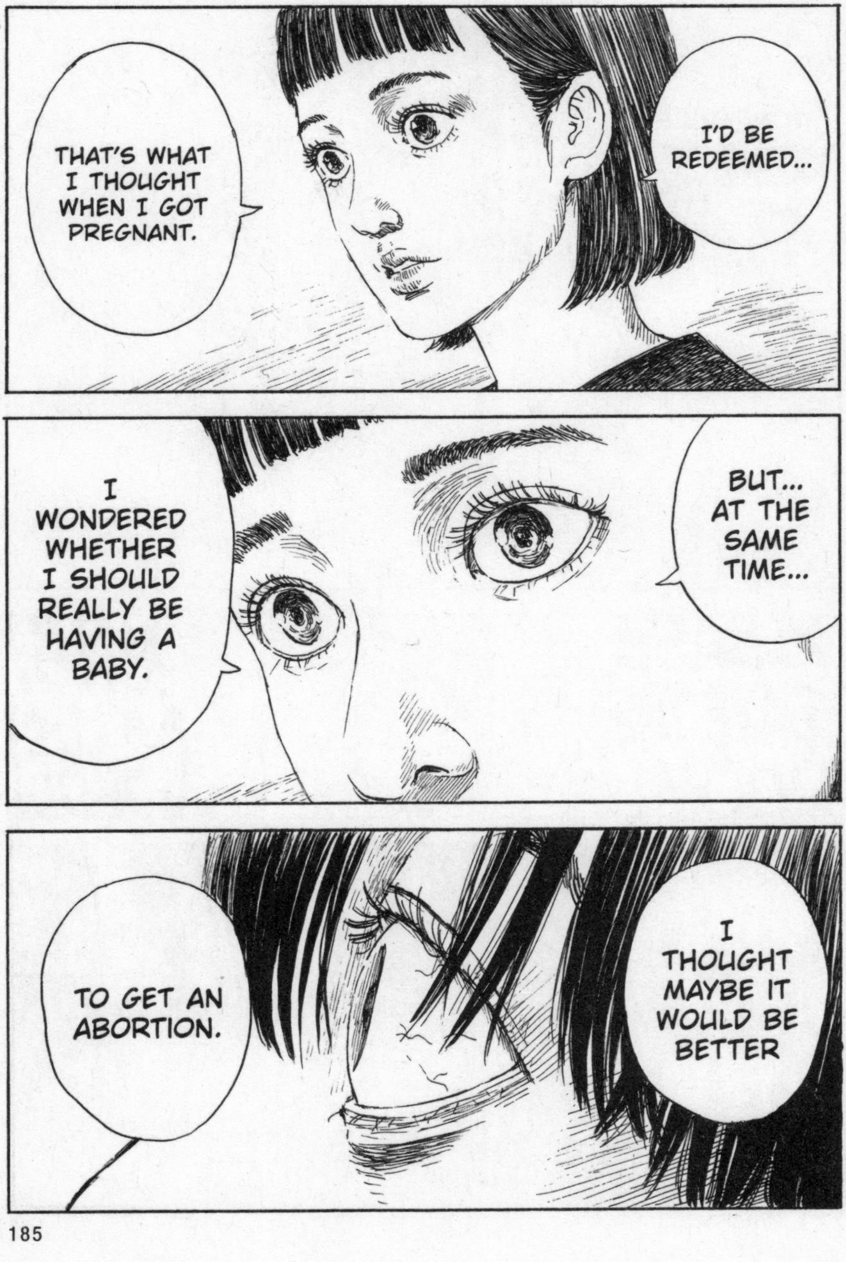
I'D BE REDEEMED...
THAT'S WHAT I THOUGHT WHEN I GOT PREGNANT.
BUT... AT THE SAME TIME...
I WONDERED WHETHER I SHOULD REALLY BE HAVING A BABY.
I THOUGHT MAYBE IT WOULD BE BETTER
TO GET AN ABORTION.

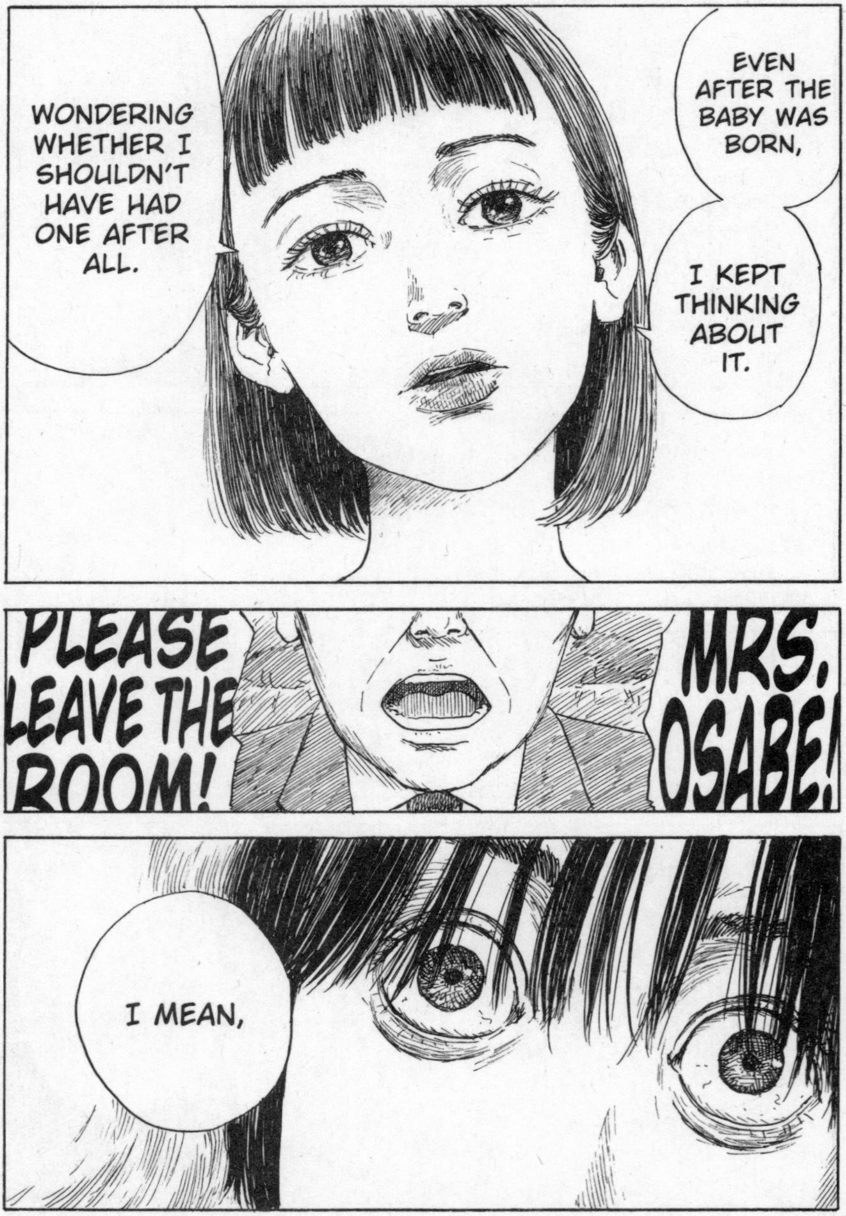
EVEN AFTER THE BABY WAS BORN,
I KEPT THINKING ABOUT IT.
WONDERING WHETHER I SHOULDN'T HAVE HAD ONE AFTER ALL.
MRS. OSABE!
PLEASE LEAVE THE ROOM!
I MEAN,

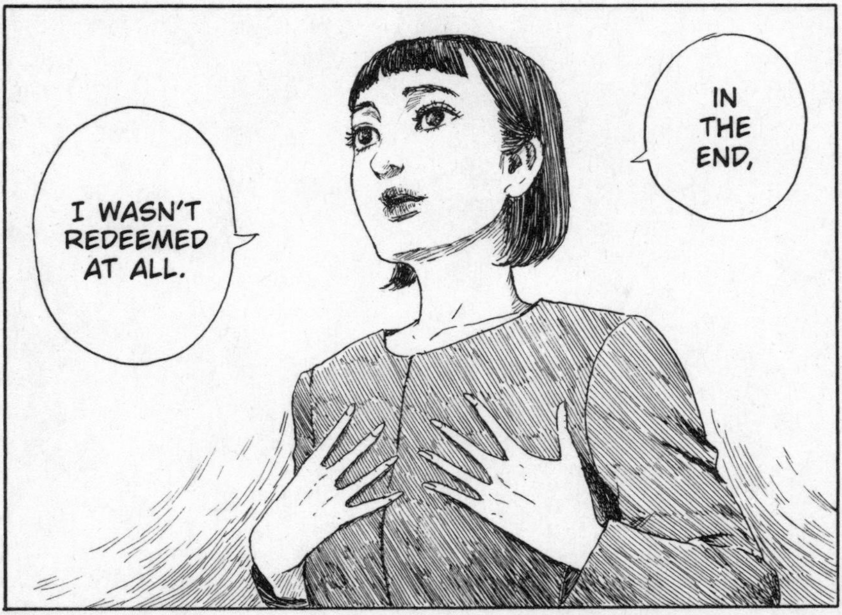
IN THE END,
I WASN'T REDEEMED AT ALL.

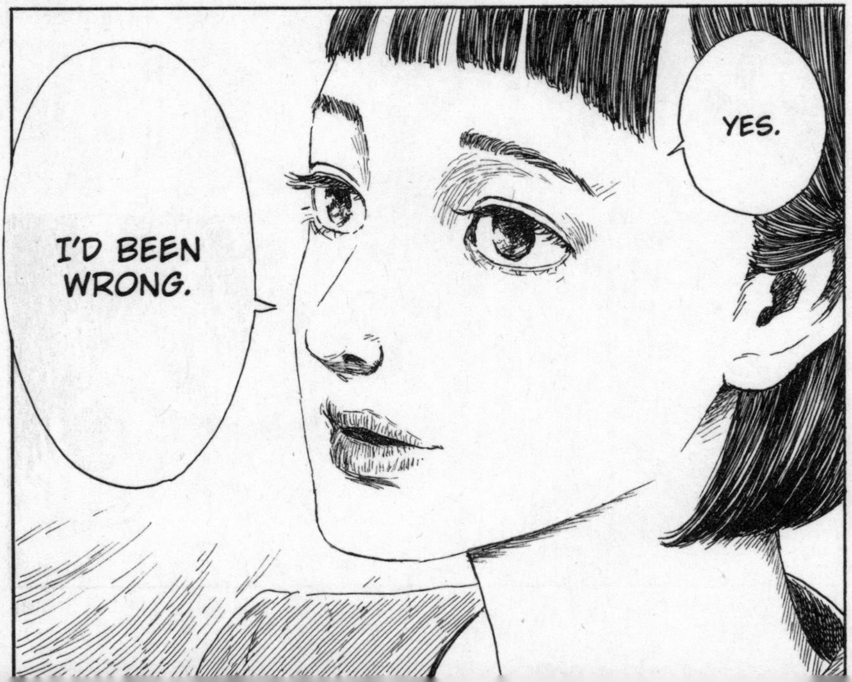
YES.
I'D BEEN WRONG.

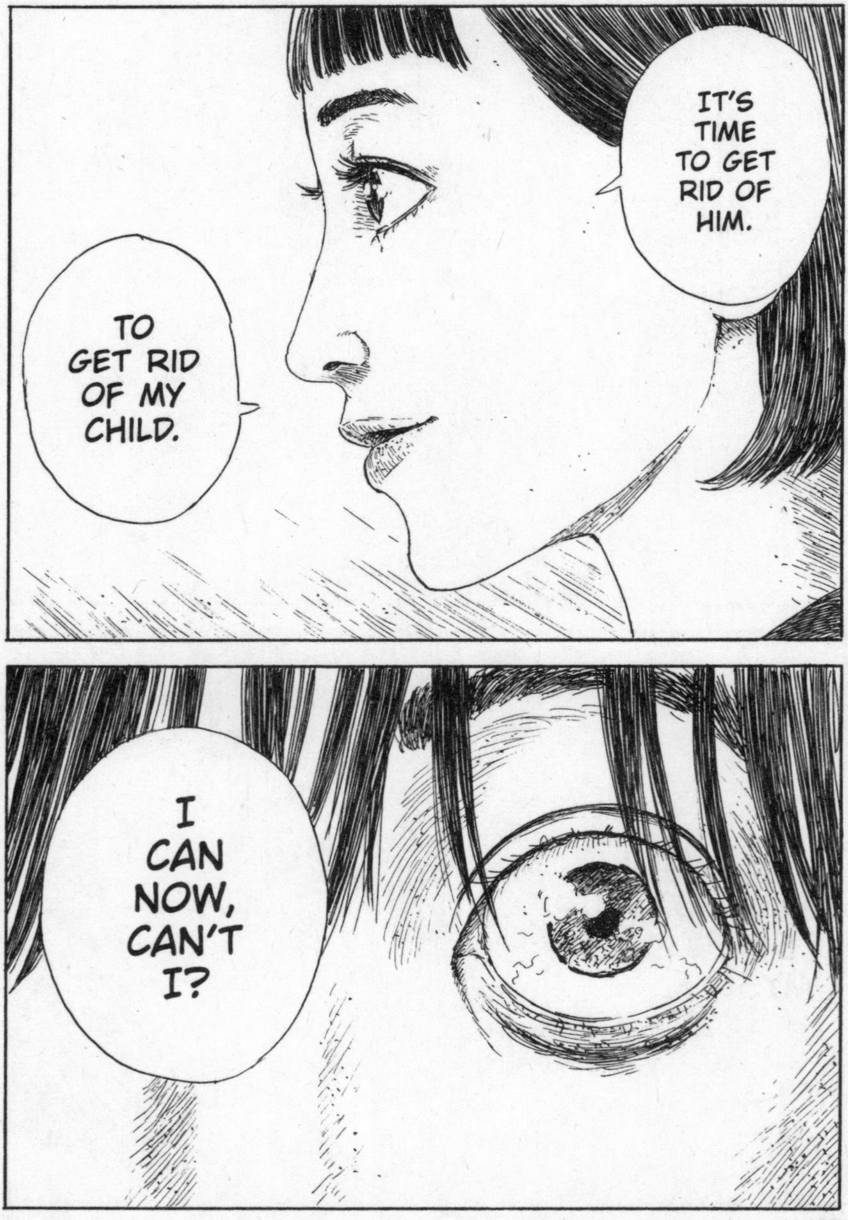
IT'S TIME TO GET RID OF HIM.
TO GET RID OF MY CHILD.
I CAN NOW, CAN'T I?

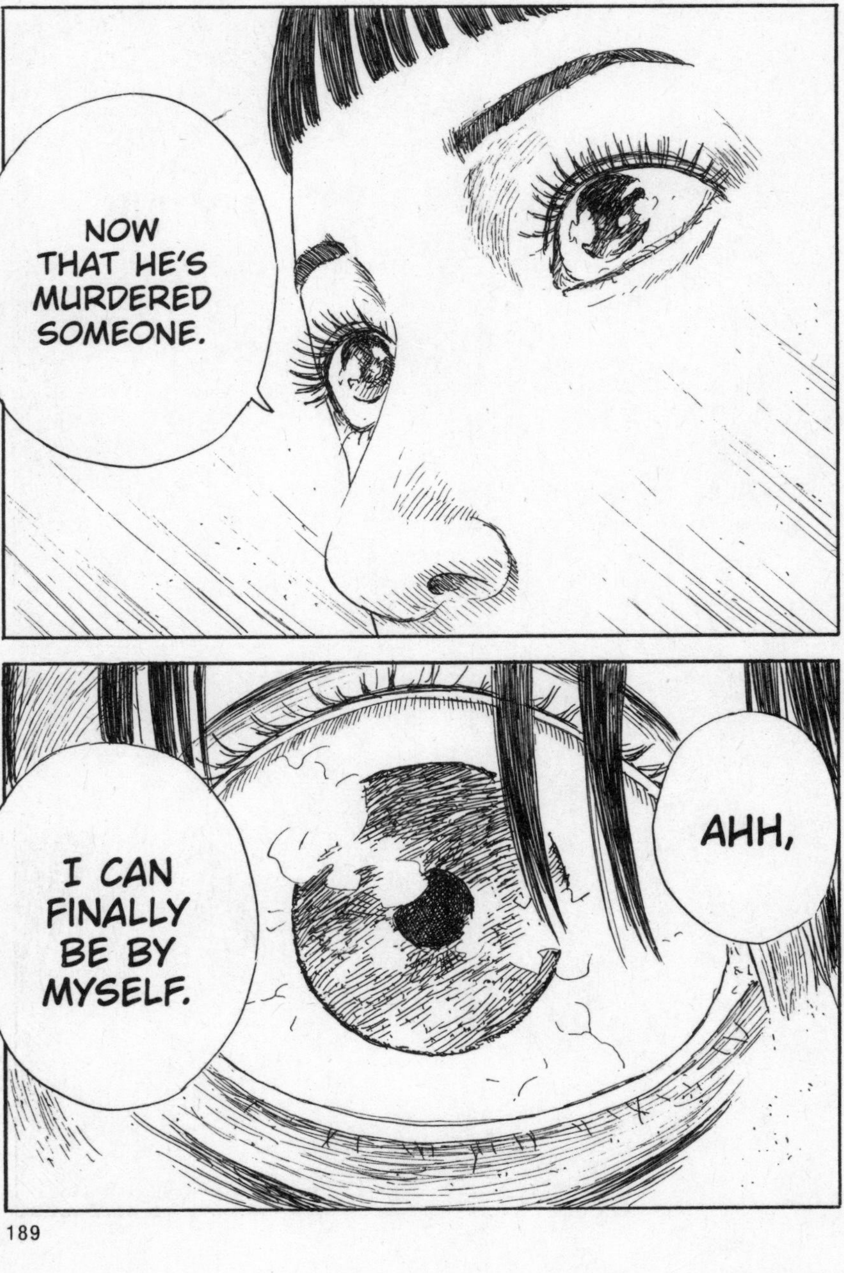
NOW THAT HE'S MURDERED SOMEONE.
AHH,
I CAN FINALLY BE BY MYSELF.

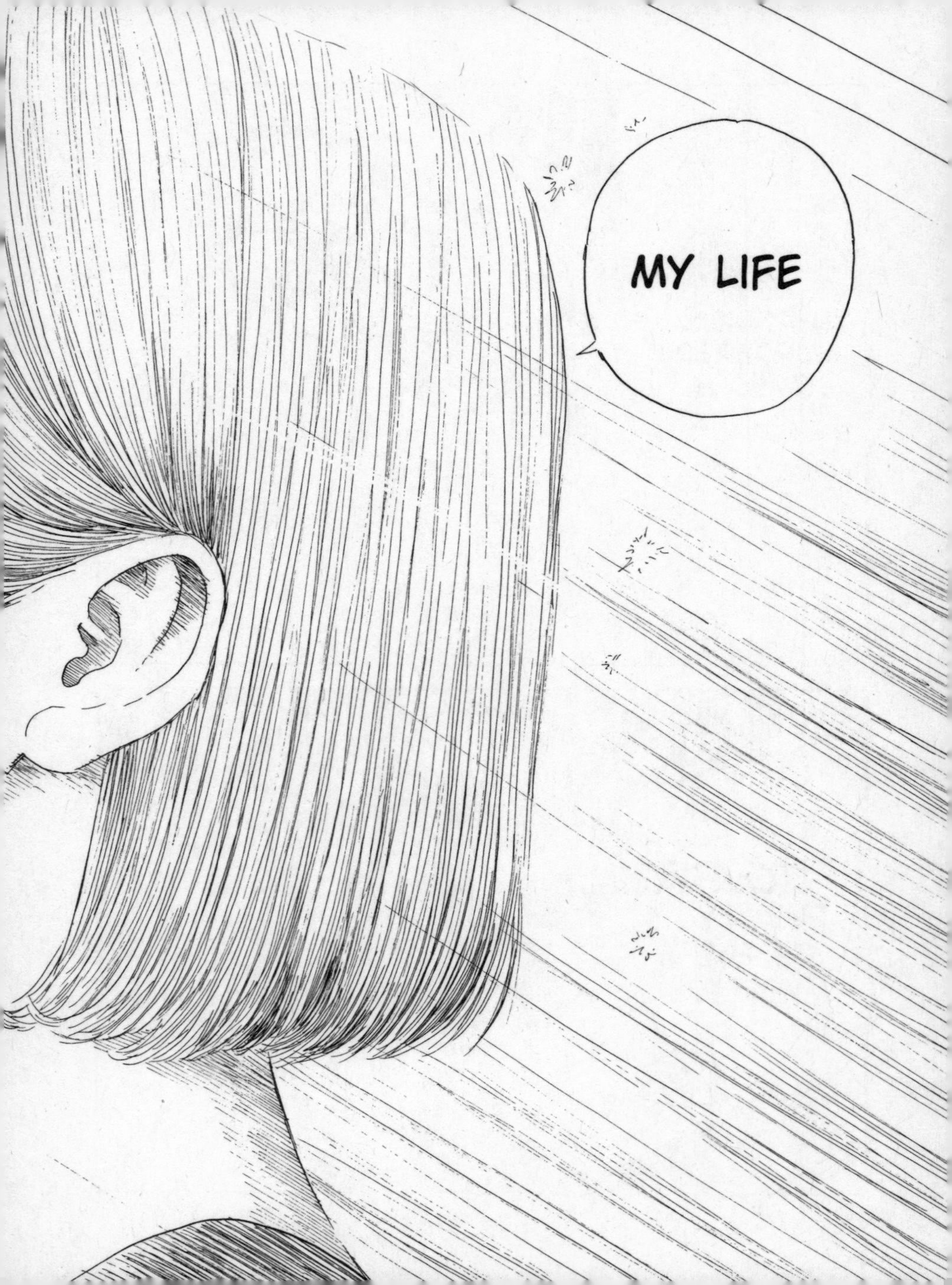
MY LIFE

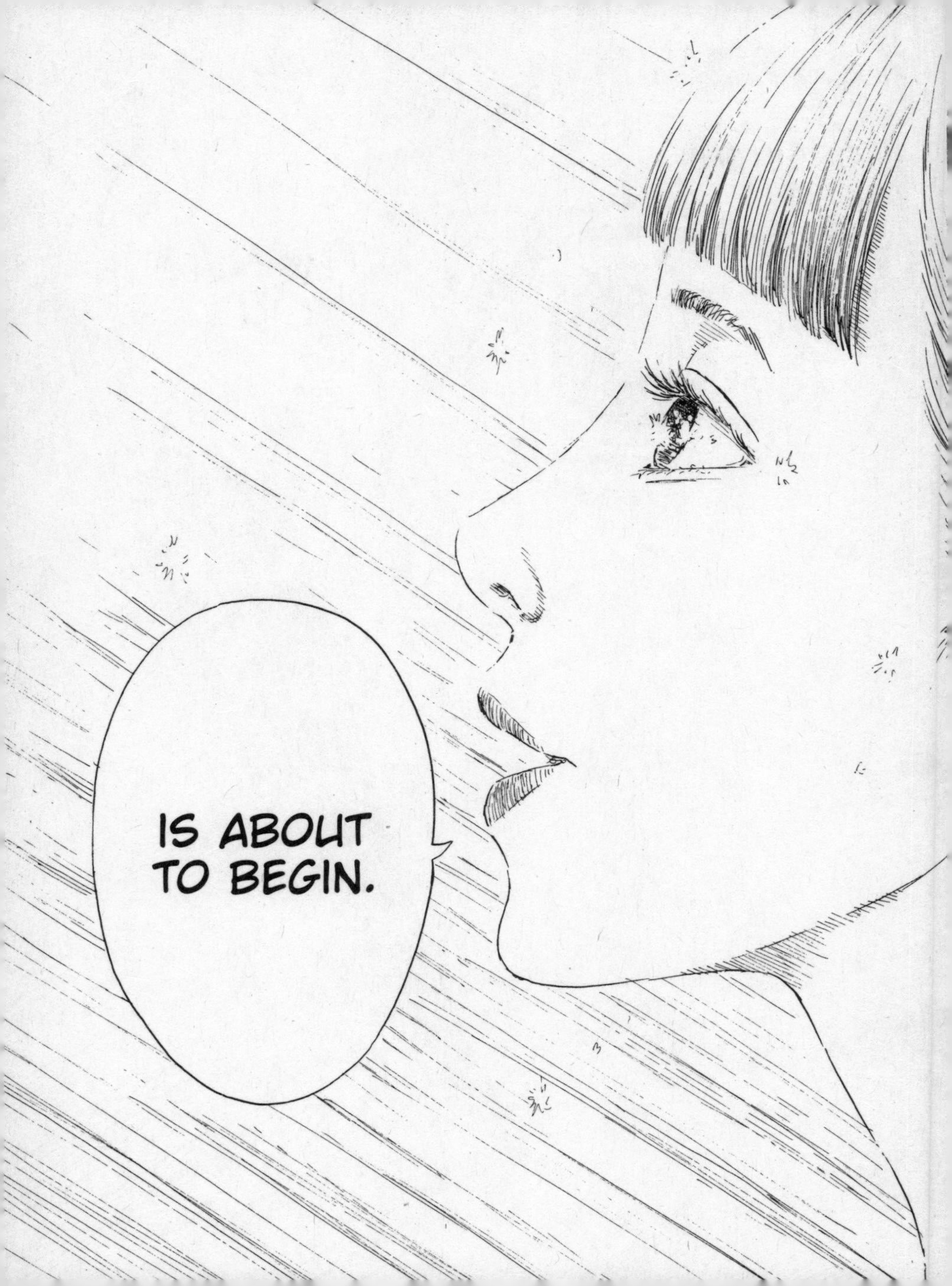
IS ABOUT TO BEGIN.

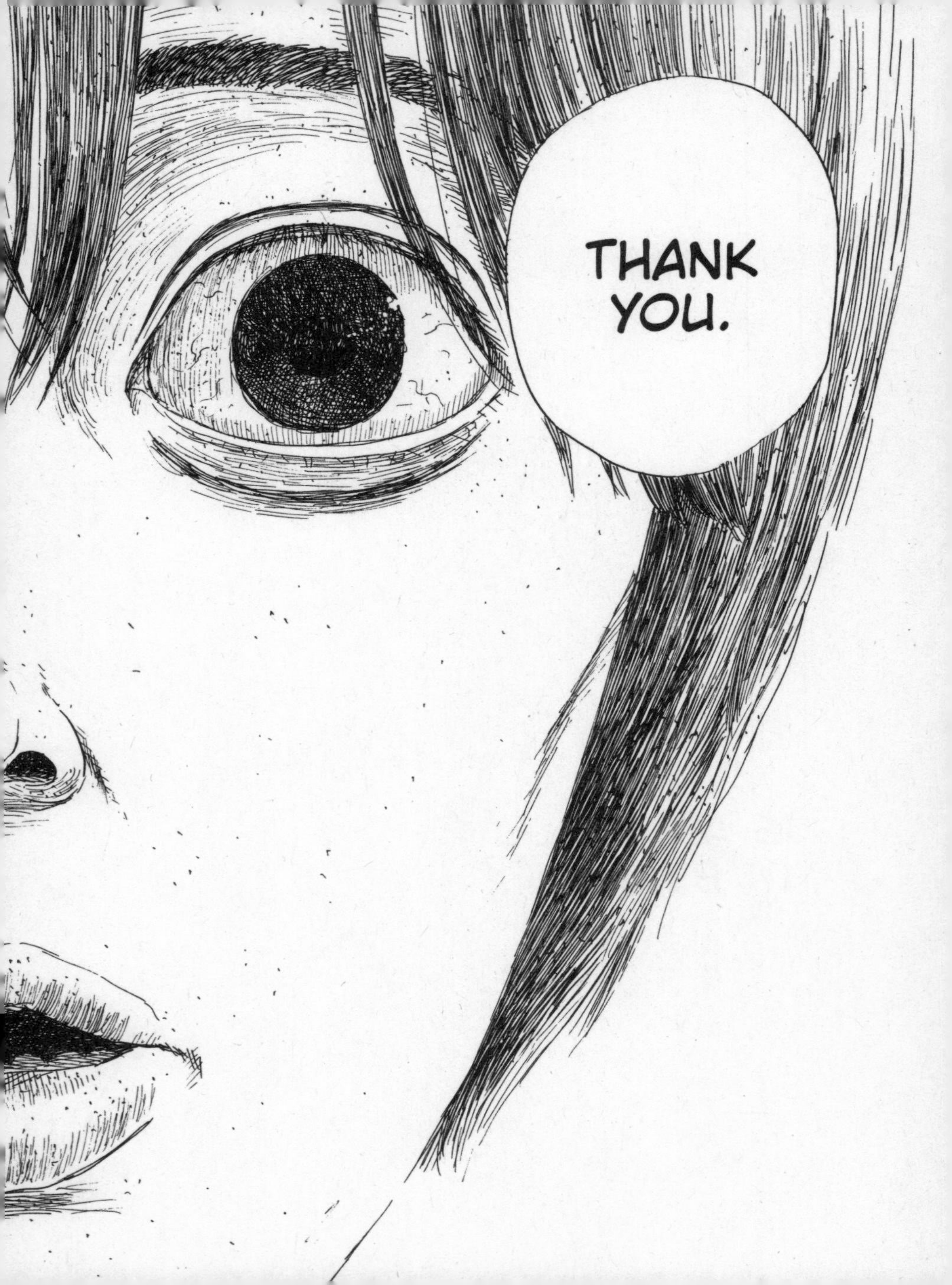
THANK YOU.

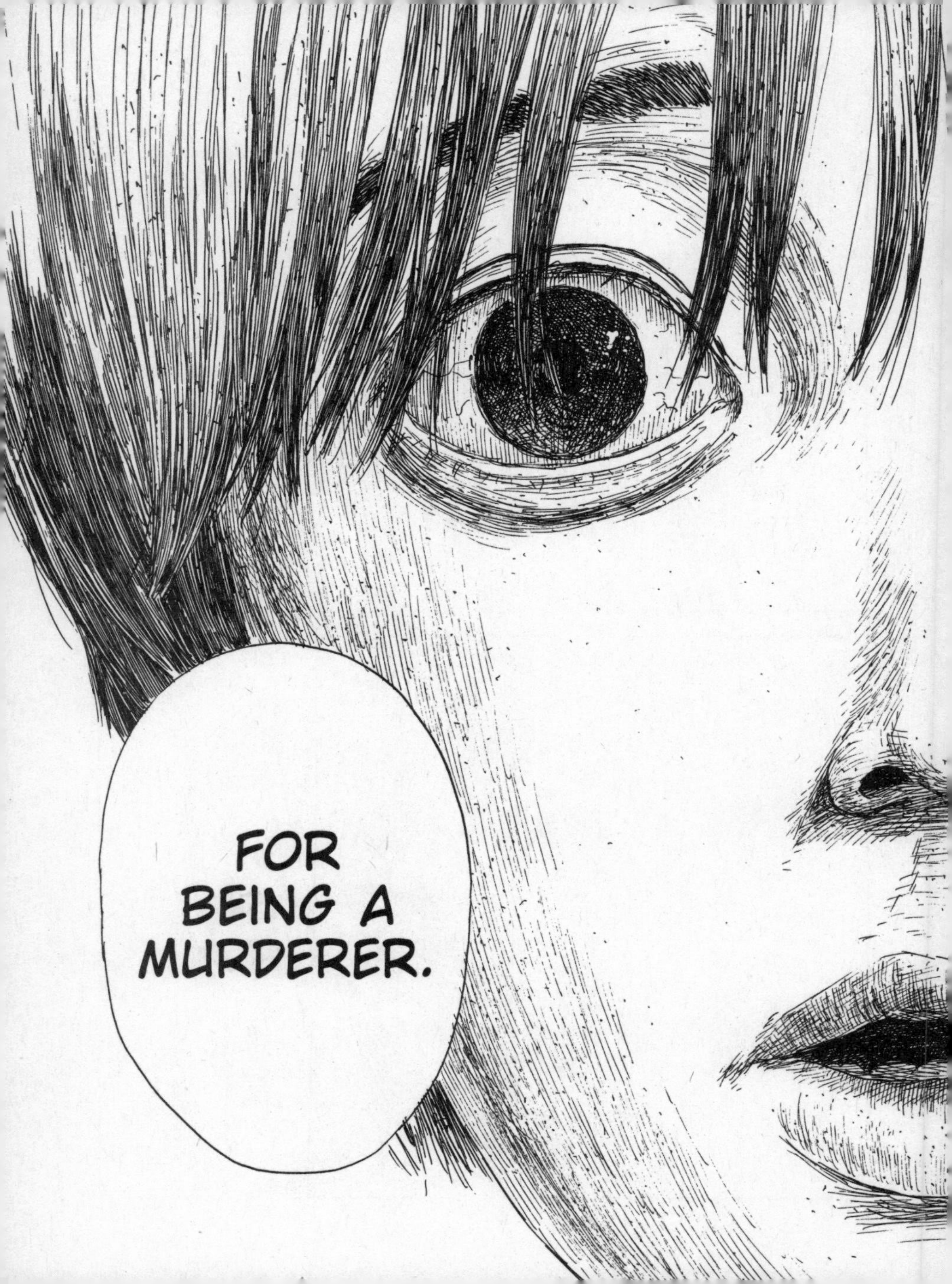
FOR BEING A MURDERER.

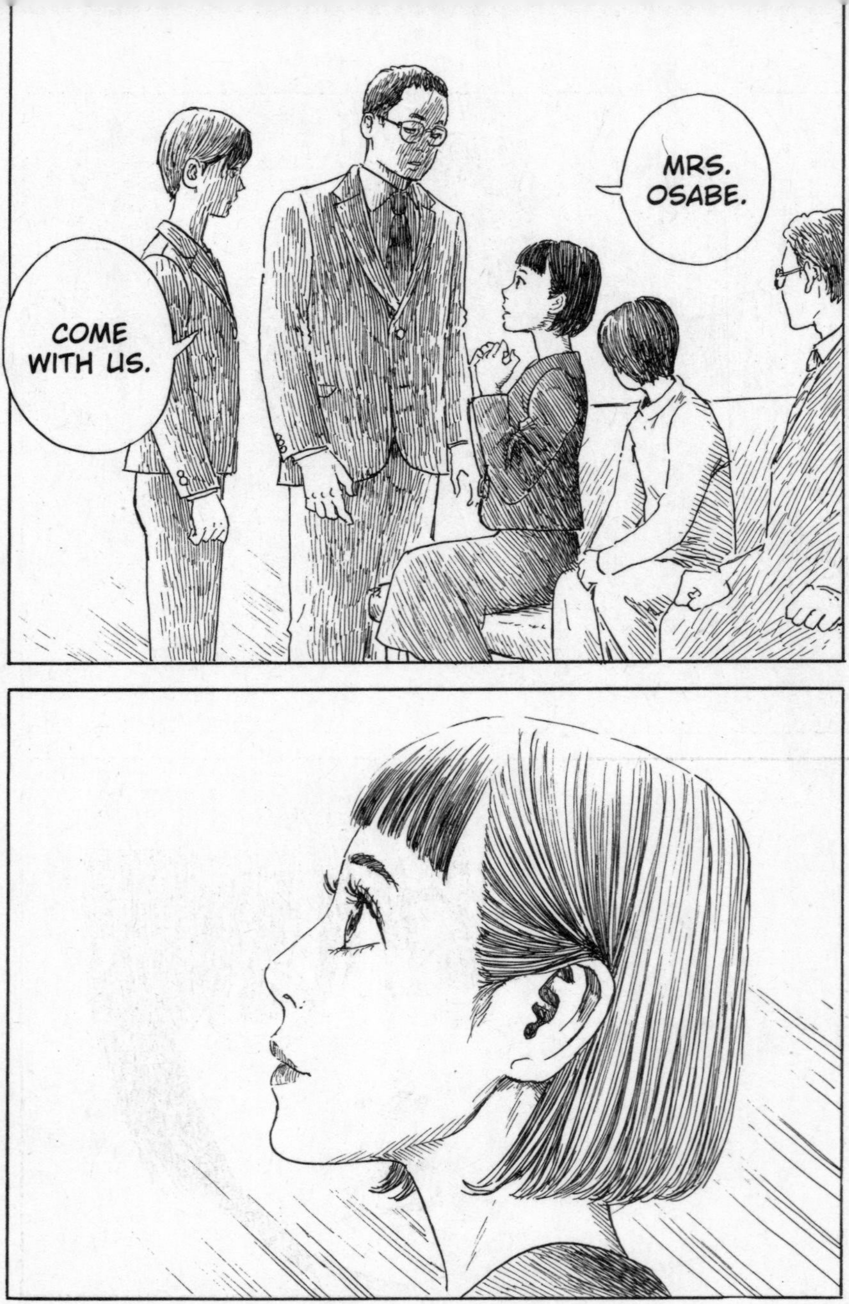
MRS. OSABE.
COME WITH US.

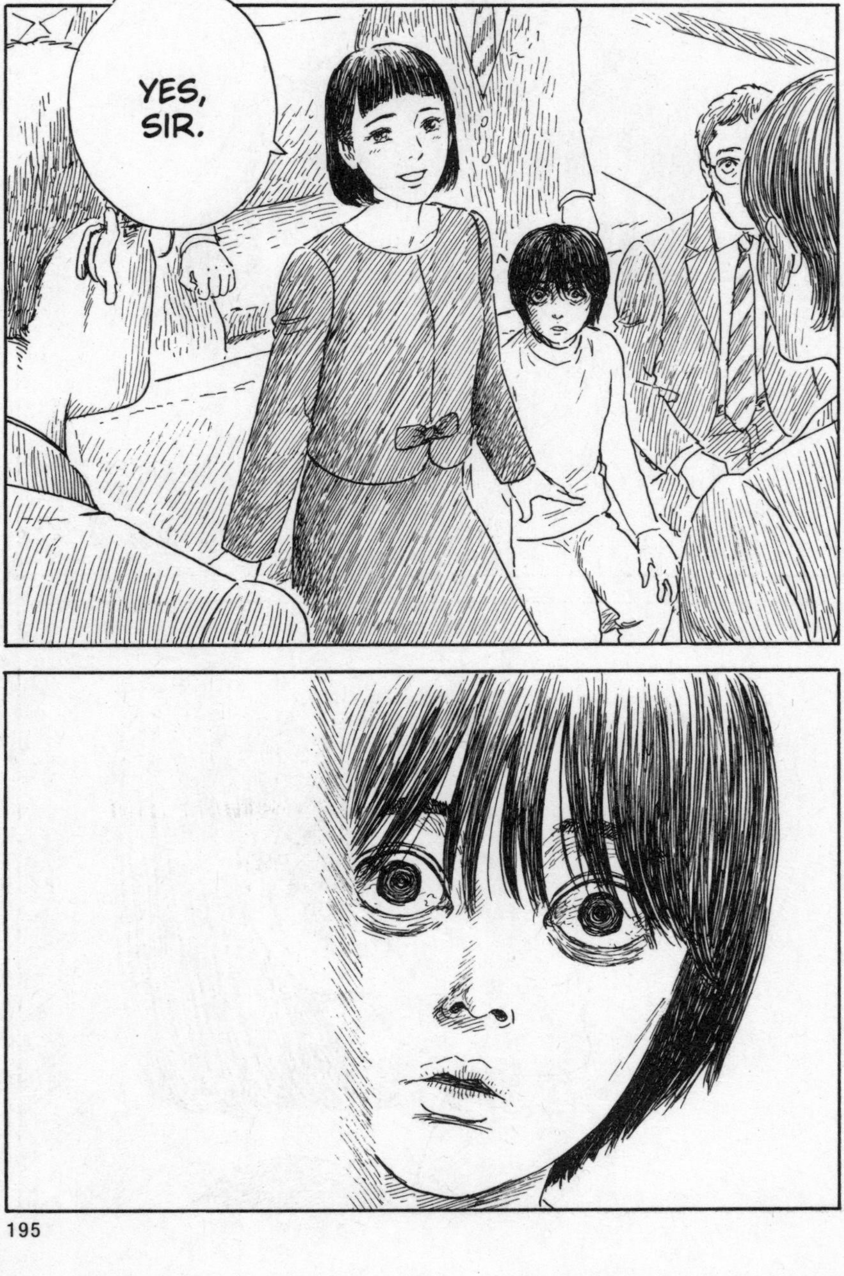
YES, SIR.

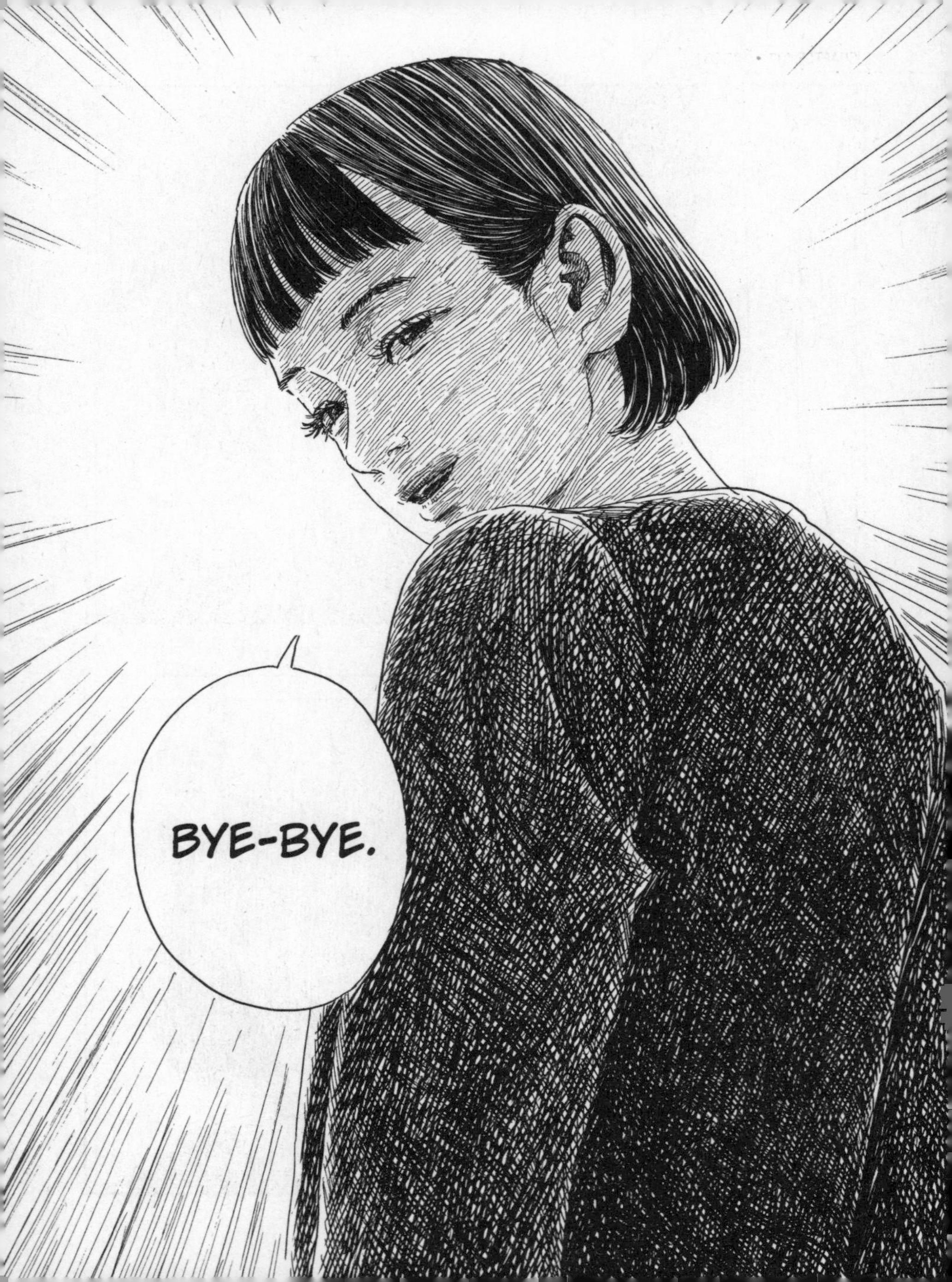
BYE-BYE.

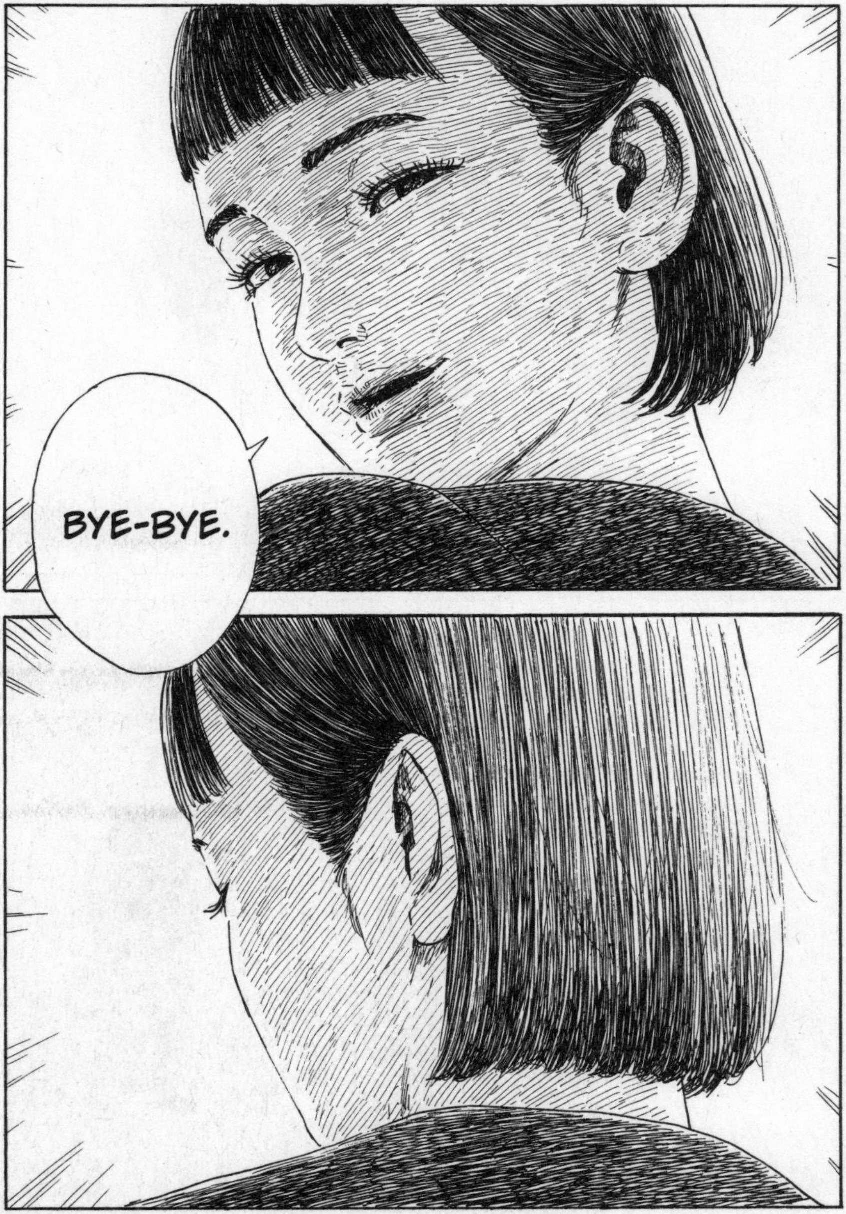
BYE-BYE.

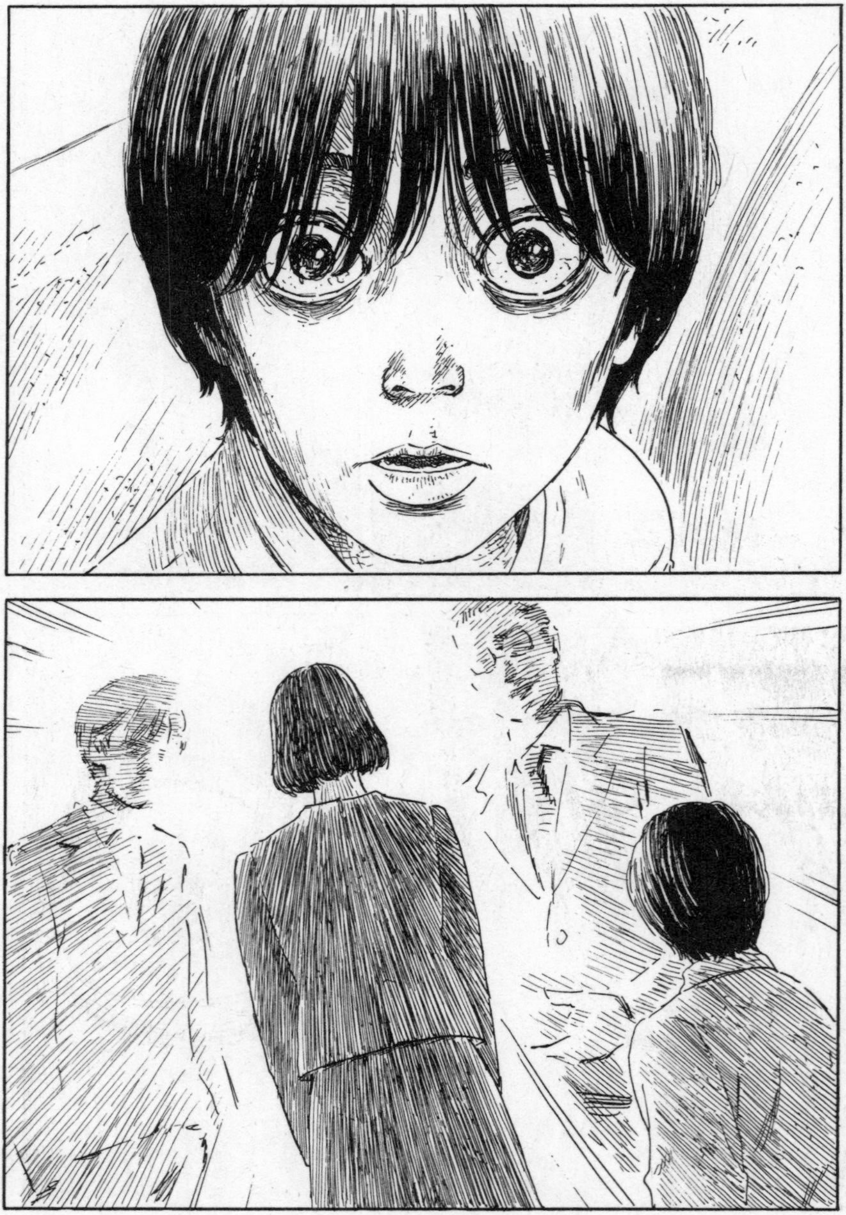

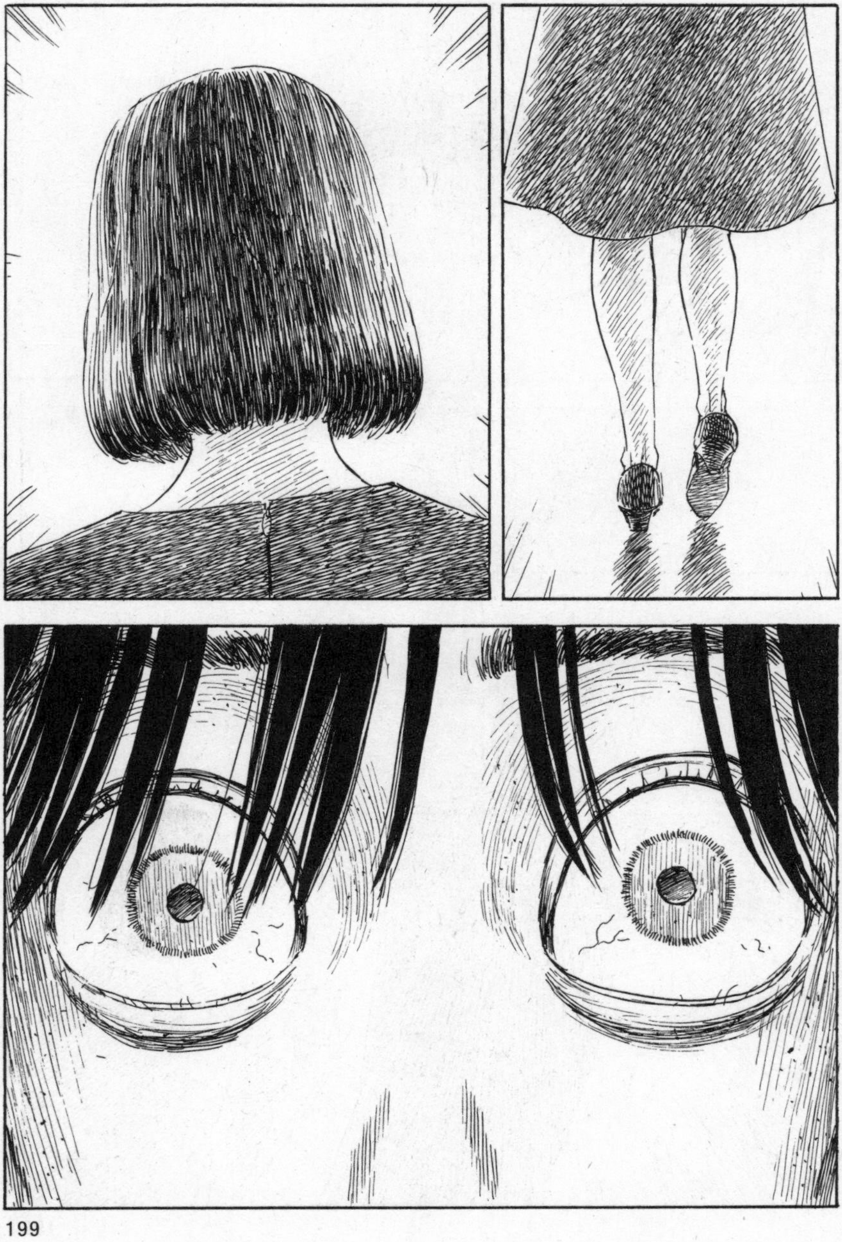

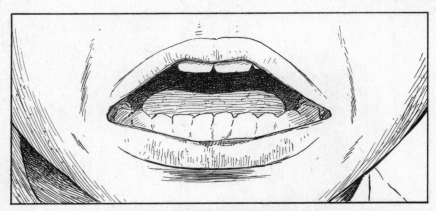

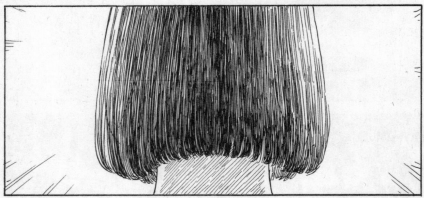

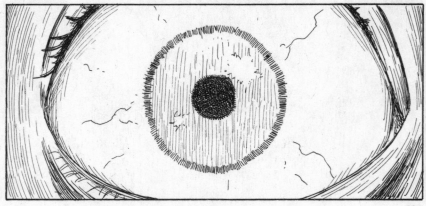

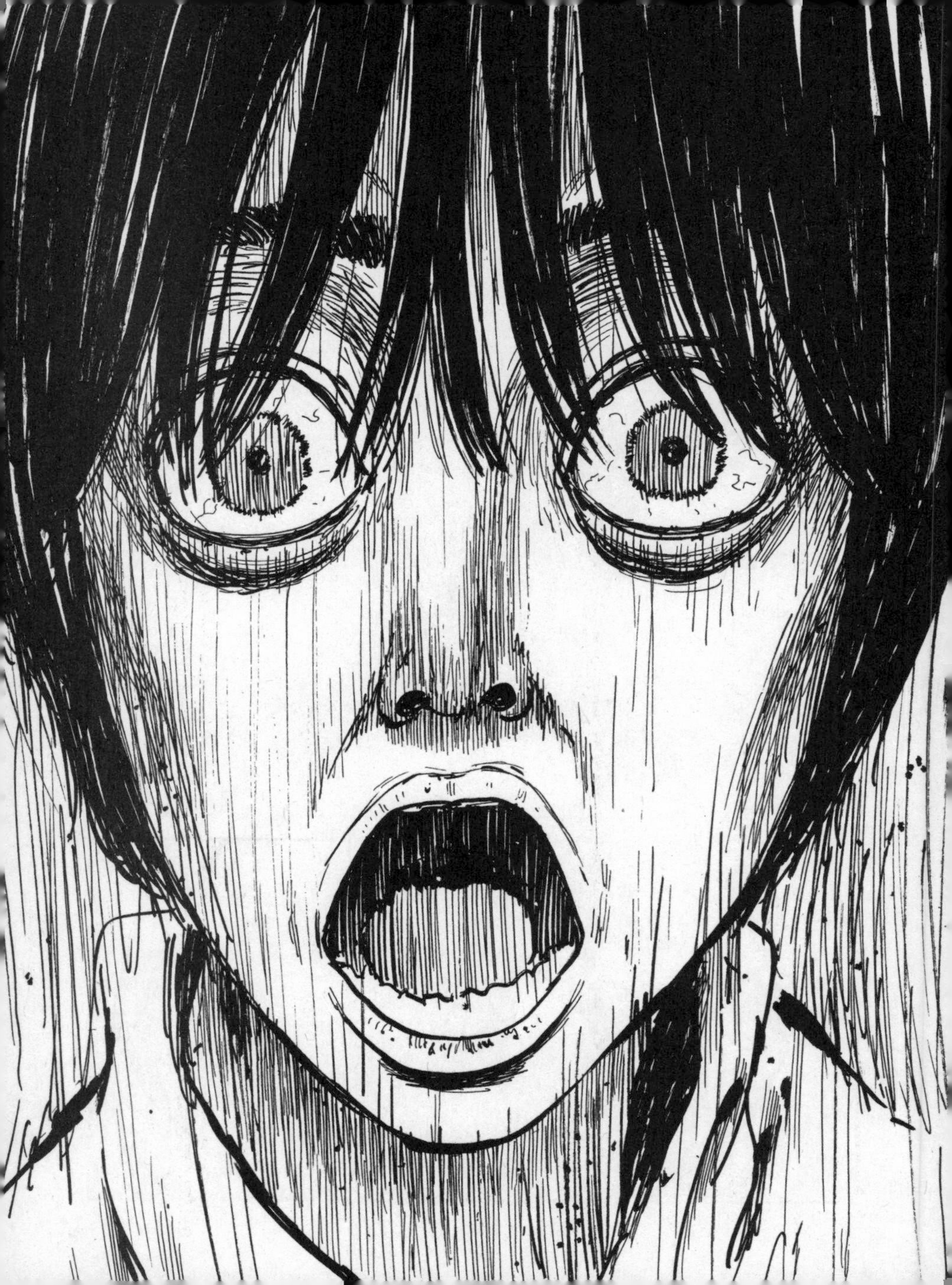

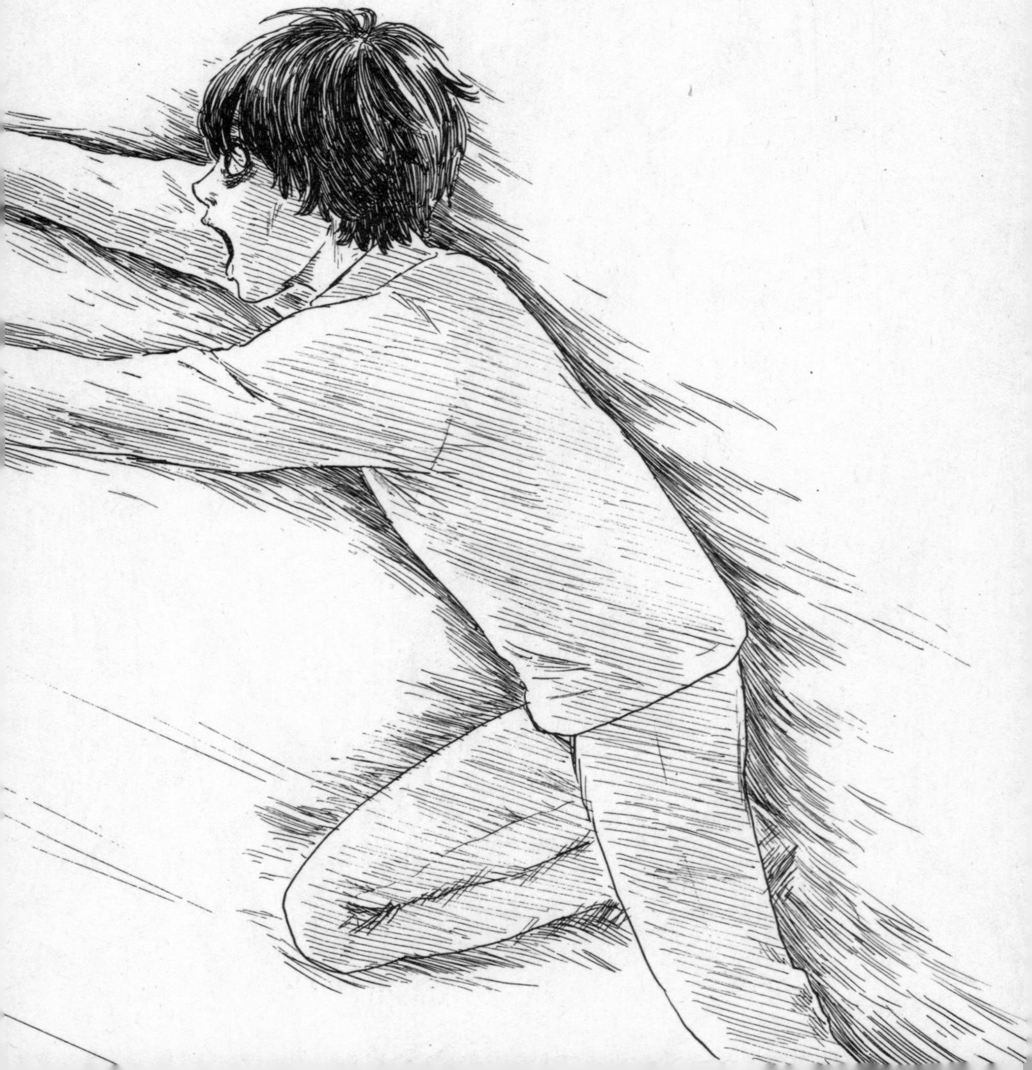

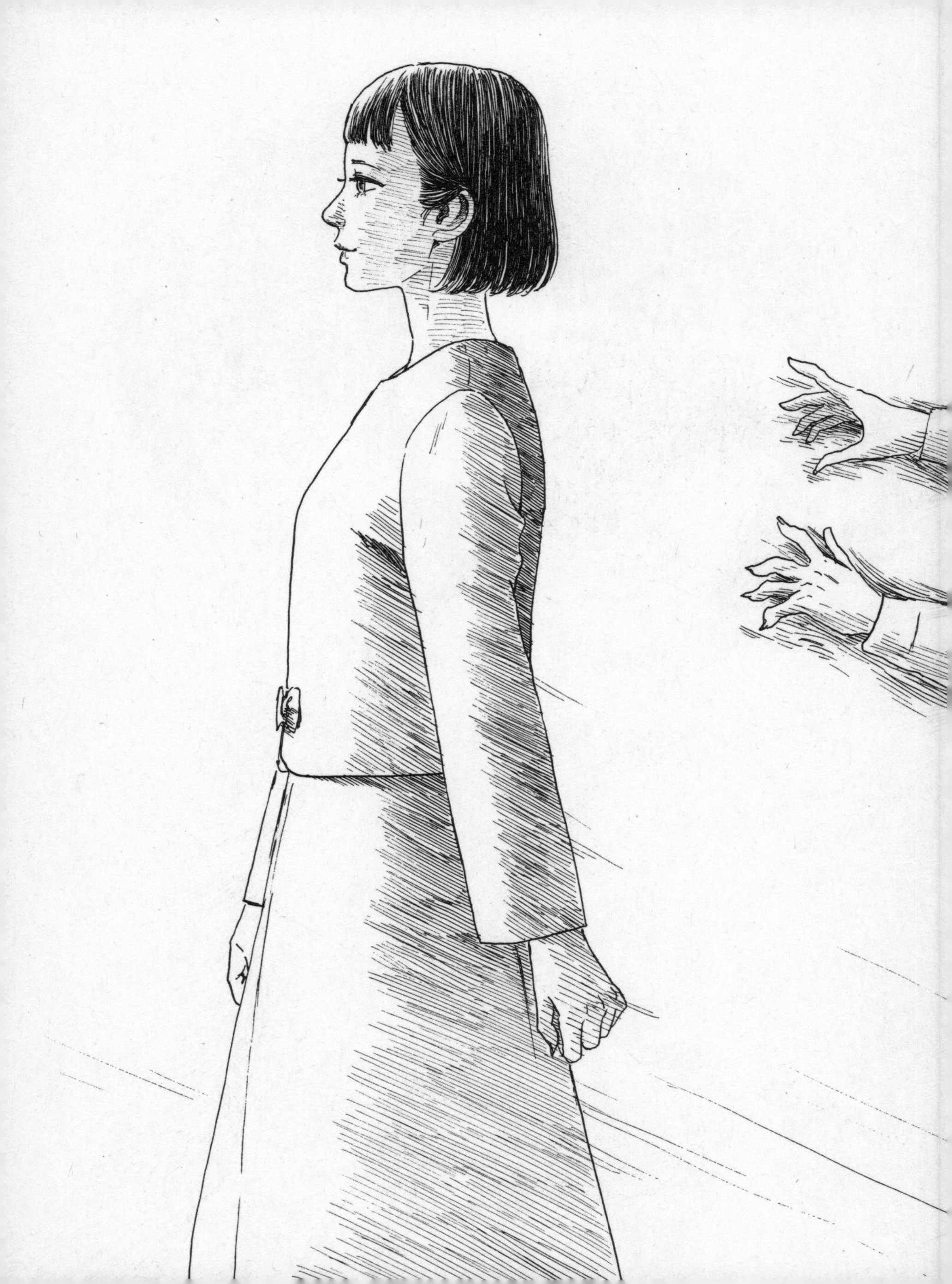

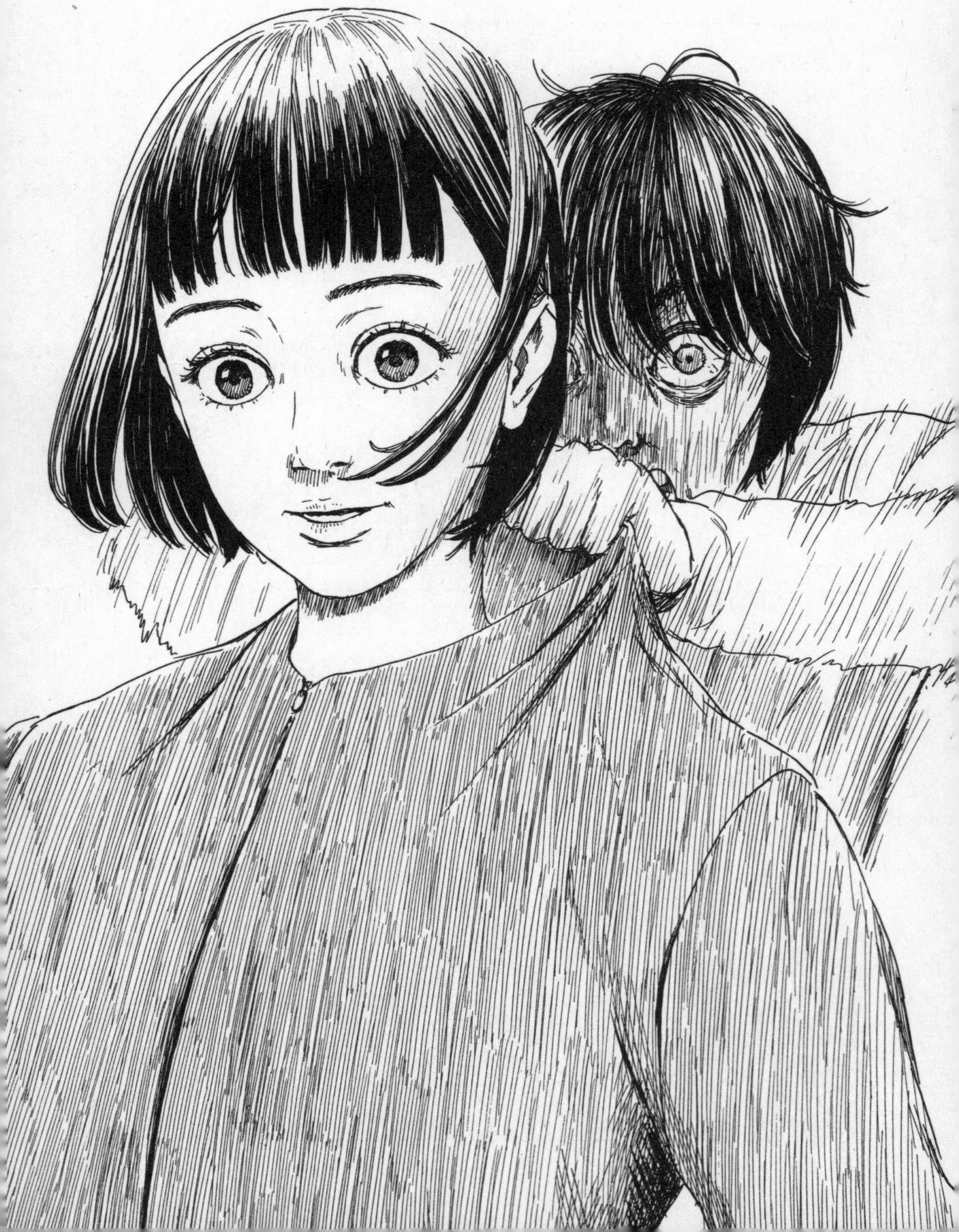

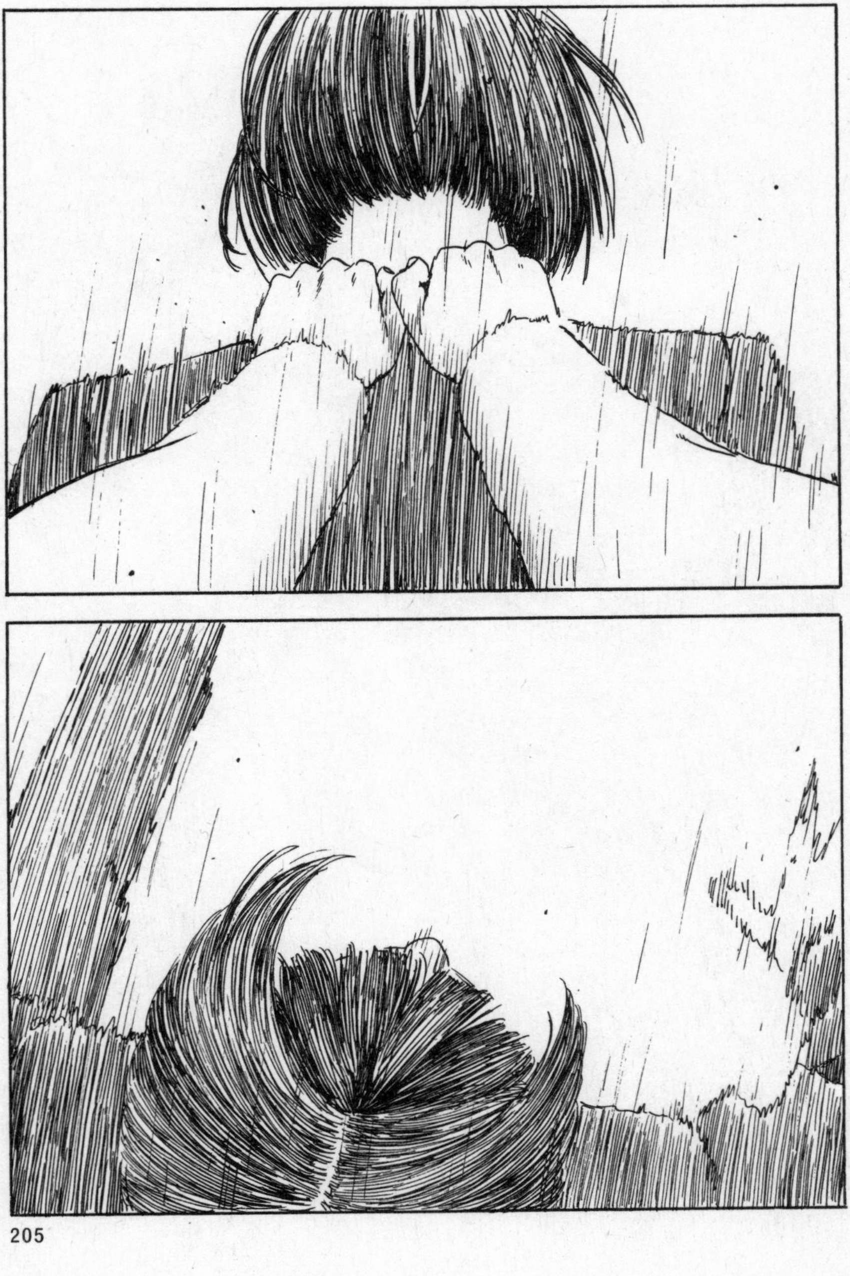

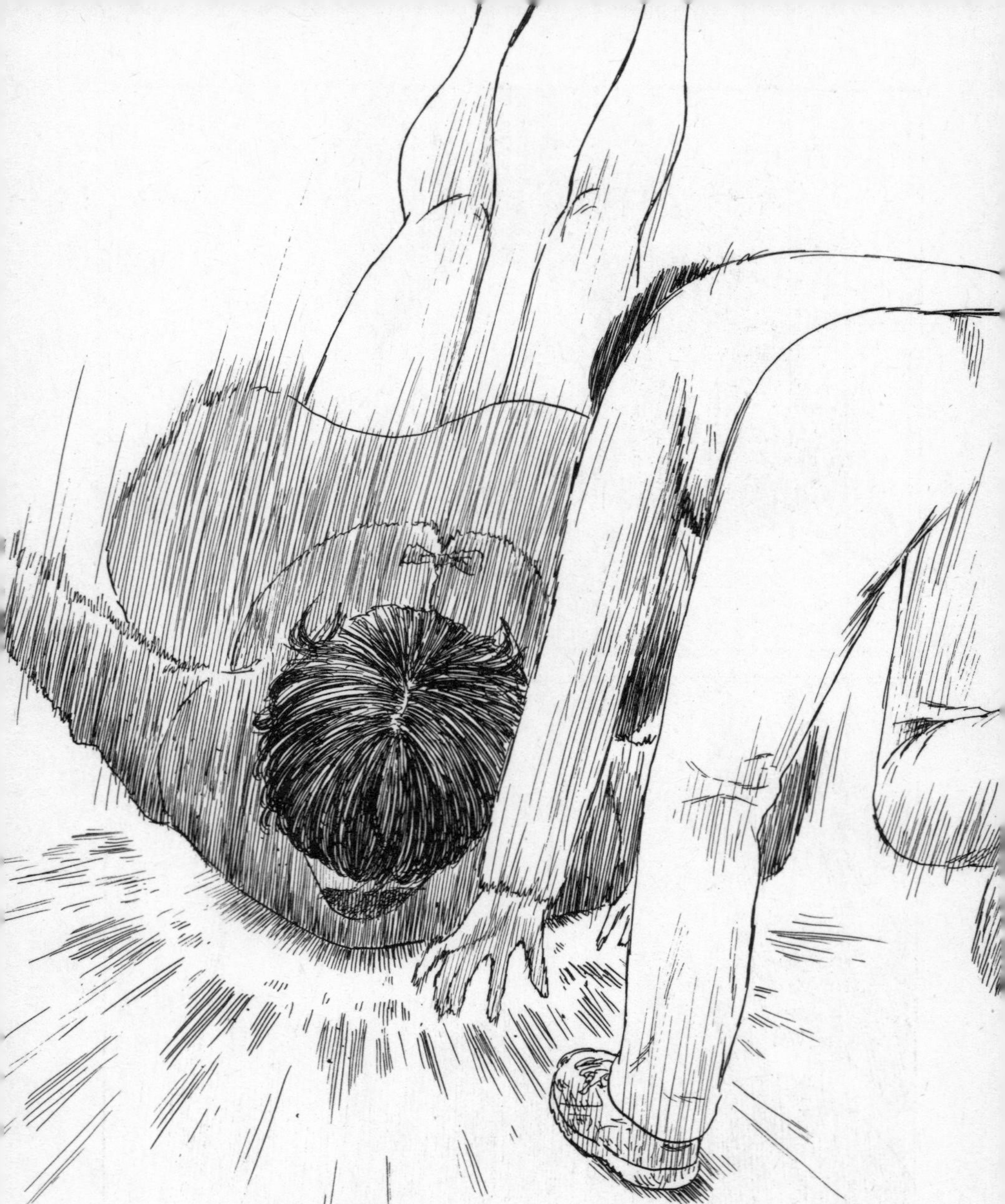

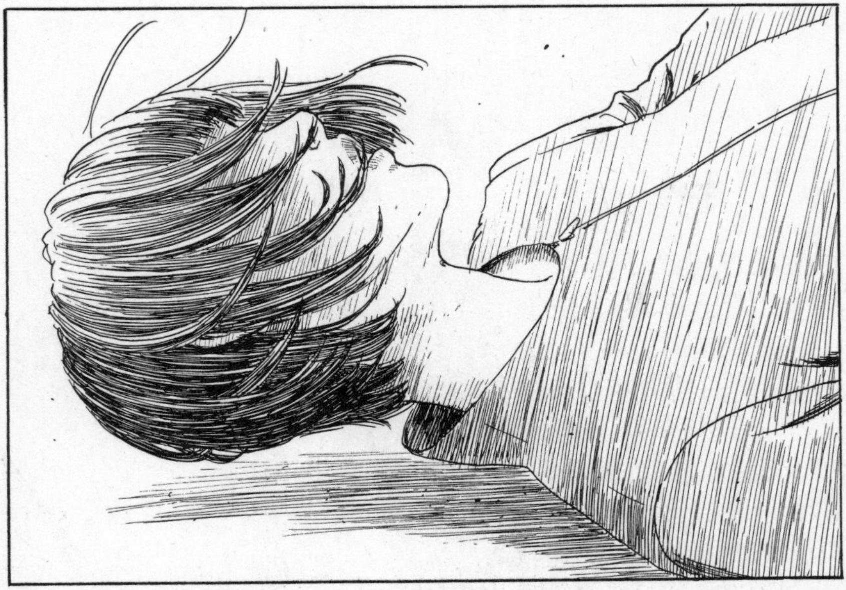

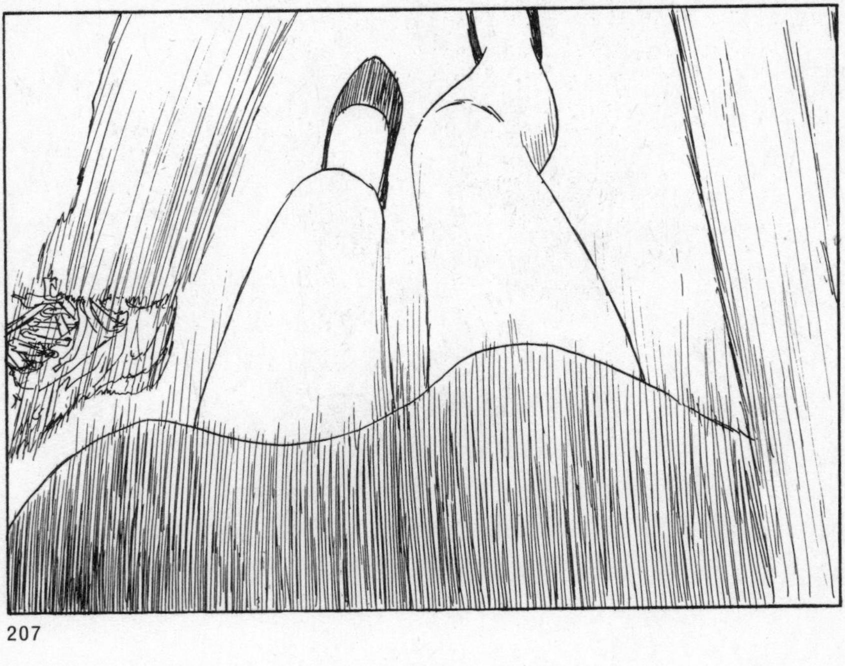

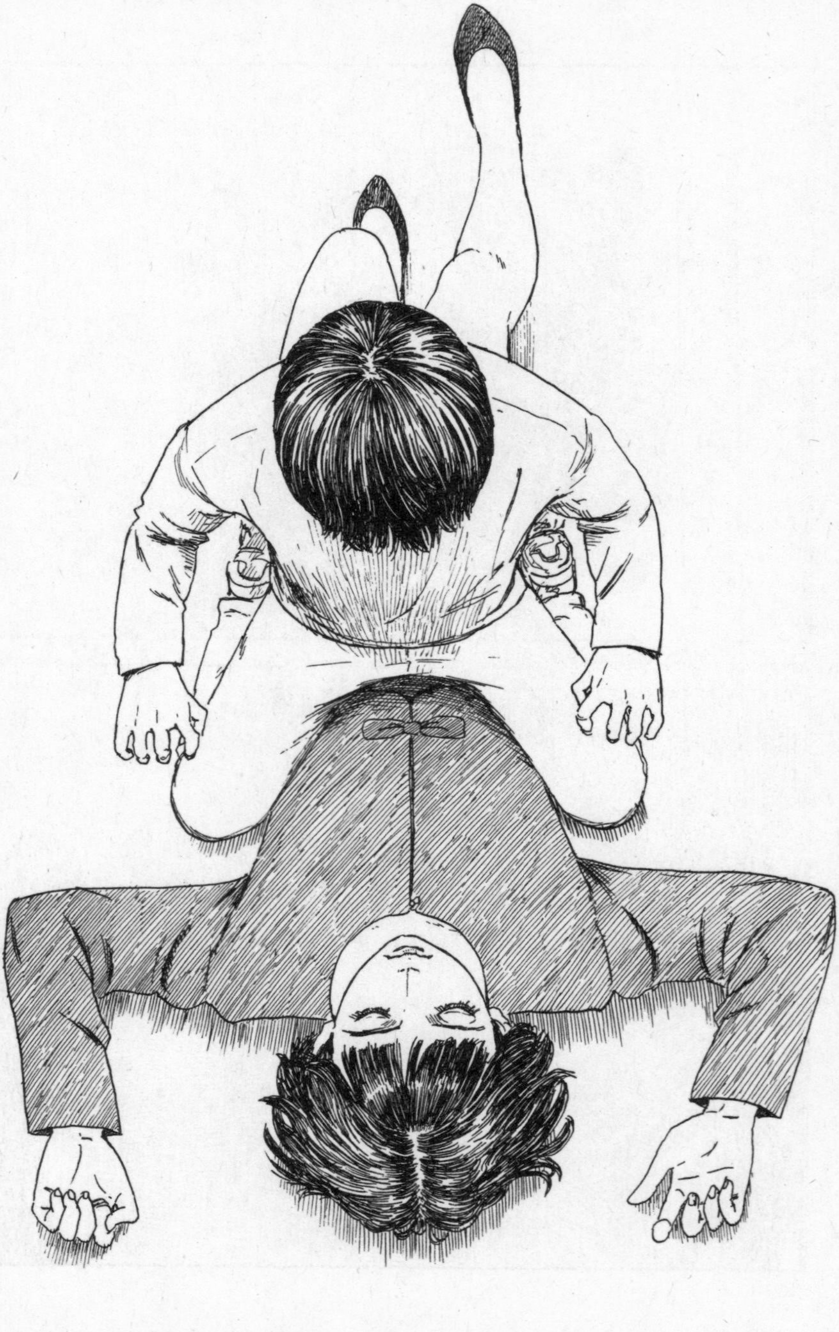

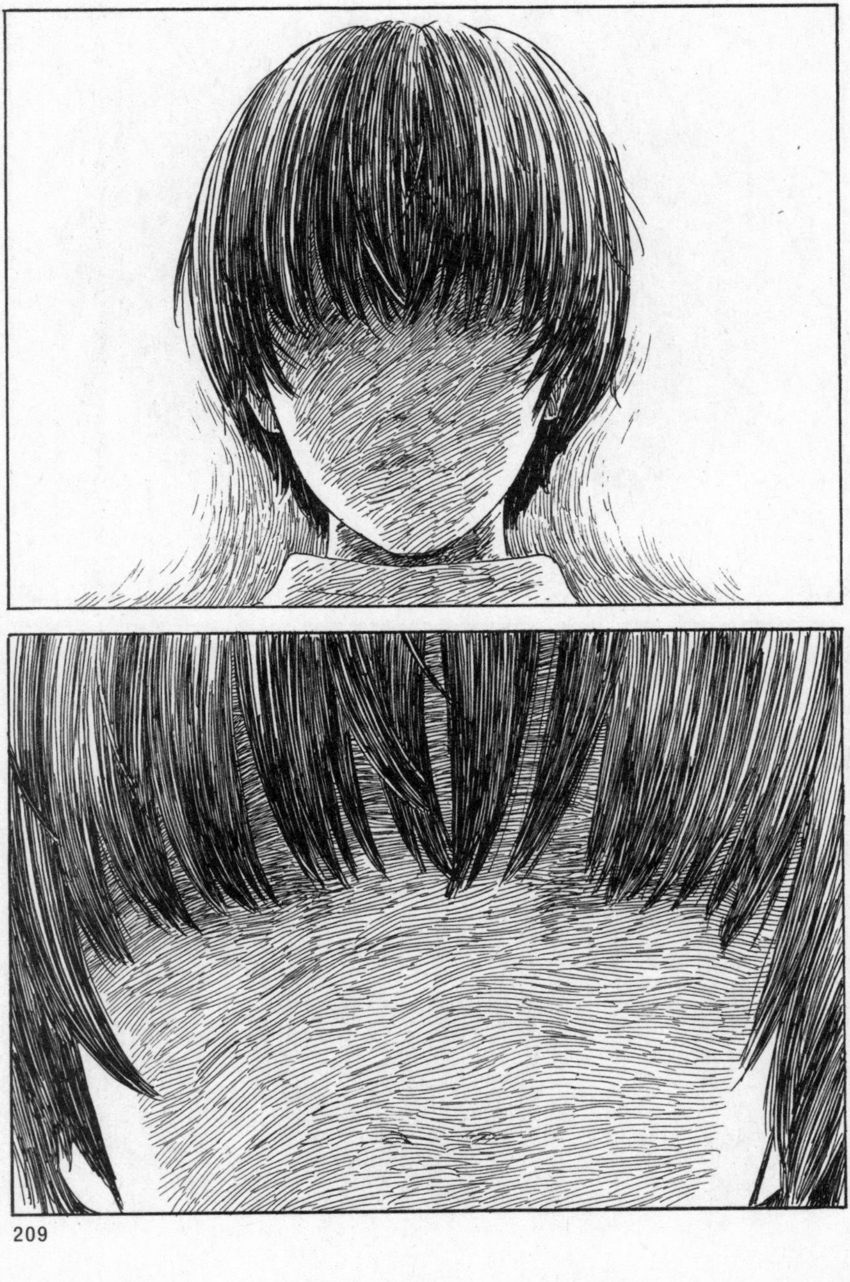

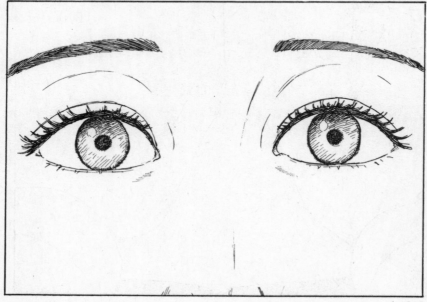

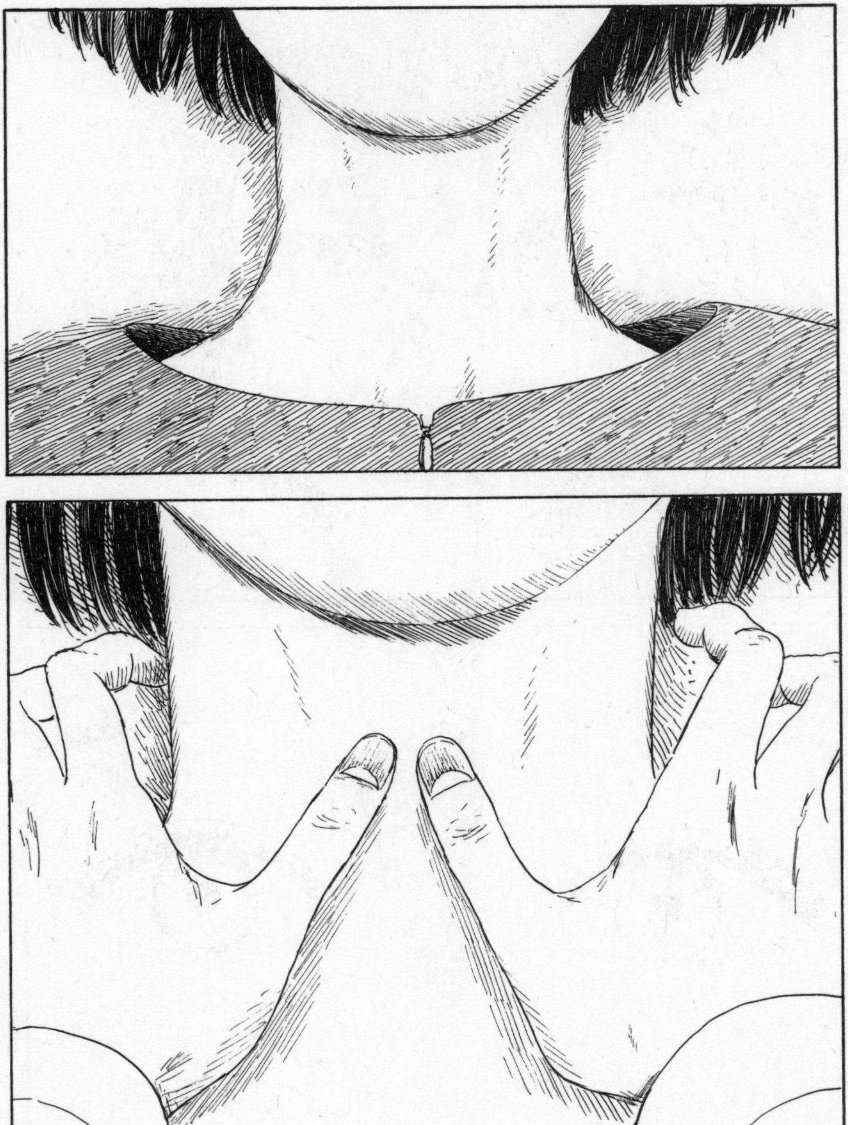

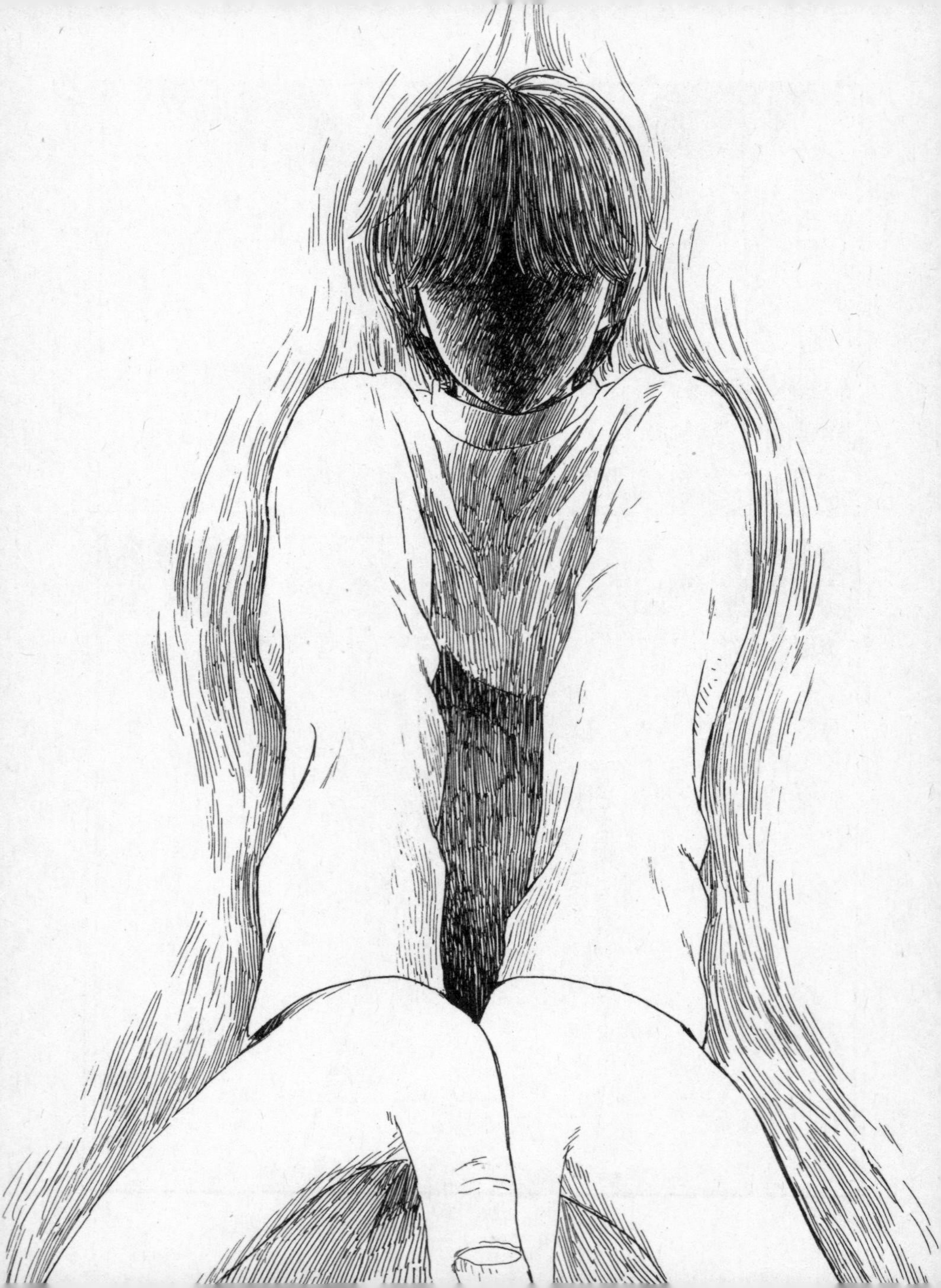

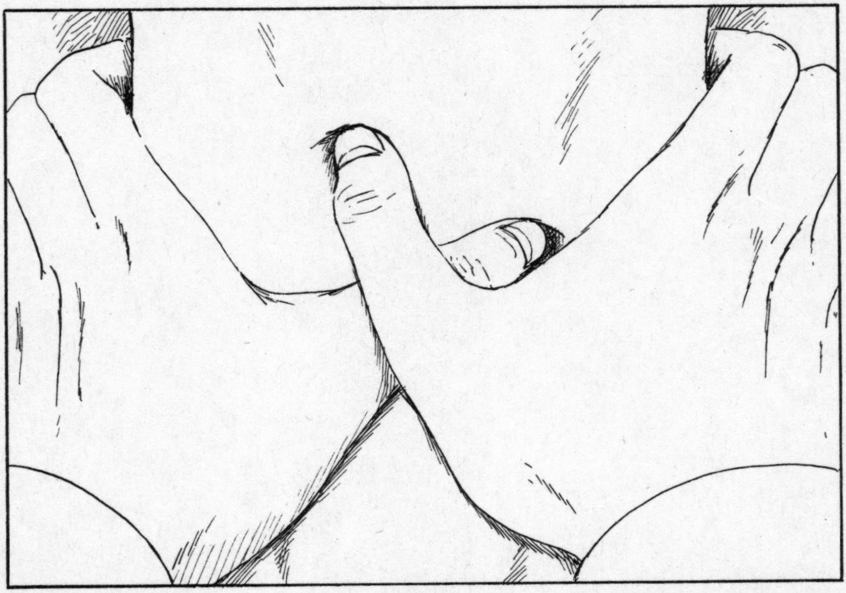
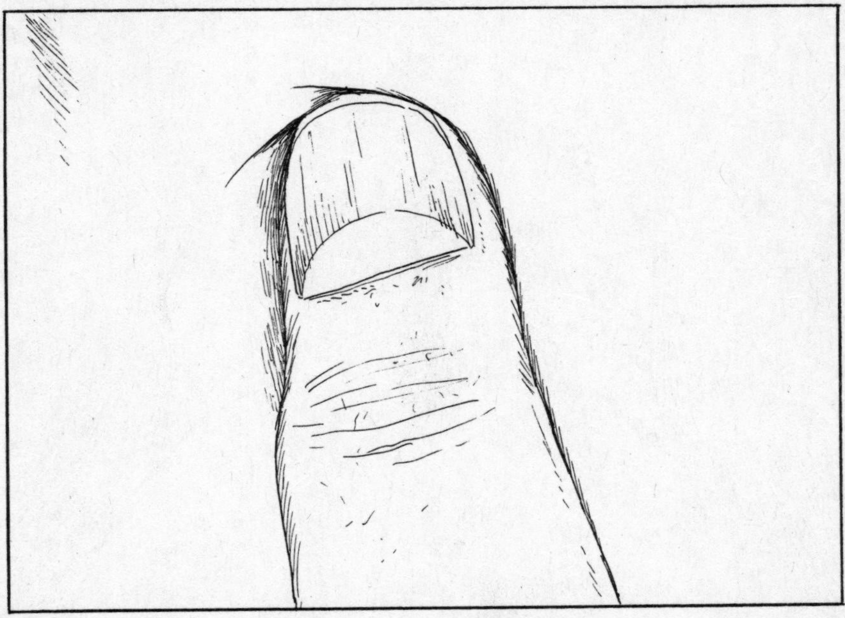

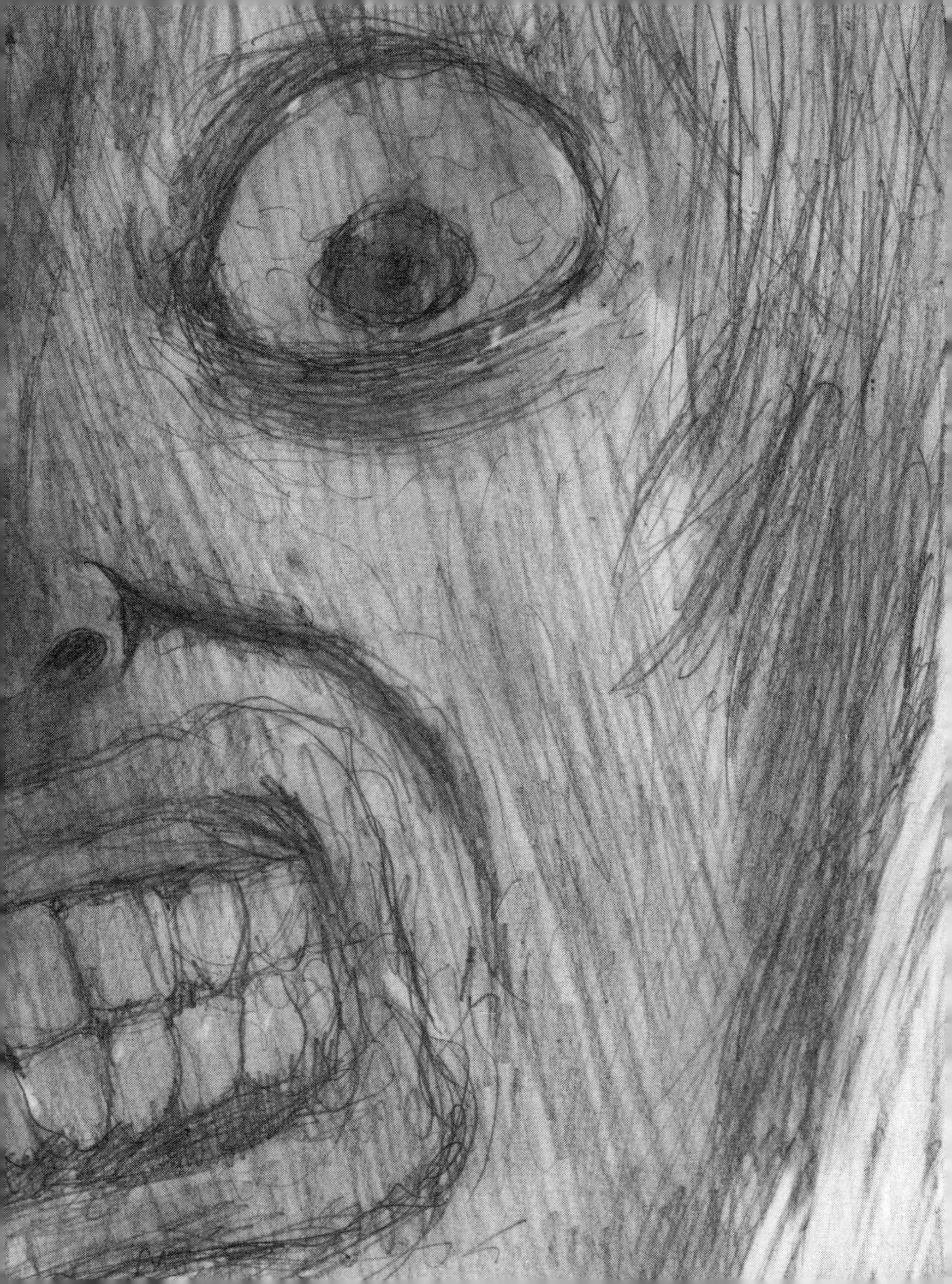

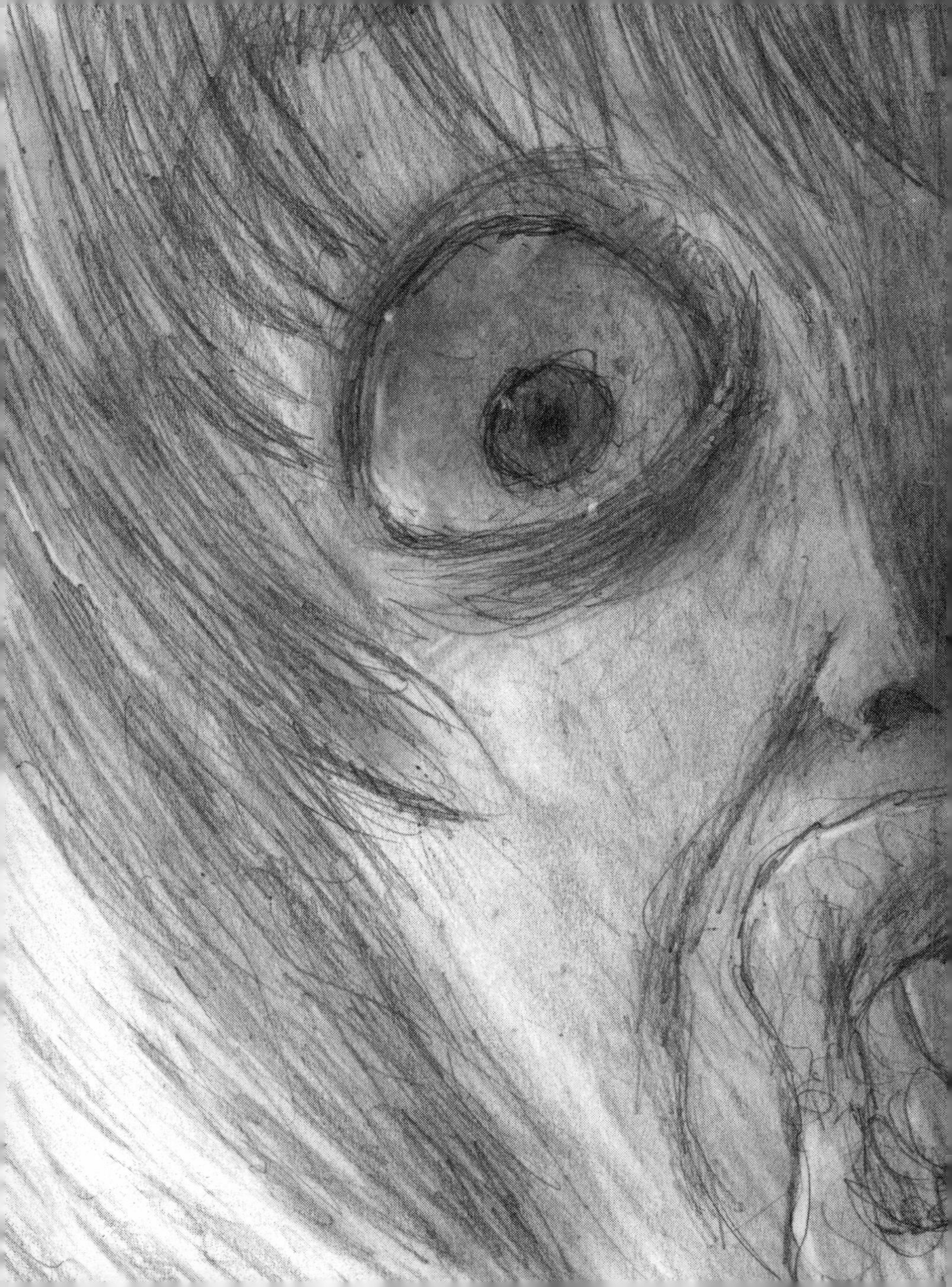

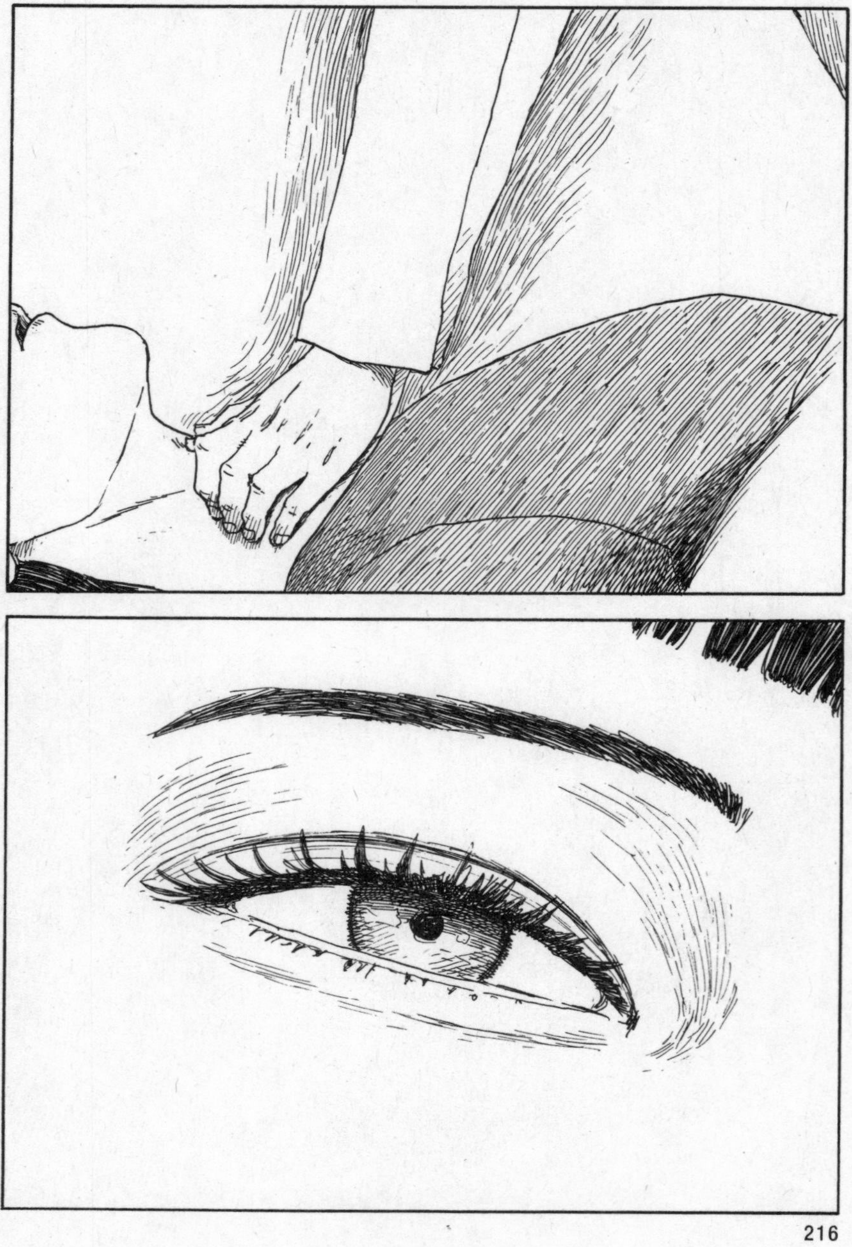

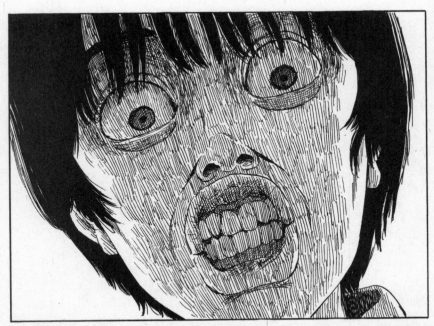

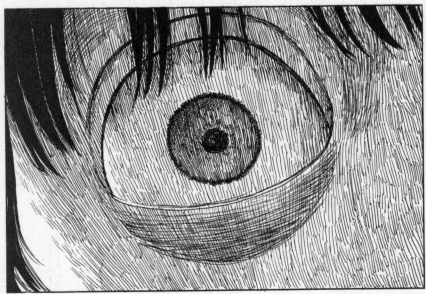

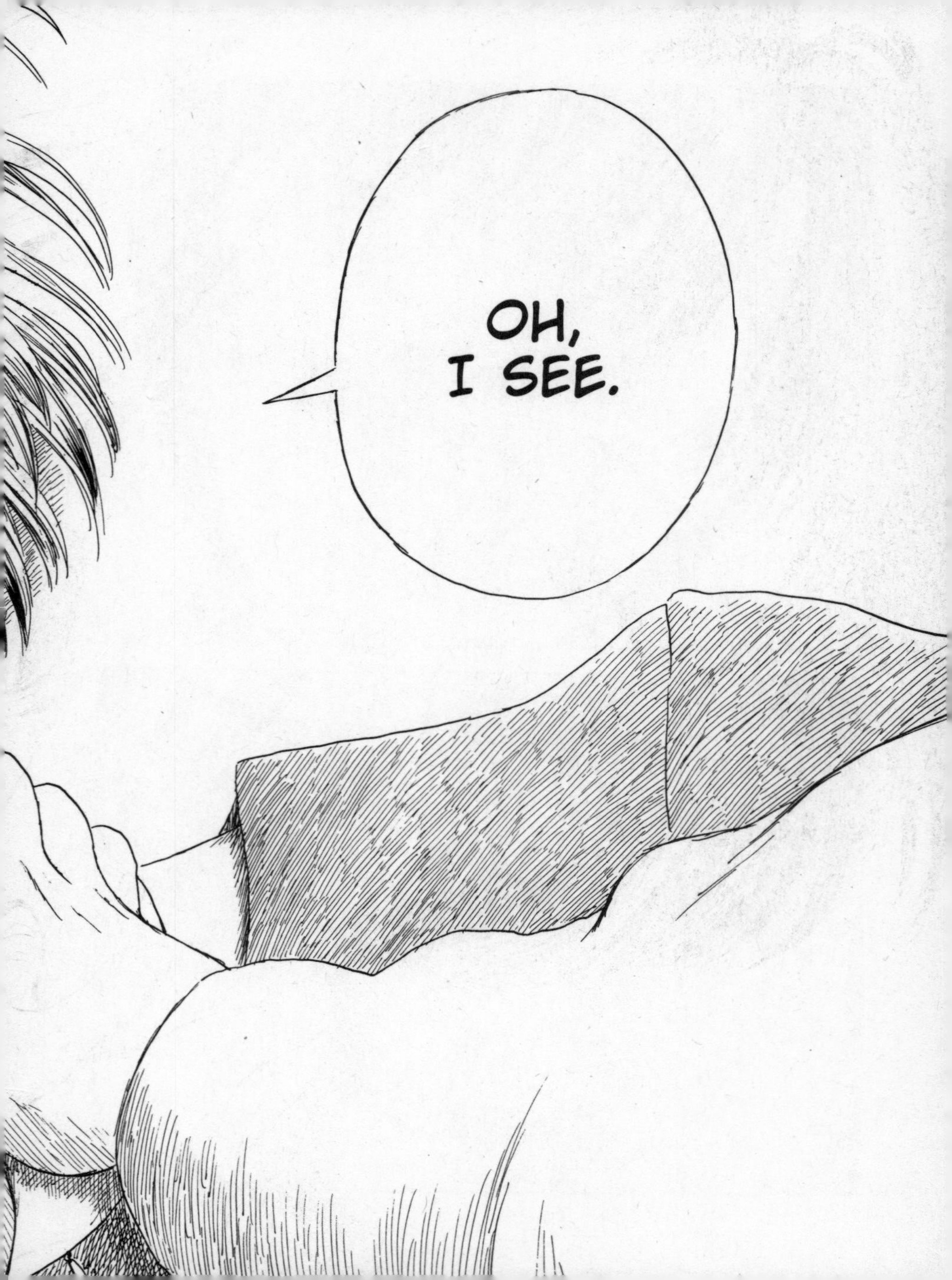
OH, I SEE.

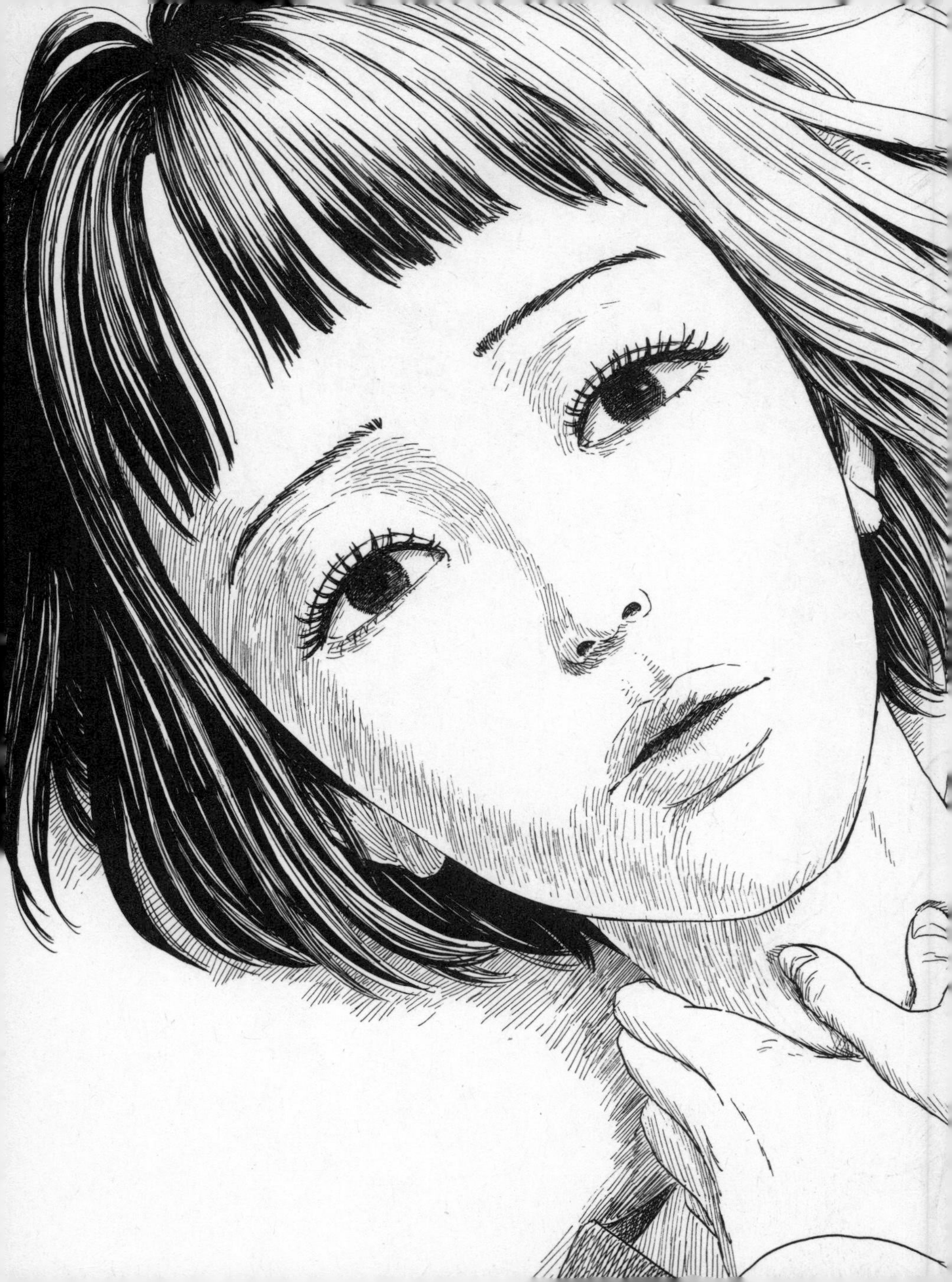

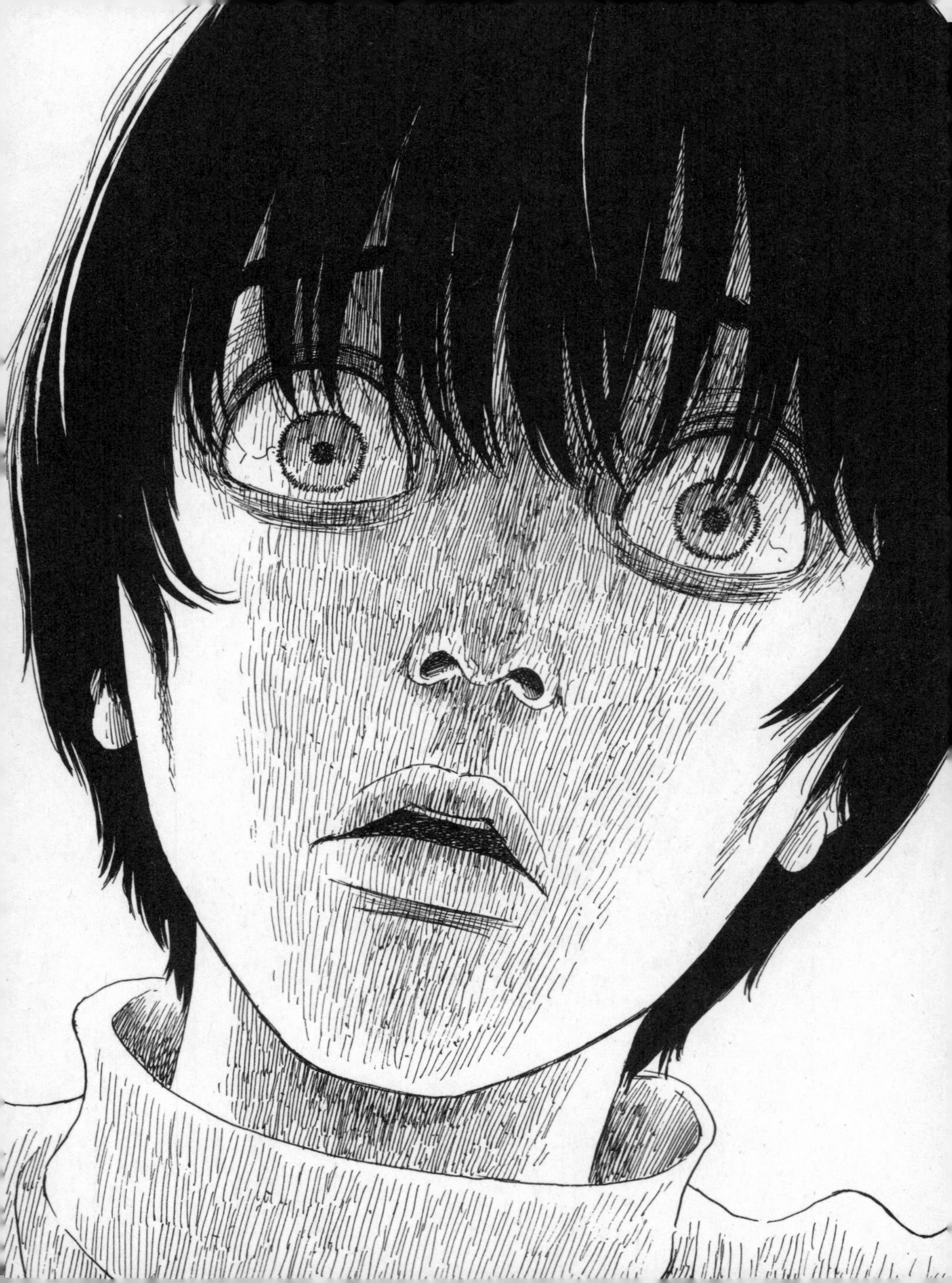

CHAPTER 108 Disposition

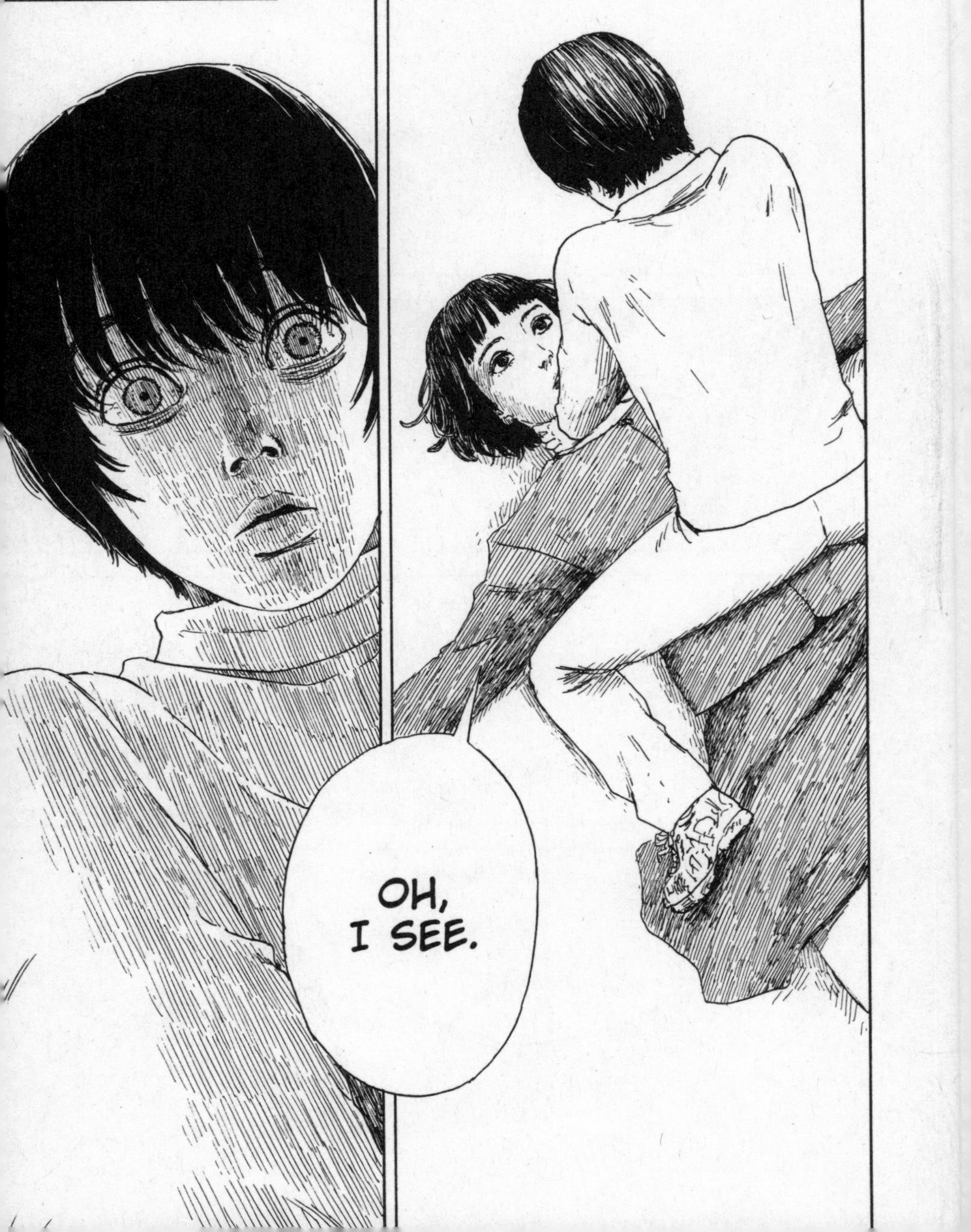
OH, I SEE.

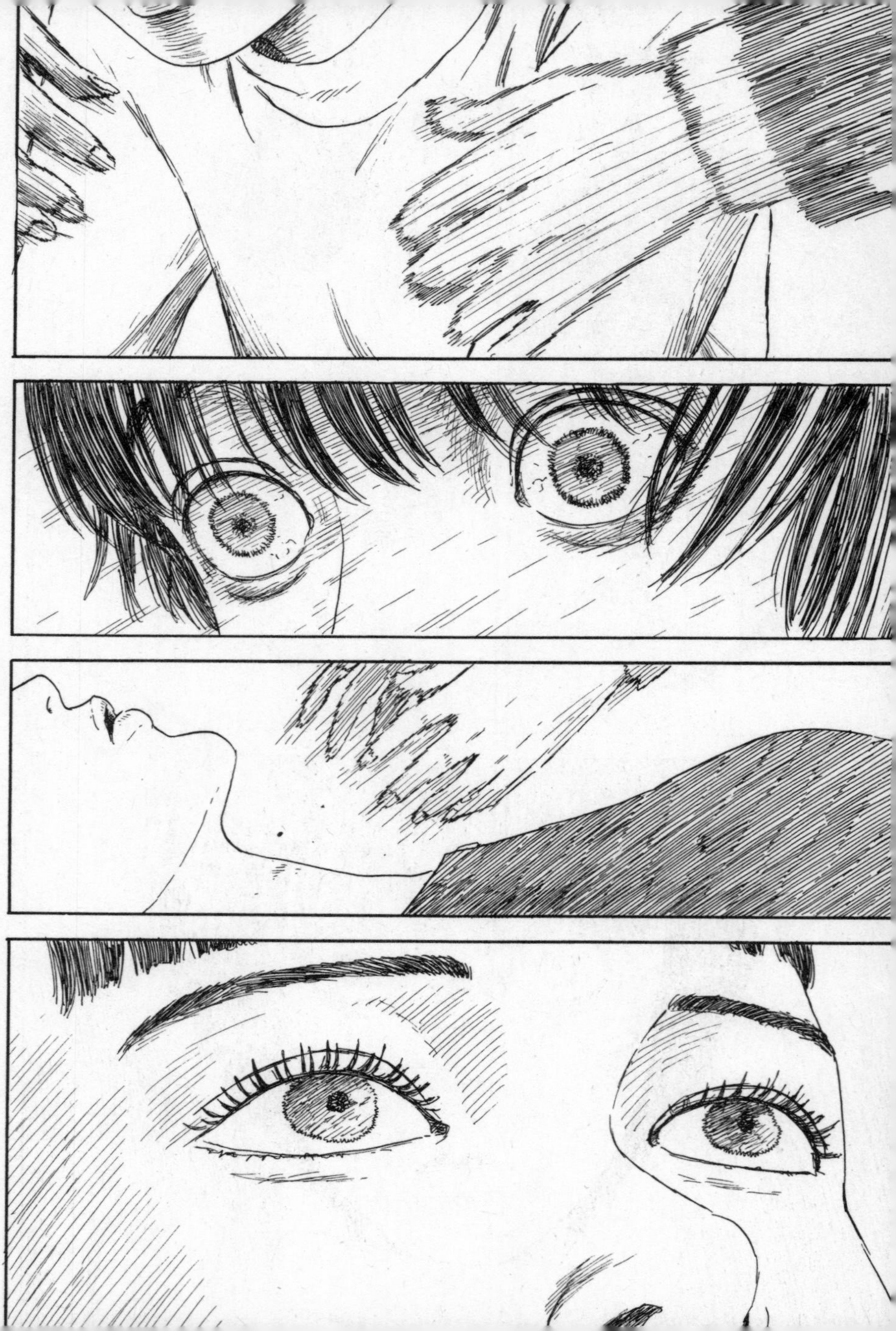

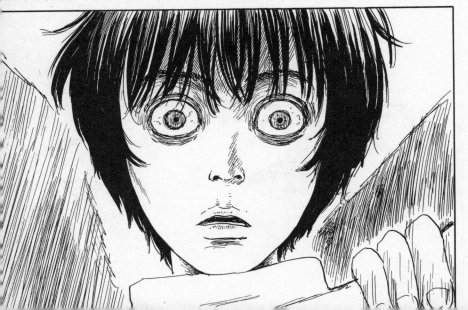

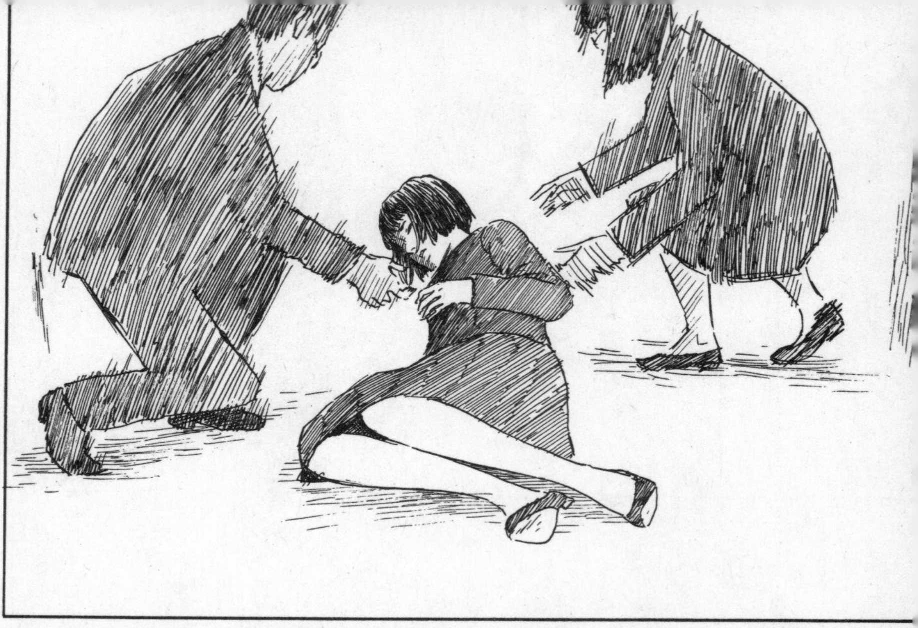

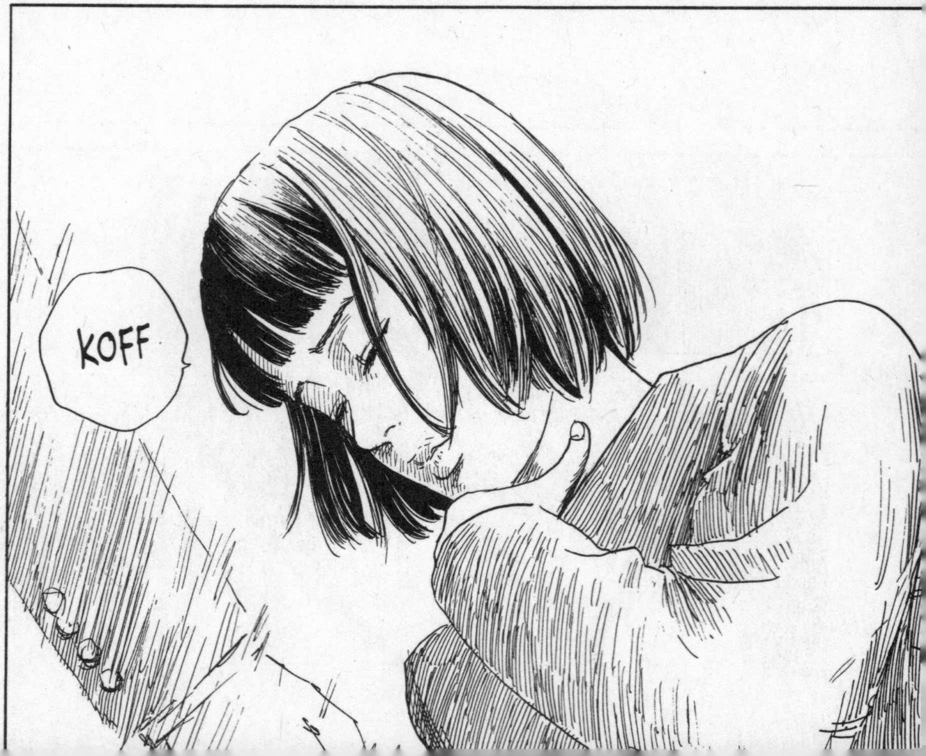
KOFF

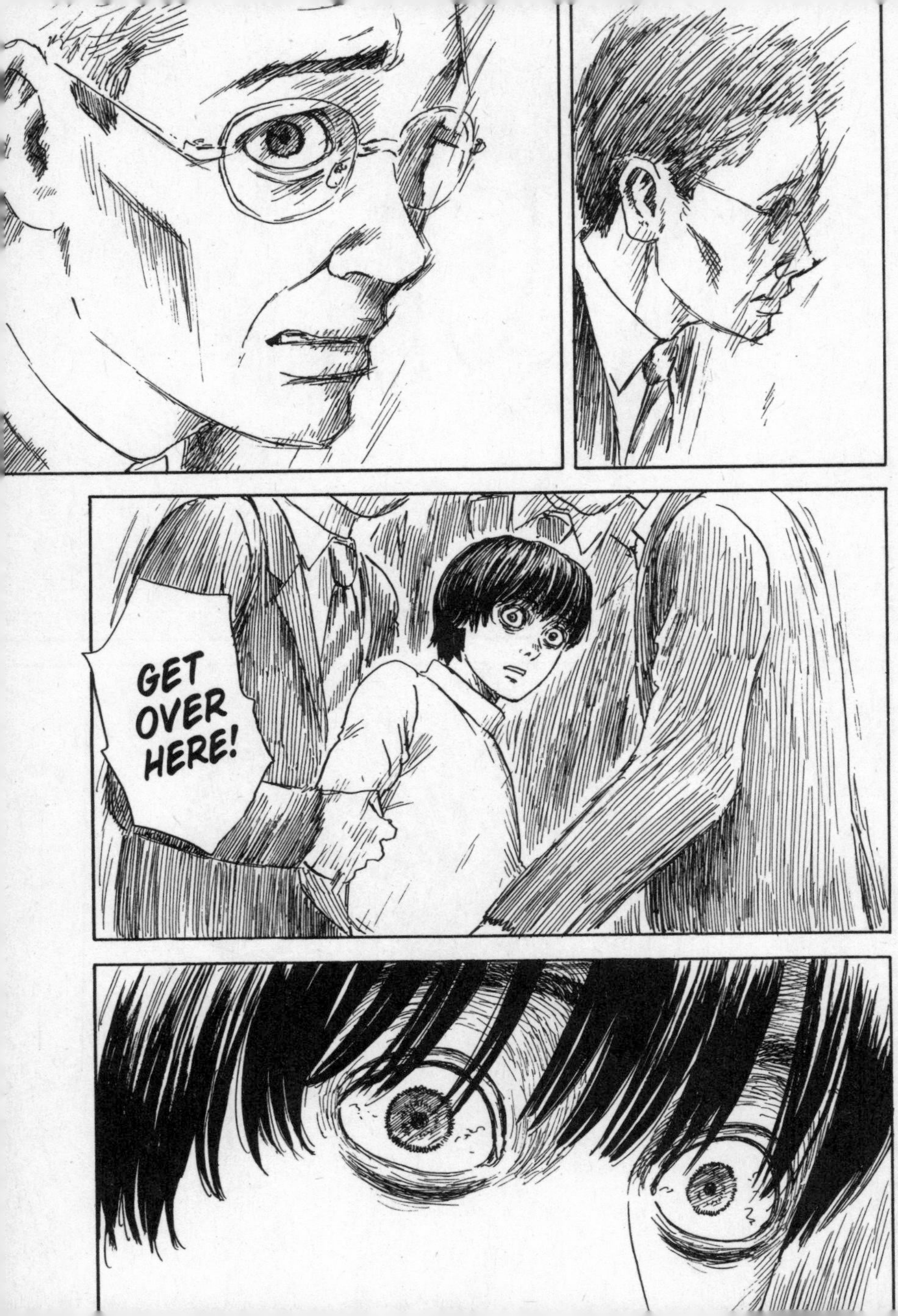
GET OVER HERE!

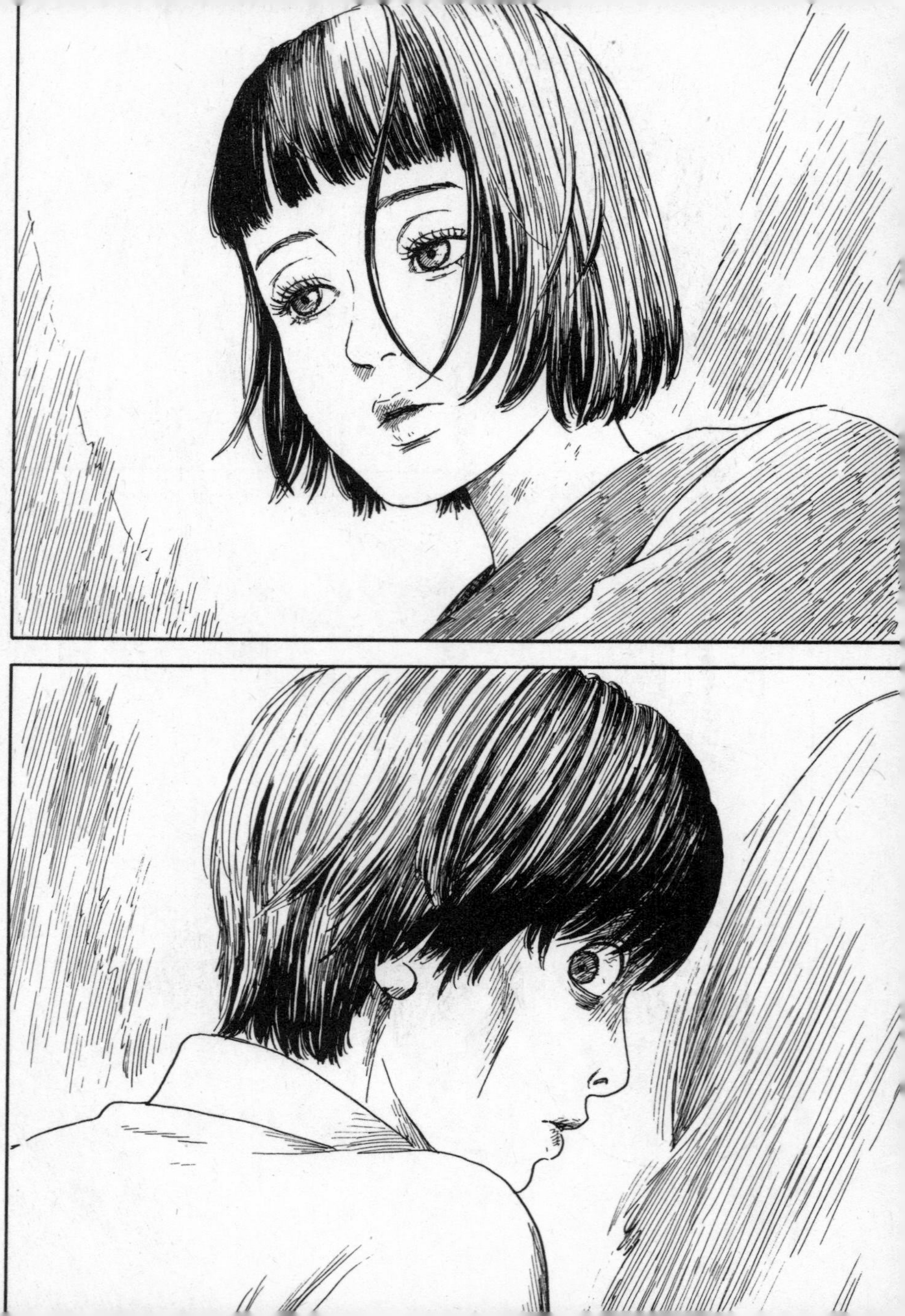

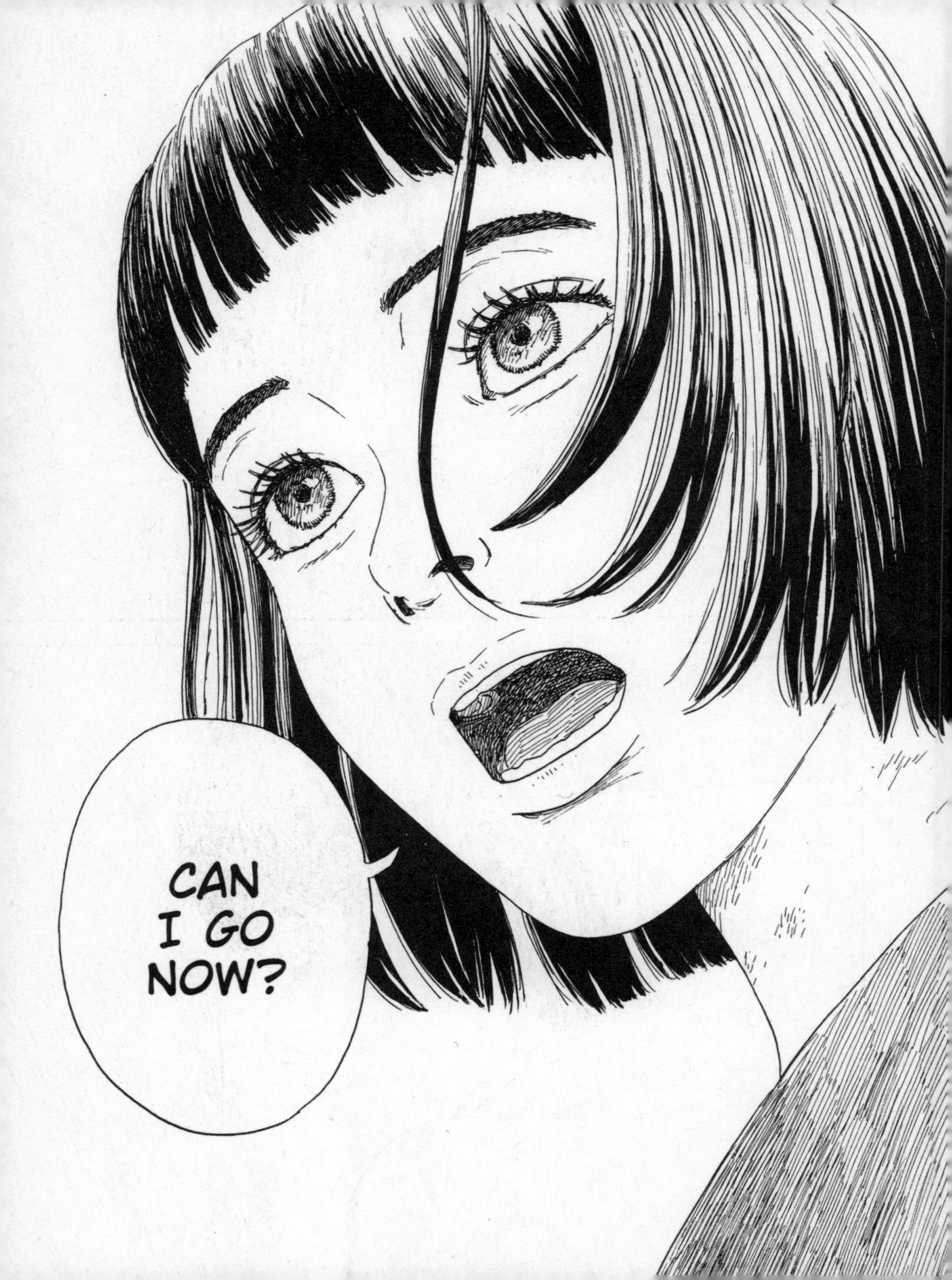
CAN I GO NOW?

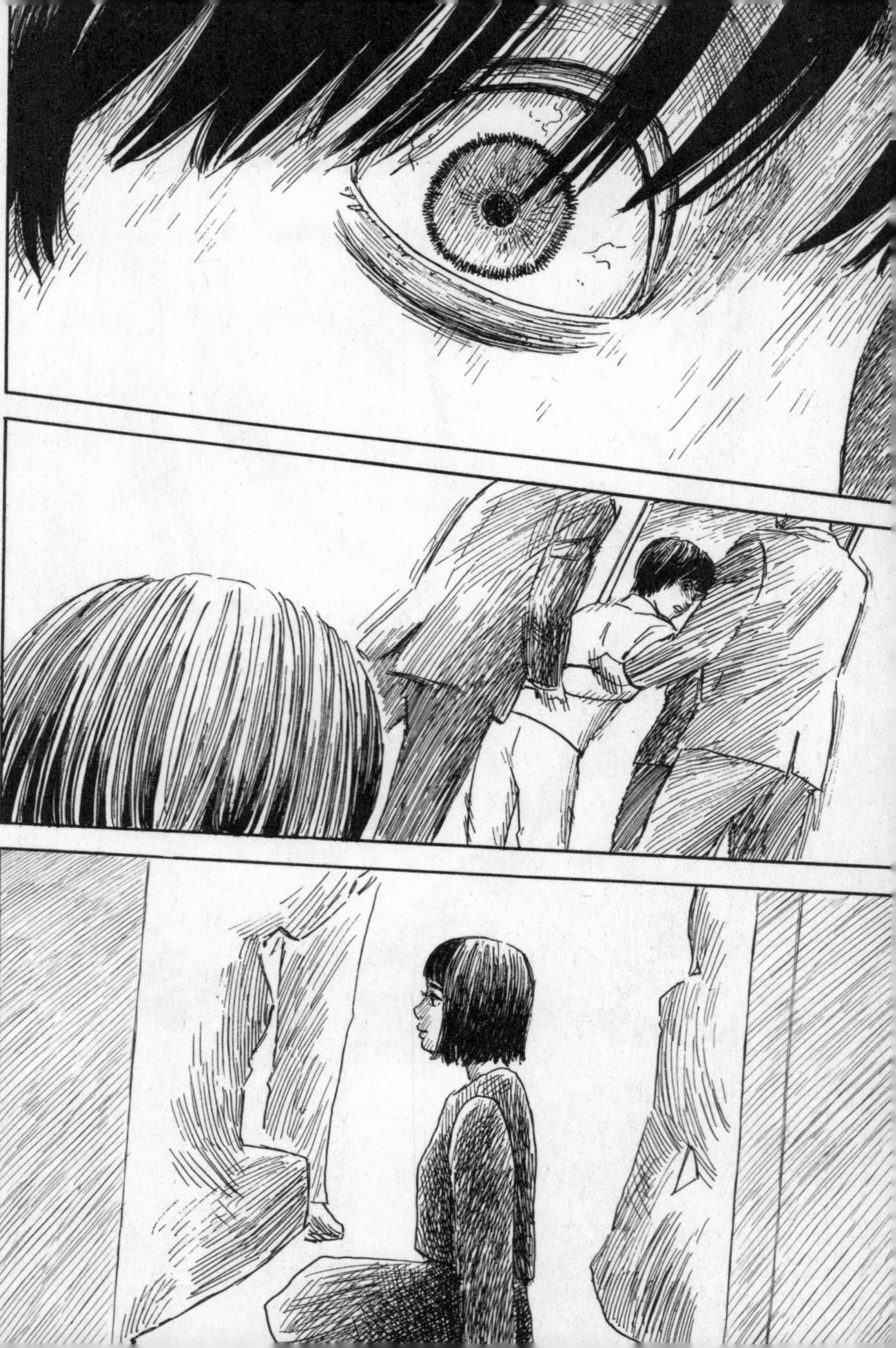

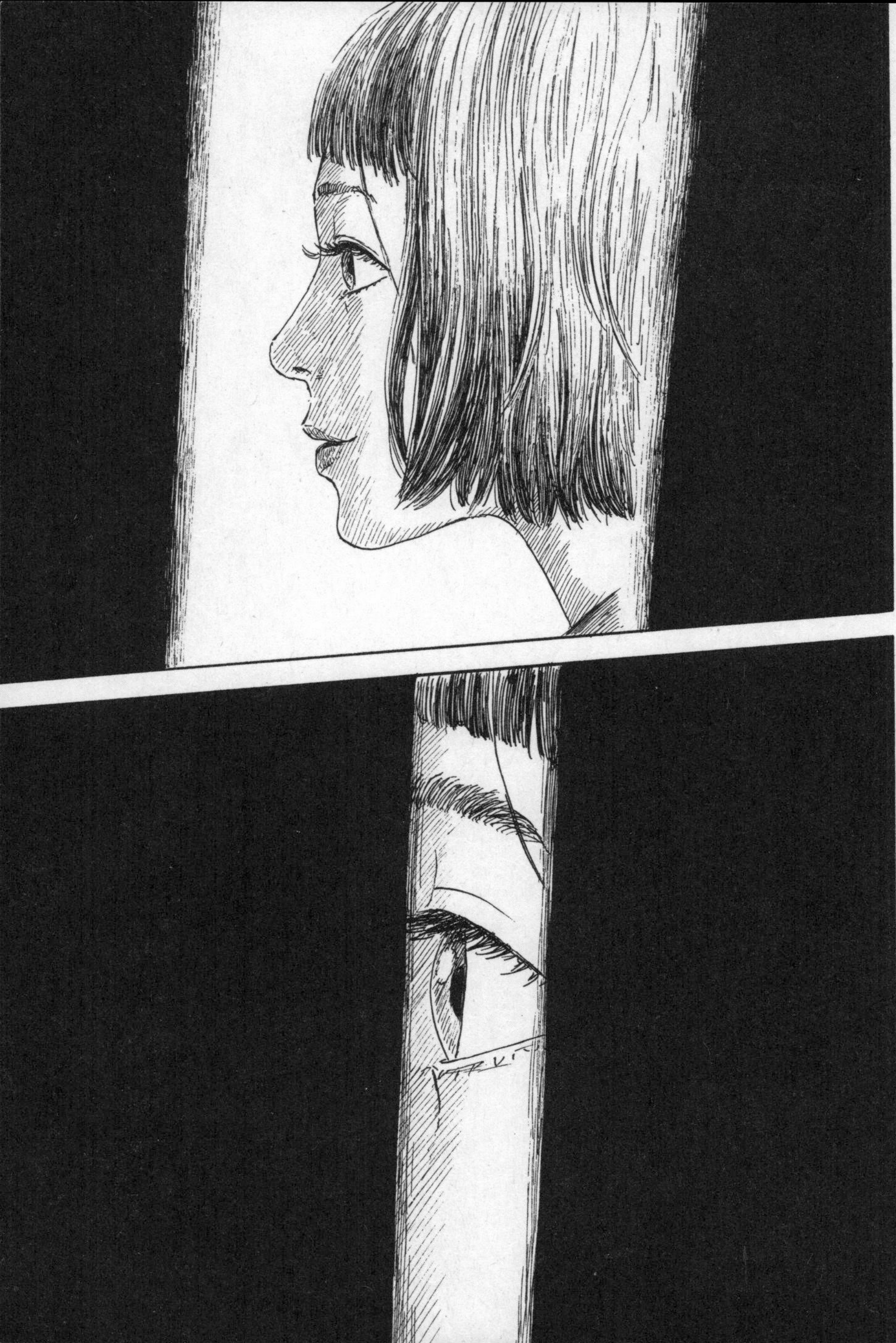

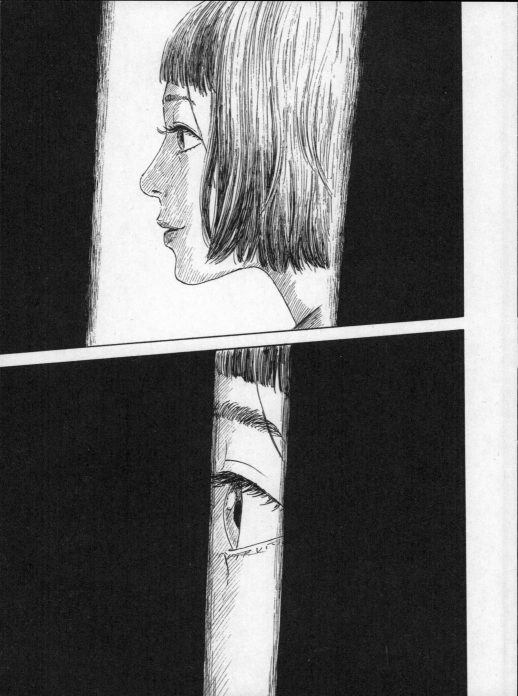

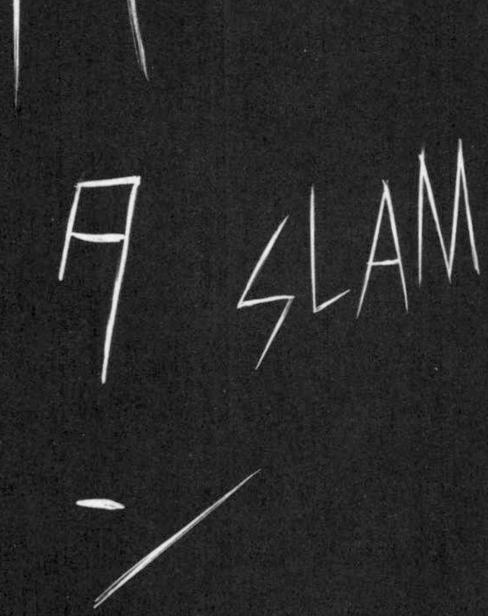
SLAM

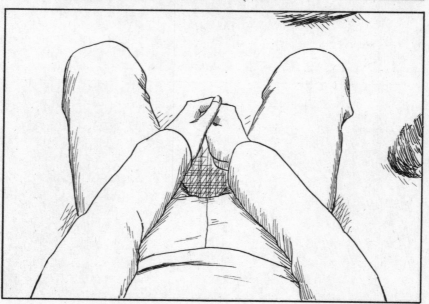

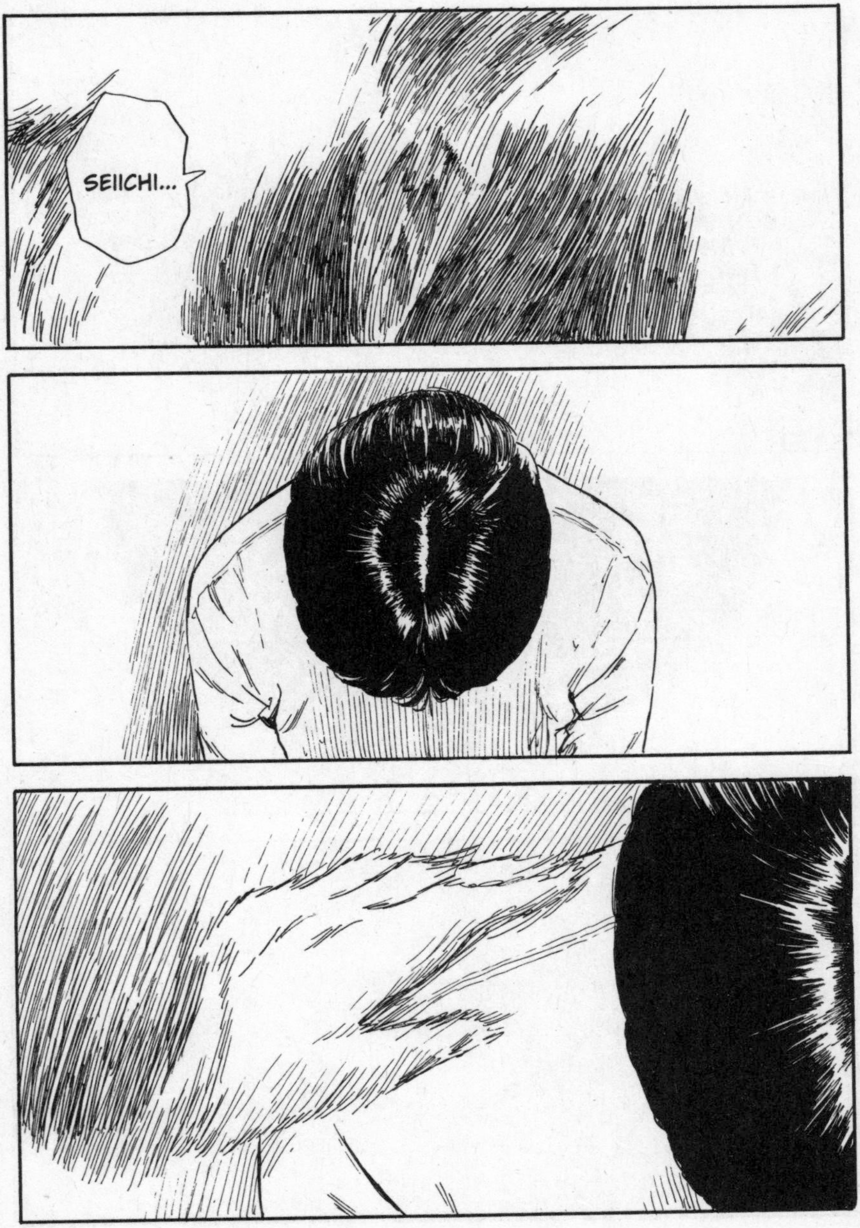
SEIICHI...

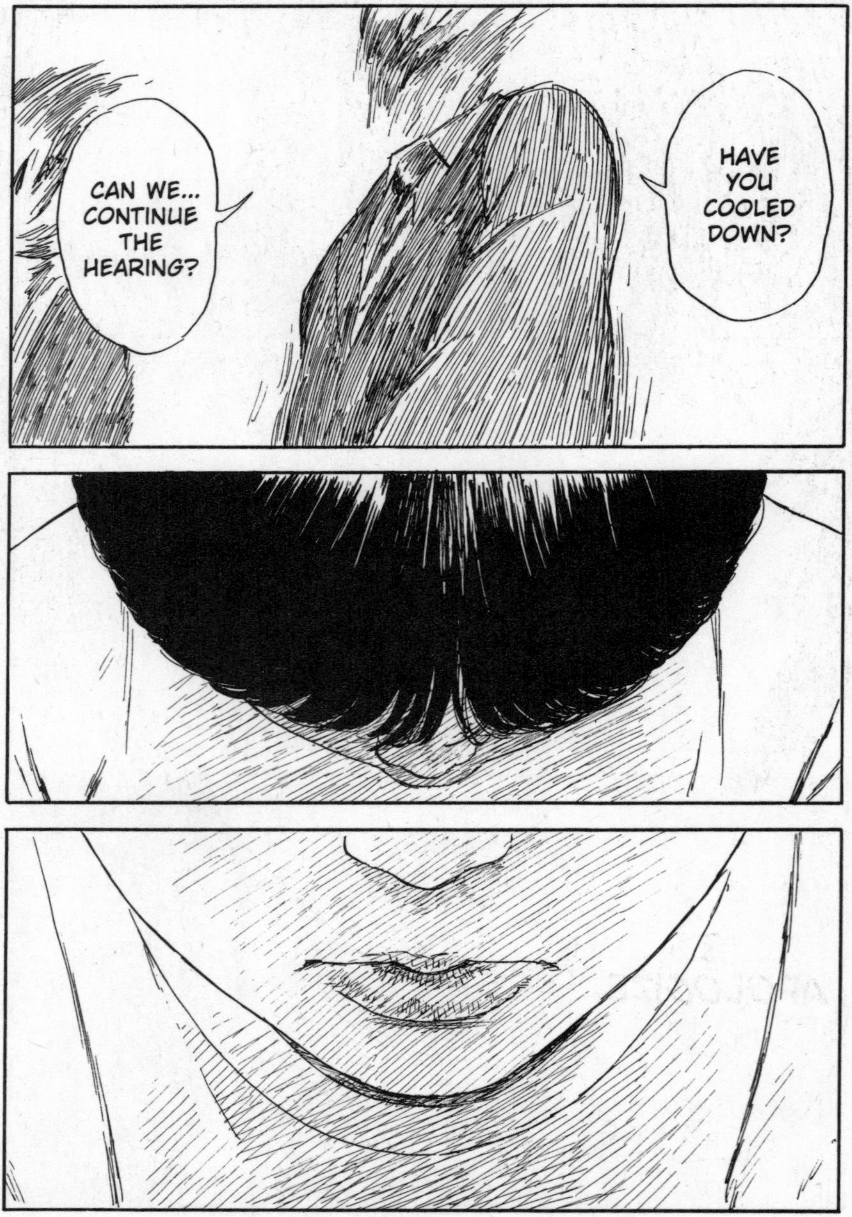
HAVE YOU COOLED DOWN?
CAN WE... CONTINUE THE HEARING?

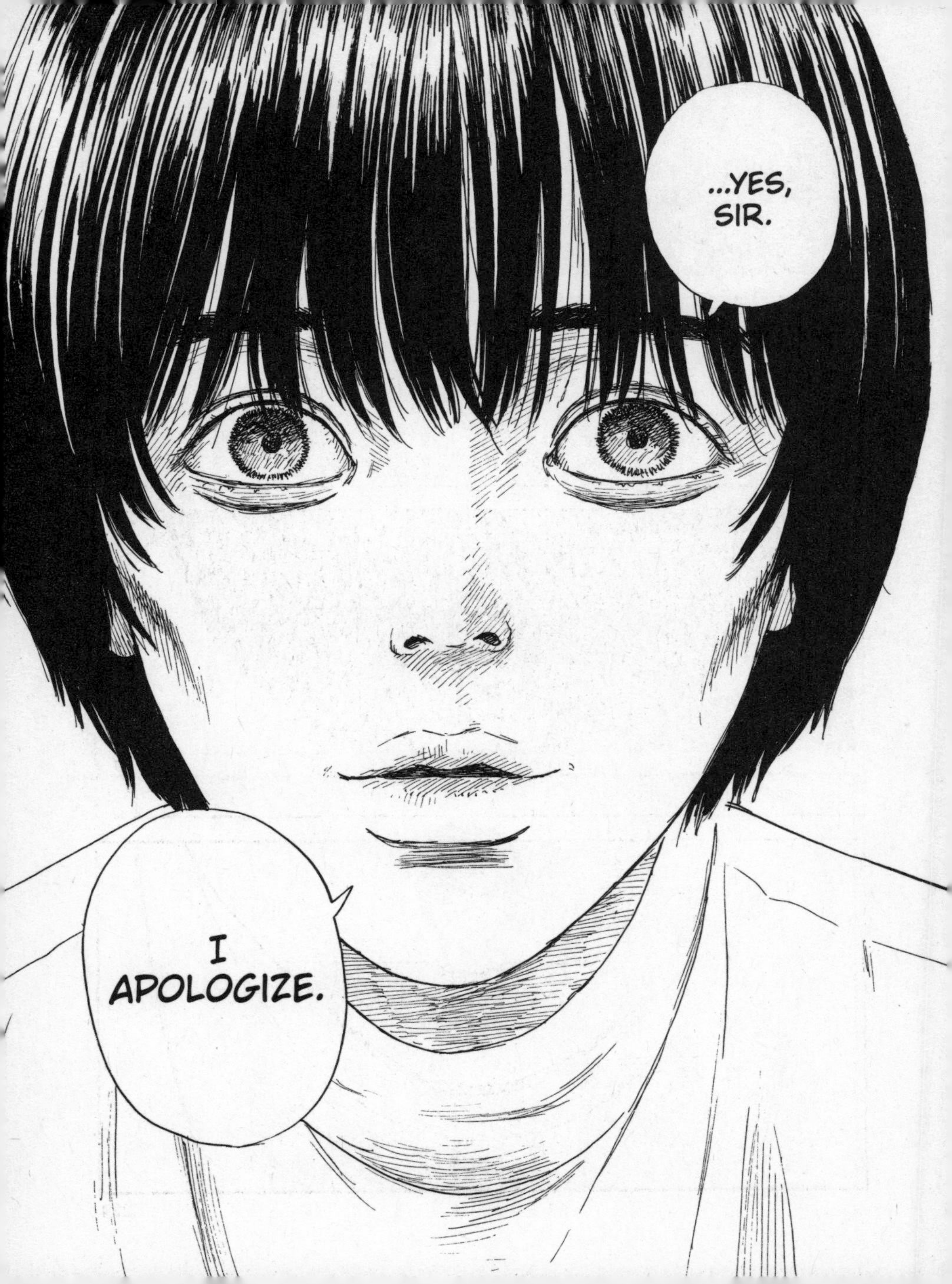
...YES, SIR.
I APOLOGIZE.

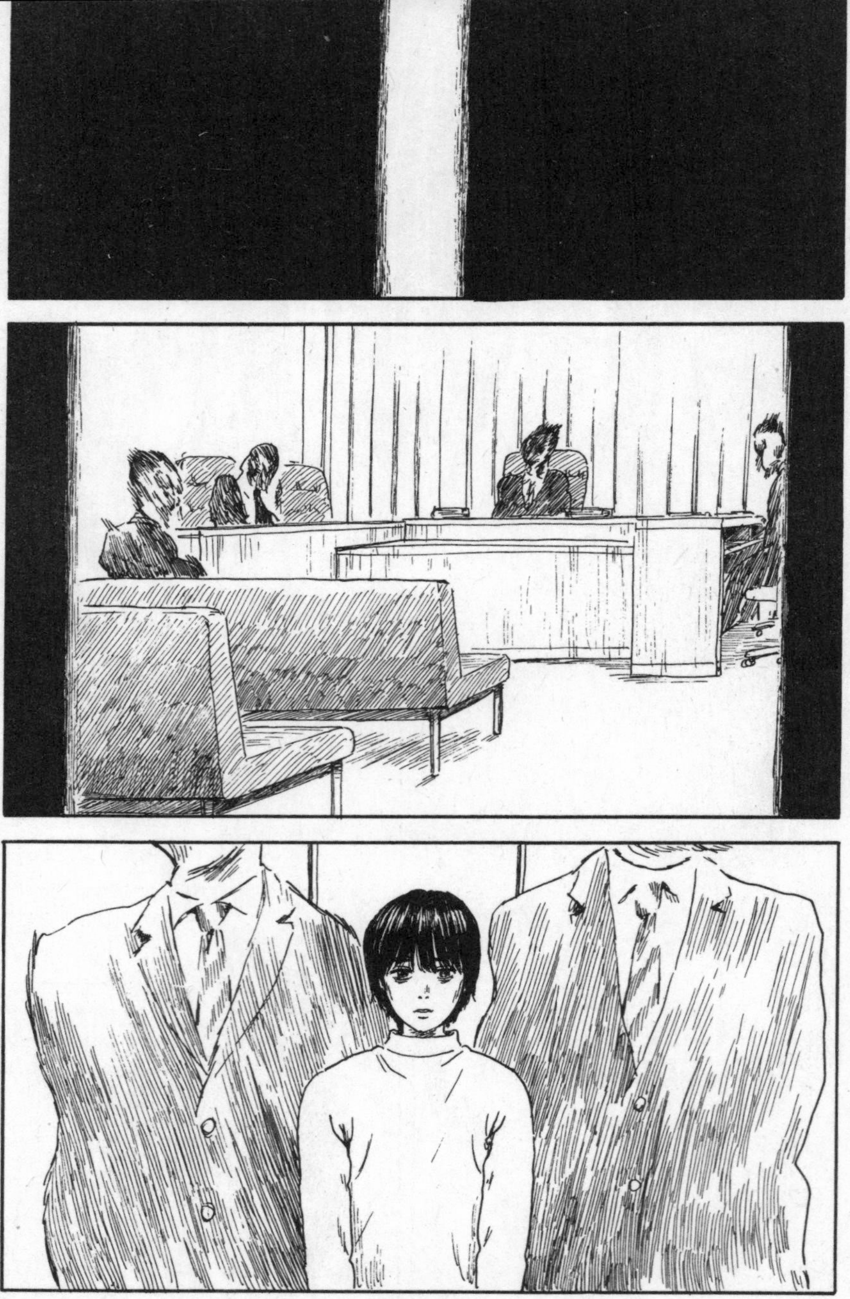

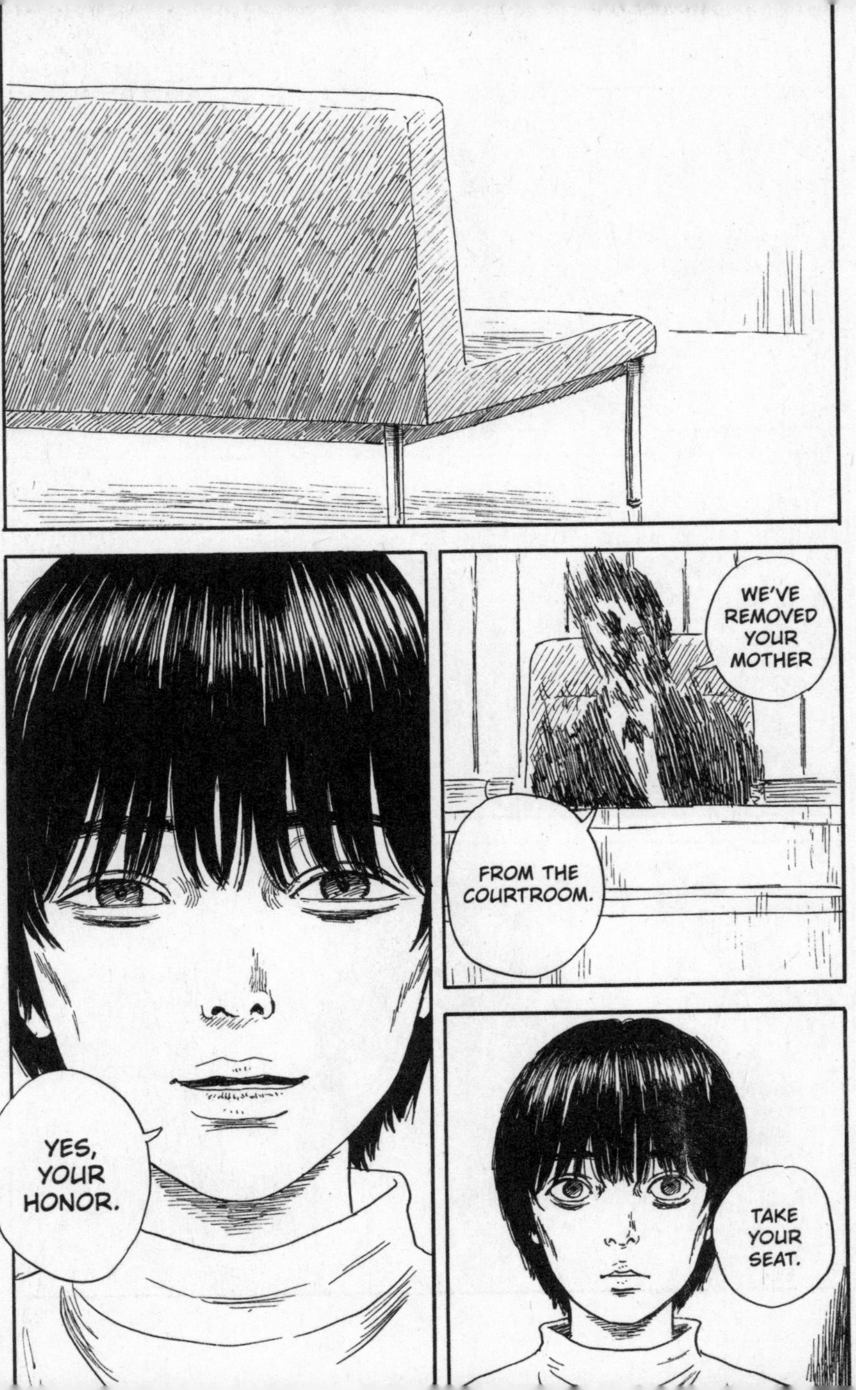
WE'VE REMOVED YOUR MOTHER
FROM THE COURTROOM.
TAKE YOUR SEAT.
YES, YOUR HONOR.

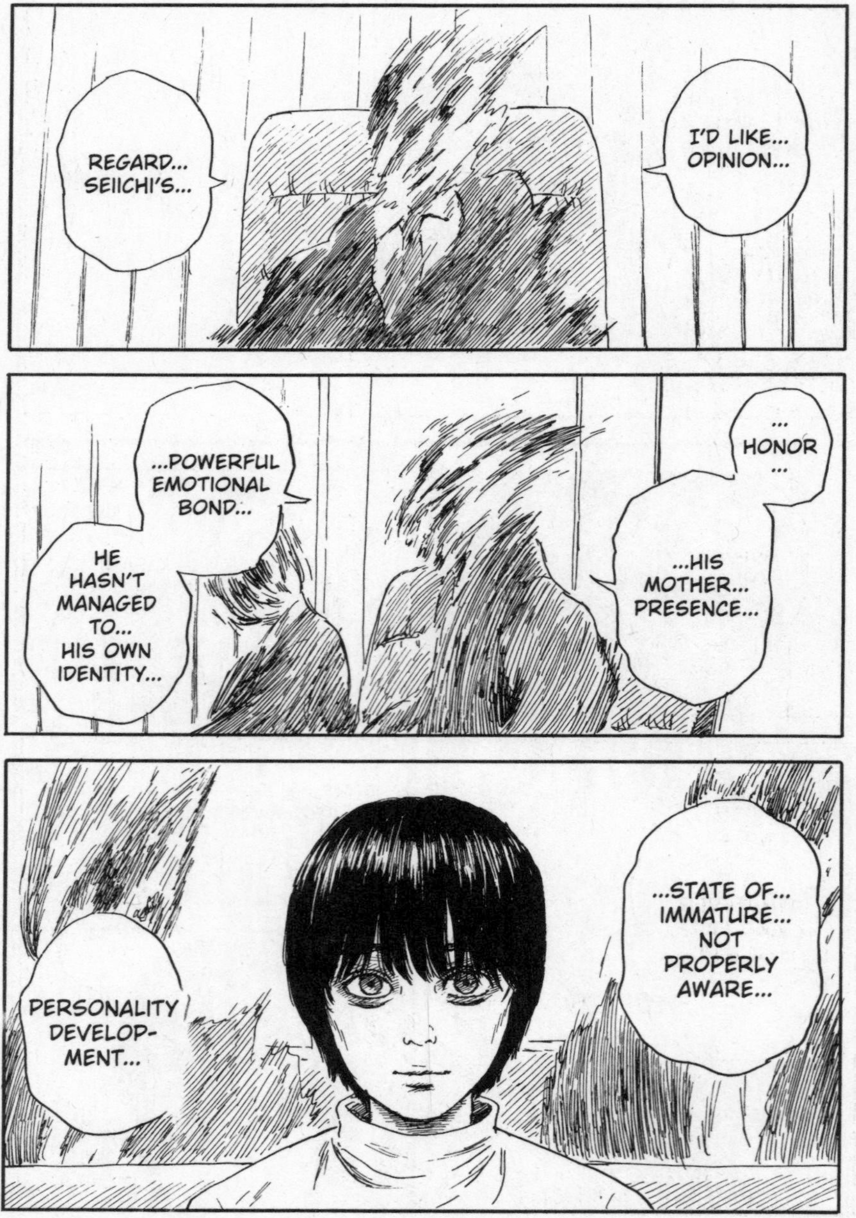
I'D LIKE... OPINION...
REGARD... SEIICHI'S...
... HONOR ...
...HIS MOTHER... PRESENCE...
...POWERFUL EMOTIONAL BOND...
HE HASN'T MANAGED TO... HIS OWN IDENTITY...
...STATE OF... IMMATURE... NOT PROPERLY AWARE...
PERSONALITY DEVELOP-MENT...

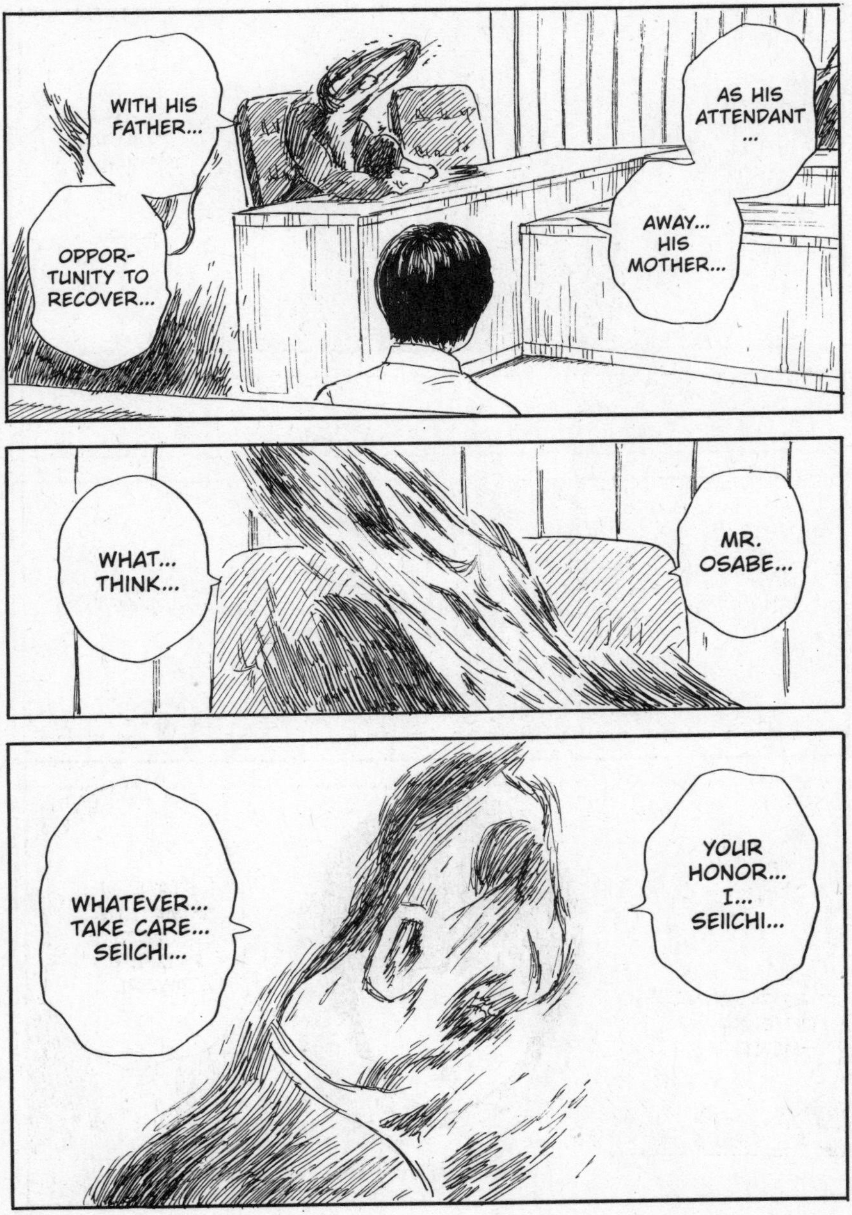
AS HIS ATTENDANT ...
AWAY... HIS MOTHER...
WITH HIS FATHER...
OPPOR-TUNITY TO RECOVER...
MR. OSABE...
WHAT... THINK...
YOUR HONOR... I... SEIICHI...
WHATEVER... TAKE CARE... SEIICHI...

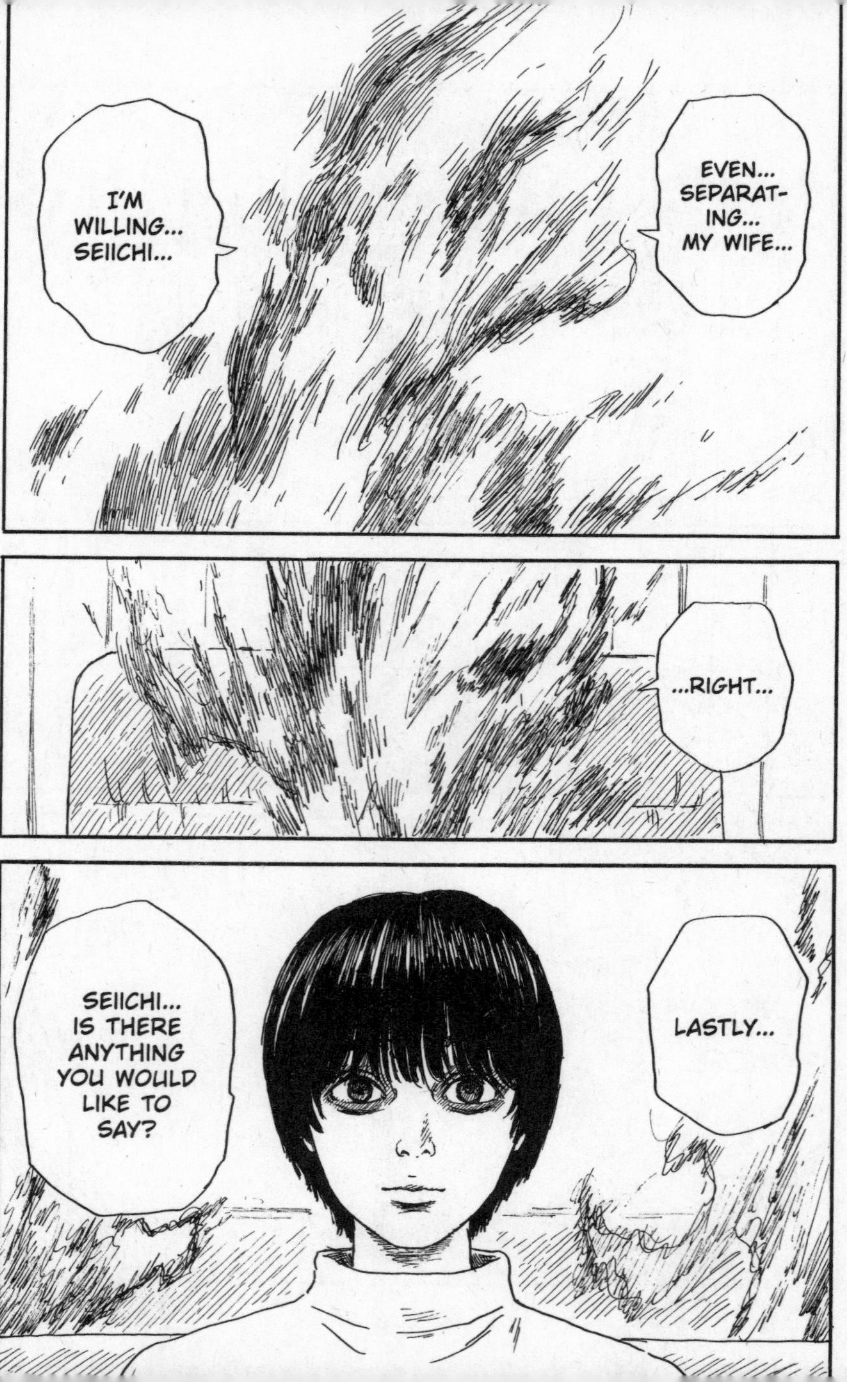
EVEN... SEPARAT-ING... MY WIFE...
I'M WILLING... SEIICHI...
...RIGHT...
LASTLY...
SEIICHI... IS THERE ANYTHING YOU WOULD LIKE TO SAY?

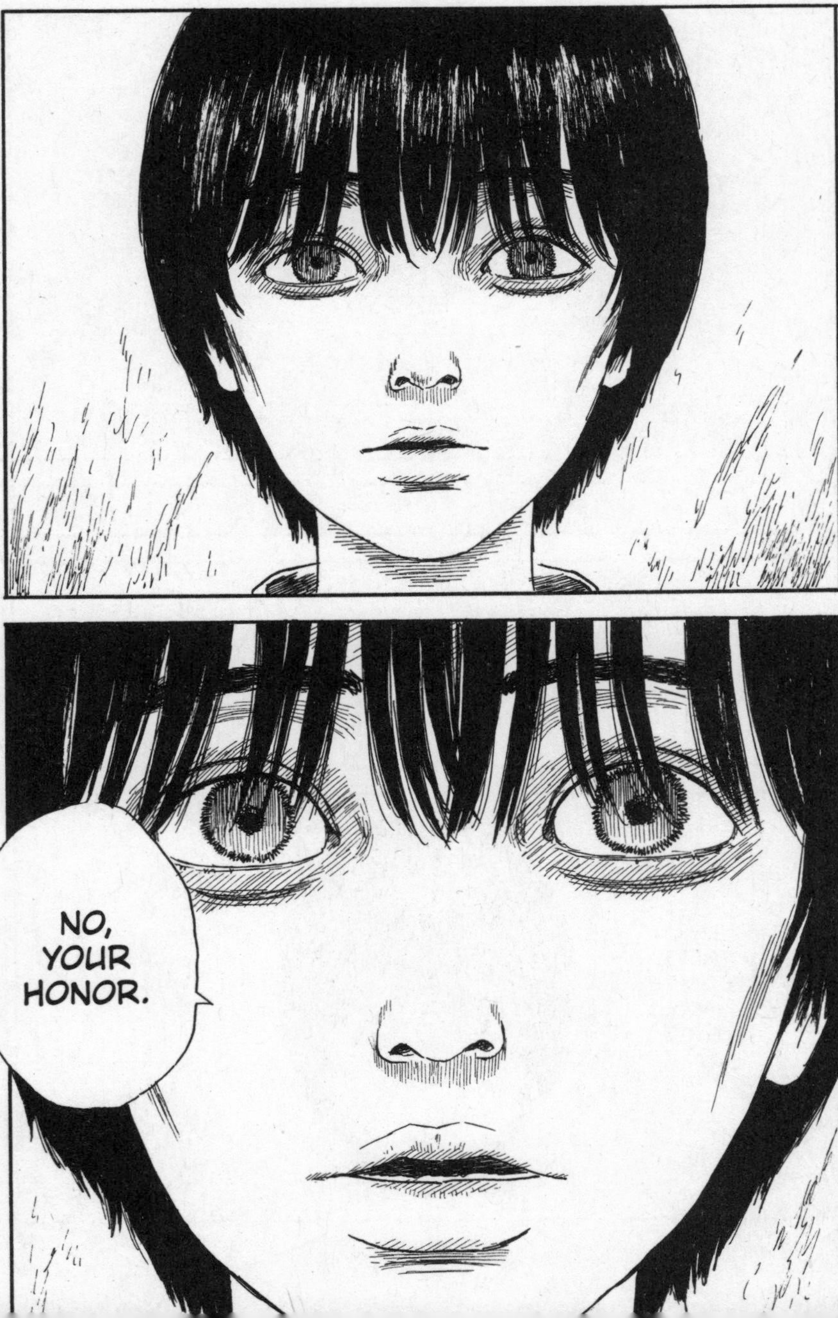
NO, YOUR HONOR.

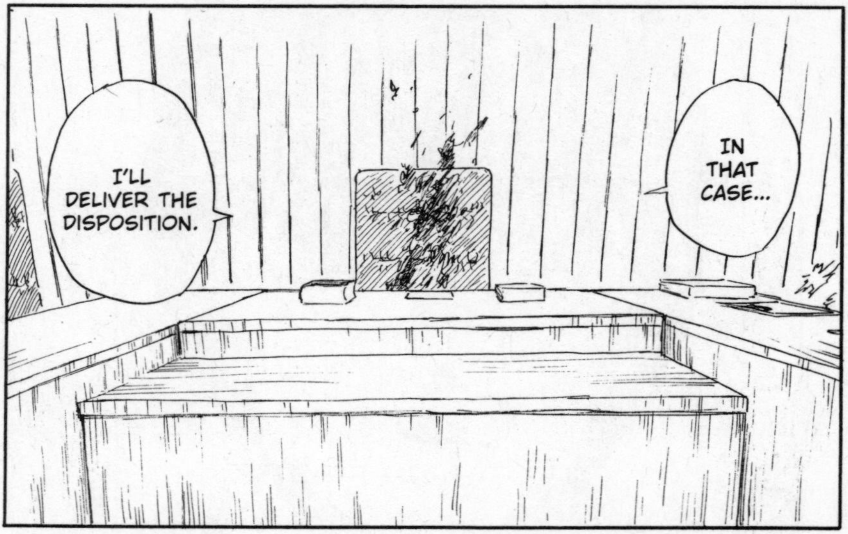
IN THAT CASE...
I'LL DELIVER THE DISPOSITION.
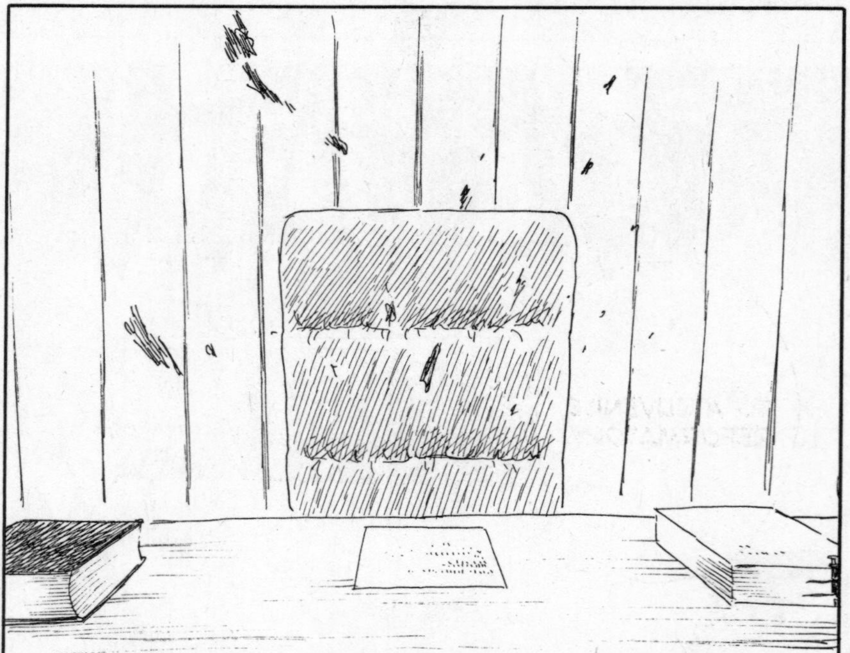

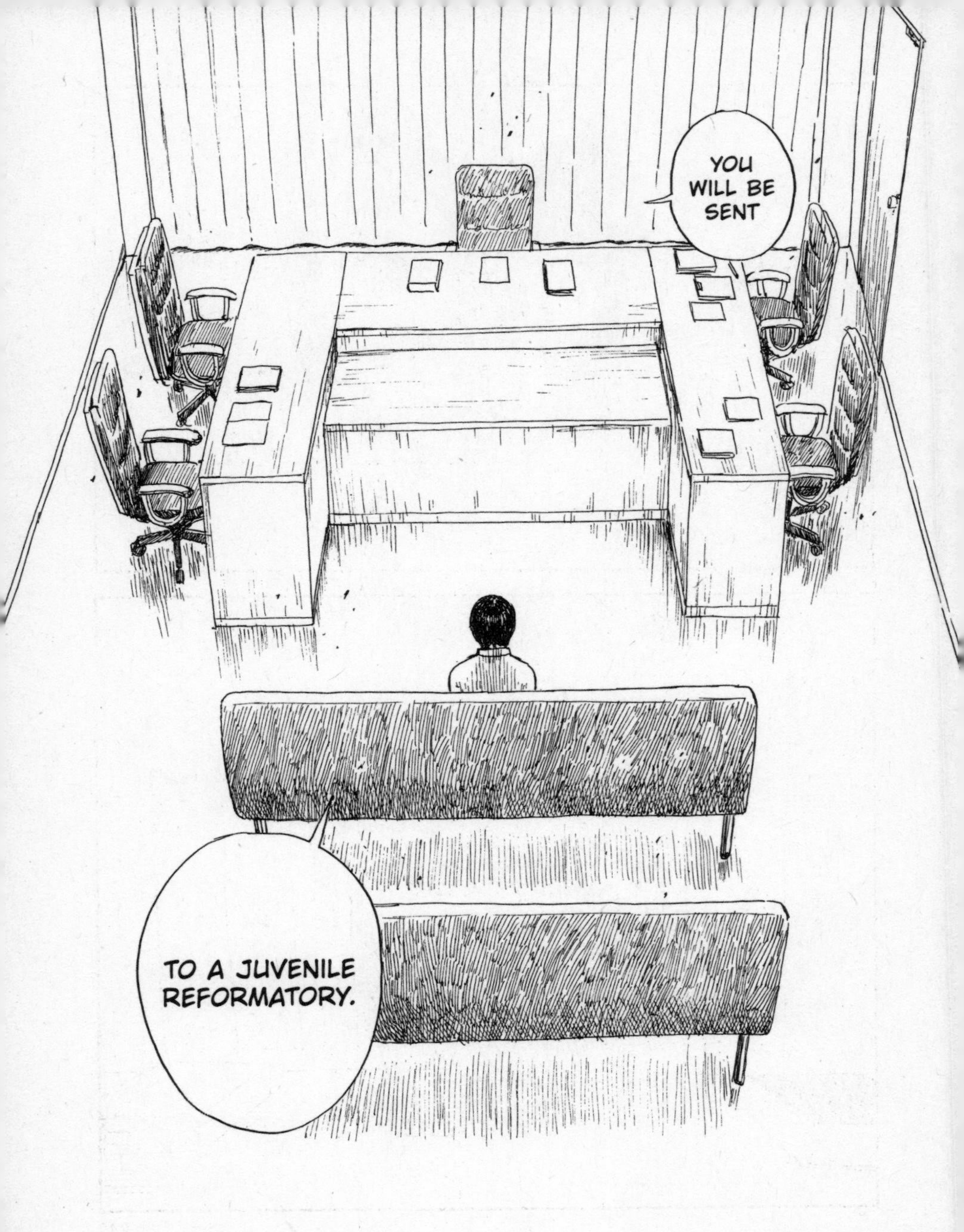
YOU WILL BE SENT
TO A JUVENILE REFORMATORY.

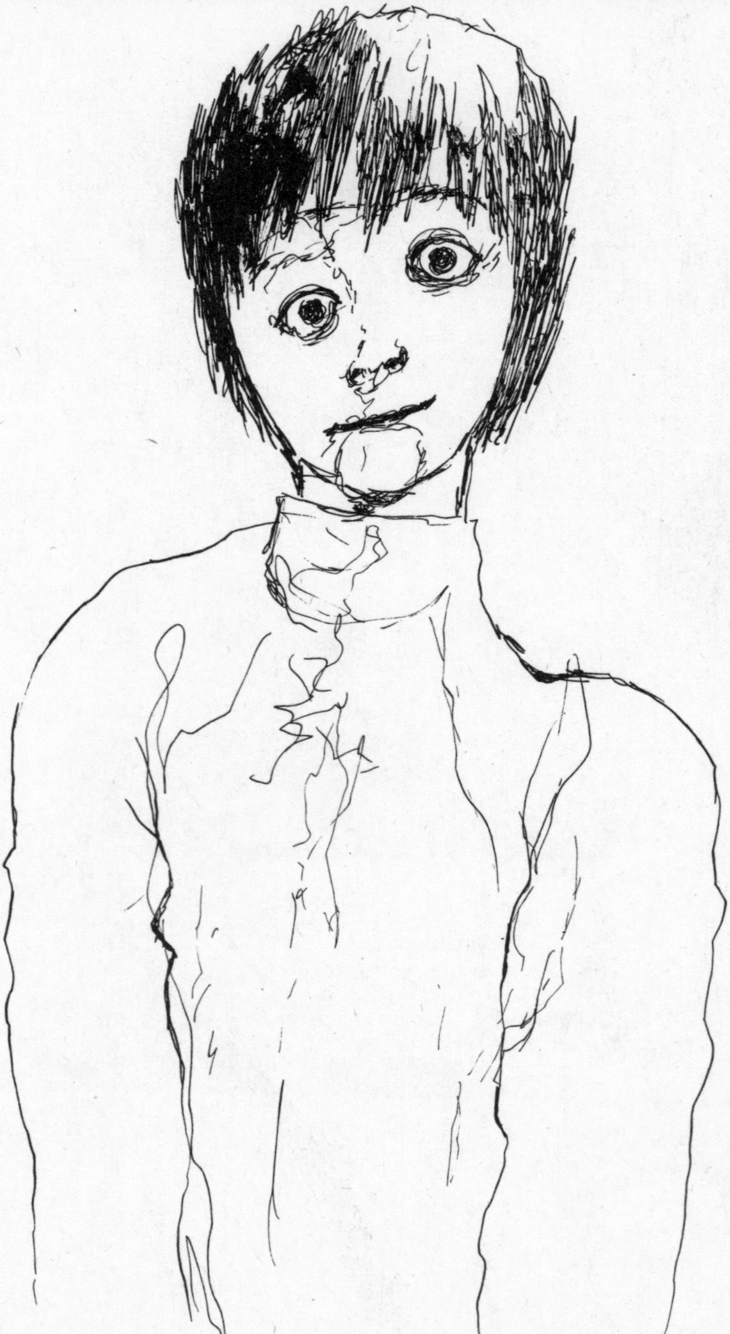

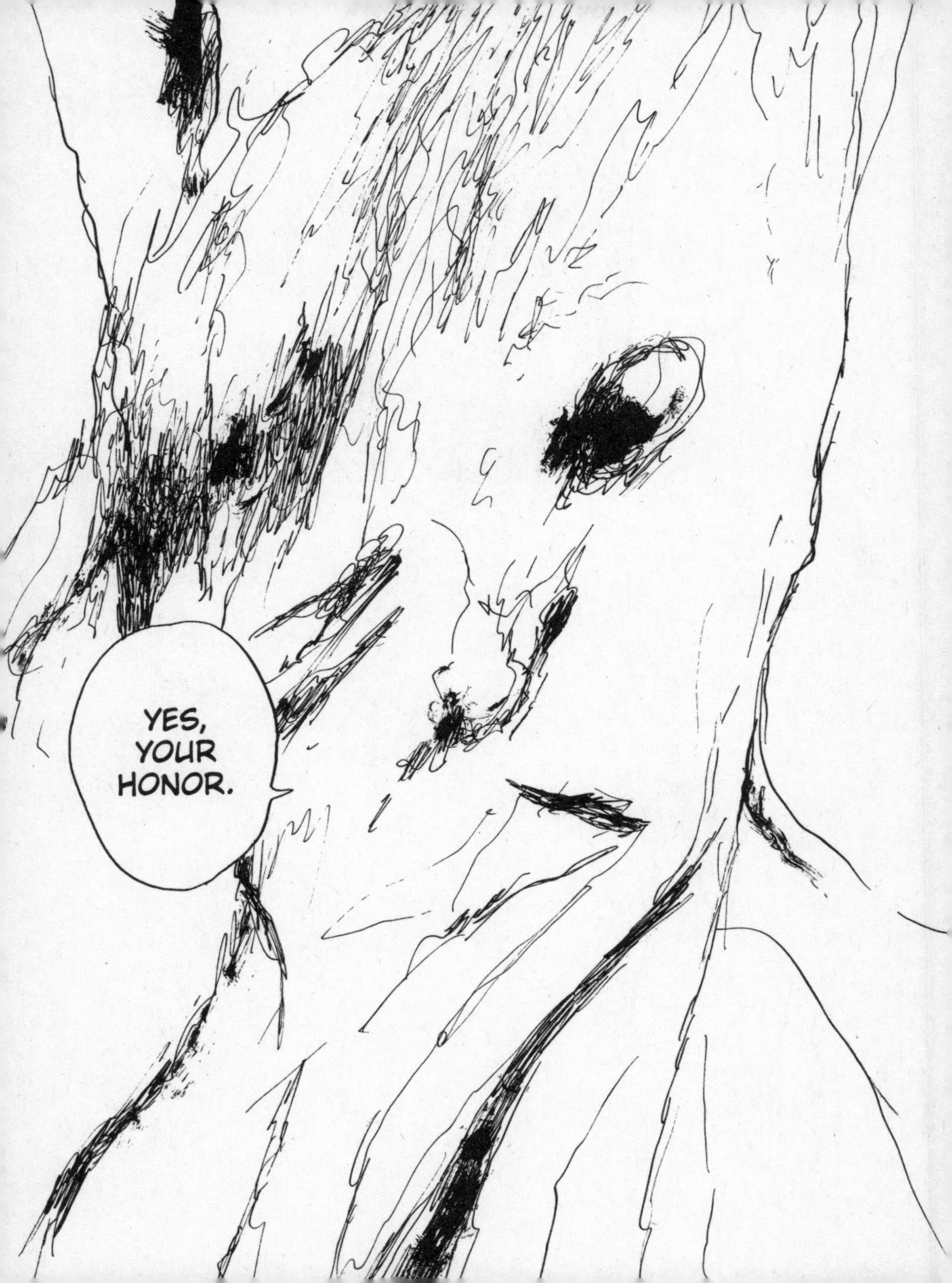
YES, YOUR HONOR.

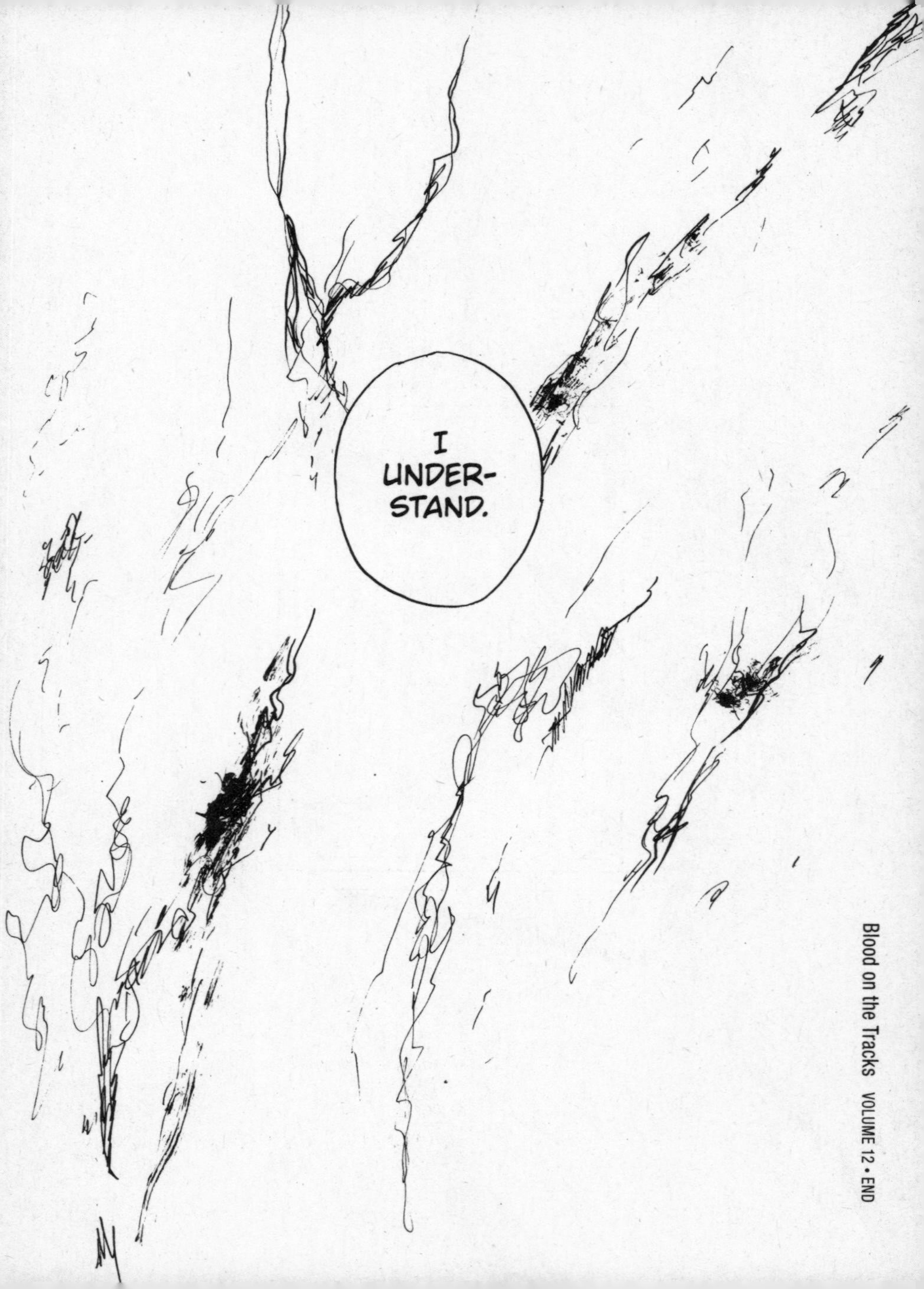
I UNDERSTAND.

Blood on the Tracks VOLUME 12 • END

precious

Memories

photo album

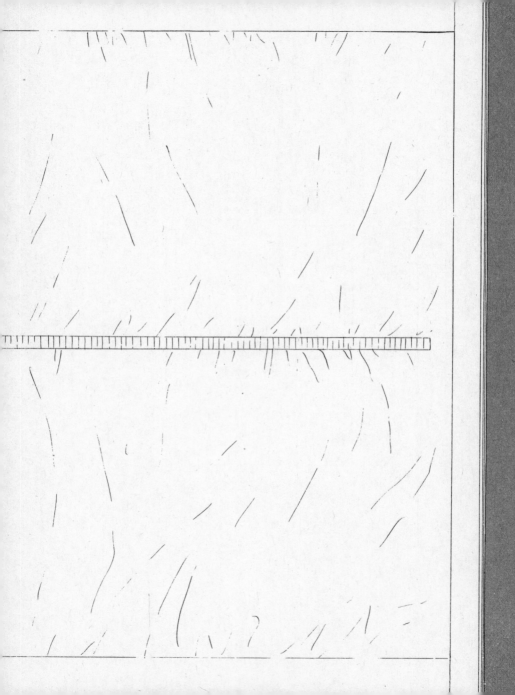

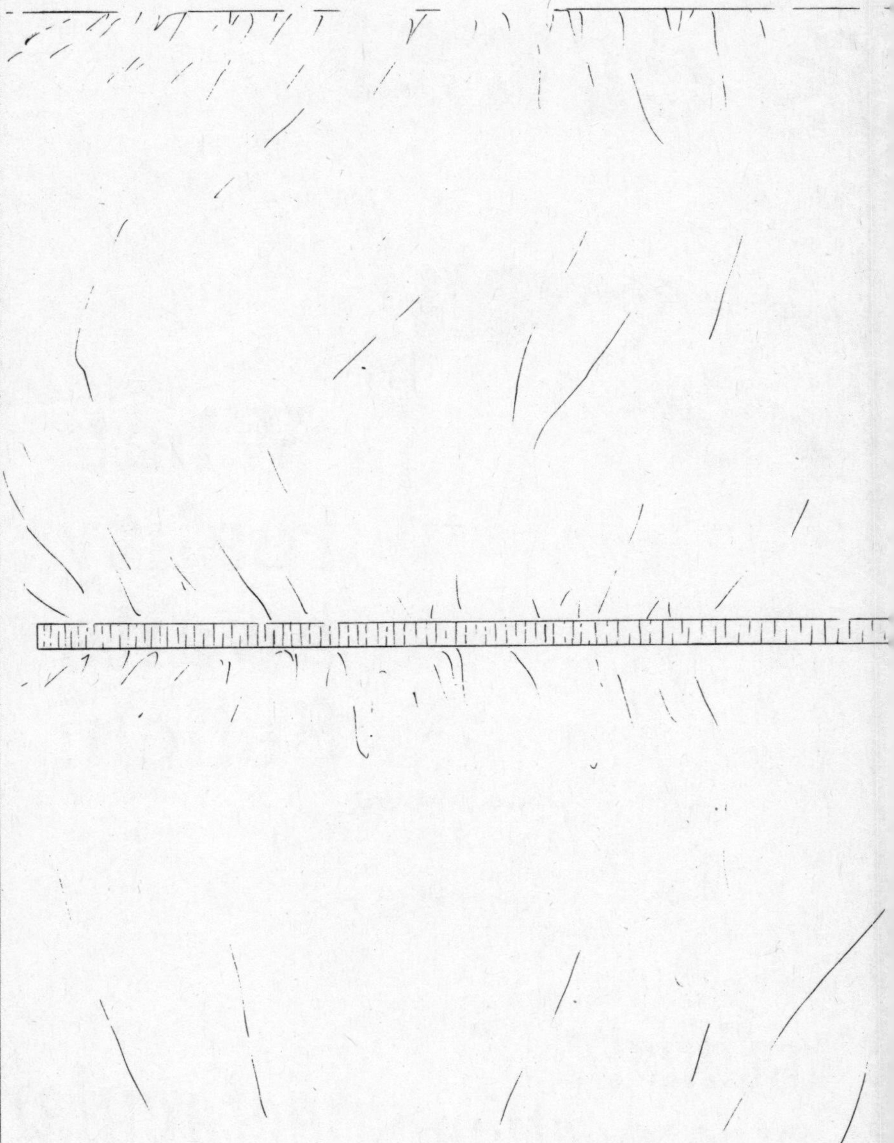

is cruel

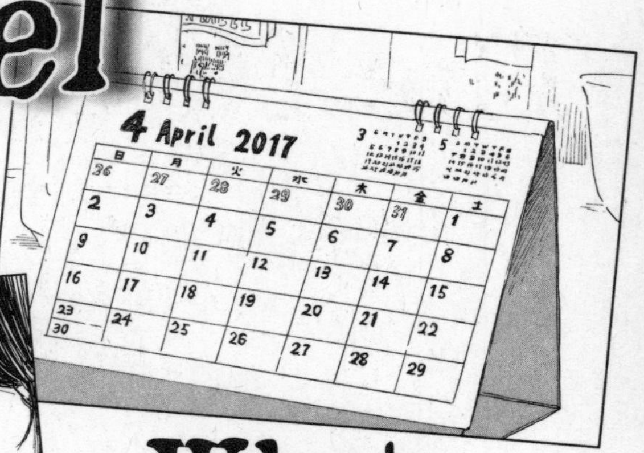
4 April 2017

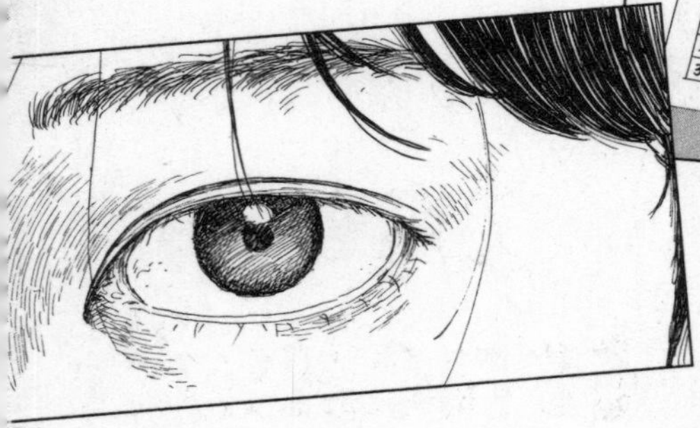

What reality awaits Seiichi

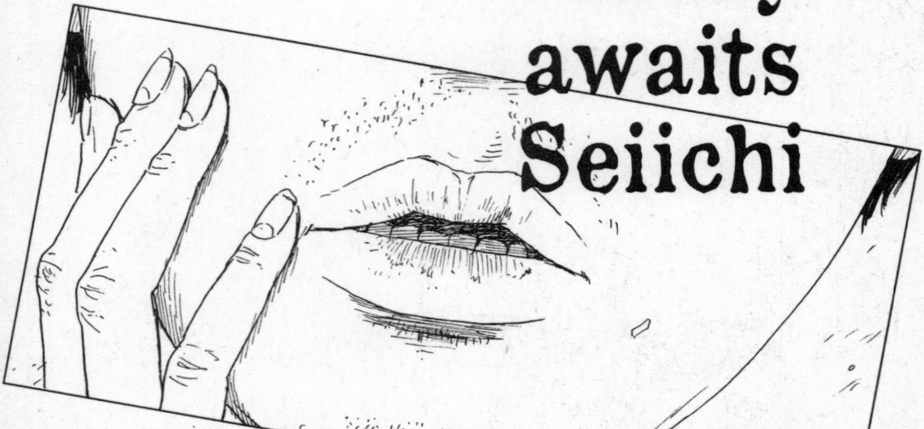

ultimate introspection spectacular!!

Volume 13 on sale Spring 2023!

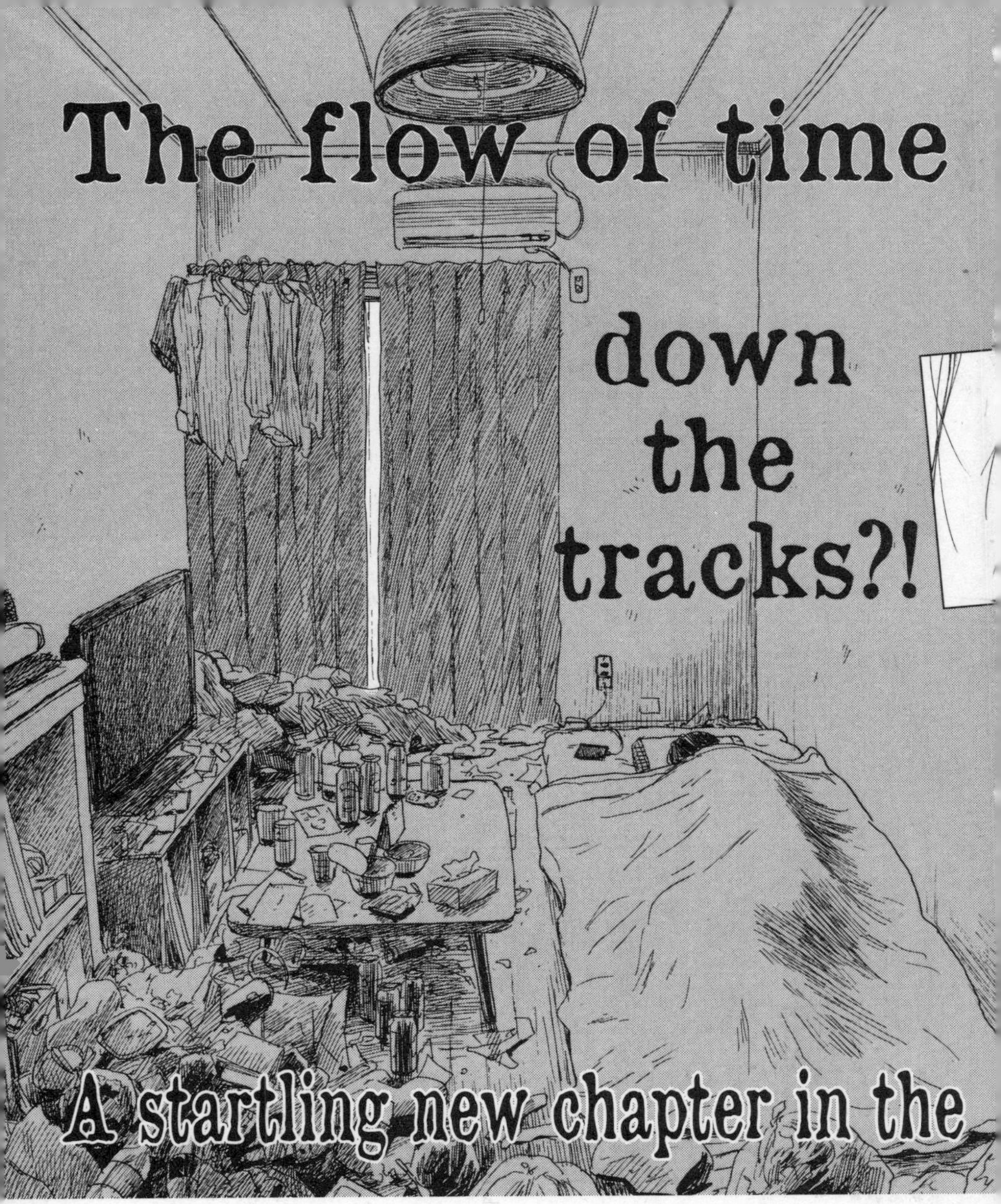
The flow of time
down the tracks?!
A startling new chapter in the

Blood on the Tracks

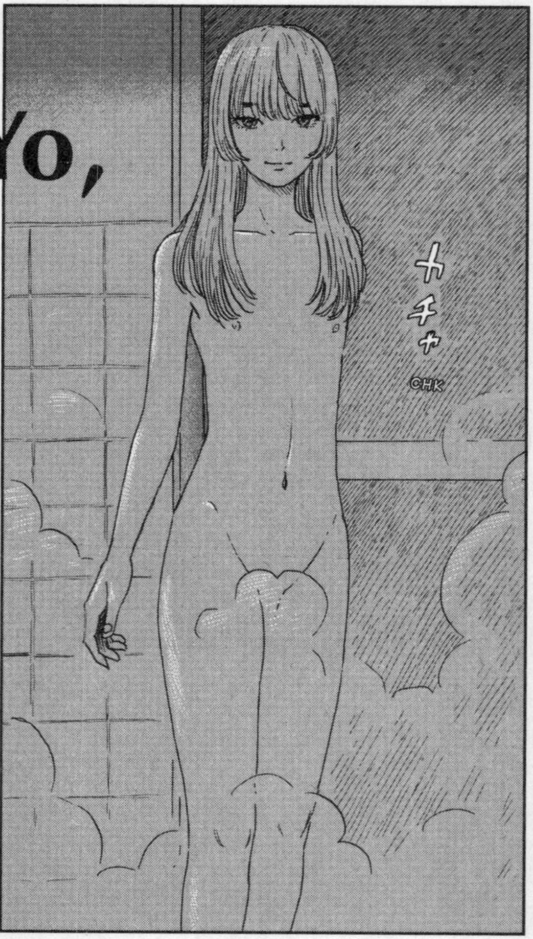
カチャ
CHK

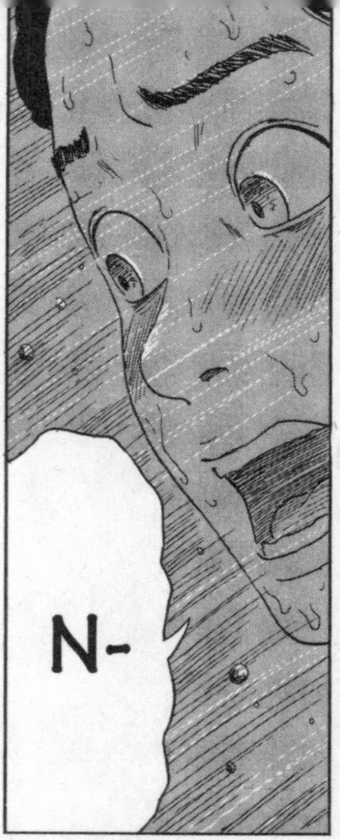
N-
Yo,

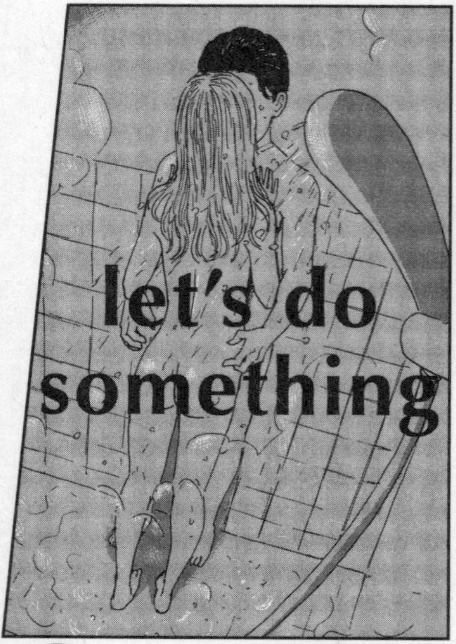
let's do something

"Sex" is stripped away. The two seek each other not as male or female, but as people. Beyond that lies...

On sale Winter 2022.

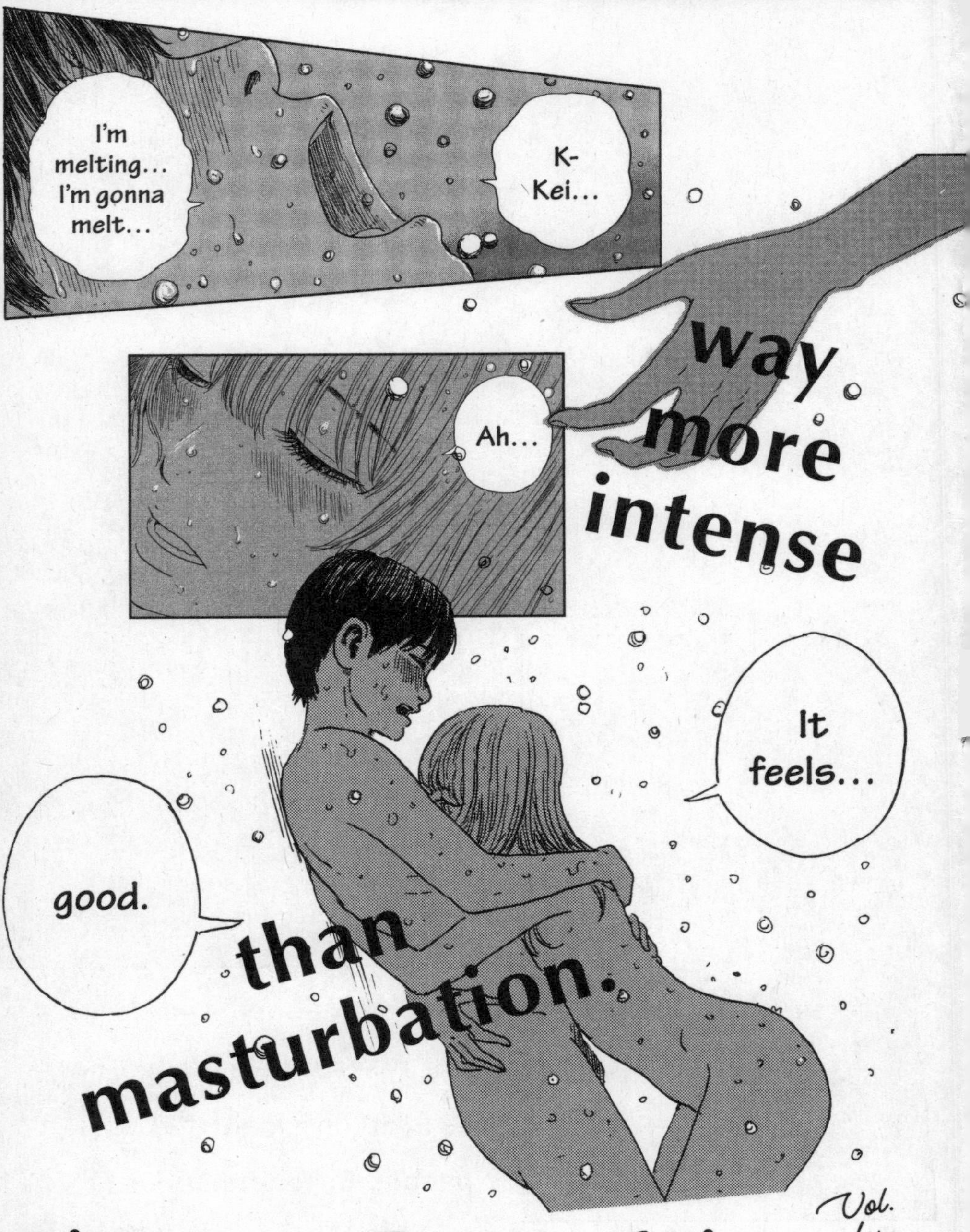
K-
Kei...
I'm melting... I'm gonna melt...
Ah...
way more intense
It feels...
good.
than masturbation.

Welcome Back, Alice Vol. 4

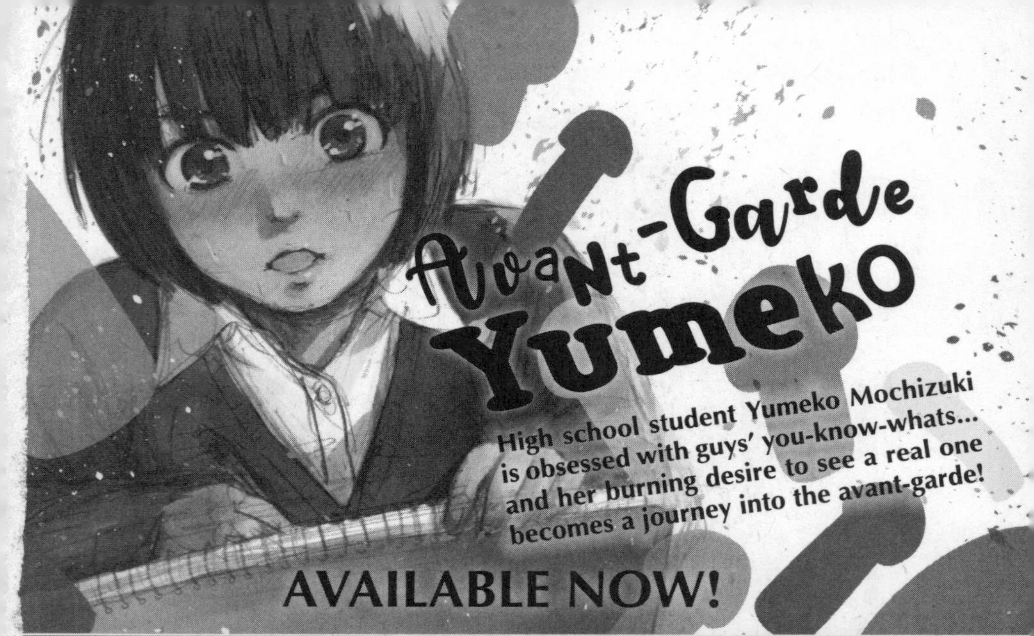
Avant-Garde Yumeko
High school student Yumeko Mochizuki is obsessed with guys' you-know-whats... and her burning desire to see a real one becomes a journey into the avant-garde!
AVAILABLE NOW!

MORE FROM SHUZO OSHIMI

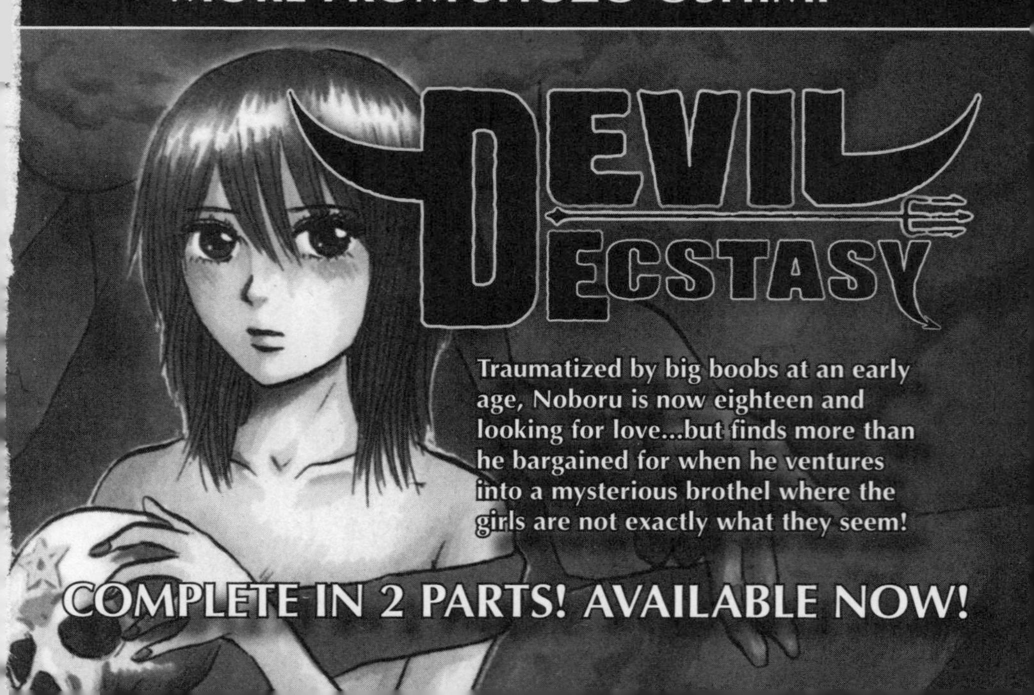
DEVIL ECSTASY
Traumatized by big boobs at an early age, Noboru is now eighteen and looking for love...but finds more than he bargained for when he ventures into a mysterious brothel where the girls are not exactly what they seem!
COMPLETE IN 2 PARTS! AVAILABLE NOW!

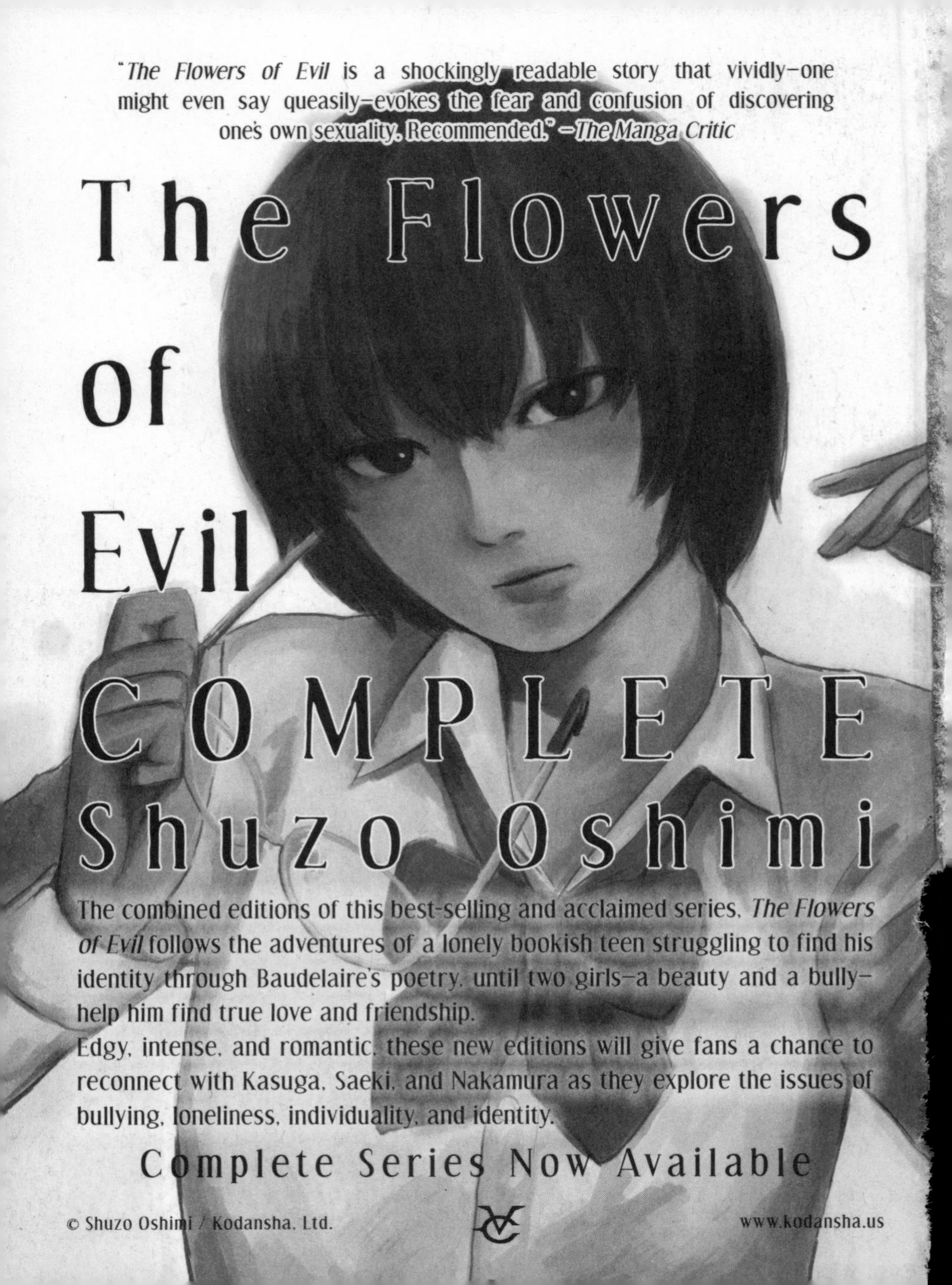
"The Flowers of Evil is a shockingly readable story that vividly—one might even say queasily—evokes the fear and confusion of discovering one's own sexuality. Recommended." —The Manga Critic
The Flowers of Evil
COMPLETE
Shuzo Oshimi
The combined editions of this best-selling and acclaimed series, The Flowers of Evil follows the adventures of a lonely bookish teen struggling to find his identity through Baudelaire's poetry, until two girls—a beauty and a bully—help him find true love and friendship.
Edgy, intense, and romantic, these new editions will give fans a chance to reconnect with Kasuga, Saeki, and Nakamura as they explore the issues of bullying, loneliness, individuality, and identity.
Complete Series Now Available
© Shuzo Oshimi / Kodansha, Ltd.
www.kodansha.us

Blood on the Tracks 12

A Vertical Comics Edition

Editor: Daniel Joseph
Translation: Daniel Komen
Production: Risa Cho
                 Pei Ann Yeap
                 Evan Hayden

CHI NO WADACHI 12
by Shuzo OSHIMI

Translation provided by Vertical Comics, 2022
Published by Vertical Comics, an imprint of Kodansha USA Publishing, LLC, New York

Originally published in Japanese as *Chi no Wadachi 12* by Shogakukan, 2021
Chi no Wadachi serialized in *Big Comic Superior*, Shogakukan, 2017-

This is a work of fiction.

ISBN: 978-1-64729-169-3

Printed in the United States of America

First Edition

Kodansha USA Publishing, LLC
451 Park Avenue South
7th Floor
New York, NY 10016
www.kodansha.us

Vertical books are distributed through Penguin-Random House Publisher Services.